WELLNESS FOR A HEALTHY ASIA

Edited by Donghyun Park, Pilipinas Quising, Gerard Bodeker, Matthias Helble, Irfan Qureshi, and Shu Tian

OCTOBER 2021

ASIAN DEVELOPMENT BANK

ADB

6 ADB Avenue, Mandaluyong City, 1550 Metro Manila, Philippines
Tel +63 2 8632 4444; Fax +63 2 8636 2444
www.adb.org

ISBN 978-92-9262-842-0 (print); 978-92-9262-843-7 (electronic); 978-92-9262-844-4 (ebook)
Publication Stock No. TCS210325
DOI: http://dx.doi.org/10.22617/TCS210325

Corrigenda to ADB publications may be found at http://www.adb.org/publications/corrigenda.

Notes:
In this publication, "$" refers to United States dollars.

ADB recognizes "Hong Kong" as Hong Kong, China; "Laos" as the Lao People's Democratic Republic; "China" as the People's Republic of China; and "Korea" and "South Korea" as the Republic of Korea.

On the cover: Wellness is the active pursuit of activities, choices, and lifestyles that lead to a state of holistic health. It covers physical, mental, emotional, and social dimensions (photos by ADB).

Cover design by Josef Ilumin.

Contents

Tables, Figures, and Boxes

Tables

Figures

Boxes

Foreword

Wellness is vital for post-pandemic recovery in developing Asia. Coronavirus disease (COVID-19) underlines the importance of wellness, or the deliberate pursuit of activities that lead to holistic health, happiness, and well-being. Public health, both physical and mental, has taken a beating during this pandemic. In Asia, as elsewhere, wellness can revive the human body, mind, and spirit, which is the first step toward rebuilding the economy and society.

Wellness is a large and growing part of the Asian economy. Even before COVID-19, Asians demanded more wellness as their incomes rose, chronic lifestyle diseases became more prevalent, and the population aged. The result has been a rapidly growing wellness economy, comprising industries that enable consumers to incorporate wellness activities into their daily lives. The wellness economy provides 11% of output in Asia, having grown annually by 10% in recent years. COVID-19 is likely to further boost demand for wellness in the coming years.

Asian wellness traditions can serve both well-being and the economy. Although modern wellness industries originated outside of Asia, the region is home to a wealth of wellness traditions. Those traditions are productive assets for the wellness economy. At the same time, tapping these traditions can promote mental and physical health in the lives of Asians. As such, the present is the opportune time for Asia to rediscover its wellness roots.

Wellness polices should be comprehensive, targeting all Asians. Government efforts to boost physical and mental well-being fall into four policy domains: creating a healthy built environment, enabling and supporting physical activity, encouraging healthy diets, and enhancing wellness in the workplace. Because healthy aging begins in childhood, a lifelong wellness policy framework such as Japan's 100-Year Life Program should complement these four policy domains. It is especially important that governments invest in wellness infrastructure and other related programs that benefit the poor, because they have fewer opportunities for wellness activities.

I would like to express my deepest appreciation to the Asian Development Bank (ADB) staff and external experts who contributed to this outstanding collective volume on a vital issue. I wholeheartedly thank Donghyun Park, who led the research project, and the other ADB coeditors—Gerard Bodeker, Matthias Helble, Pilipinas Quising, Irfan Qureshi, and Shu Tian—for their tireless efforts. My gratitude is also due to Abdul Abiad for his strategic support and guidance. This research project benefited hugely from the invaluable contributions of many external experts as well. Above all, I would like to thank Gerard Bodeker, Katherine Johnston, and Ophelia Yeung for sharing their world-class knowledge about wellness with us.

Yasuyuki Sawada
Chief Economist (Mar 2017–Aug 2021)
Asian Development Bank

Preface

COVID-19 Brings Wellness to the Fore

Wellness is conceptually distinct from happiness and well-being. It is the active pursuit of activities, choices, and lifestyles that lead to a state of holistic health. While happiness and well-being are subjective conditions when one feels happy or in a state of well-being, wellness arises from the process of actively choosing options that enable optimal health and well-being. Wellness is related to but distinct from medical health. The two overlap in preventive health care, but medical care focuses primarily on treating and curing illness, while wellness aims to improve on neutral health to achieve optimal health by, for example, exercising, eating healthy food, and meditating. Wellness is thus multidimensional and holistic in that it has physical, mental, emotional, and social dimensions.

The coronavirus disease (COVID-19) pandemic spotlights both physical and mental wellness. Medical evidence indicates much higher risk from the disease for individuals with underlying physical health conditions such as obesity, asthma, and diabetes, as well as for the elderly. Meanwhile, pandemic-induced isolation, fear, uncertainty, and economic hardship are causing stress and anxiety around the world. A recent United Nations report warns of a global mental health crisis, with current rates of mental distress at 35% in the People's Republic of China and 45% in the United States. The COVID-19 crisis thus strengthens the case for individuals to take action to improve their own physical and mental health.

Demand for wellness reflects three broad, long-term trends. These trends are higher incomes, the rising prevalence of chronic lifestyle diseases, and aging populations. Decades of rapid economic growth have left many Asians much richer than their forebears. Consequently, they are more aware of the benefits of healthier lifestyles as, most starkly, hunger for more calories gives way to a quest for better nutrition. The rise of conditions such as heart disease, stroke, diabetes, and cancer—as well as maladies caused by worsening pollution in the region—encourages Asians to exercise more, eat better, and make healthier life choices. In addition, Asia's population is aging, and older populations are vulnerable to chronic diseases, loneliness, and mental health issues.

Wellness is pro-poor and contributes to sustainable development. Wellness, or the active pursuit of well-being, aligns with the United Nations Sustainable Development Goals, in particular the third goal: Ensure healthy lives and promote well-being for all at all ages. A focus on wellness promises to bring a more balanced and holistic view of development than does measuring progress simply as increased income per capita. In principle, many wellness activities such as physical exercise are available to all. In practice, though, the poor are disadvantaged by their relative lack of money and time to devote to wellness, access to health facilities, and ready knowledge of nutritious food. These gaps can be narrowed through public investment in wellness infrastructure such as community recreation centers and green parks in poor neighborhoods, as well as health education campaigns.

The Contours of Wellness in Asia

Wellness in developing Asia is on par with the rest of world. This report constructs a Wellness Index designed to compare wellness across economies and regions. The index measures four pillars of wellness—physical, intellectual, social, and environmental—using a number of outcome indicators. The Wellness Index figure for developing Asia is 47, close to the global average of 52. Substantial differences across Asia only partly reflect variation in development stages. To be sure, rich countries such as the Republic of Korea tend to have higher wellness scores, but so do some lower-income countries, notably Bhutan.

Wellness is a large and growing part of the regional economy. The Global Wellness Institute describes the wellness economy as industries that enable consumers to incorporate wellness activities and lifestyles into their daily lives. It estimates the global wellness economy at $4.5 trillion in 2018, equal to 5% of global gross domestic product (GDP). It is an even bigger part of the economy of developing Asia. The Asian Development Bank estimates that the wellness economy provided 11% of regional GDP in 2017 and that it has been growing by about 10% annually in recent years. The rapid growth of the wellness economy reflects Asians' growing demand for wellness. Demand is likely to expand further in the wake of the COVID-19 pandemic, which has restricted physical exercise and caused significant anxiety and stress.

Holistic Pathways to Physical Wellness

Physical inactivity is a worsening threat to regional public health and is also a key lifestyle risk factor for chronic disease. While 33.2% of Asians regularly participate in recreational physical activities, this is somewhat below the global average of 35.5%. Inactivity rates are generally worse in South Asia and better in East Asia, Southeast Asia, and the Pacific. Asia has one of the world's largest and most diverse physical activity markets, valued at $240 billion in 2018, with sports and active recreation being the most popular activities. That said, many Asians spend little or no money when pursuing leisure-time physical activity on the streets, at home, or in public parks, plazas, and free sporting facilities. Governments can support participation in physical activity after COVID-19 recedes by investing in venues for sports and physical recreation.

Asia cannot afford its increasing problems with workplace wellness. The region accounted for more than two-thirds of the 2.8 million people estimated to have died worldwide in 2017 from work-related accidents or disease. Workplace wellness is still a little-known concept in Asia, benefiting primarily those who work for multinational corporations or live in the region's wealthiest areas and cities. Only 5.2% of all employed workers in Asia currently benefit from some form of workplace wellness program—barely half of the low 9.8% of workers globally. To be effective, a workplace wellness framework must be holistic and focus first on wellness challenges that arise within the workplace. Today, staying well while working from home is emerging as a new priority under widespread COVID-19 restrictions.

Community planning, zoning, and infrastructure can promote wellness. When human health and wellness are central to urban planning, real estate, and infrastructure development, the result is wellness real estate—a $134 billion industry in 2017, with Asia and the Pacific accounting for $47 billion. Public investment can similarly focus built environments on wellness. For example, governments can invest in infrastructure that encourages physical activity: pedestrian sidewalks, paths and trails, and public parks. Such planning approaches create neighborhoods and communities that are healthier for residents and that enhance their well-being and the quality of life.

The double burden of malnutrition is an additional growing risk to health. Food has become more readily available across the region, reducing malnutrition but encouraging unhealthy eating as poor choices of calorie sources provide too much sugar, salt, and fat. As a result, the region has become a global hot spot for the double burden of malnutrition: concurrent undernutrition and obesity. Poor nutrition inflicts significant economic costs. Direct medical costs from obesity, for instance, are estimated to absorb 0.8% of regional GDP. Policies can address this by favoring healthy foods, as through targeted taxes that drive down demand for sugary drinks. Public education about nutrition can guide consumers toward better diets and minimize the burden on the public health care system.

Leveraging Asian Traditions for Mental Wellness

The path to mental well-being is self-managed and evidence-based. The five pillars of mental wellness are emotional well-being, psychological well-being, resilience and balance, optimal functioning, and social well-being. Poor mental health—evidenced most commonly by depression—is the third most common cause of years lost to disability, after lower-back pain and headache. Yet many Asian economies have fewer than one mental health professional per 100,000 people. Evidence shows the benefits to mental wellness of healthy everyday habits such as eating well and seeking social support, as well as specialized wellness enablers such as meditation, tai chi, yoga, dance, and social laughter. Benefits are amplified if wellness is practiced in tune with local culture by, for example, basing optimal nutrition on local cuisine.

Asians can draw from a plethora of established wellness traditions. Asia's two major systems of traditional health knowledge—traditional Chinese medicine and Ayurvedic medicine—are grounded in principles of healthy living and wellness through the whole of life. These two systems have influenced the wellness traditions of not only East and South Asia, where they arose, but also Southeast Asia. In these traditions, lifestyle is given primary emphasis over medicine. Individual wellness practices that leverage these traditions offer a low-cost avenue to mental and overall wellness that is culturally relevant, evidence-based, and self-managed. A growing body of scientific evidence confirms the wellness benefits of Asian wellness traditions. As a bonus, these traditions can reduce public health-care costs and provide new economic opportunities.

An aging Asian population makes healthy aging an urgent priority. The share of developing Asia's population aged 65 or older is rising, from 6% in 2010 to 9% in 2020 and a projected 18% in 2050. Evidence indicates that older populations generate greater demand for wellness. For example, a 1% increase in the share of the population aged 65 or older boosts hot spring revenues by 0.29%. While mental and physical health naturally deteriorates with age, eating healthier food, including traditional Asian food, and exercising regularly can improve how well populations age. Optimizing home design helps, as does reducing isolation through technology and social support. The evidence is mixed about the impact of retirement on wellness, but it is clear that wellness in old age depends on staying mentally and physically active and fit, whether a person is retired or not.

Wellness tourism is a growing segment of the tourism industry. While almost all tourism encourages rest and relaxation and is thus beneficial to mental wellness, a key driver of rapid tourism growth in Asia is wellness tourism, which lies at the intersection of the $2.7 trillion global tourism industry and the $4.5 trillion global wellness industry. Wellness tourism, defined as travel designed to maintain or enhance personal well-being, generated $639 billion in revenue globally in 2017 and $137 billion in Asia and the Pacific. Global tourism has been hit very hard by COVID-19. Beyond the short term, economies with post-COVID-19 recovery strategies that strengthen the sustainability of wellness tourism will be among those that benefit the most from global economic recovery.

Wellness for Happiness and Inclusiveness

Subjective happiness is low in Asia relative to other regions. Sustained rapid growth has lifted developing Asia's living standards in recent decades, yet research indicates that higher incomes do not necessarily translate into greater happiness. As a result, happiness has recently attracted considerable attention. The rise of positive psychology as a field of inquiry indicates burgeoning academic interest, and Bhutan's famous Gross National Happiness Index is emblematic of growing interest among policy makers. The United Nations' *World Happiness Report 2019* states that, despite rapid economic growth, self-reported happiness in Asia averages 5.17 on a scale of 0 to 10, substantially lower than in every other region except Africa and the Middle East, and lower than the global average of 5.46. Some poorer countries such as Pakistan and the Philippines are relatively happy countries.

Empirical evidence associates wellness with happiness. The wellness economy can, in principle, generate greater well-being. Recreational physical therapy, workplace wellness programs, and spa therapy are examples of wellness enterprises geared toward better health outcomes, which are central to well-being. Empirical analysis across 146 economies confirms a significant positive association between wellness and happiness. Thus, if annual spending per capita on workplace wellness doubled from the current world average of $11 to $22, happiness would potentially improve by 0.15 units on a scale of 0 to 10.

The wellness economy can promote inclusive growth. Developing Asia has a large, fast-growing wellness economy. Wellness tourism expenditure in the region grew by 11% annually from 2015 to 2017, reaching $137 billion in 2017 as the industry directly employed 3.74 million in India, 1.78 million in the People's Republic of China, and 0.53 million in Thailand. In addition, demand for many wellness products, such as local and traditional culinary experiences and goods, can encourage micro or small enterprises to leverage local heritage and indigenous ingredients toward their creation. As many wellness-related occupations, such as complementary medicine practitioner, are dominated by women, growth in the wellness economy contributes to female employment. In these ways, the wellness economy can enable inclusive growth and reduce poverty.

Government policies that promote wellness offer broad benefits. Individuals, the economy, and society as a whole benefit when wellness makes people happier and more productive and wellness industries are a growing part of the economy. Yet, because wellness is poorly understood by governments, it is not incorporated into policy making as an overarching framework or explicit priority. Wellness can, however, bring an important perspective to policy making that complements public health, health policy, and the emerging field of happiness. Wellness policies are those that nudge people to proactively make healthy choices and live healthy lifestyles, while also creating living environments that support and encourage healthy behavior and lifestyles. Such policies are most effective if they address four crosscutting domains and take a life span approach, as explained below.

Wellness policies span four crosscutting policy domains. First, Asian governments can help create a healthy built environment by, for example, prioritizing walkability and physical movement in urban and regional planning. Second, policy makers can enable and support physical activity by funding public infrastructure, facilities, and programs for it. Third, governments can encourage healthy eating by improving consumer awareness of nutrition and diet. Finally, Asian policy makers can enhance wellness in the workplace by ensuring a safe and healthy physical work environment. Taken together, policies in these four crosscutting domains can promote mental and physical wellness.

A life span approach safeguards mental and physical health from birth. Healthy aging begins in childhood and progresses through an overarching life span framework, such as Japan's 100-Year Life Program. Preventive interventions in an individual's first 1,000 days bring lifelong benefits. Further, wellness is worth adding to the formal education system, embedded in curricula and in learning and social environments. Finally, a range of policies can support healthy aging, including lifelong learning, reskilling, personal growth and transformation, and, for seniors, better nutrition and safe homes that enable wellness. In conjunction with crosscutting wellness policies, lifelong wellness policies can help Asians navigate the uncertain, stressful COVID-19 world toward a better new normal after the pandemic.

Structure of This Book

This book is a collection of background papers prepared for the *Asian Development Outlook 2020 Update: Wellness in Worrying Times* special theme chapter. It has five parts. The first discusses the importance of addressing wellness and how COVID-19 has brought wellness again to the fore. It also provides an overview of the global wellness industry. The second part takes stock of the current state of wellness in developing Asia by presenting a Wellness Index of regional economies and providing empirical assessments of the contribution of the wellness industry to the economy. The third part examines physical wellness, while the fourth focuses on mental wellness. The last part touches on happiness and its correlation with wellness and provides policy options to policy makers.

Part 1 has two chapters. In Chapter 1, "Why Does Wellness Matter So Much in the Age of COVID-19? A Selective Literature Review," Donghyun Park and Pilipinas Quising provide a selected literature review to discuss the link between global health and economic crises and individual well-being. Past and current studies show a negative effect that strengthens the case for wellness to promote happiness and well-being. In Chapter 2, "The Global Wellness Industry and Its Implications for Asia's Development," Ophelia Yeung and Katherine Johnston examine the definitions and drivers of the global wellness industry, its current size in Asia and globally, its future prospects, and the implications of an expanding wellness industry for Asia's development.

Part 2 has two chapters. In Chapter 3, "Quantifying and Comparing Wellness across Nations: A Cross-Country Empirical Analysis," Husnain Fateh Ahmad and Irfan Qureshi present a new measure of wellness, the Wellness Index. The Wellness Index is constructed for 153 countries and is used to conduct regional and country-level analysis of wellness and its four pillars. In Chapter 4, "Tracing the Production and Employment Linkages in Developing Asia's Wellness Economies," Rafael Martin Consing III, Michael John Barsabal, Julian Thomas Alvarez, and Mahinthan Mariasingham use the system of national accounts framework to derive the wellness economy's contribution to overall domestic production and employment. Estimates based on these procedures are then provided for nine countries in developing Asia across two time periods.

Part 3 has three chapters. In Chapter 5, "The Physical Activity Economy in Asia: Market Size, Participation, Barriers, and Options to Increase Movement," Ophelia Yeung and Katherine Johnston examine the economy of physical activity in Asia, including the rates of participation in recreational physical activities across the region and the industry size and trends, using recent data on the global physical activity sector. The authors also examine the main barriers to participation in physical activity and highlight options that can encourage and support all populations to be more physically active. In Chapter 6, "Improving Workplace Wellness in Asia: A Business Case, Approaches, and Successful Practices," Ophelia Yeung and Katherine Johnston look at the state of workplace wellness in Asia and discuss a comprehensive framework for workplace wellness. In Chapter 7, "Eating in Developing Asia: Trends, Consequences, and Policies," Anne Marie Thow, Penny Farrell, Matthias Helble, and Cut Novianti Rachmi review the changing diets, food supply, and food environments in the Asia and Pacific region and then describe the prevalence and nature of undernutrition across the region. The chapter also examines the rising prevalence of diet-related risks for noncommunicable diseases.

Part 4 has four chapters. In Chapter 8, "Mental Wellness," Gerard Bodeker focuses on individual and community approaches that reduce the burden of mental illness. The author presents new directions for improving mental wellness across Asia in accordance with the principles of de-institutionalization, patient-centered care, personal responsibility for mental and physical health, community support systems, and evidence as the basis for strengthening the widespread adoption of culturally familiar pathways to mental wellness. In Chapter 9, "Asian Traditions of Wellness," Gerard Bodeker brings into focus Asia's wealth of health prevention and promotion strategies that are culturally relevant, evidence based, self-managed, and low cost, as a means of enhancing health in the region and reducing the illness burden on national health budgets. In Chapter 10, "Aging and Wellness in Asia," Gerard Bodeker, Madhavi Pundit, Pilipinas Quising, and Shu Tian take a closer look at aging and examine the demographic impact of aging on the global wellness industry, the connection between retirement and well-being, different wellness pathways, and policies to promote healthy aging. In Chapter 11, "Analysis of the Global and Asian Wellness Tourism Sector," Scott Wayne and Emma Russell analyze the wellness tourism sector with a specific focus on Asia and the Pacific. This is followed by case studies covering Thailand, India, and Sri Lanka and recommendations for Asian governments on how to further develop this sector.

Part 5 has three chapters. In Chapter 12, "Wellness for Happiness in Developing Asia," Shun Wang uses recent data on six wellness sectors from the Global Wellness Institute and self-reported happiness from the Gallup

World Poll to assess the wellness–happiness nexus empirically. In Chapter 13, "Policy Options to Promote Wellness in Asia," Katherine Johnston, Ophelia Yeung, and Gerard Bodeker discuss wellness policies that governments can embrace to encourage people to make healthy choices proactively and live healthy lifestyles, and to create living environments that support and encourage healthy behaviors and lifestyles. In Chapter 14, "Conclusion: Toward Wellness for All Asians," Donghyun Park brings together the salient findings of the various chapters and draws policy recommendations for improving and promoting wellness in Asia.

Donghyun Park
Pilipinas Quising
Asian Development Bank
Manila, Philippines

Contributors

Husnain Fateh Ahmad is an assistant professor of economics at Sewanee: The University of the South. Prior to that, he was an assistant professor of economics at Lahore University of Management Science. He obtained his doctor of philosophy (PhD) in economics from the University of Iowa, United States. He is an applied microeconomics researcher whose work applies techniques from theoretical as well as empirical and experimental economics to understand issues relevant to development. His research on auction theory and energy economics has been published in academic journals, while his more recent work focuses on the effect of information provision on individual behavior in the realms of air pollution and family planning. He has also used field and lab experiments to study individual decision-making in the presence of salient identity and contextual primes.

Julian Thomas Alvarez is a consultant at the Asian Development Bank (ADB). He earned both his master's and bachelor's degrees in economics at the University of the Philippines School of Economics. He was an economics instructor at the University of San Carlos in Cebu City from 2014 to 2017. His research interests include development economics, input–output analysis, and trade.

Michael John Barsabal is a consultant at ADB working on developing social accounting matrices and various economic indicators for different economies in Asia and the Pacific. He is a PhD (economics) candidate at the University of the Philippines Diliman, where he obtained his master's degree in the same field. His research interests include national accounting, input–output analysis, and monetary economics.

Gerard Bodeker, an Australian whose doctoral studies were at Harvard, is chairperson of the Oxford-based Global Initiative for Traditional Systems of Health and also chairs the Mental Wellness Initiative of the Global Wellness Institute. He holds a full professorship of epidemiology at Columbia University's Mailman School of Public Health in New York, currently on an adjunct basis. He has researched and taught in the Medical Sciences Division at Oxford for 2 decades and is a member of Oxford's graduate college, Green Templeton College. He is a fellow of the International Union of Pure and Applied Chemistry, editor in chief of the *World Health Organization Global Atlas of Traditional, Complementary,* and *Alternative Medicine,* and has worked with both the World Bank and several United Nations agencies, including United Nations Environment Programme, United Nations Development Programme, and Food and Agriculture Organization of the United Nations. He has published widely and is currently working on a book with Taylor & Francis titled *Healthy Ageing in Asia*.

Rafael Martin Consing III is a consultant at ADB specializing in the system of national accounts and input–output economics. His recent projects include analyses of wellness and tourism economies in developing Asia, multiregional input–output analysis of the COVID-19 pandemic's economic impact, and global value chains analysis in East Asia. His other fields of interest include environmental, health, and population economics. He undertook bachelor's, master's, and doctoral studies in economics at the University of the Philippines.

Penny Farrell is a public health researcher and veterinarian with more than 7 years of experience in health, nutrition, and agriculture policy research in Pacific island countries, Asia, and Africa. She recently completed a PhD on food security in the Pacific region and has worked previously in the nonprofit, university, and government sectors. She currently holds a position as a research fellow at the University of Sydney dedicated to researching how to build healthy and sustainable food systems globally, with a focus on low-income settings.

Matthias Helble is a senior economist in ADB's Economic Research and Regional Cooperation Department in Manila. Previously, he was a senior research fellow and cochair of the ADB Institute's Research Department in Tokyo. His research interests include international trade, health, and development. His research has been published in numerous scientific journals as well as in flagship reports of international organizations. His publication record also includes 10 books, including with Oxford University Press. Helble began his professional career at the World Bank, before joining the World Health Organization. He then worked as an economist for the World Trade Organization as well as the United Nations. He holds graduate degrees in economics from the University of Tübingen, the University of Wisconsin–Madison, and the Graduate Institute of International and Development Studies (PhD) in Geneva.

Katherine Johnston is a senior research fellow at the Global Wellness Institute. Since 2008, she has conducted pioneering research on the global wellness economy, work that has become the leading resource for wellness sector data and insights among media, industry, and government. Johnston conducts in-depth analysis of the forces shaping the future of wellness, along with deep-dive research into key industry sub-segments, including wellness communities and real estate, physical activity, workplace wellness, wellness tourism, spas, and thermal and mineral springs. Previously as a senior economist at SRI International, Johnston led dozens of studies on economic competitiveness, industry cluster and workforce development, economic development program evaluation, and economic impact analysis and modeling—both across the United States and in countries around the world. She holds a bachelor's degree from Sweet Briar College in Virginia and a master's degree from Georgetown University's School of Foreign Service.

Mahinthan Mariasingham is a senior statistician at ADB, where he leads statistical capacity-building initiatives in the economic statistics and statistical infrastructure domains. The projects he currently leads span more than 20 countries in Asia and the Pacific region. He was responsible for the development of the Asia-focused multi-region input–output database (ADB MRIO) and the statistical business register system suite (ADB-SBR). Mariasingham started his career at Statistics Canada in 1999 and specialized in system of national accounts and input–output economics. He earned a bachelor's and a master's degree in economics from Queen's University, Canada.

Donghyun Park is currently principal economist in ADB's Economic Research and Regional Cooperation Department, which he joined in April 2007. Prior to joining ADB, he was a tenured associate professor of economics at Nanyang Technological University in Singapore. He has a PhD in economics from University of California, Los Angeles, and his main research fields are international finance, international trade, and development economics. Park's research, which has been published extensively in journals and books, revolves around policy-oriented topics relevant for Asia's long-term development, including innovation, middle-income challenges, and finance sector development. He plays a leading role in the production of *Asian Development Outlook*, ADB's biannual flagship report on economic issues, and *Asia Bond Monitor*, ADB's quarterly flagship report on bond markets.

Madhavi Pundit is an economist in ADB's Economics Research and Regional Cooperation Department. She contributes to monitoring, analysis, and research for ADB's flagship publication, *Asian Development Outlook*. Her research areas are nowcasting, business cycles, international economics, economic policy, and applied econometrics with a focus on developing and emerging economies. Prior to joining ADB, Madhavi was with the National Institute of Public Finance and Policy in New Delhi, India. She holds a PhD in economics from Boston College, United States.

Pilipinas Quising is senior economics officer in ADB's Economic Research and Regional Cooperation Department. She received her bachelor's degree in business economics and master's degree in economics from the University of the Philippines. Before joining ADB as a staff member in 2000, she was consultant to an ADB cross-country poverty study and was a research associate at various institutions, working on projects on public health policy, local government decentralization, and international trade. She is coeditor, with Anil Deolalikar and Shikha Jha, of the book *Governance in Developing Asia: Public Service Delivery and Empowerment* and is part of the team that produces *Asian Development Outlook*, ADB's flagship biannual publication.

Irfan Qureshi is an economist in ADB's Economic Research and Regional Cooperation Department (ERCD). He contributes to macroeconomic surveillance, monitoring, and research while working for ADB's flagship publication, the *Asian Development Outlook (ADO)*. His research interests include monetary theory and policy, nowcasting, and macroeconomic development. His research has been published in academic journals on topics relating to monetary policy and debt dynamics in emerging markets. He joined ADB as a young professional in the Macroeconomic Research Division of ERCD, then in the Public Management, Financial Sector, and Trade Division of the Central and West Asia Department. He obtained his PhD in economics from the University of Warwick, United Kingdom. His research interests include monetary theory and policy, nowcasting, and macroeconomic development. He works on the teams that produce ADB's *Asian Development Outlook* report and conduct macroeconomic surveillance and monitoring.

Cut Novianti Rachmi is a medical doctor by training from Universitas Padjadjaran, Indonesia. She obtained her master's degree in international public health and PhD in community nutrition from the University of Sydney. Her thesis focused on the double burden of malnutrition in Indonesian children. Rachmi currently works as a consultant with Reconstra Utama Integra in Jakarta, Indonesia. She has strong research skills in both quantitative and qualitative research. She has been involved in studies, projects, and evaluation processes with Indonesia's Ministry of Health and international agency partnerships including the World Health Organization, Food and Agriculture Organization of the United Nations, United Nations Children's Fund (UNICEF), and GAIN. Her interest includes the triple burden of malnutrition and adolescent health. Rachmi is one of the cofounders of AKAR Indonesia, the association of adolescent health in Indonesia.

Anne Marie Thow is an associate professor in public policy and health at the University of Sydney and has more than 15 years of experience in policy research, including extensive policy analysis fieldwork in Africa, Latin America, Asia, and the Pacific. Her research uses theories of public policy making to explore facilitators and barriers to best practice public health nutrition policy. Thow has published more than 100 peer-reviewed articles and attracted more than $10 million in research funding. She regularly acts as a consultant and expert advisor to national governments and international organizations, most recently the World Health Organization, World Bank, and Food and Agriculture Organization of the United Nations. Prior to undertaking her PhD at the University of Sydney, she worked for the governments of Australia and Fiji on nutrition policy issues. She has trained in nutrition and has a master's degree in public policy.

Shu Tian is an economist in ADB's Economic Research and Regional Cooperation Department. Prior to joining ADB, she was an associate professor of finance at Fudan University, People's Republic of China. Her main research interests include financial services and institutions, financial market development, investments, and empirical asset pricing. Her research has been published in academic journals on topics relating to financial asset pricing, portfolio allocation, and financial market development. She works in the team that produce the *Asian Development Outlook* and *Asia Bond Monitor* reports, and is also part of the team that maintains AsianBondsOnline (https://asianbondsonline.adb.org), an online bond market data portal for ASEAN+3 bond markets under the ASEAN bond market initiative.

Shun Wang is a professor at KDI School of Public Policy and Management, Republic of Korea. He obtained a PhD in economics at the University of British Columbia, a master's degree in economics, and a bachelor's degree in business administration at Peking University. His research lies mainly in economic development, subjective well-being, and the Chinese economy. His papers have been published in the *Journal of Comparative Economics, World Development, Economic Development and Cultural Change, China Economic Review, Journal of Happiness Studies,* and others. He serves as a co-editor of the United Nations Sustainable Development Solutions Network's *World Happiness Report* series.

Scott Wayne is president of SW Associates—Sustainable Destination Services, a Washington, DC–based international development consultancy with more than 25 years of experience focused on sustainable destination development for both public and private sector clients and organizations. Wayne specializes in infrastructure; public–private partnerships; micro, small, and medium-sized enterprise tourism development; economic impact; investment; marketing; product development; policy making; and strategic planning. His clients have included ADB, World Bank, World Trade Organization, United States Agency for International Development (USAID), private sector, governments, and nongovernment organizations in more than 50 countries across every region. He is also an adjunct professor of destination planning at Georgetown University, a fellow at the Royal Geographical Society, and a member of the United Nations World Tourism Organization's Experts Panel. He holds a bachelor's degree in foreign service from Georgetown University's School of Foreign Service and a master's degree in international public administration from the University of Southern California's Schools of International Relations and Public Policy.

Ophelia Yeung has more than 20 years of experience leading research and consulting assignments for business, government, universities, and nonprofit organizations around the world, as director of the Economics Program and codirector of the Center for Science, Technology, and Economic Development at SRI International. Her recent work has focused on the wellness industry. As a senior research fellow at the Global Wellness Institute, Yeung coauthored numerous studies covering topics from the global wellness economy to healthy built environments and wellness tourism. She has presented at major industry events, written for industry publications, and given global press interviews on these topics. Yeung received a bachelor's degree in economics from Smith College and a master of public administration degree from the Princeton School of Public and International Affairs at Princeton University.

Abbreviations

ADB - Asian Development Bank
ASEAN - Association of Southeast Asian Nations
AYUSH - Ayurveda, Yoga & Naturopathy, Unani, Siddha and Homoeopathy
CASBEE - Comprehensive Assessment System for Built Environment Efficiency
CCP - critical control point
CHW - community health worker
COE - compensation of employees
COVID-19 - coronavirus disease
CVD - cardiovascular disease
DALY - disability-adjusted life year
DBM - double burden of malnutrition
DMC - developing member country
EAP - employee assistance program
EDB - Export Development Board
EIM - Exercise Is Medicine
ESG - environmental, social, and governance
FAO - Food and Agriculture Organization of the United Nations
FGID - functional gastrointestinal disorder
GBA - gut-brain axis
GBD - Global Burden of Disease
GDP - gross domestic product
GFCF - gross fixed capital formation
GNH - Gross National Happiness
GVA - gross value added
GWI - Global Wellness Institute
GWS - Global Wellness Summit
HACCP - hazard analysis and critical control point
HDI - Human Development Index
HPB - Health Promotion Board
IBEC - Institute for Building Environment and Energy Conservation
IGGI - Inclusive Green Growth Index
ILO - International Labour Organization
IOT - input–output table
IHRSA - International Health, Racquet & Sportsclub Association
ISIC - International Standard Industrial Classification of All Economic Activities
LMIC - low- and middle-income countries
MDA - marketing development assistance
NCD - noncommunicable disease
OCD - obsessive compulsive disorder
OECD - Organisation for Economic Co-operation and Development
OLS - ordinary least squares
ONS - Office of National Statistics (United Kingdom)
PCA - principal component analysis
PHC - primary health care
PPP - purchasing power parity
PRC - People's Republic of China
QOL - quality of life
ROK - Republic of Korea
SARS - severe acute respiratory syndrome
SDGs - Sustainable Development Goals
SNA - system of national accounts
SPI - Social Progress Index
SRH - self-rated health
SUT - supply and use table

TAT	-	Tourism Authority of Thailand
TCM	-	traditional Chinese medicine
ULC	-	unit labor cost
UNESCO	-	United Nations Educational, Scientific and Cultural Organization
UNWTO	-	United Nations World Tourism Organization
V-Dem	-	Variety of Democracy Initiative
WGI	-	World Governance Indicators
WHO	-	World Health Organization

PART 1

COVID-19 Brings Wellness to the Fore

CHAPTER 1

Why Does Wellness Matter So Much in the Age of COVID-19? A Selective Literature Review

Donghyun Park and Pilipinas Quising

Coronavirus disease (COVID-19) is a once-in-a-century global health and economic crisis. In this chapter, we document the link between the twin crises and individual well-being, especially mental health, by looking at past and current evidence. Past studies of the nexus between economic crisis and mental health, as well as the nexus between disaster outbreaks and mental health, point to a significant negative relationship. Emerging studies that analyze the effect of COVID-19 confirm a negative effect, which is likely to be large and persistent given the unprecedented nature of the health and economic crises. Our review thus strengthens the case for wellness, or the active pursuit of activities, choices, and lifestyles that promote happiness and well-being. Wellness will empower and enable individuals to achieve and maintain their mental well-being and physical well-being, which are invaluable assets for navigating the uncertain and stressful post-COVID-19 world.

COVID-19 Triggers a Global Health and Economic Crisis

COVID-19 is a highly infectious disease caused by a newly discovered coronavirus, which first emerged in December 2019. COVID-19 is an unprecedented, once-in-a-century shock to global health and the world economy. Although the disease initially affected the People's Republic of China (PRC) and other Asia and Pacific economies in December 2019 and January 2020, it has rapidly spread to all corners of the world. The World Health Organization (WHO) declared COVID-19 a pandemic on 11 March 2020. The pandemic has exacted a heavy toll on global public health, infecting about 54.8 million people and causing almost 1.3 million deaths worldwide by 17 November 2020. As of that date, the 12 countries with the highest number of confirmed cases were, in descending order, the United States (US), India, Brazil, the Russian Federation, France, Spain, the United Kingdom, Argentina, Italy, Colombia, Mexico, and Peru. This list of countries reflects the truly global nature of COVID-19. The future trajectory of the pandemic still remains subject to a great deal of uncertainty.

Asia too has been hit by COVID-19, which affected all subregions and economies of the continent. Although some Asian economies have been hit harder than others, none have been immune to the coronavirus. The PRC, the original epicenter of the pandemic, managed to contain it relatively effectively with stringent public health measures. The Republic of Korea (ROK), which suffered a major outbreak in late February, also brought the pandemic under control. Other Asian economies that have managed to curb the spread of the disease include Hong Kong, China;

Japan; Singapore; Taipei,China; and Viet Nam. India, on the other hand, has seen a rapid growth of cases. In addition to infecting large numbers of Asians, which has strained the health-care systems of Asian economies, the virus has also adversely affected people's mental health. Most developing Asian economies have already responded to the COVID-19 outbreak in various ways. Many governments have mobilized interagency task forces and other coordinating mechanisms to ensure a harmonized public health response.

In addition to COVID-19's devastating impact on global health, the lockdowns, travel bans, community quarantines, and other restrictions that were necessitated by the pandemic have derailed the world economy. In October, the International Monetary Fund projected that global output would contract by 4.4% and trade by 10.4% in 2020. This would mark the deepest global downturn in the postwar period, even worse than the Great Recession in the aftermath of the global financial crisis. The economies of developing Asia too will suffer a sharp downturn as a result of the pandemic. The evolution of the pandemic, and hence developing Asia's outlook, remains highly uncertain. In October 2020, the Asian Development Bank (ADB) drastically revised its 2020 regional growth forecast from April of the same year: from a slowdown of 2.2% to a contraction of 0.7%, the first regional recession in nearly 6 decades.

All of developing Asia's subregions will see their growth weaken in 2020. Global demand weakened by the pandemic will weigh on the 2020 outlook, particularly in the more open subregions and tourism-dependent economies like those in the Pacific. Growth in East Asia will dip from 5.4% in 2019 to 1.3% in 2020 before reaccelerating to 7.0% in 2021. The remaining subregions will all experience a contraction: South Asia by 6.8%, the Pacific by 6.1%, Southeast Asia by 3.8%, and Central Asia by 2.1%. Even Asian countries that managed to effectively contain the pandemic, such as the ROK, will see a sharp decline in their growth because of the deterioration of the global outlook. The pandemic of recession has spread to all subregions and economies.

Across developing Asia, governments have introduced fiscal stimulus packages and central banks have eased monetary policy to support economic activity. To support economic growth and help the most vulnerable population groups, the region's governments are ramping up spending. While countercyclical fiscal and monetary policies will help to soften the severe economic blow of the pandemic, the region clearly faces a highly uncertain economic future. In common with other parts of the world, the region faces the twin strategic challenges of tackling the health crisis while reopening and rebuilding the economy.

Global Health and Economic Crisis Brings Wellness to the Fore

The catastrophic effect of COVID-19 cannot be captured by simple numbers. Health impact figures, such as the number of confirmed cases and deaths, are informative and revealing. So too are economic impact figures such as gross domestic product (GDP) and export data. However, above all, COVID-19 has had a profound human effect. It has adversely affected billions of human lives around the world. More precisely, the pandemic has had a detrimental effect on the happiness and well-being of people in developing Asia and elsewhere. Fear of COVID-19 infection, economic hardship, uncertainty about the future, social isolation, and extended home confinement can all take a heavy toll on happiness and well-being. This is precisely why wellness, or the pursuit of happiness and well-being, is receiving significant attention from the public since the outbreak.

According to the Global Wellness Institute, wellness is the active pursuit of activities, choices, and lifestyles that lead to a state of holistic health.[1] Wellness is conceptually distinct from happiness and well-being, which refer to a subjective condition—being happy or in a state of well-being. On the other hand, wellness is associated with the process of actively making choices that lead toward optimal health and well-being. Wellness is also related

[1] Global Wellness Institute. *What Is Wellness?* https://globalwellnessinstitute.org/what-is-wellness.

to but distinct from the medical paradigm. While the two overlap when it comes to preventive health care, much of medical care is focused on treating and curing illness, whereas wellness focuses on moving from neutral to optimal health. Examples of wellness include exercising, eating healthy food, and meditating. Wellness is multidimensional and holistic in that it includes physical, mental, emotional, and social dimensions.

Even before the onset of COVID-19, Asia's demand for wellness had been growing for some time because of structural factors. In particular, higher incomes, noncommunicable diseases (NCDs), and population aging are driving the demand for wellness. Decades of rapid economic growth have left many Asians much richer than their forebears. As a result, Asians are becoming more aware of the benefits of healthier lifestyles. For instance, the quest for more calories is giving way to a quest for better nutrition. The growth of NCDs, such as heart diseases, stroke, diabetes, and cancer, in the region, is encouraging Asians to exercise more, eat better, and seek healthier life choices. In addition, Asia's population is aging. Older populations are associated with chronic diseases as well as loneliness and mental health issues. And Asia's worsening pollution presents a clear and present danger to the health of Asians.

Wellness can contribute to sustainable development as well as the mental and physical health of the poor. Wellness, or the active pursuit of well-being, is in line with the United Nations Sustainable Development Goals (SDGs), in particular SDG 3: to ensure healthy lives and promote well-being for all at all ages. A focus on wellness would also provide a more balanced and holistic view on development progress than simply pursuing increases in income per capita. In principle, many wellness activities, such as physical exercise, are available to all. In practice, the poor are at a disadvantage since they have less money and time to devote to wellness, and have more limited access to, or knowledge about, health facilities or nutritious foods. Public investment in wellness infrastructure, such as community recreation centers and green parks in poor neighborhoods, as well as health education campaigns, can help level the playing field.

To sum up, higher incomes, NCDs, population aging, and other structural factors were fueling Asians' growing demand for wellness even before the advent of COVID-19. The demand for wellness is likely to grow even more because of the pandemic, which has predictably become the overriding global concern since the outbreak and continues to do so even months after (Figure 1.1). Thus, COVID-19 will add impetus to a long-

Figure 1.1 **Top Five Global Concerns**

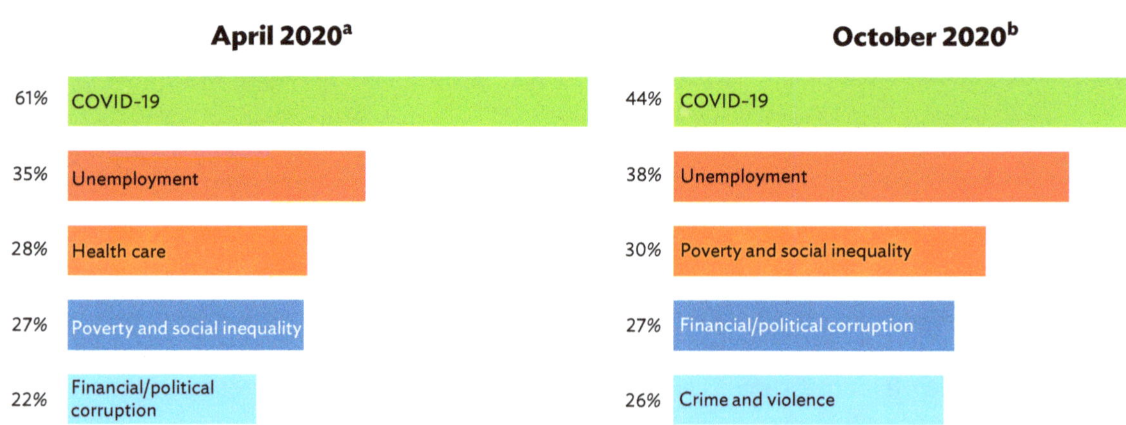

Notes:

[a] Research among adults ages 16–64 in 28 participating countries.
[b] Research among adults ages 16–64 in 27 participating countries.

Sources: For April 2020 data: Ipsos. 2020. *Coronavirus Dominates Global Worries*. https://www.ipsos.com/en/coronavirus-dominates-global-worries. For October 2020 data: Ipsos. 2020. *What Worries the World-October 2020*. https://www.ipsos.com/en-sg/what-worries-world-october-2020.

term structural trend. Given that the pandemic has led to both a health crisis and an economic crisis, it is not surprising that the general public has a wide range of concerns. The pandemic has had a negative impact on the happiness and well-being of Asians, and they are likely to actively pursue activities, choices, and lifestyles that lead to happier, more fulfilling lives.

Economic Crises and Health: Existing Evidence

COVID-19 is not a garden-variety economic crisis but a once-in-a-century economic crisis. Indeed, the current economic downturn is projected to be the worst since the Great Depression of the late 1920s and 1930s. Nevertheless, it is useful to review the existing literature on the effects of economic crises on health, which can provide us with at least some clues about the likely impact of the COVID-19 economic crisis.

There are two conflicting schools of thought on the effects of economic crises on health. One theory says that psychological and behavioral morbidity is procyclical in that it increases in good times. The other view says it is countercyclical—declining economies spell more incidence of illness.[2] Existing evidence is mixed.

According to the procyclical theory, people who lost their jobs or had their work hours reduced spent more time exercising, cooking healthy meals, sleeping, caring for children, managing the home, and gaining additional knowledge.[3] Changes in the use of time may also influence well-being in a general way by lowering the risk of contracting communicable disease[4] and lowering the incidence of vehicular accidents. Less driving during economic downturns improves the quality of air, which may lead to better health outcomes[5] and lower infant mortality.[6]

Viewed from another perspective, the daily grind, the fast pace of life, the high work stress, and the higher disposable income associated with economic expansion can lead to poorer health. A study of American adults in 1972–1981 showed an increase in reported medical problems (e.g., heart disease and back problems) during labor market expansion.[7] Mexican data from 1995 to 2010 showed a positive relationship between GDP per capita and ischemic heart disease and hypertension—diseases that are categorized as lifestyle diseases.[8]

Aside from time use changes, consumption changes may also be procyclical. For example, Ásgeirsdóttir et al. investigated the effects of the 2008 economic crisis in Iceland and found that health-compromising behaviors such as smoking, alcohol drinking, and consumption of non-healthy foods declined, but the practice of consuming fish oil and adequate sleeping improved.[9] Some studies have showed that smokers reduce the

2 R. Catalano et al. 2011. The Health Effects of Economic Decline. *Annual Review of Public Health.* 32. pp. 431–450.

3 M. Aguiar, E. Hurst, and L. Karabarbounis. 2013. Time Use during the Great Recession. *American Economic Review.* 103 (5). pp. 1664–96; M. Antillon, et al. 2014. Sleep Behavior and Unemployment Conditions. *Economics and Human Biology*. 14. pp. 22–32; T.L. Ásgeirsdóttir et al. 2014. Was the Economic Crisis of 2008 Good for Icelanders? Impact on Health Behaviors. *Economics and Human Biology*. 13. pp. 1–19. https://doi.org/10.1016/j.ehb.2013.03.005; and P. Brochu et al. 2012. The "Trendiness" of Sleep: An Empirical Investigation into the Cyclical Nature of Sleep Time. *Empirical Economics*. 43. pp. 891–913.

4 T. Barmby and M. Larguem. 2009. Coughs and Sneezes Spread Diseases: An Empirical Study of Absenteeism and Infectious Illness. *Journal of Health Economics*. 28. pp. 1012–17; and P. Cooley et al. 2011. The Role of Subway Travel in an Influenza Epidemic: A New York City Simulation. *Journal of Urban Health*. 88. pp. 982–995.

5 G. Heutel and C.J. Ruhm. 2013. Air Pollution and Procyclical Mortality. *NBER Working Paper* 18959.

6 K.Y. Chay and M. Greenstone. 2003. The Impact of Air Pollution on Infant Mortality: Evidence from Geographic Variation in Pollution Shocks Induced by a Recession. *Quarterly Journal of Economics*. 118. pp. 1121–1167.

7 C.J. Ruhm. 2003. Good Times Make You Sick. *Journal of Health Economics*. 22. pp. 637–658.

8 T. Quast and F. Gonzalez. 2014. Economic Cycles and Heart Disease in Mexico. *Social Science and Medicine*. 109. pp. 19–25. https://doi.org/10.1016/j.socscimed.2014.03.013.

9 T.L. Ásgeirsdóttir et al. 2012. Are Recessions Good for Your Health Behaviors? Impact of the Economic Crisis in Iceland; and T.L. Ásgeirsdóttir et al. 2014. Was the Economic Crisis of 2008 Good for Icelanders? Impact on Health Behaviors. *Economics and Human Biology*. 13. pp. 1–19. https://doi.org/10.1016/j.ehb.2013.03.005.

Figure 1.2 Macroeconomic Changes during Economic Downturns and Individual Responses

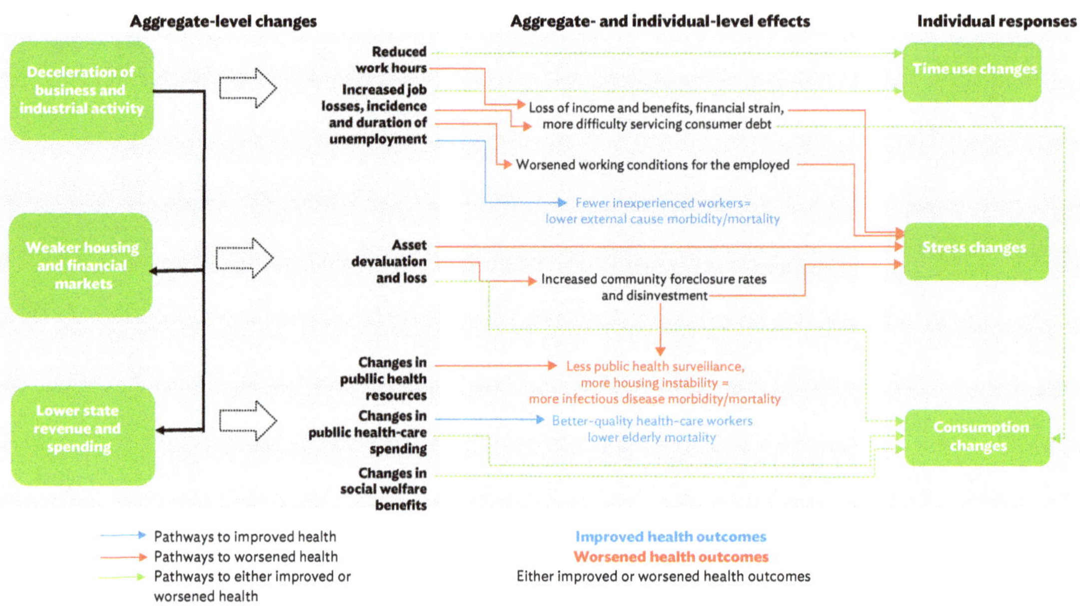

Source: S. Burgard and L. Kalousova. 2015. Effects of the Great Recession. *Annual Review of Sociology.* 41. p. 185, figure 1. https://www.annualreviews.org/doi/full/10.1146/annurev-soc-073014-112204.

number of cigarettes they smoke during recessions.[10] Similarly, cigarette smoking increases during periods of economic booms when work hours (and consequently income and stress) rise.[11]

Although we do not discount the possibility of economic crises positively affecting health, we will look primarily at the negative health effects of economic crises. There is a much larger body of evidence that supports a negative link.

There are three key macroeconomic changes associated with recessions: (i) a deceleration of economic activity that may lead to (ii) weakened housing and financial markets and (iii) lower government revenues (Figure 1.2). These changes affect an individual's resources and behaviors in ways that eventually influence their health. Following Burgard and Kalousova,[12] we will look at the links between economic crises and health, particularly mental health.

Aggregate Changes

While crises may have transitory impacts on economic activity, their effects on households and individuals may persist over the long term. At the macroeconomic level, the fiscal strain, because of the reduction of fiscal revenues during economic downturns, can force governments to implement severe cuts in public spending, including spending on health and welfare services. As a result, public health services may be unable to offer

[10] C.J. Ruhm. 2000. Are Recessions Good for Your Health? *Quarterly Journal of Economics*. 115. pp. 617–650; and C.J. Ruhm. 2005. Healthy Living in Hard Times. *Journal of Health Economics*. 24. pp. 341–363.

[11] X. Xu and R. Kaestner. 2010. The Business Cycle and Health Behaviors. *NBER Working Paper* 15737. https://www.nber.org/papers/w15737.

[12] S. Burgard and L. Kalousova. 2015. Effects of the Great Recession. *Annual Review of Sociology*. 41. pp. 181–201. https://www.annualreviews.org/doi/full/10.1146/annurev-soc-073014-112204.

services at lower rates and may be ill-equipped to absorb any surges in demand. The result may be a worsening quality of health care coupled with an increase in health-care costs. During the Asian financial crisis, real public health expenditures declined significantly in Indonesia, the ROK, the Lao People's Democratic Republic, the Philippines, and Thailand.[13] During the same period, immunization coverage in several regions in the Philippines declined.[14] In Europe during the 2008–2009 global financial crisis, the delivery of social services suffered, especially in health. Waiting lists in the health services for treatments and operations increased and patients were asked to pay a share of their treatment cost.[15]

Economic crises are sometimes associated with the collapse of financial and housing markets. The decline in asset prices leads to substantial wealth losses. In addition to wealth losses, the housing market's collapse can intensify residential crowding and homelessness. Abandoned foreclosed buildings can become hosts for insects and other disease vectors that weaken community-level immunity.[16] For example, Reisen et al.[17] found that a wave of delinquencies on adjustable-rate mortgages in Kern County, California, led to neglected swimming pools and a 276% increase in the number of human West Nile virus cases in 2007 because of increased mosquito reproduction. Even those who remain employed during recessions may face poorer work conditions, which can worsen health conditions.[18]

The economic difficulties experienced by the population will deepen existing health inequities and increase the social exclusion of vulnerable groups, which include the poor, children, young people, single-parent families, unemployed people, ethnic minorities, migrants, and older people. Research using Midlife in the US data found that the 2008/09 recession highlighted the health gap between the haves and have-nots. Comparing adults from time points before (1995–1996) and after (2011–2014) the recession, the authors found that the socioeconomic inequalities that were exacerbated by the global financial crisis were also evident in widening the health gaps.[19] Also using Midlife in the US data, Goldman, Glei, and Weinstein[20] found substantial social stratification of psychological health among American adults. The lower a person's socioeconomic status, the greater the drop in mental health. In Asia, there was a significant deterioration in the health and nutrition of mothers and children in poor communities in the short term during the 1997 Asian financial crisis.[21]

---

13 J. Knowles, E. Pernia, and M. Racelis. 1999. Social Consequences of the Financial Crisis in Asia: The Deeper Crisis. *EDRC Briefing Notes* No. 16. Asian Development Bank.

14 C.R. Reyes et al. 1999. Social Impact of the Regional Financial Crisis in the Philippines. *PIDS Discussion Paper Series* No. 99–14. Philippine Institute for Development Studies.

15 R. Hanan. 2012. The Social Impact of the Economic Crisis in Europe. *Working Notes*. Issue 69. https://www.workingnotes.ie/images/stories/Issue69/the%20social%20impact%20of%20the%20economic%20crisi%20in%20europe.pdf.

16 M. Suhrcke et al. 2011. The Impact of Economic Crises on Communicable Disease Transmission and Control: A Systematic Review of the Evidence. *PLOS One*. 6 (6): e20724. doi:10.1371/journal.pone.0020724.

17 W.K. Reisen et al. 2008. Delinquent Mortgages, Neglected Swimming Pools, and West Nile Virus, California. *Emerging Infectious Diseases*. 14 (11). pp. 1747–1749. https://doi.org/10.3201/eid1411.080719.

18 S. Modrek and M. Cullen. 2013. Job Insecurity during Recessions: Effects on Survivors' Work Stress. *BMC Public Health*. 13 (929). https://bmcpublichealth.biomedcentral.com/track/pdf/10.1186/1471-2458-13-929.pdf; S. Burgard and K. Lin. 2013. Bad Jobs, Bad Health? How Work and Working Conditions Contribute to Health Disparities. *American Behavioral Scientist*. 57 (8). pp. 1105–1127. https://doi.org/10.1177%2F0002764213487347; and M. Tausig and R. Fenwick. 1999. Recession and Well-Being. *Journal of Health and Social Behavior*. 40. pp. 1–16. https://doi.org/10.2307/2676375.

19 J.A. Kirsch and C.D. Ryff. 2016. Hardships of the Great Recession and Health: Understanding Varieties of Vulnerability. *Health Psychology Open*. https://doi.org/10.1177/2055102916652390; and J.A. Kirsch et al. 2019. Scientific Imperatives Vis-à-vis Growing Inequality in America. *American Psychologist*. 74 (7). pp. 764–777. https://doi.org/10.1037/amp0000481.

20 N. Goldman, D. Glei, and M. Weinstein. 2018. Declining Mental Health among Disadvantaged Americans. *Proceedings of the National Academy of Sciences*. 115 (28). pp. 7290–7295. DOI: 10.1073/pnas.1722023115.

21 Z. Bhutta et al. 2008. *The Impact of Food and Economic Crisis on Child Health and Nutrition*. https://www.researchgate.net/publication/228384646_The_Impact_of_Food_and_Economic_Crisis_on_Child_Health_and_Nutrition/link/0fcfd50a4d64f21c23000000/download.

Economic crisis and unemployment have a devastating impact on families, particularly children. Economic pressure, through its influence on parental mental health, marital interaction, and parenting, affects the mental health of children and adolescents.[22]

Individual Responses

Individual responses consist of time use changes, consumption changes, and stress changes.

Time Use Changes

Economic contraction can improve health when the reduced time at work enables a person to have more time available for productive and healthy practices (e.g., exercise or monitoring the health of chronically ill relatives). However, the opposite can also happen as individuals manage the consequences of lost jobs or lost income. Kumar et al.[23] showed that, without paid sick days, the employed may stay at work even when ill, increasing the risk of spreading infections. In addition, working conditions worsen in firms that have laid off many workers,[24] which could increase stress levels and mental and physical morbidity.

Consumption Changes

Households and individuals who lose income will forego consumption of healthy goods and services that they consider less essential. Catalano et al.[25] refer to this change in behavior as effect budgeting. The coping mechanisms they adopt may have deleterious consequences. For example, lower quantity and quality of food intake and less utilization of health services may lead to deterioration of household nutrition and health outcomes. Strategies like these were observed among Argentinian households in 2001 when the country was in deep economic and financial crisis,[26] among Asians during the Asian financial crisis of 1997/98,[27] and in Europe[28] and the US during the 2008/09 global financial crisis.[29]

Another form of coping mechanism is the increase in the consumption of unhealthy substances such as cigarettes, drugs, and alcohol. Using repeated cross-section individual-level data from 1984 to 1995, Dee showed that binge drinking in the US increased substantially during economic downturns.[30] Similarly, drug use and distribution and cigarette smoking rose among teens and young adults during economic downturns.[31]

---

[22] K. Conger, M. Rueter, and R. Conger. 2012. *The Role of Economic Pressure in the Lives of Parents and Their Adolescents: The Family Stress Model*. https://www.researchgate.net/publication/232543712_The_role_of_economic_pressure_in_the_lives_of_parents_and_their_adolescents_The_Family_Stress_Model; and R.D. Conger and K.J. Conger. 1992. A Family Process Model of Economic Hardship and Adjustment of Early Adolescent Boys. *Child Development*. 63 (3). pp. 526–541. doi:10.1111/1467-8624.ep9207061028.

[23] S. Kumar et al. 2013. Policies to Reduce Influenza in the Workplace: Impact Assessments Using an Agent-Based Model. *American Journal of Public Health*. 103. pp. 1406–1411.

[24] M. Tausig and R. Fenwick. 1999. Recession and Well-Being. *Journal of Health and Social Behavior*. 40. pp. 1–16. https://doi.org/10.2307/2676375.

[25] R. Catalano et al. 2011. The Health Effects of Economic Decline. *Annual Review of Public Health*. 32. pp. 431–450.

[26] A. Fiszbein, P.I. Giovagnoli, and I. Addriz. 2003. The Argentine Crisis and Its Impact on Household Welfare. *CEPAL Review*. 79. pp. 143–158. https://www.cepal.org/en/publications/10935-argentine-crisis-and-its-impact-household-welfare.

[27] J. Knowles, E. Pernia, and M. Racelis. 1999. Social Consequences of the Financial Crisis in Asia: The Deeper Crisis. *EDRC Briefing Notes* No. 16. Asian Development Bank.

[28] W. Bartlett and M. Uvalic. 2013. *The Social Consequences of the Global Economic Crisis in South East Europe*. https://www.researchgate.net/publication/257298392_The_Social_Consequences_of_the_Global_Economic_Crisis_in_South_East_Europe/download; N. Habibov et al. 2018. Effects of the 2008 Global Financial Crisis on Population Health. *The International Journal of Health Planning and Management*. 34 (1). pp. e327–e353. https://doi.org/10.1002/hpm.2652; and M. Ramesh. 2009. Economic Crisis and Its Social Impacts. *Global Social Policy*. 9. https://journals.sagepub.com/doi/pdf/10.1177/1468018109106886.

[29] S.A. Burgard and J.M. Hawkins. 2014. Race/Ethnicity, Educational Attainment, and Foregone Health Care in the United States in the 2007–2009 Recession. *American Journal of Public Health*. 104. pp. e134–e40.

[30] T.S. Dee. 2001. Alcohol Abuse and Economic Conditions: Evidence from Repeated Cross-Sections of Individual-Level Data. *Health Economics*. 10. pp. 257–270.

[31] J. Arkes. 2007. Does the Economy Affect Teenage Substance Use? *Health Economics*. 16 (1). pp. 19–36; and J. Arkes. 2012. How Does Youth Cigarette Use Respond to Weak Economic Periods? Implications for the Current Economic Crisis. *Substance Use & Misuse*. 47 (4). pp. 375–382.

Stress

Studies have shown that an economic crisis is a major source of stress that negatively affects health, especially mental health.[32] Stress is linked to a rise in unemployment; increased workload; difficulty in meeting financial obligations; wage and income reduction; and declines in institutional resources and social capital, which characterizes economic recessions.

The effects of economic crises on mental health can be categorized into four types: (i) psychological well-being (as measured by mental health distress, self-rated health [SRH], and well-being or quality-of-life variables); (ii) common mental disorders (such as depression, anxiety, and somatoform disorders); (iii) substance-related disorders; and (iv) suicidal behaviors.[33]

Using balanced panel data for 2008–2011 covering 26 European countries, Brzezinski[34] found that the incidence of low SRH increased during the crisis. The rise in low SRH was attributed mainly to the rise of material deprivation and job loss. Individual country studies also showed the same results during the economic recession in Greece,[35] Italy,[36] Spain,[37] Sweden,[38] and Japan.[39] Mental distress can also arise from an inability to service debt,[40] or from wealth losses. One study of Americans showed that those with large stock holdings prior to the global financial crisis were 50% more likely to feel depressed and 20% less likely to report excellent or very good health.[41]

Although the employed may not be as severely affected as the unemployed, they may also be affected by way of a more negative perception of the future. Giorgi et al.[42] looked at the effect of fear of the crisis on the mental health of the employed in Italy during the global financial crisis. The authors found that the fear of the economic crisis lessens the practice of social support as individuals become more preoccupied with their own situations. The decline in social support among employees, in turn, increases job-related stress, which naturally affects workers' mental well-being.

---

32 For a systematic review of studies correlating stress with economic crises, refer to N. Mucci et al. 2016. The Correlation Between Stress and Economic Crisis: A Systematic Review. *Neuropsychiatric Disease and Treatment*. 12. pp. 983–993. https://doi.org/10.2147/NDT.S98525.

33 D. Frasquilho et al. 2016. Mental Health Outcomes in Times of Economic Recession: A Systematic Literature Review. *BMC Public Health*. 16 (115). https://bmcpublichealth.biomedcentral.com/track/pdf/10.1186/s12889-016-2720-y.pdf.

34 M. Brzezinski. 2019. What Accounts for the Rise of Low Self-Rated Health during the Recent Economic Crisis in Europe? *International Journal for Equity in Health*. 18 (21).

35 N. Drydakis. 2015. The Effect of Unemployment on Self-Reported Health and Mental Health in Greece from 2008 to 2013: A Longitudinal Study before and during the Financial Crisis. *Social Science and Medicine*. 128. pp. 43–51. https://doi:10.1016/j.socscimed.2014.12.025; D. Zavras et al. 2013. Impact of Economic Crisis and Other Demographic and Socio-economic Factors on Self-Rated Health in Greece. *European Journal of Public Health*. 23 (2). pp. 206–210. doi:10.1093/eurpub/cks143; E. Simou and E. Koutsogeorgou. 2014. Effects of the Economic Crisis on Health and Healthcare in Greece in the Literature from 2009 to 2013: A Systematic Review. *Health Policy*. 115. pp. 111–119; and S. Vandoros et al. 2013. Have Health Trends Worsened in Greece as a Result of the Financial Crisis? A Quasi-Experimental Approach. *European Journal of Public Health*. 23. pp. 727–731.

36 L. Minelli et al. 2014. Employment Status and Perceived Health Condition: Longitudinal Data from Italy. *BMC Public Health*. doi:10.1186/1471-2458-14-946.

37 X. Bartoll et al. 2014. The Evolution of Mental Health in Spain during the Economic Crisis. *European Journal of Public Health*. 24 (3). pp. 415–418. doi:10.1093/eurpub/ckt208.

38 S. Blomqvist, B. Burström, and M. Backhans. 2014. Increasing Health Inequalities between Women in and out of Work—The Impact of Recession or Policy Change? A Repeated Cross-Sectional Study in Stockholm Country, 2006 and 2010. *International Journal for Equity in Health*. 13 (51). https://www.ncbi.nlm.nih.gov/pmc/articles/PMC4126349/pdf/1475-9276-13-51.pdf.

39 N. Kondo et al. 2008. Economic Recession and Health Inequalities in Japan: Analysis with a National Sample, 1986–2001. *Journal of Epidemiology and Community Health*. 62 (10). pp. 869–875. https://doi.org/10.1136/jech.2007.070334.

40 M. Keese and H. Schmitz. 2014. Broke, Ill, and Obese: Is There an Effect of Household Debt on Health? *Review of Income and Wealth*. 60. pp. 525–524; and E. Turunen and H. Hiilamo. 2014. Health Effects of Indebtedness: A Systematic Review. *BMC Public Health*. 14 (489). https://doi.org/10.1186/1471-2458-14-489.

41 M. McInerney, J.M. Mellor, and L.H. Nicholas. 2013. Recession Depression: Mental Health Effects of the 2008 Stock Market Crash. *Journal of Health Economics*. 32. pp. 1090–1104.

42 G. Giorgi et al. 2015. Economic Stress in Workplace: The Impact of Fear the Crisis on Mental Health. *Work*. 1. pp. 135–142. https://doi.org/10.3233/WOR-141844.

According to WHO, close to 800,000 people die of suicide every year, making it the 18th-leading cause of death in 2016, the latest year data is available. Suicide is a global phenomenon with many causes. However, studies have shown that there is a substantial increase in the prevalence of suicidal thoughts and attempts and actual suicide cases during and after economic recessions. The Asian financial crisis also saw a rise in suicide cases. There was a marked increase in suicide rates in a number of East Asian and Southeast Asian economies in the late 1990s.[43]

In a population-level study of suicide in 54 countries before and after the global financial crisis, Chang et al.[44] found that there were 4,884 more suicides in 2009 than what would have been expected based on trends between 2000 and 2007, prior to the crisis. European, North American, and South American countries drove the trend, as did men. In the 27 European countries studied, the suicide rate for men increased by 4.2%, while there was no increase for women. In the 18 countries in the Americas included in the analysis, suicide rates for men increased by 6.4%, compared with 2.3% for women. More recently, Economou et al.[45] found similar results for Greece in 2009 and 2011. People suffering from depression, men, married individuals, people experiencing financial strain, people with low interpersonal trust, and individuals with a history of suicide attempts were found to be particularly vulnerable to committing suicides.

Durkheim[46] proposed a possible explanation to the above phenomenon. According to Durkheim, during economic crises, the risk of suicide of certain individuals increases because they fail to adjust to the sudden deterioration in their socioeconomic status. The risk is intensified when society or institutions fail to help these individuals readapt.[47] The stress caused by economic recessions disrupts the equilibrium of the body and "evoke[s] a set of nonspecific physiological responses" that allow the body to cope.[48] However, if the exposure is intense, prolonged, or repeated, the physical and mental ability of the person to cope weakens, rendering the body more susceptible to illness and altering normal behavioral patterns.

Another unwelcome manifestation of this behavioral change is the rise in domestic violence. Stressful experiences increase the likelihood of experiencing other stressors not directly associated with the economy. These include marital difficulties or family conflicts. Actual economic hardship can cause abusive behavior. In addition, increasing uncertainty and the resulting fear and anxiety can affect the quality of relationships. For example, Schneider, Harknett, and Mclanahan[49] show that the adverse behavioral effects of unemployment shocks persisted even after controlling for individual-level measures of unemployment and material hardship. Unfortunately, domestic violence or marital conflicts affect not only the partners themselves. In particular,

[43] S. Chang et al. 2009. Was the Economic Crisis 1997–1998 Responsible for Rising Suicide Rates in East/Southeast Asia?; H. Kim et al. 2014. Changes in Mortality after the Recent Economic Crisis in South Korea. *Annals of Epidemiology*. 14 (6). pp. 442–446. doi:10.1016/j.annepidem.2003.09.018; J.J. Lin and T.H. Lu. 2008. 1971–2005. *BMC Public Health*. 8 (6.); Y.H. Khang, J.W. Lynch, and G.A. Kaplan. 2005. Impact of Economic Crisis on Causes Specific Mortality in Korea. *International Journal of Epidemiology*. 34. pp. 1291–1301; P. Thomyangkoon, A.A. Leenaars, and D. Wasserman. 2005. Suicide in Thailand, 1977 to 2002. *Archives of Suicide Research*. 9. pp. 361–368; K. Ueda and Y. Matsumoto. 2003. National Strategy for Suicide Prevention in Japan. *The Lancet*. 361 (882); and P.S. Yip et al. 2010. The Impact of Epidemic Outbreak: The Case of Severe Acute Respiratory Syndrome (SARS) and Suicide among Older Adults in Hong Kong. *Crisis*. 31. pp. 86–92.

[44] S.S. Chang et al. 2013. Impact of 2008 Global Economic Crisis on Suicide: Time Trend Study in 54 Countries. *The BMJ*. 347: f5239. doi:10.1136/bmj.f5239.

[45] M. Economou et al. 2013. Suicidal Ideation and Reported Suicide Attempts in Greece during the Economic Crisis. *World Psychiatry*. 12 (1). pp. 53–59.

[46] E. Durkheim. 1952. *Suicide, a Study in Sociology*. London: Routledge & K. Paul.

[47] World Health Organization. 2011. *Impact of Economic Crisis on Mental Health*. Denmark. See box comparing the unemployment rate and suicide rates in Sweden and Spain from 1980 to 2005.

[48] J.F. Phifer, K.Z. Kaniasty, and F.H. Norris. 1988. The Impact of Natural Disaster on the Health of Older Adults: A Multiwave Prospective Study. *Journal of Health and Social Behavior*. 29 (1). pp. 65–78.

[49] D. Schneider, K. Harknett, and S. Mclanahan. 2016. Intimate Partner Violence in the Great Recession. *Demography*. 53 (2). https://www.jstor.org/stable/24757065?seq=1.

children may suffer trauma from witnessing parental violence, and/or experience parental neglect as a consequence of violence.[50]

Disease Outbreaks and Mental Health

COVID-19 is both a health crisis and an economic crisis. As such, it is worthwhile to briefly take stock of the impact of a health crisis on mental health. Since COVID-19 is a new disease and much about it is still unknown, a high degree of fear and anxiety is engulfing the general population. The highly contagious nature of the disease causes fear, and anxiety is especially pronounced among the most vulnerable groups, including health-care providers, the elderly, and those with preexisting health conditions. As the coronavirus pandemic spreads and its impacts are felt widely, a sense of helplessness, loneliness, and depression; the use of alcohol, drugs, and other toxic substances; and self-harm or suicidal attempts are expected to rise. Historically, outbreaks of epidemics and pandemics have been found to trigger elevated levels of stress, fear, and anxiety, which can harm the psychological well-being of the population. Studies on the severe acute respiratory syndrome (SARS) epidemic outbreak in 2003, the Ebola outbreak in Sierra Leone, and the H1N1 influenza virus outbreak in 2009 all showed an increase in depression, anxiety, somatoform disorders, and suicidality.[51]

Brooks et al.[52] reviewed 24 studies covering 10 countries to document the psychological impact of quarantine during SARS, Ebola, 2009 and 2010 H1N1 influenza, Middle East respiratory syndrome, and equine influenza. Most of the reviewed studies reported negative psychological effects, including post-traumatic stress symptoms, confusion, and anger, with some individuals suffering long-lasting effects. Identified stressors include longer quarantine duration, infection fears, frustration, boredom, inadequate supplies, inadequate information, financial loss, and stigma. The potential fallout of an economic downturn on mental health is pronounced for those directly affected and their caregivers. For example, the SARS epidemic in 2003 was associated with a 30% increase in suicide in those aged 65 years and older, about 50% of recovered patients remained anxious, and 29% of health-care workers experienced emotional distress.

Lack of accurate information and the abundance of misinformation, often aided by sensationalist popular media headlines and articles, have been shown to fuel health-related fears and phobias.[53] The explosive growth of social media in recent years is further fueling misinformation, popularly known as fake news, which can spread and intensify fear and anxiety.

[50] A.E. Appel and G.W. Holden. 1998. The Co-occurrence of Spouse and Physical Child Abuse: A Review and Appraisal. *Journal of Family Psychology*. 12 (4). pp. 578–599. https://doi.org/10.1037/0893-3200.12.4.578; and E. Nicklas and M. Mackenzie. 2012. Intimate Partner Violence and Risk for Child Neglect during Early Childhood in a Community Sample of Fragile Families. *Journal of Family Violence*. 28. doi:10.1007/s10896-012-9491-8.

[51] M.Y. Chong et al. 2004. Psychological Impact of Severe Acute Respiratory Syndrome on Health Workers in a Tertiary Hospital. *British Journal of Psychiatry*. doi:10.1192/bjp.185.2.127; P. Wu et al. 2009. The Psychological Impact of the SARS Epidemic on Hospital Employees in [the People's Republic of] China: Exposure, Risk Perception, and Altruistic Acceptance of Risk. *Canadian Journal of Psychiatry*. 54 (5). pp. 302–311. doi:10.1177/070674370905400504; P.S. Yip et al. 2010. The Impact of Epidemic Outbreak: The Case of Severe Acute Respiratory Syndrome (SARS) and Suicide among Older Adults in Hong Kong. *Crisis*. 31. pp. 86–92; L. Page et al. 2011. Using Electronic Patient Records to Assess the Impact of Swine Flue (influenza H1N1) on Mental Health Patients. *Journal of Mental Health*. 20 (1). pp. 60–69; and S. Kamara et al. 2017. Mental Health Care during the Ebola Virus Disease Outbreak in Sierra Leone. *Bulletin of the World Health Organization*. 1 December. 95 (12). pp. 842–847. https://www.ncbi.nlm.nih.gov/pmc/articles/PMC5710077.

[52] S. Brooks et al. 2020. The Psychological Impact of Quarantine and How to Reduce It: Rapid Review of the Evidence. *The Lancet*. 395 (10227). pp. 912–20.

[53] S. Taylor and G.J.G. Asmundson. 2004. *Treating Health Anxiety: A Cognitive-Behavioral Approach*. New York: Guilford Press.

The COVID-19 Pandemic and Mental Health

The previous sections make it abundantly clear that both economic crisis and outbreaks of diseases have significant adverse effects on mental health. Therefore, the fact that COVID-19 is a once-in-a-century economic crisis as well as a health crisis is likely to amplify its negative impact on mental health. Although the COVID-19 pandemic is still evolving and far from over, its effects are already being felt. Emerging evidence shows that the deterioration in mental health can be deep and long-lasting. The pronounced and persistent effect on mental health, in turn, may further deepen the economic consequences of the twin crises.

In less than a year since WHO declared COVID-19 a pandemic, many studies have already delved into its mental health effects. Canadian psychology researchers, for example created a database of studies documenting the effects of COVID-19 on mental health.[54] At the time of writing, this database already includes 56 studies. The most common symptom citied in the studies is anxiety. Anxiety was associated with impaired sleep[55] and even delirium.[56]

Also, female gender, being a student, having symptoms suggestive of COVID-19, having young children and/or high-risk people living in their homes, and having poor perceived health were associated with higher rates of anxiety and depression. On the other hand, the availability of accurate information and the use of specific preventive measures, such as handwashing, seemed to mitigate negative thoughts.[57] A number of studies have also documented the mental health issues facing health care workers, including frontline medical personnel.[58] Recently, researchers have coined the term "coronaphobia" to refer to the fear and the emotional and social strain experienced by the general public in response to COVID-19.[59] Obsessive behaviors, distress, avoidance reaction, panic, anxiety, hoarding, paranoia, and depression are some of the known manifestations of coronaphobia.[60]

COVID-19 and the Urgent Case for Wellness

Emerging evidence that looks directly at the effects of COVID-19, as well as evidence from the large existing literature on the effects of economic and health crises on health, especially mental health, strongly suggest that the pandemic will have a significant negative impact on the happiness and well-being of humanity. Economic crisis inflicts substantial economic pain on individuals—for example, unemployment or loss of income. Likewise, disease outbreaks heighten individuals' health-related worries and anxiety—for example, fears and even paranoia

[54] Bronfenbrenner Center for Translational Research. 2020. *What Are the Mental Health Effects of COVID-19?* https://www.psychologytoday.com/us/blog/evidence-based-living/202008/what-are-the-mental-health-effects-covid-19; Medical research on COVID-19 is also available through Elsevier's Novel Coronavirus Information Center (https://www.elsevier.com/connect/coronavirus-information-center?dgcid=_SD_banner#research) and is updated frequently.

[55] See, for example, H. Xiao et al. 2020. The Effects of Social Support on Sleep Quality of Medical Staff Treating Patients with Coronavirus Disease 2019 (COVID-19) in January and February 2020 in [the People's Republic of] China. *Medical Science Monitor*. 26: e923549; R. Rossi et al. 2020. *COVID-19 Pandemic and Lockdown Measures Impact on Mental Health among the General Population in Italy. An N=18147 Web-Based Survey*. https://www.researchgate.net/publication/340642451_COVID-19_pandemic_and_lockdown_measures_impact_on_mental_health_among_the_general_population_in_Italy_An_N18147_web-based_survey; and S. Liu et al. 2020. Online Mental Health Services in [the People's Republic of] China during the COVID-19 Outbreak. *The Lancet Psychiatry*. 7 (4). pp. e17–e18. https://doi.org/10.1016/S2215-0366(20)30077-8.

[56] E. Deans. 2020. Mental Health Effects of COVID-19 Infection. *Psychology Today*.

[57] D. Wang et al. 2020. Clinical Characteristics of 138 Hospitalized Patients with 2019 Novel Coronavirus–Infected Pneumonia in Wuhan, [People's Republic of] China. *Journal of the American Medical Association*. 323. pp. 1061–1069. doi:10.1001/jama.2020.1585 pmid:32031570.

[58] B. Tan et al. 2020. Psychological Impact of the COVID-19 Pandemic on Health Care Workers in Singapore. *Annals of Internal Medicine*. https://doi.org/10.7326/M20-1083; H. Xiao et al. 2020. The Effects of Social Support on Sleep Quality of Medical Staff Treating Patients with Coronavirus Disease 2019 (COVID-19) in January and February 2020 in [the People's Republic of] China. *Medical Science Monitor*. 26: e923549; and C. Zhang et al. 2020. Survey of Insomnia and Related Social Psychological Factors among Medical Staff Involved in the 2019 Novel Coronavirus Disease Outbreak. *Frontiers of Psychiatry*. 11. https://www.frontiersin.org/articles/10.3389/fpsyt.2020.00306/full.

[59] See PubMed.gov https://pubmed.ncbi.nlm.nih.gov/32078967 for a list of studies referring to coronaphobia.

[60] J. Watson. 2020. COVID-19's Psychological Impact Gets a Name. *Medscape Pediatrics*. https://www.medscape.com/viewarticle/938253.

of infection. Given the unprecedented nature of COVID-19, which has wrought havoc on global health systems and the world economy in a matter of weeks, it may leave a large, lasting footprint on the well-being of individuals in Asia and beyond. The pandemic strengthens the case for wellness, or the active pursuit of activities, choices, and lifestyles that promote well-being, for a number of specific reasons.

First, COVID-19 underscores the importance of being physically fit and healthy, which boosts our immune systems that protect us from disease. Although the virus that causes COVID-19 infects people of all ages, evidence to date confirms that fitter and healthier individuals are less vulnerable. According to WHO, older people (people over 60 years old) and those with underlying medical conditions (such as cardiovascular disease, diabetes, chronic respiratory disease, and cancer) are more vulnerable.[61] These findings have been corroborated by clinical studies of COVID-19 patients.[62] The Centers for Disease Control and Prevention of the US has identified obesity, or a body mass index of 40 kilogram per square meter (kg/m^2) or higher, as another risk factor.[63] This is not surprising, as obesity has been associated with greater risk of type 2 diabetes, cardiovascular disease, and hypertension. These conditions are classified in the medical profession as lifestyle diseases that can be prevented by physical activity.

Just as individuals with preexisting physical illness are more likely to fall ill from COVID-19, people with existing mental issues are also at greater risk of experiencing more serious mental illness as a result of COVID-19. These people are at a greater risk of relapse, owing to fear, anxiety, and social rhythm disruption. For example, staying with family may harm a patient who suffers from post-traumatic stress disorder because of past family trauma. Another example is people who have a preexisting condition known as obsessive compulsive disorder (OCD). Patients suffering from one type of OCD, known as contamination OCD, frequently and repeatedly wash their hands. The COVID-19 pandemic can blur the boundary between health safety and compulsion.

Growing medical evidence points to the lingering effects of the virus in the patient's body even after he or she recovered. This was revealed in blood tests done by Chinese doctors on 34 COVID-19 patients. Results show that many biological markers of those who survived did not return to normal.[64] Similar evidence was found in discharged COVID-19 patients in Hong Kong, China. They had difficulty doing the same activities they did in the past. In short, COVID-19 survivors would need to continue to engage in activities that improve their physical condition, such as regular exercise.

Second, although community lockdowns and quarantines are curtailing the spread of the disease, the restrictions are encouraging physical inactivity and greater reliance on processed food and canned goods, which may increase the risk of metabolic diseases in the population. Staying at home disrupts social rhythms and deprives people of their social-coping mechanisms for dealing with stress, leading to loneliness, depression, and erosion of mental function.

[61] WHO. 2020. Coronavirus Disease (COVID-19) Advice for the Public: Myth Busters. https://www.who.int/emergencies/diseases/novel-coronavirus-2019/advice-for-public/myth-busters.

[62] For example, R. Huang et al. 2020. *Clinical Findings of Patients with Coronavirus Disease 2019 in Jiangsu Province, China: A Retrospective, Multi-Center Study*. https://ssrn.com/abstract=3548785; D. Wang et al. 2020. Clinical Characteristics of 138 Hospitalized Patients with 2019 Novel Coronavirus–Infected Pneumonia in Wuhan, [People's Republic of] China. *Journal of the American Medical Association*. 323. pp. 1061–1069. doi:10.1001/jama.2020.1585 pmid:32031570; J. Yang et al. 2020. Prevalence of Comorbidities in the Novel Wuhan Coronavirus (COVID-19) Infection: A Systematic Review and Meta-Analysis. *International Journal of Infectious Diseases*. 94. pp. 91–95. https://www.sciencedirect.com/science/article/pii/S1201971220301363; S. Garg et al. 2020. Hospitalization Rates and Characteristics of Patients Hospitalized with Laboratory-Confirmed Coronavirus Disease 2019—COVID-NET, 14 States, 1–30 March. *Morbidity and Mortality Weekly Report*. 69. pp. 458–464. DOI: http://dx.doi.org/10.15585/mmwr.mm6915e3; and W. Liang et al. 2020. Clinical Characteristics and Outcomes of Hospitalised Patients with COVID-19 Treated in Hubei (Epicenter) and Outside Hubei (Non-Epicenter): A Nationwide Analysis of [the People's Republic of] China. *European Respiratory Journal*. https://doi.org/10.1183/13993003.00562-2020.

[63] Centers for Disease Control and Prevention. 2020. Groups at Higher Risk of Severe Illness. https://www.cdc.gov/coronavirus/2019-ncov/need-extra-precautions/groups-at-higher-risk.html.

[64] D. Wu et al. 2020. Plasma Metabolomic and Lipidomic Alterations Associated with COVID-19. *National Science Review*. https://doi.org/10.1093/nsr/nwaa086.

Leading theories of suicide emphasize the key role that social connections play in suicide prevention. Individuals having suicidal thoughts often lack connections to other people and often disconnect from others.[65] Also, what if the individual is living in a toxic home environment? Then spending more time at home without access to the usual support networks could be extremely stressful. Thus, the public health strategy that is central to stopping the spread of the disease may be triggering another kind of crisis centered on social isolation and loneliness.

Third, wellness activities play an important role in boosting the immune system to fight coronavirus. Proper hygiene, good nutrition, adequate sleep, meditation, regular exercise, and a positive attitude can reduce stress and build the body's resistance against infections and other illnesses. Health experts have also issued warnings against smoking, vaping, and alcohol consumption.[66] Smoking cigars and cigarettes, using drugs, and vaping can damage the lungs and contribute to pneumonia—a possibly fatal complication of coronavirus. Similarly, drinking alcohol damages the liver and reduces the presence of white blood cells and other helpful microorganisms in the body that help fight off infections.

Fourth, when the pandemic recedes, post-COVID-19 care will emerge as a top priority. People who survived the virus have to engage in wellness activities to help them fully recover and get their lives back. Not only do we have to think about the patients, but also the health-care providers who may be physically as well as mentally and emotionally exhausted. Another social issue that must be tackled is the social stigma and discrimination toward infected people and their family members.

Finally, we cannot rule out the danger of a pandemic-induced burnout. When people are forced to stay at home and do their work from home, then the lines between home and work and between the personal and the professional become blurred. Coupled with the pressure to be more productive because we now have more time, being busy now becomes part of our own coping mechanism. Since we are doing work remotely, in the comforts of our home, the tendency to overwork is stronger and the risk of burnout may increase. That is, people may overwork without knowing it since they are working in the comfort of their home.

Concluding Observations

COVID-19 is a once-in-a-century global health and economic crisis. In this paper, we document the link between the twin crises and individual well-being, especially mental health, by looking at past and current evidence. Past studies of the nexus between economic crisis and mental health, as well as the nexus between disaster outbreaks and mental health, point to a significant negative relationship. Emerging studies analyzing the effect of COVID-19 confirm a negative effect, which is likely to be large and persistent given the unprecedented nature of the health and economic crises. Our review thus strengthens the case for wellness, or the active pursuit of activities, choices, and lifestyles that promote happiness and well-being. Wellness will empower and enable individuals to achieve and maintain their mental and physical well-being, which are invaluable assets for navigating the uncertain and stressful post-COVID-19 world.

Importantly, wellness is not the exclusive preserve of richer countries or richer individuals. During COVID-19, poor and vulnerable groups bore a disproportionate share of the health and economic pain—for example, African Americans in the US. And developing countries with weak health-care infrastructures have seen health disasters morph into humanitarian disasters, with their hospitals unable to cope with surging cases. But wellness can contribute to sustainable development as well as the mental and physical health of the poor.

[65] N. Darvishi et al. 2015. Alcohol-Related Risk of Suicidal Ideation, Suicide Attempt, and Completed Suicide: A Meta-Analysis. *PLOS One*. 10 (5): e0126870. doi: 10.1371/journal.pone.0126870.

[66] National Institute on Drug Abuse (NIDA). 2020. COVID-19: Potential Implications for Individuals with Substance Use Disorders. https://www.drugabuse.gov/about-nida/noras-blog/2020/04/covid-19-potential-implications-individuals-substance-use-disorders.

Further Reading

C. Coile, P. Levine, and R. McKnight. 2012. Recessions, Older Workers, and Longevity: How Long Are Recessions Good For Your Health? *NBER Working Paper* No. 18361.

S. Lee. 2020. Coronavirus Anxiety Scale: A Brief Mental Health Screener for COVID-19 Related Anxiety. *Death Studies*. 44 (7). pp. 393–401. doi: 10.1080/07481187.2020.1748481.

E. Morselli. 1882. *Suicide: An Essay on Comparative Moral Statistics*. New York: D. Appleton and Company. https://archive.org/details/suicide00morsgoog/page/n22/mode/2up.

N. Moukaddam. 2019. Fears, Outbreaks, and Pandemics: Lessons Learned. *Psychiatric Times*. 36. https://www.psychiatrictimes.com/anxiety/fears-outbreaks-and-pandemics-lessons-learned/page/0/1.

M. Narici et al. 2020. Impact of Sedentarism Due to the COVID-19 Home Confinement on Neuromuscular, Cardiovascular and Metabolic Health: Physiological and Pathophysiological Implications and Recommendations for Physical and Nutritional Countermeasures. *European Journal of Sport Science*. https://doi.org/10.1080/17461391.2020.1761076.

C. Nicomedes and R. Avila. 2020. *An Analysis on the Panic of Filipinos during COVID-19 Pandemic in the Philippines*. 10.13140/RG.2.2.17355.54565.

Office for National Statistics. 2020. Coronavirus and the Social Impacts on Great Britain: 7 May 2020. https://www.ons.gov.uk/peoplepopulationandcommunity/healthandsocialcare/healthandwellbeing/bulletins/coronavirusandthesocialimpactsongreatbritain/latest#main-points.

H.W. Tsang, R.J. Scudds, and E.Y. Chan. 2004. Psychosocial Impact of SARS. *Emerging Infectious Diseases*. 10. pp. 1326–1327.

CHAPTER 2

The Global Wellness Industry and Its Implications for Asia's Development

Ophelia Yeung and Katherine Johnston

Wellness is a word that was not often spoken or seen in print just 10 years ago. Yet in the last few years it has become ubiquitous in consumer and trade media and has entered the vernacular all around the world. Consumer interest in all things related to wellness is accelerating, and wellness has become a selling point for all kinds of products and services—from food and vitamins to real estate and vacation packages, and from gym memberships and health-care plans to meditation apps and DNA testing kits. The wellness economy is estimated to be a $4.5 trillion market in 2017–2018.[1] *This chapter examines the definitions and drivers of the global wellness industry, its current size in Asia and globally, its future prospects, and the implications of an expanding wellness industry for Asia's development.*

Introduction and Background

Wellness: A Modern Industry with Ancient Roots

Wellness has emerged as an industry only recently, but as a concept and practice it has existed for thousands of years. The key tenets of wellness as both preventive and holistic can be traced back to ancient civilizations from the East to the West. Ayurveda, an ancient health-care system that was recorded more than 2,000 years ago in sacred Hindu texts, strives to create harmony between body, mind, and spirit.[2] Traditional Chinese medicine (TCM), another one of the world's oldest systems of medicine, is influenced by Buddhist and Taoist philosophies and extends the concept of health through harmony from the individual to the family, community, and environment.[3] Hippocrates, the ancient Greek physician, was possibly the

[1] Global Wellness Institute (GWI). 2019. *Move to Be Well: The Global Economy of Physical Activity*. https://globalwellnessinstitute.org/industry-research/global-economy-physical-activity; and GWI. 2018. *Global Wellness Economy Monitor 2018*. https://globalwellnessinstitute.org/industry-research/2018-global-wellness-economy-monitor.

[2] A. Guha. n.d. Ayurvedic Medicine. *Taking Charge of Your Health & Wellbeing*. Earl E. Bakken Center for Spirituality & Healing, University of Minnesota. https://www.takingcharge.csh.umn.edu/explore-healing-practices/ayurvedic-medicine (accessed 19 November 2018).

[3] C. Hafner. n.d. Acupuncture and Traditional Chinese Medicine. *Taking Charge of Your Health & Wellbeing*. Earl E. Bakken Center for Spirituality & Healing, University of Minnesota. https://www.takingcharge.csh.umn.edu/explore-healing-practices/acupuncture (accessed 19 November 2018).

first member of the medical profession to emphasize the prevention of disease; his wellness concept is captured in the modern Hippocratic Oath: "I will prevent disease wherever I can, for prevention is preferable to cure."[4]

A variety of intellectual, religious, and medical movements, which developed in parallel with conventional medicine in the 19th-century United States (US) and Europe, have provided a firm foundation for wellness today. These focused on holistic and natural approaches, self-healing, and preventive care, including homeopathy, osteopathy, chiropractic, and naturopathy. These kinds of wellness-focused, holistic modalities have gained more visibility since the 1960s and the 1970s through the writings and thought leadership of an informal network of American physicians and thinkers (such as Halbert Dunn, Jack Travis, Don Ardell, and Bill Hettler), who have informed much of the healthy-living, self-help, well-being, fitness, diet, and spirituality movements that are flourishing today.[5]

In regions around the world, the popular understanding and usage of the word "wellness" may vary because of cultural, historical, and linguistic differences. For example, in Europe, wellness is often used in association with activities such as spas, health resorts, thalassotherapy, and the types of nonmedical treatments offered at such facilities. Many Europeans use the term "well-being" when referring to a concept of holistic health. In Asia, many ancient spiritual traditions, healing modalities, and life philosophies, including yoga, Ayurveda, TCM, tai chi, reiki, meditation, herbal medicines, and *ikigai*, are deeply ingrained in the culture and daily life. However, in Asia, these activities may not be associated with the word "wellness" like they are in the West. For example, in the Chinese language, the concept closest to wellness is *yangsheng*, which means "looking after one's health" or "keeping fit," while the English word "wellness" is translated simply as "health" in Chinese.

As the popularity of wellness practices has grown in recent years, the understanding and usage of the term "wellness" is gradually converging to a universal definition. Simply put, wellness is closely related to, and complementary with, health. Since 1948, the World Health Organization (WHO) has defined "health" as a state of complete physical, mental, and social well-being and not merely the absence of disease or infirmity.[6] This definition is significant for going beyond a physical state of simply being free of disease, and also emphasizing a holistic approach that includes the social and mental dimensions.

Notwithstanding some regional variations in the usage of the term, several common threads stand out in the definitions of wellness.

(i) **Wellness is multidimensional.** It incorporates physical, mental, emotional, social, and other dimensions.
(ii) **Wellness is holistic.** Each dimension influences the other dimensions of wellness, and they must work in harmony.
(iii) **Wellness changes over time and along a continuum.** Wellness is not a static state or an end point, but is experienced along a continuum where an individual attempts to move toward an optimal sense of health and well-being.

[4] P. Tyson. 2001. The Hippocratic Oath Today. *Public Broadcasting Service (PBS)*. https://www.pbs.org/wgbh/nova/article/hippocratic-oath-today.
[5] SRI International and Global Spa Summit. 2010. *Spas and the Global Wellness Market: Synergies and Opportunities.* https://globalwellnessinstitute.org/industry-research/spas-global-wellness-market.
[6] WHO. 1948. *Constitution of World Health Organization: Principles.* https://www.who.int/about/mission/en.

(iv) **Wellness is individual and environmental.** Wellness depends upon individual choices, behaviors, and lifestyles, but is also significantly influenced by the physical, social, and cultural environments in which people live.

(v) **Wellness is a self-responsibility.** Wellness requires individuals to be aware and proactively make choices that lead to better health and well-being.

Wellness is often used synonymously with terms such as health, well-being, and happiness. While there are common elements among these concepts, especially the multidimensional and holistic aspects, wellness is distinguished from the others by not referring to a static state of being (i.e., being happy, in good health, or in a state of well-being); rather, wellness is associated with a process of being aware and actively making choices that lead toward an outcome of optimal health. The authors and the Global Wellness Institute (GWI) now use and advocate a definition of wellness that emphasizes its active qualities: "Wellness is the active pursuit of activities, choices, and lifestyles that lead to a state of holistic health."[7]

Quantification of the Global Wellness Industry

The quantification of the global wellness industry is a recent endeavor, and it remains limited and incomplete. The recent measurement of the global wellness economy as a $4.5 trillion industry is based on the work of the authors conducted under the auspices of GWI. This work originated in 2008 with the measurement of the global spa industry, a study that was launched to support a newly founded, knowledge-sharing, and "visioning" event known as the Global Spa Summit. Over time, this annual event (renamed the Global Wellness Summit [GWS] in 2015) has grown in both scope and attendance to include more than 600 wellness industry executives across a broad spectrum of wellness segments (e.g., spa, fitness, healthy eating, mental wellness, integrative medicine, and public health) and occupations (e.g., investors, technology experts, physicians, academics, real estate developers, and architects).[8] In 2015, the nonprofit GWI was established by GWS founders and leadership to support the activities that are championed by GWS delegates and other wellness industry stakeholders throughout the year. Wellness industry research is one of GWI's major focuses.

Over the last 10 years, the authors have conducted a number of studies under the auspices of GWI and GWS to quantify six wellness sectors: spas, thermal and mineral springs, wellness tourism, workplace wellness, wellness real estate, and physical activity. For each of these six sectors, the authors created a conceptual framework to define the industry and its boundaries and estimated the sectors' sizes country by country to arrive at globally aggregated figures. To our knowledge, these are the only studies that have estimated the size of these six sectors across all the economies in the world using a consistent framework.[9]

[7] GWI. 2018. *Global Wellness Economy Monitor 2018*. https://globalwellnessinstitute.org/industry-research/2018-global-wellness-economy-monitor.

[8] GWS. *About Us*. https://www.globalwellnesssummit.com/about-us.

[9] GWI. *Wellness Industry Research*. https://globalwellnessinstitute.org/industry-research.

In 2014, GWI and GWS commissioned the authors to estimate the size of the global wellness industry for the first time. The authors identified 10 key wellness sectors, estimated their global size at $3.4 trillion in 2013, and created the term "global wellness economy" to describe these 10 sectors collectively.[10] For the four sectors where we do not produce original country-level data, we employ a variety of secondary sources to derive a global aggregate for each one: healthy eating, nutrition, and weight loss; personal care, beauty, and anti-aging; preventive and personalized medicine and public health; and traditional (indigenous) and complementary medicine. To our knowledge, this was the first time that wellness was defined and measured as a global industry. GWI's global wellness economy figure has been updated since, most recently in 2019 (using 2017 and 2018 data).[11] However, a considerable amount of work remains to be done on sector definitions, data collection, and estimation, especially in the four remaining wellness sectors that have not been studied in detail by GWI, in order to measure the size of the overall wellness industry by domestic economy and by region (for Asia and the Pacific and other regions around the world).

The authors acknowledge that other researchers, economists, and industry analysts may have differing opinions on what constitutes the global wellness industry or the wellness economy. The data and estimates put forth in this chapter are based on our decade of work via GWI and GWS, as well as our collaborations with industry stakeholders worldwide, to understand the history and concept of wellness, how it is translated into economic activities, and how these activities can be defined and quantified. The next sections will present our definitions and measurements of the global wellness economy, both worldwide and in the Asia and Pacific region.

The Global Wellness Economy: Definitions, Data, Drivers, and Growth

What Is Wellness?

Measuring the size of the wellness economy first requires a clear definition of wellness. In previous research for GWI, the authors have defined wellness as the active pursuit of activities, choices, and lifestyles that lead to a state of holistic health. There are two important aspects to this definition. First, wellness is not a passive or static state, but rather an "active pursuit" that is associated with intentions, choices, and actions. Second, wellness is linked to holistic health, that is, it extends beyond physical health and incorporates many different dimensions, including physical, mental, emotional, spiritual, social, and environmental dimensions (Figure 2.1).

While this definition aligns with the most common understanding and practice of wellness as it has developed in recent years, other conceptual frameworks for wellness may incorporate additional dimensions such as intellectual wellness, occupational wellness, or financial wellness. The important point is not which specific dimensions are or are not included in the wellness framework, but merely that wellness is multidimensional and is about more than just physical health.

---

10 GWI. 2014. *Global Spa & Wellness Economy Monitor*. https://globalwellnessinstitute.org/industry-research/global-spa-wellness-economy-monitor-2014.

11 GWI. 2019. *Move to Be Well: The Global Economy of Physical Activity*. https://globalwellnessinstitute.org/industry-research/global-economy-physical-activity; and GWI. 2018. *Global Wellness Economy Monitor 2018*. https://globalwellnessinstitute.org/industry-research/2018-global-wellness-economy-monitor.

Figure 2.1 **Wellness Is Multidimensional**

Source: Global Wellness Institute.

Wellness is about more than just physical health. Most models of wellness include at least 6 dimensions (sometimes up to 9 or 12).

- **Physical.** A healthy body through exercise, nutrition, sleep, etc.
- **Mental.** Engagement with the world through learning, problem-solving, creativity, etc.
- **Emotional.** Being in touch with, aware of, accepting of, and able to express one's feelings (and those of others).
- **Spiritual.** Our search for meaning and purpose in human existence.
- **Social.** Connecting with, interacting with, and contributing to other people and our communities.
- **Environmental.** A healthy physical environment free of hazards; awareness of the role we play in bettering rather than denigrating the natural environment.

What Is the Wellness Economy?

With this conceptual understanding of wellness, the authors define the wellness economy as "industries that enable consumers to incorporate wellness activities and lifestyles into their daily lives." Further, the authors identified 10 sectors that are associated with the wellness economy (Figure 2.2). By aggregating the size of these industries, the authors and GWI estimate the global wellness economy to be worth $4.5 trillion in 2017–2018.[12] See Box 2.1 for research scope and methodology.

[12] Note that the $4.5 trillion wellness economy figure combines sector-specific estimates from two years; the estimate for physical activity is for 2018, while estimates for all other sectors are for 2017.

Figure 2.2 **The Global Wellness Economy**

b = billion.

Source: Global Wellness Institute.

Box 2.1 **Research Scope and Methodology**

The global wellness economy and industry data presented in this report are for 2017 and 2018. The definitions, conceptual framework, and estimation models for the various wellness sectors are developed by the authors under the auspices of the Global Wellness Institute (GWI), consistent with the data and methodologies used in prior GWI studies over the last decade. The authors have developed original, country-level data estimates for six wellness economy sectors: spas, wellness tourism, thermal and mineral springs, workplace wellness, wellness real estate, and physical activity, based on GWI's proprietary models and databases. Global figures for the other four wellness sectors are aggregated from secondary sources.

The 10 wellness sectors that the authors and GWI measure in detail or in aggregate are not defined as industries in national accounts or in national or international industry classification systems; therefore, they are not tracked by governments, and very little data exist to measure them. Similar to the challenges of measuring "high-tech" industries or "green" industries, wellness-related activities cut across traditional industry boundaries, include a mixture of products and services, and are not easily categorized. Most wellness sectors are not well defined or understood across countries and first require definition before they can be measured, especially for very new and emerging segments such as wellness tourism and wellness real estate. The estimation methodologies were developed by the authors, sector by sector, over a span of 11 years, to address the needs of public and private sector stakeholders who are interested in understanding these sectors and their growth. The estimation methodologies are not consistent across each sector because they are driven by each sector's definition, the availability of data inputs, and the need to develop estimates that are easily communicated to key audiences. For example, some sectors (such as spas and thermal and mineral springs) lend themselves to a "bottom-up" approach, where we can count or estimate the number of business establishments, and then estimate revenues and employment based on key benchmark figures across different subcategories, sizes, and regional contexts. Other sectors (such as wellness tourism and wellness real estate) use a "top-down" approach because overall tourism or construction and real estate expenditures data are available across different countries and regions, and we can estimate the "wellness

continued on next page

Box 2.1 *continued*

portion" out of these totals. Since wellness industry measurement is a new and challenging endeavor, the figures and methodologies are still a work in progress, and the authors welcome and encourage others to help add rigor to these figures and contribute to definitional and data collection efforts.

The figures presented in this chapter are based on extensive primary and secondary research conducted in 2018–2019, including literature reviews, data research, and dozens of expert interviews. Key public and private sources consulted include Euromonitor International, World Bank, International Monetary Fund, World Health Organization, International Labour Organization, World Travel & Tourism Council, World Tourism Organization United States (US). Bureau of Labor Statistics, US National Institutes of Health, International Spa Association, International Health, Racquet & Sportsclub Association, and global travel promotion and booking websites, along with numerous country-specific and industry-specific organizations, databases, publications, and media sources (e.g., the *2018 Global Wellness Trends Report* by the Global Wellness Summit, *Spa Business Handbook*, and *Spa Business Magazine*).

The authors also benefited from industry insights and technical inputs from several GWI initiatives, including the Wellness Tourism Initiative, the Wellness Communities Initiative, the Wellness at Work Initiative, and the Hot Springs Initiative.

Source: Authors.

The 10 sectors in the wellness economy are defined as follows:

(i) **Wellness real estate.** Expenditures on construction of residential and commercial or institutional (e.g., office, hospitality, mixed-use or multifamily, medical, and leisure) properties that incorporate intentional wellness elements in their design, materials, and building as well as their amenities, services, and/or programming.

(ii) **Workplace wellness.** Expenditures on programs, services, activities, and equipment by employers aimed at improving their employees' health and wellness. These expenditures aim to raise awareness; provide education; offer incentives that address specific health risk factors and behaviors (e.g., lack of exercise, poor eating habits, stress, obesity, and smoking); and encourage employees to adopt healthier lifestyles.

(iii) **Wellness tourism.** The aggregation of all expenditures made by wellness tourists (primary and secondary, international and domestic), including spending on lodging, food and beverage, activities and excursions, shopping, and in-country transportation.

(iv) **Spa economy.** Includes the revenues of spa facilities and the related cluster of sectors that support and enable spa businesses, such as spa education, spa consulting, spa capital investments, spa associations, and spa-related media and events.

(v) **Thermal and mineral springs.** Encompasses the revenues of business establishments associated with the wellness, recreational, and therapeutic uses of water with special properties, including thermal water, mineral water, and seawater.

(vi) **Physical activity.** Consumer spending associated with intentional physical activities performed during leisure and recreation, including three recreational activity subsectors (sports and active recreation, fitness, and mindful movement) and three enabling subsectors (technology, equipment and supplies, and clothing and apparel).

(vii) **Healthy eating, nutrition, and weight loss.** Includes consumer expenditures on vitamins and supplements, fortified or functional foods and nutraceuticals, natural and organic foods, health foods, sports nutrition, nutrition and dietary services, and weight loss or management products and services.

(viii) **Personal care, beauty, and anti-aging.** Includes consumer expenditures on beauty and salon services (excluding spas); skin, hair, and nail care services and products; cosmetics, toiletries, and other personal care products; dermatology; and prescription pharmaceuticals for skin care, as well as products and services that specifically address age-related health and appearance issues, such as cosmetics and cosmeceuticals for skin/face/body care, hair care or growth, and pharmaceuticals and supplements that treat age-related health conditions.

(ix) **Preventive and personalized medicine and public health.** Includes expenditures on medical services that focus on treating "well" people, preventing disease, or detecting risk factors—for example, routine physical exams, diagnostic and screening tests, and genetic testing. Personalized health uses sophisticated information and data for individual patients (including genetic, molecular, and environmental screening, analysis, and diagnostics; personalized disease management services; and health information technology such as electronic health records, telemedicine, and remote patient monitoring) to provide tailored approaches for preventing disease, diagnosing and managing risk factors, or managing and treating conditions.

(x) **Traditional and complementary medicine.** Encompasses expenditures on diverse medical, health care, holistic, and mentally or spiritually based systems, services, and products that are not generally considered to be part of conventional medicine or the dominant health-care system, including homeopathic, naturopathic, chiropractic, TCM, Ayurveda, energy healing, and traditional or herbal remedies and supplements. The nomenclature for this sector is evolving alongside growing consumer adoption of traditional and indigenous, complementary, alternative, and integrative medical practices outside of the conventional or Western medical system.

The Wellness Economy: Size and Projections

The authors estimate that the wellness economy is currently a $4.5 trillion market, accounting for roughly 5.5% of global economic output in 2017. By comparison, global health expenditures were estimated at $7.4 trillion in 2016.[13] From 2013 to 2017, the wellness economy grew from $3.4 trillion to $4.2 trillion, or by 5.8% annually, a growth rate more than five times as fast as global economic growth (1.1% annually).[14] Figure 2.3 illustrates the average annual growth rates of nine sectors included in the wellness economy from 2013 to 2017.[15] During this period, the fastest-growing sectors were wellness real estate, fitness and mind–body, and preventive and personalized medical and public health.[16]

Within a relatively short span of time, wellness has emerged globally as a dominant lifestyle value, driving consumer interest in exercise, healthy eating, self-care, mindfulness, stress reduction, healthy aging, complementary medicine, holistic health, and other wellness practices. For an expanding set of consumers, wellness has become an important value system used to filter daily life and decision-making, with a growing focus

[13] Authors' analysis of health expenditures data is from WHO. *Global Health Expenditures Database.* http://apps.who.int/nha/database/Home/Index/en. The year 2016 is the most recent year available.

[14] Global gross domestic product (GDP) data is from the International Monetary Fund. *World Economic Outlook Database.* October 2019 Edition. https://www.imf.org/external/pubs/ft/weo/2018/02/weodata/index.aspx.

[15] The 10th sector, traditional and complementary medicine, is not included in this figure because the definition and measurement of this sector was changed by GWI in 2017, and therefore the size estimates cannot be directly compared as a time series.

[16] In the past year, the authors have defined and measured a new segment within the wellness economy, "physical activity," which replaces the segment previously called "fitness and mind–body." The $4.5 trillion figure for the wellness economy reflects the new 2018 figures for physical activity, combined with 2017 figures for the other nine segments. The $4.5 trillion figure is not directly comparable with the $4.2 trillion figure published by the authors and GWI in 2017 (or earlier figures for the wellness economy) because of the change in the definition of this segment. Therefore, when analyzing growth rates, the authors are using 2017 figures for the wellness economy and its segments, because they can be directly compared as a time series with previous years.

Figure 2.3 **Average Annual Market/Revenue Growth, 2012–2017**

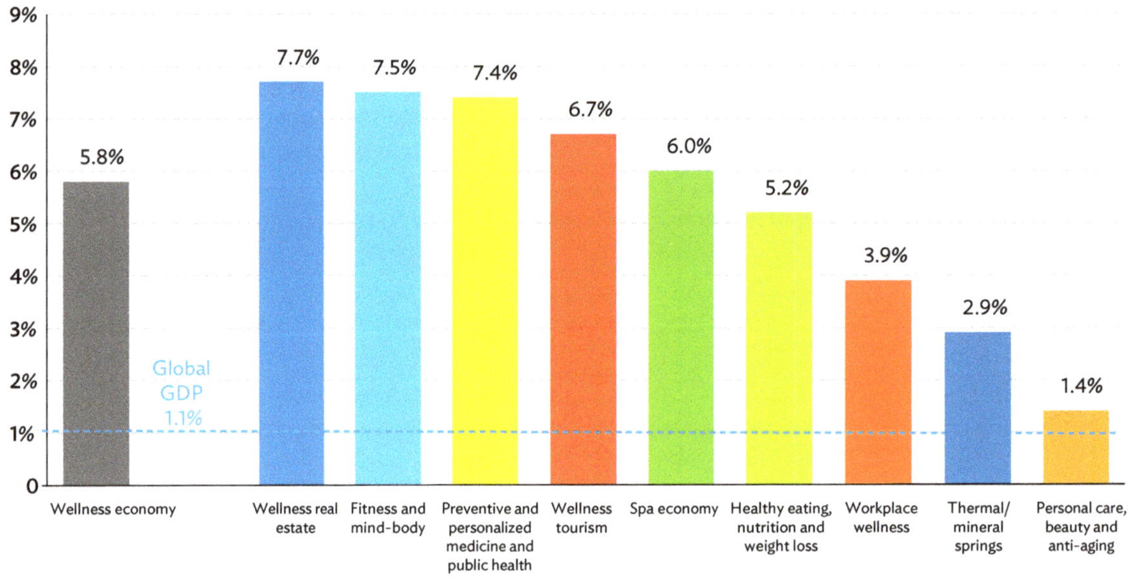

GDP = gross domestic product.

Source: Global Wellness Institute.

Figure 2.4 **Projected Average Annual Growth Rate, 2017–2022**

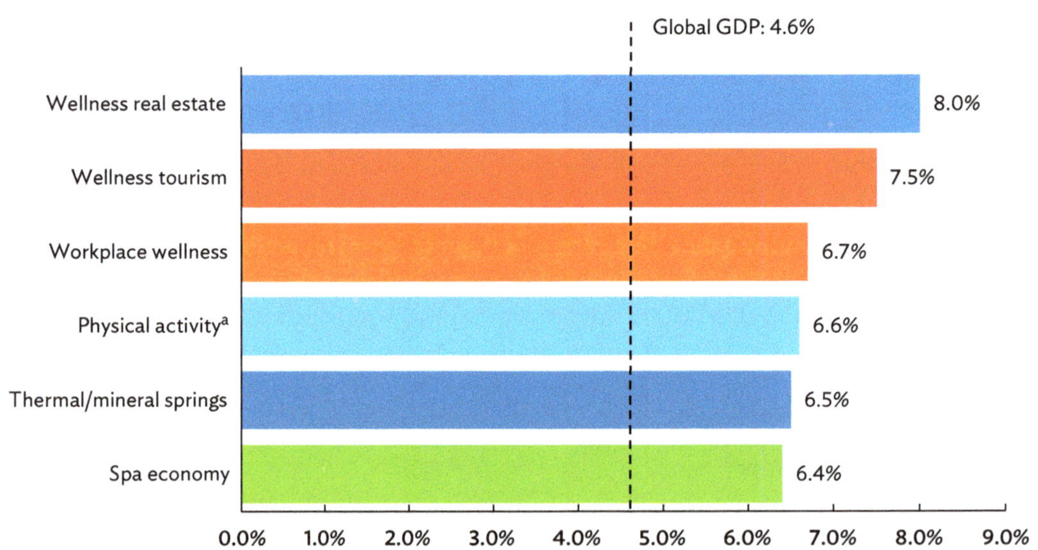

[a] Projection for physical activity segment is for 2018–2023.

GDP = gross domestic product.

Sources: Global Wellness Institute. Global GDP data from International Monetary Fund. *World Economic Outlook Database*. October 2019 edition.

on issues such as food quality and the way food is prepared and consumed, mitigating stress and boosting mental wellness, incorporating movement into daily activities, environmental consciousness, the yearning for connection, the desire for self-actualization, and a search for happiness. There is no sign that this trend is slowing down. For the next 5 years, the authors project robust growth in the six wellness sectors that we track in detail (Figure 2.4). The upward momentum for the wellness economy is strong because the underlying trends that propel it remain as compelling as ever (see the following section).

Macro Drivers of the Global Wellness Economy

In recent decades, vast economic, technological, social, demographic, and environmental changes have brought both positive and negative impacts for human health and well-being. The growth of the wellness economy is fundamentally a consumer response to these megatrends, and this response is turning into a major societal and economic force.

The World's Population Is Growing Sicker, Lonelier, and Older

Consumers are seeking different approaches and models in their personal lives, in order to deal not only with aging, but also with rising chronic and lifestyle diseases, alongside increasing stress and mental health issues. Global statistics in these areas are alarming.

(i) **Lifestyle and environmental disease.** Noncommunicable diseases (NCDs) are now the leading causes of death (replacing communicable and infectious diseases), collectively responsible for 71% of deaths worldwide. More than three-quarters of global NCD-related deaths occur in low-income and middle-income countries.[17] According to WHO, at least 80% of heart disease, stroke, and type 2 diabetes, as well as 40% of cancers, could be prevented by addressing key risk factors.[18] Consumers are becoming aware that they can reduce risks through physical activity, healthy diets, moderated use of tobacco and alcohol, lower levels of stress, and healthier lifestyles overall.

(ii) **Loneliness and mental health.** In 2017, there were an estimated 1.1 billion cases reported worldwide of mental and substance use disorders (affecting about 15% of the world's population).[19] According to WHO, depression increased by more than 18% from 2005 to 2015, and it is the leading global cause of illness and disability.[20] Policy makers and physicians in developed countries are also worried about the rise of loneliness and isolation as a public health epidemic. A recent cross-country survey found that 9% of adults in Japan, 22% in the US, and 23% in the United Kingdom (UK) report always or often feeling lonely or socially isolated.[21] Loneliness is closely linked with physical and mental illness and has significant health impacts. The growing visibility of mental health and illness and its gradual de-stigmatization have opened the door to people seeking help through wellness modalities, such as meditation, mindfulness, and yoga.

---

[17] WHO. 2018. *Fact Sheet: Noncommunicable Diseases.* http://www.who.int/en/news-room/fact-sheets/detail/noncommunicable-diseases.

[18] WHO. 2005. *Preventing Chronic Diseases: A Vital Investment—Misunderstanding #4.* https://www.who.int/chp/chronic_disease_report/part1/en/index11.html.

[19] Authors' analysis of data from Institute for Health Metrics and Evaluation. *Global Health Data Exchange.* http://ghdx.healthdata.org (accessed 30 November 2018).

[20] WHO. 2017. "Depression: Let's Talk" Says WHO, as Depression Tops List of Causes of Ill Health. *WHO News Release.* http://www.who.int/en/news-room/detail/30-03-2017--depression-let-s-talk-says-who-as-depression-tops-list-of-causes-of-ill-health.

[21] B. DiJulio, et al. 2018. *Loneliness and Social Isolation in the United States, the United Kingdom, and Japan: An International Survey.* https://www.kff.org/other/report/loneliness-and-social-isolation-in-the-united-states-the-united-kingdom-and-japan-an-international-survey.

(iii) **Population aging.** Globally, the population aged 60 and over is growing faster than all younger age groups.[22] In 2020, adults over age 65 will outnumber children under age 5,[23] and by 2050 all regions of the world except Africa will have nearly a quarter or more of their populations at age 60 and above (footnote 22). With aging populations also comes the rise of chronic disease. For individuals, the important question is no longer about increasing life span, but how to maximize healthy life span (compression of morbidity). This aging population, which has collectively amassed considerable wealth, is an important market force behind the wellness economy.

The Environmental Crisis Is Also a Health Crisis

As the world heads into an environmental crisis, governments around the world are not treating it with adequate urgency, partly because the ramifications of things like climate change may seem remote or indirect to most people. However, there is mounting evidence that environmental degradation and its causes are also causing immediate, direct, severe, and widespread harm to human health and well-being.

(i) **Pollution and health.** Modern living and human activities release enormous amounts of toxins into our air, water, soil, and food that harm human health. Pollution is now the largest environmental cause of disease and premature death, responsible for 9 million avoidable premature deaths worldwide (or 16% of all deaths) in 2015. More than 90% of these deaths were in low-income and middle-income countries.[24] Nearly three-quarters of these deaths were because of outdoor and indoor air pollution, which increases the incidences of asthma, lung cancer, heart disease, stroke, and other chronic diseases.[25] In low-income regions, people who cook with coal or biomass fuels face particularly high risks from indoor air pollutants, suffering as many as 4 million premature deaths every year from these practices.[26] Even in high-income countries, where research on "sick-building syndrome" is only emerging, studies have shown that indoor air pollution can be twice or five times worse than outdoors.[27] The shifting of focus from environmental to human welfare is also beginning to bring attention to some of the sustainability practices that can be harmful to health, such as sealing windows and insulating buildings with toxic materials and substances.

(ii) **Agriculture, food, and health.** Another area of consumer wellness interest that has grown out of environmental concern is the modern agricultural system. The impacts of monoculture, reduction of biodiversity, nutrient depletion in soil, pesticides and runoff, genetically modified organisms, and greenhouse gas emissions are not merely environmental, but are also profoundly adverse to human health. The proliferation of the modern, industrialized system of farming and food production, distribution, and marketing is linked to the spread of unhealthy, nutrition-poor, highly processed Western diets, which contribute to the rise of obesity and chronic disease worldwide. According to the Global Burden of Disease study, poor diet is a factor in one out of five deaths around the world.[28] In addition,

[22] United Nations. n.d. *Global Issues: Ageing*. http://www.un.org/en/sections/issues-depth/ageing (accessed 30 November 2018).

[23] W. He, D. Goodkind, and P. Kowall. 2016. An Aging World: 2015. U.S. Census Bureau. *International Population Reports*. Washington, DC: U.S. Government Publishing Office. https://www.census.gov/content/dam/Census/library/publications/2016/demo/p95-16-1.pdf.

[24] P.J. Landrigan et al. 2018. The *Lancet* Commission on Pollution and Health. *The Lancet*. 391 (10119). pp. 462–512. https://doi.org/10.1016/S0140-6736(17)32345-0.

[25] WHO. n.d. *Air Pollution*. https://www.who.int/airpollution/en (accessed 30 November 2018).

[26] WHO. 2018. *Household Air Pollution and Health Fact Sheet*. http://www.who.int/mediacentre/factsheets/fs292/en.

[27] US Environmental Protection Agency. n.d. *Volatile Organic Compounds' Impact on Indoor Air Quality*. https://www.epa.gov/indoor-air-quality-iaq/volatile-organic-compounds-impact-indoor-air-quality (accessed 30 November 2018).

[28] S. Boseley. 2017. Poor Diet Is a Factor in One in Five Deaths, Global Disease Study Reveals. *The Guardian*. https://www.theguardian.com/society/2017/sep/14/poor-diet-is-a-factor-in-one-in-five-deaths-global-disease-study-reveals. Cites data from *The Lancet*. Global Burden of Disease Study. https://www.thelancet.com/gbd.

contaminated foods are responsible for 600 million illnesses (nearly 1 in 10 people) and 420,000 deaths every year, resulting in the loss of 33 million healthy life years.[29]

(iii) **Car dependence and unwell lifestyles.** The growing dominance of the automobile over the last century is not only a major contributor to pollution and climate change, but also has enormous health ramifications. Rising rates of car ownership and congestion, along with urban planning that invests in driving over active or public transit, contribute to stress, sedentary behavior, lack of time for social and leisure activities, and other unhealthy lifestyle risk factors for chronic disease. While North America has long been the epicenter of these issues, these development patterns are now spreading throughout other rapidly urbanizing regions around the world.

Health Systems Fail to Keep Up, While the Economic Burden Rises

Health systems around the world are largely based on the paradigm of conventional Western medicine and focused on "sick care," and they are failing to meet the needs of a growing number of aging, chronically ill, and mentally ill patients. While global health expenditures grew from 8.6% of global GDP in 2000 to 10.0% in 2016,[30] only about 4%–5% of the $7.4 trillion in annual health expenditures is on prevention, risk reduction, and public health.[31] Meanwhile, research now indicates that up to 80%–90% of our health outcomes may be determined by external and environmental factors that are outside the purview of the health-care system.[32] The burden of disease is immense, affecting families (e.g., out-of-pocket costs, lost work and income, and suffering); businesses (e.g., rising health premiums for employees, lost productivity, and absenteeism); and governments (e.g., rising costs for national health-care systems). Thus, it is not surprising that consumers, employers, and even governments are turning to wellness approaches to complement and address deficiencies in existing health-care systems.

Consumer Demographics, Value Systems, and Lifestyles Are Rapidly Evolving

Rapidly evolving global demographics, lifestyles, and value systems are increasing consumer interest in, knowledge of, and access to wellness modalities, products, and services, even as these developments create more need for wellness.

(i) **Urbanization and growth of the middle class.** September 2018 marked a "tipping point" when more than 50% of the global population (3.8 billion people) are now "middle class" or "rich." Most of the new entrants to the middle class are Asian and from developing countries.[33] Middle-class consumers drive global economic growth, with their large numbers and their discretionary funds to spend on enhancing quality of life or searching for fulfilment and happiness (e.g., health, education, travel, entertainment, and experiences). The wellness economy has benefited from this growing consumer base. Parallel to this development is rapid urbanization. In 2018, 55% of the global population was living in urban areas, and their share will reach 68% by 2050. Much of this growth will come from developing countries, especially India, the People's Republic of China (PRC), and Nigeria.[34] The twin phenomena of urbanization and a growing middle class have upended

[29] WHO. 2017. *Food Safety Fact Sheet*. http://www.who.int/news-room/fact-sheets/detail/food-safety.

[30] Authors' analysis of WHO *Global Health Expenditures Database*, and WHO data cited in World Bank. *World Development Indicators*. https://data.worldbank.org/indicator/SH.XPD.CHEX.GD.ZS (accessed 30 November 2018).

[31] Authors' analysis of WHO *Global Health Expenditures Database*.

[32] GWI. 2018. *Build Well to Live Well: Wellness Lifestyle Real Estate and Communities*. https://globalwellnessinstitute.org/industry-research/wellness-real-estate-communities-research.

[33] H. Kharas and K. Hamel. 2018. A Global Tipping Point: Half the World Is Now Middle Class or Wealthier. *Brookings*. https://www.brookings.edu/blog/future-development/2018/09/27/a-global-tipping-point-half-the-world-is-now-middle-class-or-wealthier.

[34] United Nations. 2018. *World Urbanization Prospects: The 2018 Revision—Key Facts*. https://esa.un.org/unpd/wup/Publications/Files/WUP2018-KeyFacts.pdf.

traditional lifestyles and aspirations, including living arrangements, eating habits, physical activities, work, families, communities, values, tastes, and much more. This "new" lifestyle has many unhealthy aspects, such as automobile dependency, consumption of processed foods, sedentary lives, stress, loneliness and social isolation, and increased exposure to pollutants,[35] which in turn increase the risk factors for chronic disease, as well as the demand for wellness.

(ii) **Consumer awareness, openness, and self-responsibility.** Wellness first took hold in the industrialized countries 30 to 40 years ago, when the interest of baby boomers in complementary and non-Western health modalities, wellness, foods, and mind–body brought practices, such as chiropractic, yoga, meditation and mindfulness, acupuncture, TCM, herbal remedies, and vitamins and supplements, into the mainstream culture. More recently, aging baby boomers have fueled the birth and growth of the modern fitness, spa, organic and healthy food, and workplace wellness industries. Meanwhile, the values of younger generations are driving further cultural, social, and economic shifts, especially as they head into their peak earning years. Millennials now account for more than 31% of the world's population,[36] and nearly 9 out of 10 millennials live in developing countries.[37] Core values of this generation include meaningful work and self-fulfillment, work-life balance and flexibility, collaboration and connection, diversity, experience, and authenticity. These values are driving growth and major shifts in health and wellness, travel, media, technology, and many other industries.

(iii) **Technology and connectivity.** Technological innovations, especially in information and communication technology, have brought both positive and negative impacts for human health and well-being. The rise of the internet and digital technologies have exposed billions of people to different healing practices, health-care approaches, and philosophies and beliefs across countries and cultures, supporting the rising interest in and business growth around non-Western and traditional wellness modalities, such as yoga, Ayurveda, TCM, reiki, and balneotherapy. Technology also brings new wellness and preventive health opportunities, including wellness apps and trackers for individuals, DNA screening and analysis, new diagnostic methods and tools, and personalized medicine.

However, technology is also a double-edged sword. Some of its adverse effects on well-being include (i) reduced sleep quantity and quality; (ii) inactivity, obesity, and other physiological effects from prolonged sitting and screen time; (iii) reduced mental wellness linked with screen time and social media usage (including depression, anxiety, and childhood cognitive development and attention); (iv) reduced quality of social relationships and loneliness; (v) distraction and safety issues (e.g., texting while driving); and (vi) reduced productivity because of an always-on culture and stress.[38] Growing consumer awareness of the many unhealthy aspects of technology is supporting a burgeoning backlash; recognition of the need to disconnect, slow down, and be more mindful; and growth of many wellness-related movements and offerings, such as digital detox and digital-free zones, nature-based therapies and getaways (e.g., forest bathing, thermal bathing), off-the-grid travel, silent retreats, bans on after-hours emails in workplaces, a new industry of sleep-related therapies and products, and much more.

[35] H. Kharas. 2017. *The Unprecedented Expansion of the Global Middle Class: An Update.* Brookings Global Economy & Development Working Paper 100. Washington, DC: Brookings. https://www.brookings.edu/wp-content/uploads/2017/02/global_20170228_global-middle-class.pdf.

[36] L.J. Miller and W. Lu. 2018. Gen Z Is Set to Outnumber Millennials within a Year. *Bloomberg.* https://www.bloomberg.com/news/articles/2018-08-20/gen-z-to-outnumber-millennials-within-a-year-demographic-trends.

[37] K. Hamel, K. Fenz, and M. Hofer. 2018. How to Harness the Spending Power of Millennials: Move beyond the US. *Brookings.* https://www.brookings.edu/blog/future-development/2018/04/30/how-to-harness-the-spending-power-of-millennials-move-beyond-the-us; and C. Tilford. 2018. The Millennial Moment—In Charts. *Financial Times.* https://www.ft.com/content/f81ac17a-68ae-11e8-b6eb-4acfcfb08c11.

[38] J. McCarthy, et al. 2018. *Wellness in the Age of the Smartphone.* Global Wellness Institute: Digital Wellness Initiative. https://globalwellnessinstitute.org/wp-content/uploads/2018/06/pdfs/Wellness-in-the-Age-of-the-Smartphone-Whitepaper.pdf.

The Asian Wellness Economy: Data and Developments in Six Sectors

As discussed in the first part of this chapter, the quantification of the wellness industry in individual economies remains incomplete. Therefore, at this moment, there is no estimate for the size of the overall wellness industry in Asia. However, country-level data exists in six wellness sectors where the authors have developed estimates under the auspices of GWI. This section focuses on those six sectors.

Wellness Real Estate

In the 2018 GWI report *Build Well to Live Well: Wellness Lifestyle Real Estate and Communities,* the authors define wellness real estate as "the construction of residential and commercial/institutional properties that incorporate intentional wellness elements into their design, materials, and building as well as their amenities, services, and/or programming."[39] Valued at $46.8 billion in 2017, the Asia and the Pacific wellness real estate market represents more than one-third of the global market ($134.3 billion). Compared with the broader construction and real estate sector in Asia, wellness real estate is a nascent industry. Consumers are only recently beginning to recognize that the built environment has a major impact on healthy lifestyles, health outcomes, and longevity.

In Asia, wellness lifestyle real estate projects tend to take several forms: (i) high-end, mixed-use, and master-planned communities in rapidly growing metropolitan areas; (ii) luxury multifamily high-rise buildings in urban centers (which are most likely to use formal wellness or sustainability certification schemes); (iii) luxury vacation or second homes built as part of wellness resorts and destination spas, especially in Southeast Asia and the PRC; and (iv) co-living-style projects that appeal to young singles living in cities, especially in the PRC. Many of the wellness lifestyle real estate developments currently ongoing across the region are hospitality focused. These projects typically cater to foreign guests, expatriates, and local residents who are looking to incorporate wellness as part of their destination experience, or who are seeking preventive or medical care that is augmented by wellness facilities and offerings.

Workplace Wellness

In the 2016 GWI research report *The Future of Wellness at Work*, the authors define the workplace wellness market as the "expenditures made by employers to improve employee wellness."[40] This market includes a wide variety of services, products, and platforms (such as health screening assessments; diagnostic tests; in-house amenities or subsidized memberships for fitness clubs and exercise classes; healthy food offerings at company cafeterias; wearable devices; health fairs, educational programming, and counseling services for wellness; and incentives for participation in wellness activities), which serve a wide range of employee needs, from exercise, healthy eating, and sleep, to chronic illness, obesity, addiction, depression, and stress. Much of this spending is motivated by employers' desires to lower health-care costs; improve morale, retention, and recruitment; and increase productivity and competitiveness. Estimated at $9.3 billion, the workplace wellness market in Asia and the Pacific represented about 20% of global workplace wellness expenditures in 2017.

However, these workplace wellness expenditures are modest when viewed from the perspective of employee coverage, mainly benefiting workers who work for multinational corporations and in knowledge-intensive industries (e.g., finance, investment, consulting, information technology, high-tech, higher education, and creative industries). Across the region, a far greater share of the workforce suffers from dire and often life-threatening issues related to

[39] GWI. 2018. *Build Well to Live Well: Wellness Lifestyle Real Estate and Communities*. https://globalwellnessinstitute.org/industry-research/wellness-real-estate-communities-research.
[40] GWI. 2016. *The Future of Wellness at Work*. https://globalwellnessinstitute.org/industry-research/the-future-of-wellness-at-work.

Figure 2.5 Asia and the Pacific Wellness Sector Highlights (2017 and 2018)

Wellness real estate (2017)

Wellness real estate market: $46.8 billion (7.3% CAGR from 2015 to 2017)
Wellness lifestyle real estate (residential) project pipeline: 293 projects

Workplace wellness (2017)

Number of workers with access to workplace wellness programs and services: 97.8 million (5.2% of employed workers)
Expenditures on workplace wellness: $9.3 billion (5.1% CAGR from 2015 to 2017)

Physical activity (2018)

Expenditures on physical activity: $240.4 billion
Share of population participating regularly in recreational physical activities: 33.2%

Wellness tourism (2017)

Number of wellness trips: 257.6 million (15.3% CAGR from 2015 to 2017)
Wellness tourism expenditures: $136.7 billion (10.9% CAGR from 2015 to 2017)
Average expenditure per trip: $1,741 for internationalor inbound (33% premium); $268 for domestic (120% premium)

Spas (2017)

Number of spas: 48,679 (12.0% CAGR from 2015 to 2017)
Spa revenues: $26.5 billion (11.2% CAGR from 2015 to 2017)
Spa employment: 918,675 (12.8% CAGR from 2015 to 2017)

Thermal and mineral springs (2017)

Number of thermal and mineral springs establishments: 25,916 (13.4% CAGR from 2015 to 2017)
Thermal and mineral springs establishment revenues: $31.6 billion (4.0% CAGR from 2015 to 2017)
Thermal and mineral springs establishment employment: 1,244,661 (17.5% CAGR from 2015 to 2017)

CAGR = compound annual growth rate.

Source: Global Wellness Institute.

exploitation, workplace safety and health threats, and lack of living wages or a secure job. These issues are not being adequately addressed by government regulation or by workplace wellness programs in their current incarnation.

Physical Activity

The physical activity market is defined by the authors as consumer spending associated with intentional physical activities performed during leisure and recreation, in the 2019 GWI research report *Move to Be Well: The Global Economy of Physical Activity*.[41] The core of the market is the services that allow consumers to participate in three

[41] GWI. 2019. *Move to Be Well: The Global Economy of Physical Activity*. https://globalwellnessinstitute.org/industry-research/global-economy-physical-activity.

categories of recreational physical activities: fitness, sports and active recreation, and mindful movement. The market also includes three supporting sectors that enable and facilitate consumer participation in these activities: technology, equipment and supplies, and apparel and footwear.

Valued at $240.4 billion in 2018, the physical activity market in Asia and the Pacific is large, diverse, and dynamic. It accounts for 29% of the total global economy for physical activity ($828.2 billion). The Asia and Pacific region is the second-largest regional market in the world for physical activity, after North America. In Asia, direct consumer spending to participate in recreational physical activities (primarily sports and active recreation, fitness, and mindful movement) accounts for $116.6 billion (48% of the physical activity market). The remaining 52%, or $125.5 billion, represents consumer expenditures in the enabling and supporting sectors, primarily clothing and footwear, along with fitness equipment, sporting goods, and related supplies, and fitness- and exercise-related technologies.

Importantly, many people in Asia conduct their leisure-time sports and recreational physical activities in public places and free venues (e.g., in public parks and plazas, in free sporting facilities such as neighborhood basketball courts or ball fields, in vacant lots, in the streets, and at home). Recognizing the growing public health crisis associated with inadequate levels of physical activity, a number of governments across Asia have recently committed to increasing participation rates through greater public investment in exercise and sports facilities and infrastructure.

Wellness Tourism

In two prior research studies, the authors defined wellness tourism as "travel associated with the pursuit of maintaining or enhancing one's personal well-being." Based on this definition, the authors have estimated the size of the global wellness tourism industry (since 2013) by aggregating expenditures made by two types of tourists:[42]

(i) **Primary wellness tourist.** A tourist whose trip or destination is motivated primarily by wellness.
(ii) **Secondary wellness tourist.** A tourist who seeks to maintain wellness while traveling, or who participates in wellness experiences while taking any type of trip, for leisure or business.

In 2017, the market for wellness tourism in Asia and the Pacific was estimated at $136.7 billion, constituting 257.6 million inbound and domestic wellness tourism trips. The expenditures by wellness tourists include lodging, food and beverage, activities and excursions, shopping, in-country transportation, and other services—some of which may be specifically wellness-related (such as getting a massage, attending a meditation retreat, or staying at a wellness hotel), while others may be generic (such as hiring a local car). In 2017, the Asia and Pacific region accounted for 21.4% of global wellness tourism expenditures and 31.0% of all wellness tourism trips. The authors estimated that wellness tourism accounted for 10.1 million direct jobs in the region.

Not only is wellness tourism a sizable and high-growth market, it is also high-yield compared with the general tourism sector. Wellness tourists—whether international or domestic—spend more than the average tourist. In 2017, inbound or international wellness tourists in Asia and the Pacific on average spent $1,741 per trip, 33% more than the typical international tourist. The premium for domestic wellness tourists was

[42] GWI. 2013 and 2018. *The Global Wellness Tourism Economy 2013* and *Global Wellness Tourism Economy 2018*. https://globalwellnessinstitute.org/industry-research.

even higher, with average spending of $268 per trip or 120% more than the typical domestic tourist. This is because wellness travelers are typically more affluent, educated, well-traveled, and willing to seek out new and novel experiences.

Spas

Spas are defined as "establishments that promote wellness through the provision of therapeutic and other professional services aimed at renewing the body, mind, and spirit." The authors created this definition for the first time in a 2008 report for the Global Spa Summit.[43] Since then, this definition has been employed to estimate the global revenues of spas, which include: hotel or resort spas; day, club, or salon spas; destination spas and health resorts; medical spas; thermal and mineral springs spas; and other spa facilities, such as cruise ship spas, airport spas, mobile spas, and historically or culturally based facilities that have incorporated spa-like services into their offerings (e.g., hammams, Ayurveda centers, and *onsens*). The authors estimated that there were more than 48,000 spas in Asia and the Pacific in 2017, earning $26.5 billion in revenues and representing 28.3% of the global spa market.[44]

Asia and the Pacific region hosts the largest number of spas in the world, and it also gained the greatest number of new spas from 2015 to 2017. Much of this growth is catering to an increasing number of wellness tourists. More broadly, the underlying demand for the Asian spa industry is driven by growing consumer interest in living healthier lives. It is increasingly common for consumers to turn to body work to relieve stress and chronic pain, and to seek treatments that help maintain vitality and good health. In many Asian metropolises, spas have turned into urban sanctuaries where guests seek much more than just a facial or massage, but a full range of holistic wellness services (e.g., body work, hydrotherapy, sound healing, energy treatments, and coaching or spiritual guidance).

Thermal and Mineral Springs

The authors define the thermal and mineral springs industry as encompassing "revenue-earning business establishments associated with the wellness, recreational, and therapeutic uses of waters with special properties." For 2017, the authors estimated that there were 25,916 thermal or mineral springs establishments in Asia and the Pacific, earning $31.6 billion in revenues and employing more than 1.2 million workers. The global thermal and mineral springs industry is heavily concentrated in Asia and the Pacific; the region accounted for 76% of all establishments and 56% of all revenues in the global sector in 2017 (footnote 44).

The Asia and Pacific region has vast thermal water resources and bathing traditions dating back thousands of years. As economies begin to recognize thermal springs' potential for wellness tourism and economic development, a growing number of destinations (including Australia; Japan; the Lao People's Democratic Republic; New Zealand; Taipei,China; and Viet Nam) are highlighting their springs-based attractions to international visitors and are investing in undeveloped and underdeveloped thermal sites and regions. The Chinese hot springs sector is enormous and is increasingly integrated with wellness tourism, but it mainly caters to domestic visitors. While South Asian and Southeast Asian economies also have considerable thermal resources, their hot springs sectors are generally at earlier stages of development.

[43] Global Spa Summit and SRI International. 2008. *The Global Spa Economy 2007*. https://globalwellnessinstitute.org/industry-research/global-spa-economy.

[44] GWI. 2018. *Global Wellness Economy Monitor 2018*. https://globalwellnessinstitute.org/industry-research/2018-global-wellness-economy-monitor.

Opportunities and Potential Development Impacts of Wellness Industries in Asia

Wellness is an important strategy to embrace in developing countries (i) as a concept of holistic health encompassing physical, mental, social, and other dimensions; (ii) as a lifestyle choice focusing on disease prevention and thriving; and (iii) as an attitude characterized by personal responsibility and individual agency. Low-income and marginalized populations are the most vulnerable to chronic disease, which is growing in developing countries; disease and health-care cost burdens are rising when they can scarcely afford it. So wellness is very relevant for developing countries to frame economic and human development strategies.

As an industry, wellness has many potentially crosscutting impacts in Asian economies, not only for economic development, but also in the arenas of social and cultural affairs, health, workforce, competitiveness, urban planning, environmental and cultural sustainability, equity, and other development impacts.

Wellness Drives Economic Growth

The $4.5 trillion economy of wellness is fast-growing, resilient, and pervasive. The forces driving consumers to spend on wellness are sufficiently strong that wellness industry growth around the world has been robust and has exceeded GDP growth (even in years in which the global economy shrank). These trends are expected to continue, with much of the industry's growth driven by domestic demand and met by domestic supply.

(i) **Employment creation and small business development.** A large portion of wellness activities and businesses are service-oriented and, therefore, help create jobs. In addition, many wellness sectors are dominated by small and locally owned enterprises that serve a local clientele and use local products and services (e.g., yoga studios, fitness studios, spas, retail, traditional or indigenous and complementary medicine practitioners, and nutritionists). A growing wellness industry, therefore, creates opportunities for micro and small enterprises, entrepreneurship, and new business models.

(ii) **Promotion of locally sourced, produced, and branded products.** Wellness consumers increasingly favor authentic, organic, locally sourced, and sustainable products (e.g., fresh produce and foods, skincare and personal care products, and herbal and traditional remedies), and are often willing to pay a premium for them. The development of the wellness industry can stimulate the development of homegrown products and services, while encouraging regions to value their own heritage and unique place-based products and offerings.

(iii) **Women's empowerment and benefits to families.** The majority of wellness consumers are women, and many wellness-related occupations are traditionally dominated by women (e.g., massage therapists, traditional healers, and tourism and retail workers). Therefore, growth of this industry supports job creation for women. In addition, traditional wellness knowledge (e.g., healing modalities, herbal remedies) is often transmitted through matrilineally based lines, passing from grandmother to mother to daughter. The rise of the wellness industry creates economic and entrepreneurship opportunities for women at all levels, while strengthening the preservation of cultural heritage and indigenous knowledge. The benefits of female economic empowerment to families are extensive, including greater investment in health and education for children, especially girls. However, an ongoing challenge is that because many wellness jobs and skills are traditionally considered to be "female," such as hands-on caring and healing, serving, teaching, food production, and gardening, they are under-valued in most societies and have below-average wages. Worse, sometimes wellness occupations face stigma and misunderstanding (e.g., conflating massage therapists with sex workers).

Wellness Improves Public Health

People's lifestyles, behaviors, health outcomes, and longevity are largely determined by social and environmental factors that are outside the purview of health-care systems. Expansion of the wellness industry can help address the rising global health epidemic, improve public health, and improve the financial sustainability of health-care systems.

(i) **Mitigating rising health-care costs.** In countries worldwide, health-care expenditures are growing at an unsustainable rate, driven by the rise of chronic disease and mental illness. Wellness services that focus on prevention and healthy behaviors are the only way to address critical risk factors (e.g., sedentary life, unhealthy diets, and smoking) and the social and environmental determinants of health (e.g., loneliness, food inequity). According to WHO, even a limited set of interventions to address noncommunicable diseases (NCDs) in developing countries would yield a return of $7 for every $1 invested, not only from a direct reduction of health care costs, but also from a reduction in premature death and disability and the resulting increase in employment and productivity.[45]

(ii) **Improving health equity by engaging wellness workers in the community.** A critical issue in public health today is how to improve health delivery to all people at all income levels, across geographically dispersed areas. As outlined in a paper by Sachs and Sachs, leveraging community health workers (CHWs), especially in low-resource settings, is critical to achieving the United Nations Sustainable Development Goal 3.[46] CHWs in Asia, large numbers of whom practice traditional or indigenous medicine, represent an important resource to deliver preventive health services and health-care education. Because they are local, trusted, and embedded in the communities they serve, CHWs are well-positioned to help adapt nutritional guidelines and healthy lifestyle habits to local contexts, provide culturally based framing of health messages, and engage in mental wellness conversations.

(iii) **Addressing the growing mental health epidemic.** The wellness movement is a leading force that draws attention to the rise of stress, anxiety, loneliness, and other mental health issues around the world. This public conversation helps reduce the stigma of mental illness and shifts attention to the critical importance of mental wellness. The wellness industry is a channel for delivering new solutions to address mental health both within and outside the medical system, including meditation and mindfulness activities, sleep-focused products and solutions, coaching and counseling, stress-reducing and social and built environments, and much more.

(iv) **Harnessing wellness knowledge, traditions, and modalities indigenous to Asia.** Wellness industry growth spurs the revival, modernization, and mainstreaming of numerous wellness traditions and healing modalities originating in Asia—from TCM, Ayurvedic medicine, and Tibetan medicine to yoga, meditation, tai chi, qigong, and Japanese forest bathing. As consumers increasingly seek out these approaches, more and more scientific research is being conducted on their efficacy. Individuals have a growing number of options to engage in traditionally based healthy lifestyle activities, while evidence-based and cost-effective modalities are being adopted into the conventional or Western medical system alongside or as a substitute for allopathic treatments (e.g., acupuncture for migraines or back pain, manual therapy for neck pain, spa therapy for Parkinson's, and fish oil substitutes for preventing heart attacks).[47] However, far more research is needed across all modalities to provide evidence of the treatment and cost-effectiveness of traditional, complementary, and integrative approaches.

[45] WHO. 2018. Investing in Noncommunicable Disease Control Generates Major Financial and Health Gains. *WHO News Release*. https://www.who.int/news-room/detail/16-05-2018-investing-in-noncommunicable-disease-control-generates-major-financial-and-health-gains.

[46] S. Sachs and J. Sachs. 2018. *The Community Health Worker Revolution. Achieving SDG 3: Policy Brief Series 2018*. Sustainable Development Solutions Network. http://unsdsn.org/wp-content/uploads/2018/10/181020-Policy-Brief-Series-5.pdf.

[47] P.M. Herman et al. 2012. Are Complementary Therapies and Integrative Care Cost-Effective? A Systematic Review of Economic Evaluations. *BMJ Open*. 2 (5). https://doi.org/10.1136%2Fbmjopen-2012-001046.

Wellness Supports Protection of Natural and Cultural Assets

As wellness consumers become more sophisticated and discerning, they start to care more about where products come from, how things are produced, and how their purchases impact local people and communities. The rise of the wellness economy increases incentives to communities and regions to protect their unique natural and cultural assets, and to build upon these as an economic development strategy.

(i) **Environmental protection.** There is a growing recognition that individual wellness is inextricably linked to wellness of place and planet. Therefore, wellness products, services, and businesses are increasingly focusing on sustainability and environmental health alongside delivering health and wellness to the consumer. Regions and policy makers are encouraged to pursue development strategies that consider environmental sustainability alongside human and social sustainability.
(ii) **Preserve and celebrate local culture and heritage.** Wellness consumers seek out things that are authentic, local, and unique; in response, wellness industries and businesses are increasingly supporting and developing local culture and heritage rather than cookie-cutter, mass-produced offerings. In turn, this supports regional efforts toward community-building, diversity and inclusion, and quality of life, as well as market differentiation (place-based branding) and discovery of new local and culturally rooted products and services in the self-care, nutritional, and medical categories.
(iii) **Mitigate tourism-related challenges.** Successful wellness tourism development depends upon environmentally and socially sustainable destinations that preserve and celebrate the uniqueness of local natural and cultural assets. Wellness tourism brings tourists with higher spending patterns, interest in getting "off the beaten path," and interest in traveling off-season. Therefore, it provides opportunities for regions to address a number of growing tourism-related challenges, including seasonality, mass tourism, and overtourism. In particular, the vast thermal and mineral spring resources across Asia offer opportunities to spread the benefits of wellness to less-traveled areas. In this sector, the development, operation, and promotion of *onsens* and *ryokans* in Japan could offer a useful model.

Wellness Supports Workforce Development and Worker Welfare

The wellness movement is bringing new attention to the critical relationship between individual health and well-being and business productivity and growth. Workplace wellness is a growing segment of the wellness economy that is developing new models and solutions that can benefit both businesses and their workers.

(i) **Worker development, retention, and recruitment.** Businesses around the world face challenges with employees' physical and mental health, absenteeism, and disengagement or presenteeism, and their negative impacts on productivity, competitiveness, health care costs, and the "bottom line." Well-run and targeted workplace wellness initiatives can help improve employee health, motivation, productivity, and retention, while enhancing recruitment efforts. At a regional level, efforts to improve worker and population health can also support workforce development and business retention and attraction more broadly. However, the effectiveness of different types of workplace wellness initiatives is not adequately studied or understood, and these initiatives are still concentrated in wealthier countries and larger companies. Thus, far more work is needed to identify the most effective models and their replicability across different types of organizations, industries, worker populations, and regional contexts.
(ii) **Worker welfare.** Workers around the world face innumerable challenges, which range from abusive working arrangements and environments in some countries and industries (including within the wellness industry) to fair pay, equity and discrimination, work conditions and safety, work-related stress, work–life balance, and relationships with coworkers and management, even among the most privileged workers. The wellness movement is bringing a burgeoning awareness of these issues and is encouraging businesses to explore new models and solutions (e.g., occupational safety and health initiatives, pay

equity, diversity initiatives, flexible work, new leadership and management approaches, and triple bottom line and for-benefit enterprises). Importantly, the workplace wellness industry is also bringing attention to models and approaches that can be benchmarked and replicated. Simultaneously, some employers are starting to recognize that caring for employees as a number one priority is critical to the future success of their businesses, and a small but growing body of research is providing evidence of this reality.

Wellness Enhances Quality of Life and Social Capital

Our living environments have an immense influence on individual lifestyles, behaviors, health, and happiness, as well as on relationships, communities, and social capital. While the green and sustainable building movement has gone from niche to mainstream over the last few decades, the newer wellness real estate movement is beginning to shift development, infrastructure, and planning approaches toward human-focused aims that simultaneously enhance quality of life and individual, community, and planetary well-being.

(i) **Urban and community planning, zoning, and infrastructure.** Wellness real estate incorporates human health and wellness as a central concept in urban planning, real estate, and infrastructure development, rationalizing and reinforcing other development priorities, such as sustainability, community safety, walkability, livability, and diversity, in addition to health. Key features of wellness-focused built environments include design and infrastructure that encourage physical activity (e.g., sidewalks and walkability, paths and trails, parks, and active transit options); healthy eating (e.g., community gardens, farmers markets, and edible landscaping); social connections (e.g., public spaces and plazas, housing density and setbacks, mixed-use zoning, and community events and programming); and mental and emotional wellness (e.g., green space, biophilic design, and public art). These kinds of planning approaches serve multiple purposes. They not only create neighborhoods and communities that are healthier for residents, but also enhance quality of life, happiness, well-being, sustainability, and economic growth.

(ii) **Social capital and trust.** A new but growing body of evidence is demonstrating that the built environment has an enormous effect on relationships and civic life within communities. In recent decades, many urban planning approaches have reinforced individual and societal patterns toward loneliness, isolation, segregation, and distrust. Wellness-focused design and infrastructure emphasizes parks, plazas, and other social and community spaces as a critical part of a healthy living environment for individuals. Simultaneously, the investment in design, upkeep and maintenance, and equitable distribution of these kinds of civic assets and public spaces also encourages trust in public institutions and other people, civic engagement and pride, and other types of social capital that are critical to civil society and a healthy democracy.[48]

[48] Center for Active Design. 2018. *Introducing the Assembly: Civic Design Guidelines.* https://centerforactivedesign.org/assembly.

PART 2

Contours of Wellness in Asia

CHAPTER 3

Quantifying and Comparing Wellness across Nations—A Cross-Country Empirical Analysis

Husnain Fateh Ahmad and Irfan Qureshi

The lack of a measure of national well-being, and the use of gross domestic product (or gross domestic product per capita) as a proxy, has been a cause of concern since the latter's inception. Recently, there has been a renewed effort to understand the weaknesses of growth-led policy along with a call for better and more holistic measures of a nation's ability to provide for its citizens—measures that capture the well-being of citizens and not just their average level of income. This chapter illustrates a new measure of wellness, the Wellness Index, which is comprised of four pillars: physical, intellectual, environmental, and social wellness. The Wellness Index is constructed for 153 countries and is used to conduct regional and country level analysis of wellness and its four pillars.

Introduction

In this chapter, we propose and construct a new index that allows us to measure ordinally a country's ability to cater to the wellness needs of its populace. The Wellness Index presented in this paper uses open data that is mostly readily available to create a cross-country ranking of wellness by extending the Global Wellness Institute (GWI) definition of individual wellness to the national level. The index aims to fill an important gap in the literature by providing an estimate of (relative) wellness across countries and serving as an easy-to-use measure of the average level of individual wellness. By updating the Wellness Index over time, policy makers can also use it to benchmark the success of their interventions.

Historically, per capita gross domestic product (GDP) has been used as the de facto measure of a country's success and well-being. However, GDP is not a measure of wellness, but rather a simple exercise of national income accounting. Indeed, its own architects warned against its use as a measure of well-being.[1] Regardless, over time it came to be a measure of a country's success and a benchmark for policy makers across the world. After the Great Recession, the Stiglitz-Sen-Fitoussi Commission of 2009 highlighted the urgent need to move past growth-focused policy. It not only laid out the shortcomings of GDP as a measure of well-being, but also called for policy makers and academics to move toward more holistic benchmarks of well-being and move beyond growth.

1 S. Kuznets. 1934. *National Income, 1929–1931*. Senate Document. United States of America: 73rd US Congress.

A shift toward wellness policy requires measures of well-being that can allow policy makers to benchmark their performance. In this section, we propose one such measure: an index that captures the level of well-being of the average citizen in a country. We argue that this Wellness Index provides key policy insights and identifies key areas for policy interventions that would allow nations to reap the maximum benefits of their material wealth, when used in conjunction with GDP.

In the context of developing Asia, as the region moves toward middle-income status, policy makers have already begun to move beyond growth-focused policy, with renewed interest in areas of health, education, and individual well-being. Therefore, there is a preexisting need for such an index. The Wellness Index aims to fill this gap in the policy toolbox and is designed to aid policy makers in identifying areas of strengths and weakness across four dimensions of individual wellness. Further, it is designed not as a replacement for GDP, but rather is intended to be used in conjunction with GDP. As a complement to preexisting indicators, the index is also in line with the recent recommendations made by the International Monetary Fund that call for new measures of well-being to augment those of growth.[2]

The Wellness Index takes a bottom-up approach and defines wellness at the individual level, which distinguishes it from other aggregate measures of national well-being. It uses the GWI's definition of individual wellness and focuses on four pillars of wellness: physical, intellectual (mental), environmental, and social wellness. Physical wellness captures a nation's ability to cater to the health needs of its populace, while intellectual wellness measures both the quality of and access to education. Social and environmental wellness measure the quality of the social and physical environment. While measures of well-being beyond growth have been formulated and put forward, from the Human Development Index (HDI) to the World Happiness Index, none to the best of our knowledge model wellness as an individual-level phenomenon aggregated at the country level.

While wellness is not directly observable, we are able to create an ordinal measure of wellness by leveraging the variance in closely related indicators. Cross-country analysis of wellness based on data from the last 5 years allows us to identify areas of strength and weakness for each country in our sample, which enables us to highlight areas that need more targeted policy interventions. We also find a positive correlation between wellness and GDP, though the remarkable variation in wellness among countries at similar levels of economic growth suggests that the relationship is not causal. We argue that policy is needed to link growth to wellness. The results highlight the complementary role of GDP and wellness; the choice between wellness and growth is not either/or, rather policy makers need to give wellness and growth equal footing. Proactive policy is needed to invest the material gains from growth to increase the well-being of a country's citizens.

In the sections that follow, we define wellness first and outline the methodology used to create our index. Results from our analysis are discussed, with a special focus on developing Asia and its performance relative to the rest of the world. Then the index is compared with preexisting measures of well-being, followed by analysis of the relationship between wellness and growth.

A New Index of Wellness

We join a rich literature that seeks to create a comprehensive measure of wellness and the efforts of other multilateral organizations as they aim to better understand and measure the well-being of their citizens—for example, Strategy 2030 of the Asian Development Bank (ADB).[3]

---

2 M.B. Reinsdorf. 2020. *Measuring Economic Welfare: What and How?* International Monetary Fund Policy Paper.

3 ADB. 2018. *Strategy 2030: Achieving a Prosperous, Inclusive, Resilient, and Sustainable Asia and Pacific.* Manila.

In this section, we detail the construction and methodology of the Wellness Index, present results for the developing Asia region, and compare the region's performance with the 153 countries in our sample. Finally, we compare our index to other similar indexes, and highlight both its strengths and its weaknesses in relation to preexisting measures.

Building the Index

Our objective was to use available data to build an index that aims to capture the well-being of the average citizen in each country. Therefore, we began our analysis with a well-established definition of individual well-being. We utilized the GWI's definition of wellness and focused on the four pillars of wellness they identify—physical, intellectual, environmental, and social wellness.

With the push toward more wellness-centric policy, ideally, we would have utilized specifically collected microdata, but, given current data constraints, we leveraged aggregate country-level indicators that allowed us to proxy for individual wellness. When selecting indicators, we took an output over input approach. We focused on indicators that reflected the current state of wellness in the country and not policy decisions that may influence future outcomes. For example, we focused on mortality rates as a measure of the physical wellness of citizens in a country, rather than using government expenditure on health. While the latter may reflect a government's policy priority, inefficiencies in implementation may not yield higher levels of wellness, which is what we were interested in measuring.

Data Collection Strategy

We utilized available sources of open data to allow easy replication and modifications as needed by policy makers. Therefore, we required, first and foremost, that all indicators used should be easily available to the public. Data used must also be collected in a consistent manner and collated by a single agency.

Availability of data varied across indicators and countries, so we first established a list of "core countries of interest." The list includes 25 ADB members with a wide variation in size, economic growth, and geography that are known to have good data coverage from previous studies, such as ADB's Inclusive Green Growth Index (IGGI). These core countries (a list of which is provided in Appendix 1) helped guide our data collection and identification strategy.

For an indicator to be selected, it had to meet the following requirements for our core countries of interest:

(i) Indicator values must not be older than 2014 (5-year period for data collection).
(ii) The latest year for available data is defined as the most recent year (post-2014) when data is available for at least 75% of our core countries of interest.
(iii) Where a country has missing values for the latest year, enough information from past observations must be available to allow time trend imputation.
(iv) For a core country, if a sub-indicator is missing such that time trend imputation is not possible, cross-indicator imputation is allowed if no more than 25% of indicators are missing in a pillar.

Following our strategy, we identified 22 unique indicators across our four pillars of wellness (Figure 3.1) for a total of 153 countries.

Indicators selected for physical wellness proxy for physical well-being of individuals by using data on health outcomes, in particular indicators for mortality rates, undernourishment, and disease burden. Intellectual wellness utilizes objective measures of both the level of educational attainment and the quality of education.

Figure 3.1 **List of Indicators by Pillar**

Physical

- Life expectancy at birth
- Maternal mortality rate
- Child (under 5) mortality rate
- Prevalence of undernourishment
- DALY noncommunicable diseases
- DALY communicable diseases

Intellectual

- Adult literacy rate
- Mean years of schooling
- Harmonized test scores

Environmental

- Mortality rate attributed to household and ambient air pollution, age-standardized
- PM2.5 air pollution, mean annual exposure (micrograms per cubic meter)
- Protected areas total
- Population weighted average NO_2 levels
- Imperviousness level in most populous city

Social

- Gender Parity Index, literacy rate, youth (ages 15 to 24)
- Gini Index (World Bank estimate)
- Ratio of female to male labor force participation rate (%)
- World Bank Control of Corruption: (World Bank estimate)
- World Bank: Rule of Law: (World Bank estimate)
- V-Dem: Social class equality in respect for civil liberties
- V-Dem: Social group equality in respect for civil liberties
- V-Dem: Power distributed by social group

DALY = disability-adjusted life year, NO_2 = nitrogen dioxide, V-Dem = Variety of Democracy Initiative.

Note: PM2.5 refers to atmospheric particulate matter that has a diameter of less than 2.5 micrometers.

Source: Authors.

Indicators used to measure environmental wellness underlined our focus on individual wellness and distinguish the Wellness Index from other measures of environmental quality. Unlike most measures, we do not focus on sustainable development, but rather on attributes of the individual's experienced environment. So we used measures of pollution and proxies for green spaces. However, note that, by not incorporating sustainability, we are not dismissing its importance. We believe that, like growth, sustainability is indeed an important area of policy, but it is essentially beyond the scope of an individual measure of wellness. Of course, policy makers should prioritize sustainability and employ indicators such as the ADB's IGGI to measure it.

Finally, social wellness seeks to measure the level of inclusivity in a society. This is the only pillar where we employ subjective measures (in addition to available objective measures), relying on the World Bank World Governance Indicators (WGI) to measure corruption and rule of law, and the Variety of Democracy Initiative (V-Dem) indicators for equity. Both WGI and V-Dem indicators are widely trusted indicators that are used both directly by policy makers, and as inputs in many other indexes (see, for example, Fragile State Indicators and the Social Progress Index). The WGI rely on individual and firm-level surveys, while V-Dem uses a panel of country experts to create its indexes.

While, as an exercise in measuring the average wellness of citizens of a country, we began from the well-established definition of individual wellness, it is interesting to note that the current formulation also lines up well with the recommendations of the Stiglitz-Sen-Fitoussi Commission on Wellness.[4] The Wellness Index, in seeking to measure individual wellness independent of material wellness (income, consumption, and wealth), covers five of the seven dimensions of nonmaterial well-being identified by the commission.[5]

Methodology

While collapsing a complex phenomenon, such as wellness, into a single index has some drawbacks, a single number provides an easy summary statistic of wellness and allows easier digestion by the public at large. This is perhaps one of the reasons for the popularity of GDP as a measure of wellness, despite its weaknesses; it takes something as complex and multidimensional as national income accounting and collapses it into one number.

Therefore, to create our index, we must collapse our diverse set of indicators. We utilize principal component analysis (PCA) at the pillar level to create, for each pillar, a pillar score. PCA is a technique that allows us to extract common information from a set of variables. By analyzing the correlation between variables, it identifies the orthogonal linear combinations that best capture the variance between variables.[6] This weighted average (typically called "PCA values") forms the basis of our score for each pillar.

While primarily a dimensionality reduction tool, PCA can be used to proxy for an unobserved variable using variance in related indicators. It is widely used in the development literature to create wealth or standard of living indexes using data on household assets, an approach first proposed by Filmer and Pritchett.[7] The intuition behind the technique is that it leverages the variance in variables that are correlated to our unknown to produce an ordinal ranking in the unobservable dimension of interest. For example, consider physical wellness. While we are unable to measure physical wellness itself, we do have variables that capture information that may be correlated to physical well-being. It is reasonable to assume that those with "high" physical wellness, for example, would have lower incidence of disease. PCA uses such related indicators and finds the linear combination that captures the most variance in the sample across countries. This linear sum allows us to create an ordinal ranking that is correlated to physical wellness; the higher the PCA values, the higher the relative position of a country.

The use of PCA imposes some constraints on what is, otherwise, a subjective exercise. An alternative method of creating the index would be to identify our indicators of interest, and then take averages based on subjectively chosen weights. While the selection of any weighing method, including PCA, is subjective, PCA chooses weights in a way that captures the most variance in the data and places more weight on indicators that have higher variance in the sample.

---

4 J. Stiglitz, A. Sen, and J. Fitoussi. 2009. *Report by the Commission on the Measurement of Economic Performance and Social Progress*. Paris.

5 The Stiglitz-Sen-Fitoussi Commission identified eight dimensions of well-being: (i) material living standards, (ii) health, (iii) education, (iv) personal activities including work, (v) political voice and governance, (vi) social connections, (vii) environment, and (viii) insecurity.

6 B.F. Manly and J.A. Alberto. 2016. *Multivariate Statistical Methods, a Primer*. CRC Press. Boca Raton. Consider the physical pillar. PCA would generate six weights (w_i) corresponding to each sub-indicator (i). Then, for a country, its PCA value in the physical dimension will be calculated by taking a weighted average of all demeaned indicator values (v_i), i.e. $\sum w_i v_i$.

7 D. Filmer and L.H. Pritchett. 2001. Estimating Wealth Effects without Expenditure Data—or Tears: An Application to Educational Enrollments in States of India. *Demography*. 38 (1). pp. 115–132.

Pillar Scores and the Wellness Index

The first step in PCA analysis converts the raw data into z-scores, i.e., for any indicator, it converts it into a variable with mean zero and unit variance across the sample. Principal components then use these normalized values to find the linear combinations that capture the most variance in the underlying data. The core idea is that this linear dimension proxies from our pillar, as countries with high wellness in each pillar should consistently be above the mean in their component indicators, while those with low wellness would consistently lie below the mean.

To allow comparison across pillars, and to aggregate to a single score of wellness (the Wellness Index), we convert pillar values to pillar scores using the maximum-minimum normalization. The maximum-minimum normalization takes the pillar values for all countries in our sample and subtracts the lowest sample value. It then divides this by the range of scores and multiplies by 100. The transformation gives the country with the highest wellness in a pillar a score of 100 and the country with the lowest score of 0.[8]

Finally, we aggregate all pillar scores by taking a simple average. The average wellness score captures average wellness across our four dimensions of wellness and serves as the Wellness Index. Table 3.1 reports the Wellness Index for all ADB members in our sample and their global rank. Appendix 2 includes details of the 153 countries for which the complete index is constructed. Finally, Figure 3.2 illustrates the global variation in wellness for the 153 countries in our sample.

As can be seen, there is tremendous variation in the level of wellness across ADB members in our sample.

At first glance, there seems to be a correlation between economic development and wellness, but there is significant variance in performance, with middle countries at various levels of economic development filling out the middle tertile of wellness. For example, comparing Bhutan and Thailand, we see that, despite having a GDP per capita, adjusted for purchasing power parity (PPP), that is about half that of Thailand, Bhutan outperforms Thailand. The difference is consistent across all pillars, except intellectual wellness, where Thailand is ranked higher than Bhutan. These differences highlight the need for policy to focus on wellness in addition to growth, as Bhutan's higher ranking may be because of its focus on wellness above growth and its use of gross national happiness (GNH) to guide policy.

Intuitively, these results suggest that, while there may be a correlation between GDP and wellness, the relationship is not straightforward. Policy may be the missing link between GDP and wellness, and there appears to be space for policy to help achieve higher wellness at all levels of growth. In later sections, we analyze both the relationship between wellness and growth and use our index to identify priority areas for policy makers in developing Asia.

Wellness across Developing Asia

Focusing on wellness in developing Asia, Figure 3.3 presents the average wellness score as captured by the Wellness Index and its four pillars for developing Asia (ADB members in our sample, minus Japan), the global average, and comparative groups, as well as the interregional variance wellness.

[8] Formally, the pillar score $= 100 \times \dfrac{\textit{country value} - \textit{lowest value}}{\textit{highest value} - \textit{lowest value}}$

Table 3.1 **Wellness across ADB Members in the Study Sample**

Country	Physical	Intellectual	Environmental	Social	Wellness Index	Global Rank
Japan	100.00	100.00	58.32	84.76	85.77	21
Singapore	99.68	97.60	52.79	65.77	78.96	30
Republic of Korea	98.41	98.19	34.00	73.12	75.93	39
Maldives	91.03	64.72	95.75	47.37	74.72	40
Armenia	87.16	81.13	61.73	62.05	73.02	43
Kazakhstan	84.75	93.54	66.46	45.26	72.50	45
Fiji	72.96	82.10	86.49	46.43	72.00	47
Georgia	83.72	84.41	60.87	58.75	71.94	48
Sri Lanka	89.28	69.57	82.20	36.09	69.29	52
Malaysia	89.13	77.46	65.74	44.17	69.12	54
Bhutan	76.57	32.72	91.22	67.61	67.03	59
Vanuatu	69.38	48.60	85.70	62.75	66.61	60
Viet Nam	84.23	78.23	55.38	45.48	65.83	63
Kyrgyz Republic	80.37	75.37	60.88	41.34	64.49	66
Azerbaijan	80.35	81.03	59.85	29.78	62.76	71
Mongolia	75.00	74.94	40.54	54.42	61.22	76
Thailand	89.43	65.12	59.31	23.75	59.40	81
Uzbekistan	77.94	77.51	53.76	23.82	58.26	83
Indonesia	75.65	62.64	60.18	32.33	57.70	87
Philippines	72.80	69.38	53.26	21.69	54.28	97
Tajikistan	75.66	77.94	51.63	11.20	54.11	98
Turkmenistan	73.41	70.21	60.11	12.00	53.93	99
People's Republic of China	89.31	69.95	30.89	20.56	52.68	101
Lao People's Democratic Republic	63.90	50.48	70.56	20.34	51.32	105
Cambodia	71.36	53.83	71.98	7.51	51.17	107
Papua New Guinea	50.97	31.50	80.11	37.32	49.98	109
Myanmar	65.45	46.52	57.38	23.31	48.17	116
Nepal	73.46	34.46	22.66	49.14	44.93	121
Bangladesh	73.88	41.05	37.47	19.82	43.06	125
India	69.37	40.78	10.97	34.74	38.96	133
Pakistan	58.17	26.99	20.20	3.58	27.24	149
Afghanistan	40.89	16.74	25.38	11.22	23.56	151

Source: Authors' estimates using 2014–2019 data.

Figure 3.2 Global Distribution of Wellness

Central Asia	
Armenia	73.02
Azerbaijan	62.76
Georgia	71.94
Kazakhstan	72.50
Kyrgyz Republic	64.49
Tajikistan	54.11
Turkmenistan	53.93
Uzbekistan	58.26
East Asia	
Mongolia	61.22
PRC	52.68
Republic of Korea	75.93
Pacific	
Fiji	72.00
Maldives	74.72
Papua New Guinea	49.98
Vanuatu	66.61
South Asia	
Afghanistan	23.56
Bangladesh	43.06
Bhutan	67.03
India	38.96
Nepal	44.93
Pakistan	27.24
Sri Lanka	69.29
Southeast Asia	
Cambodia	51.17
Indonesia	57.70
Lao PDR	51.32
Malaysia	69.12
Myanmar	48.17
Philippines	54.28
Singapore	78.96
Thailand	59.40
Viet Nam	65.83
Other Asia	
Australia	90.19
Japan	85.77
New Zealand	93.67
North America	
Canada	89.16
United States	82.31

LANIC	
Argentina	67.82
Barbados	78.05
Bolivia	61.29
Brazil	62.92
Chile	72.86
Colombia	62.65
Costa Rica	76.50
Cuba	76.66
Dominican Republic	57.76
Ecuador	64.69
El Salvador	57.49
Guatemala	49.46
Guyana	60.22
Haiti	35.52
Honduras	57.29
Jamaica	69.16
Mexico	61.10
Nicaragua	56.95
Panama	67.84
Paraguay	60.72
Peru	60.42
Suriname	65.92
Trinidad and Tobago	73.79
Uruguay	79.07
Venezuela	61.58
MENA	
Algeria	58.39
Bahrain	49.94
Egypt, Arab Rep.	39.73
Iran, Islamic Rep.	51.18
Iraq	37.58
Jordan	63.14
Kuwait	49.28
Lebanon	55.74
Malta	76.69
Morocco	55.99
Oman	65.06
Qatar	47.43
Saudi Arabia	47.53
Tunisia	62.88
United Arab Emirates	57.76

SSA	
Angola	30.94
Benin	42.41
Botswana	63.39
Burkina Faso	38.65
Burundi	42.91
Cameroon	34.36
Cape Verde	68.38
Central African Republic	14.17
Chad	8.38
Comoros	51.90
Cote d'Ivoire	35.36
Equatorial Guinea	39.61
Eritrea	37.90
Ethiopia excluding Eritrea	40.56
Gabon	54.45
Gambia	43.08
Ghana	49.28
Guinea	33.30
Guinea-Bissau	33.29
Kenya	54.31
Lesotho	49.60
Liberia	38.41
Madagascar	46.00
Malawi	52.42
Mali	29.79
Mauritania	32.14
Mauritius	78.06
Mozambique	41.41
Namibia	55.95
Niger	27.46
Nigeria	23.75
Rwanda	53.34
Sao Tome and Principe	61.59
Senegal	44.70
Sierra Leone	28.86
South Africa	57.80
Sudan	31.48
Swaziland	50.21
Tanzania	51.41
Togo	41.82
Uganda	44.66
Zambia	49.07
Zimbabwe	47.75

EUROPE	
Albania	72.21
Austria	89.27
Belarus	76.03
Belgium	88.07
Bosnia and Herzegovina	70.01
Bulgaria	77.03
Croatia	79.28
Cyprus	81.18
Czech Republic	86.96
Denmark	94.23
Estonia	91.09
Finland	96.24
France	85.79
Germany	93.75
Greece	74.56
Hungary	78.41
Iceland	90.56
Ireland	90.34
Italy	80.83
Latvia	85.47
Luxembourg	95.71
Macedonia, FYR	66.06
Moldova	71.08
Netherlands	87.96
Norway	94.41
Portugal	83.39
Russian Federation	71.40
Slovak Republic	82.68
Slovenia	92.23
Sweden	94.49
Switzerland	92.96
Turkey	55.63
Ukraine	68.66
United Kingdom	87.06

Legend: 96 / 52 / 8

Notes:

Full tables are available in Appendix 2.

Lao PDR = Lao People's Democratic Republic, MENA = Middle East and North Africa, PRC = People's Republic of China.

Source: Authors' estimates using 2014–2019 data.

Data show that developing Asia, on average, performs close to the global average. This is in line with country-level scores in Table 3.1; countries in the region are spread evenly across the global ranking, with nations placing across the tertiles of the global rankings. The dimensions in which developing Asia performs relatively poorly are social and environmental wellness. This seems to be driven primarily by its weak performance on social indicators and those relating to equal opportunities across gender, as well as the high levels of pollution and lack of green spaces in its largest urban areas.

There is significant heterogeneity across subregions, with no single region consistently performing higher than others. East Asia ranks highest in physical wellness, Central Asia in intellectual wellness, and the Pacific in environmental and social wellness.

The result hints at a positive relationship between GDP and at least two pillars of wellness—physical and intellectual. This makes intuitive sense, as regions that perform well have higher GDP and therefore more resources available to allocate to health and education.

We build on these insights in later sections when we study the relationship between material well-being (as measured by GDP) and the Wellness Index and its pillars. We also dive deeper into the distribution of wellness among ADB members, as we use the Wellness Index to highlight areas of weakness and strength.

Figure 3.3 Comparing Average Wellness

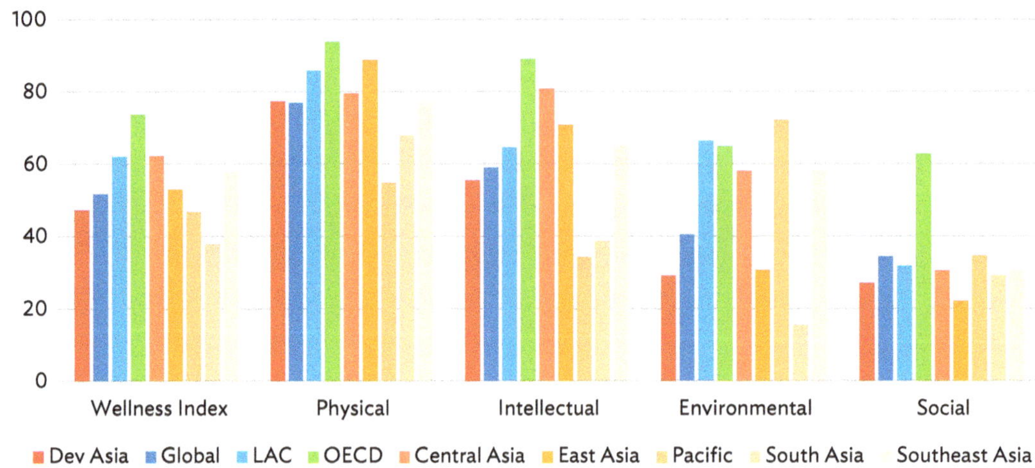

Dev Asia = developing Asia, NIE = newly industrialized economy, LAC = Latin America and the Caribbean, OECD = Organisation for Economic Co-operation and Development.

Subregion definitions and coverage are listed in Figure 3.2.

Note: Regional averages are population weighted of country scores.

Source: Authors' estimates.

Comparison with Other Measures of Well-Being

A wide variety of measures have been designed to capture various aspects of well-being. Some incorporate material well-being (as captured by GDP), while others, like our Wellness Index, do not. As mentioned earlier, the current default measure for well-being is GDP. GDP (and its predecessor, gross national product) were not designed to measure well-being, but rather were simple calculations of a nation's "income." GDP measures the total production in a country (or any geographical area) over a certain period, and aggregates it using the prices of each product. Even though those who formulated GDP warned against its use as a measure of well-being,[9] it has become the yardstick by which a nation's success is measured.

GDP's weakness as a measure of well-being should be obvious: it only measures a nation's income and nothing else. Even as a measure of income, it is an aggregate measure and does not account for inequality within the country. The Wellness Index seeks to measure wellness beyond growth with the aim to complement GDP. Therefore, it incorporates aspects of wellness that are missing in the GDP, and it explicitly disregards measures of wealth. This is not to argue that wealth is not important, but rather that the Wellness Index seeks to become a tool used by policy makers in conjunction with GDP; it is not a substitute, but a complement. Given the importance of GDP in policy and academic discourse, we also analyze the relationship between the Wellness Index and GDP in later sections.

Given the historic focus on GDP, attempts have been made to propose alternatives to GDP that seek to better capture well-being. Before we discuss these alternatives, note that, when comparing them to the Wellness Index, we anchor the conversation around the Wellness Index. Note that some of the indexes, given their different approaches, also incorporate concepts that are beyond the scope of the Wellness Index.

[9] S. Kuznets. 1934. *National Income, 1929–1931*. Senate Document. United States of America: 73rd US Congress.

One of the earliest measures of well-being is the Happiness Development Index (HDI) proposed by Amartya Sen and Mahbub Ul Haq and curated yearly by the United Nations Development Programme. HDI measures well-being in the dimensions of health, education, and material wealth by incorporating measures of life expectancy, literacy, and GDP, respectively. While it is a more comprehensive measure of wellness when compared with GDP, the HDI is incomplete as it does not incorporate multiple dimensions of well-being, and even in those that it does measure, it uses a very limited number of indicators.

Like the HDI, the Happy Planet Index relies on preexisting indicators and data from the Gallup World Poll to incorporate satisfaction, life expectancy, inequality, and ecological footprint. It relies on subjective surveys of well-being conducted by Gallup and other preexisting data to create a measure of well-being and sustainability. While more comprehensive than the HDI, the Happy Planet Index is still lacking in coverage of all aspects of well-being. Not surprisingly, given its name, however, it does capture some aspects of emotional well-being that are not included in the Wellness Index because the underlying data is proprietary.

Other indexes that capture more specific aspects of wellness include the Indigo Wellness Index and the World Happiness Report. The former utilizes measures of health and consumption across countries to capture some aspects of physical wellness. The World Happiness Report measures, as the name implies, happiness by utilizing subjective survey data on happiness. Both indexes are limited in their approach when compared with the Wellness Index but do contain some indicators distinct from those used in the current exercise.

More recently, three indexes have been proposed that take a more comprehensive view of well-being. The Organisation for Economic Co-operation and Development (OECD) Better Life Index takes direct inspiration from the Stiglitz-Sen-Fitoussi Commission and creates 11 indexes capturing various aspects of wellness for a sample of 50 countries.[10] Compared with the Wellness Index, their use of indicators is limited, as is their coverage of countries.

The Inclusive Green Grown Index (IGGI) is another recent addition to indicators that seek to augment GDP. As the IGGI's focus is on sustainable and equitable growth, it incorporates social inclusion, environmental well-being, and growth to provide policy makers with an easy-to-understand index. Like the Wellness Index, it relies on preexisting and open data. However, given its primary focus on green growth, the IGGI's methodology and coverage of indicators are, understandably, significantly different.

Finally, the Social Progress Index (SPI) is perhaps the closest in both motivation and methodology to the current exercise. The SPI identifies three basic foundations of social progress, each with four subcategories, covering various aspects of societal well-being, from access to necessities to personal freedoms. It utilizes 52 indicators and, like the Wellness Index, uses subcategory factor analysis to create an aggregate index. Like the Wellness Index, the SPI aims to measure well-being. However, the approaches are significantly different. As its starting point, the SPI defines three areas of social progress at the national level and uses them to create what can be viewed as a top–down measure of social progress. In contrast, the Wellness Index uses personal well-being as its starting point and focuses on the current and *live-d* experience of the average citizen with regard to wellness. While the SPI utilizes both inputs and outputs (e.g., access to necessities), the Wellness Index only uses outcomes. These differences in motivation result in significantly different approaches.

In addition to cross-country indexes, many countries have their own internal measures of well-being. While beyond the scope of this cross-country exercise, two that deserve mention are the GNH index used by Bhutan and the Canadian Index of Wellbeing.[11] The GNH was one of the first wellness indexes proposed and one that is used heavily to

10 OECD. 2011. *How's Life? Measuring Well-being*. OECD Publishing.

11 K. Ura et al. 2012 *A Short Guide to Gross National Happiness Index*. The Centre for Bhutan Studies; Canadian Index of Wellbeing. 2016. *How Are Canadians Really Doing: The 2016 CIW National Report*. Waterloo: Canadian Index of Wellbeing and University of Waterloo.

inform policy in the country. Both indexes rely on surveys that are unique to each country and include both subjective and objective measures of well-being. While not comparable with a cross-country exercise, they suggest promising directions for future global data collection exercises, especially if well-being is to become an integral part of policy.

Caveats

As formulated, the Wellness Index leverages data that are available over the past 5 years to rank countries ordinally. The use of PCA analysis relies on the assumption that each pillar represents a unique dimension of wellness that, while unobservable directly, affects the sub-indicators in a consistent manner. The resulting index must be understood for what it is, ordinal and sample-dependent. Its purpose is to allow us to compare countries across dimensions of wellness, not to assign a definitive value on wellness itself.

The ordinal ranking we achieve is sample-dependent, that is, the weights generated by principal components are a result of the underlying variation in country-level indicators that may change with time. We have attempted to clearly lay out the methodology of the index to allow easy replication in the future by using newer data. However, with newer data, the weights may change, and care must be taken when comparing rankings across different time periods.

Further, the sample dependence may also be a strength of the current methodology. While it only allows comparisons across years with respect to changes in ranking, the weights in principal components reflect underlying variance in indicators. As countries focus on improving their population's wellness, lower variance in improved indicators would result in higher weights assigned to other dimensions, updating the policy priority automatically.[12]

Replication is also one of the core reasons for using open access and nonproprietary data. Given their needs, policy makers and researchers can and should add or remove variables to the analysis, if certain proprietary variables are more suitable for their purposes. The Wellness Index is an attempt to create a "general" ranking of well-being across nations and should be interpreted as such.

Gross Domestic Product and Wellness

By leaving measures of growth and GDP out from the composition of the Wellness Index, we can study the relationship between the two indexes. In this section, we try to understand the relationship between wellness and GDP, both at the aggregate and at the pillar level. The analysis highlights the remarkable variance in wellness across each GDP level, across each pillar, as well as on aggregate.

Gross Domestic Product and Wellness Index: A Positive Relationship Overall

Figure 3.4 illustrates the relationship between the Wellness Index and the natural log of GDP per capita at purchasing power parity (PPP) (based on the latest available figures from 2018).[13] Each point on the plot represents a different nation in our sample, differentiating ADB members using blue dots.

[12] However, note that this effect can work both ways. In the unlikely event that all countries get *worse* in a dimension and reduce the variance with a race to the bottom, the weight of that indicator would also decrease.

[13] Throughout this chapter, we use GDP per capita at PPP, using constant 2010 US dollar. The underlying distribution of GDP per capita has a lot of clustering at the bottom. Taking a concave transformation, the natural log allows cleaner exposition. If a transformation is made, note that the relationship is not linear, as may be assumed from the graph, but rather log linear.

Figure 3.4 **Wellness and Gross Domestic Product**

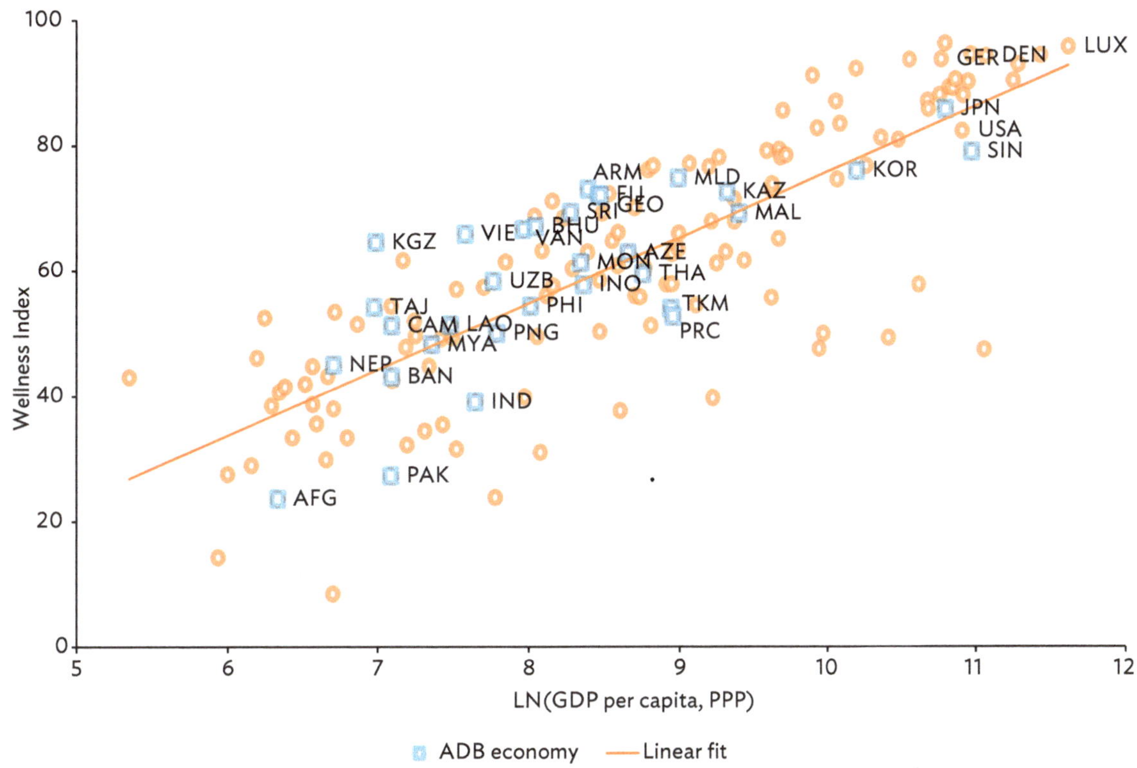

ADB = Asian Development Bank, AFG = Afghanistan, ARM = Armenia, AZE = Azerbaijan, BAN = Bangladesh, BHU = Bhutan, CAM = Cambodia, DEN = Denmark, FIJ = Fiji, GDP = gross domestic product, GEO = Georgia, GER = Germany, INO = Indonesia, IND = India, JPN = Japan, KAZ = Kazakhstan, KGZ = Kyrgyz Republic, KOR = Republic of Korea, LAO = Lao People's Democratic Republic, LUX = Luxembourg, MAL = Malaysia, MLD = Maldives, MON = Mongolia, MYA = Myanmar, NEP = Nepal, PAK = Pakistan, PHI = Philippines, PNG = Papua New Guinea, PPP = purchasing power parity, PRC = People's Republic of China, SIN = Singapore, SRI = Sri Lanka, TAJ = Tajikistan THA = Thailand, TKM = Turkmenistan, USA = United States, UZB = Uzbekistan, VAN = Vanuatu, VIE = Viet Nam.

Source: Authors' estimates.

As can be seen, the data suggest that there is a positive relationship between the Wellness Index and GDP, with countries with higher GDP performing better on the Wellness Index. The correlation perhaps then justifies the historic focus on GDP, which is further supported by intuition. Countries with higher GDP per capita may intuitively have access to more resources to provide their citizens with more services and better cater to their wellness needs.

However, this intuitive result ignores that the bridge between GDP and wellness is policy. The wide dispersion in wellness at all GDP levels highlights the fact that, in order to utilize material resources, a country needs proactive policy to focus on wellness. The link between GDP and wellness is not direct, and countries need wellness-focused policies to gain the maximum benefits of their material resources.

As the Wellness Index is the average of wellness scores across four dimensions, Figure 3.5 shows the relationship between growth and the pillars of the Wellness Index. We find that all four pillars display a positive relationship, though once again there is wide dispersion at every level of GDP.

Figure 3.5 Relationship between Growth and the Pillars of Wellness

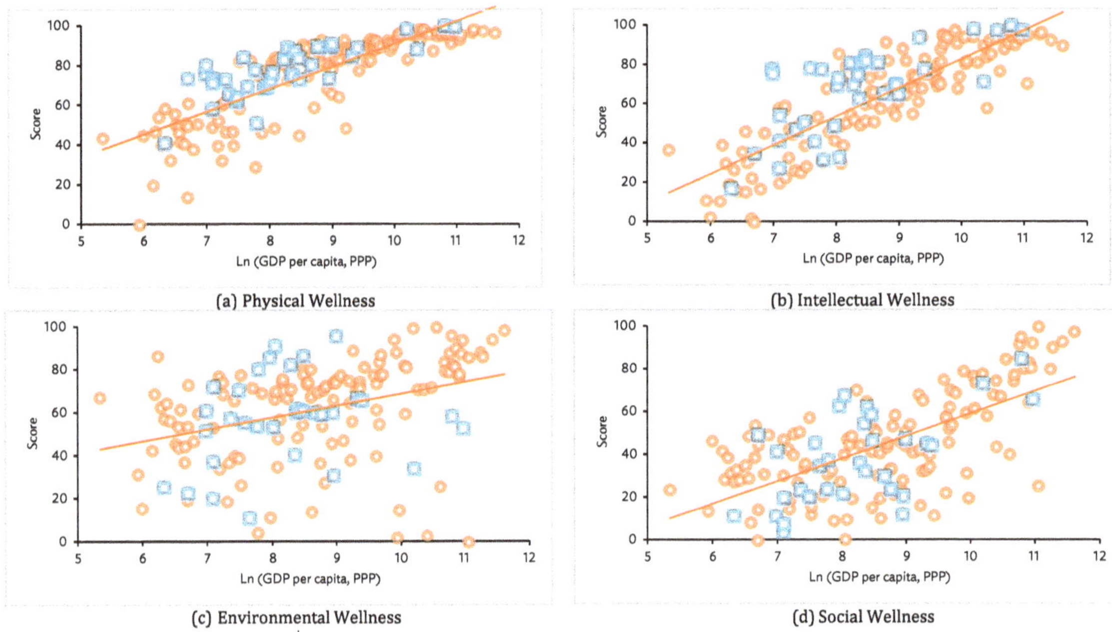

ADB = Asian Development Bank, GDP = gross domestic product, PPP = purchasing power parity.

Note: As before ln (GDP per capita PPP) is on the X-axis, with each pillar score on the Y-axis. Blue dots represent ADB members.

Source: Authors' estimates.

Need for Policy to Prioritize Wellness

While there is a positive relationship between wellness and GDP, the dispersion at all GDP per capita levels suggests that there is need for policy that focuses on wellness, beyond simply material well-being (as captured by GDP).

To better understand this point, consider more closely the case of Viet Nam. Like the majority of developing Asia, Viet Nam is a middle-income country with a nominal GDP per capita in 2018 of $2,566.60 ($1,964 at PPP using constant 2010 US dollar). Analyzing the subset of countries (Figure 3.6) that have similar GDP per capita (PPP) to Viet Nam, we find it outperforms all countries that have GDP similar to it (we allow for GDP to vary by ±10%). Not only this, we find that Viet Nam is able to compete on wellness with countries with significantly higher GDP per capita (PPP). For example, it outperforms Brazil, which has a GDP per capita (PPP) that is nearly five times larger.

Similarly, at the pillar level, we find major variation in performance. Consider the subset of countries that have GDP per capita (PPP) between $1,085 and $1,205. We find variance in each country's level of wellness, both overall and for each pillar. Interestingly, the Kyrgyz Republic, which has the lowest GDP, outperforms all its GDP peers. Of course, each nation will have different dynamics and historical contexts, but the comparison shows that, by only comparing and focusing on GDP, policy makers may be ignoring wellness and may wish to use the Wellness Index to identify areas of priority (Figure 3.7).

Figure 3.6 **Gross Domestic Product and Wellness for Countries within 10% Bands of Viet Nam**

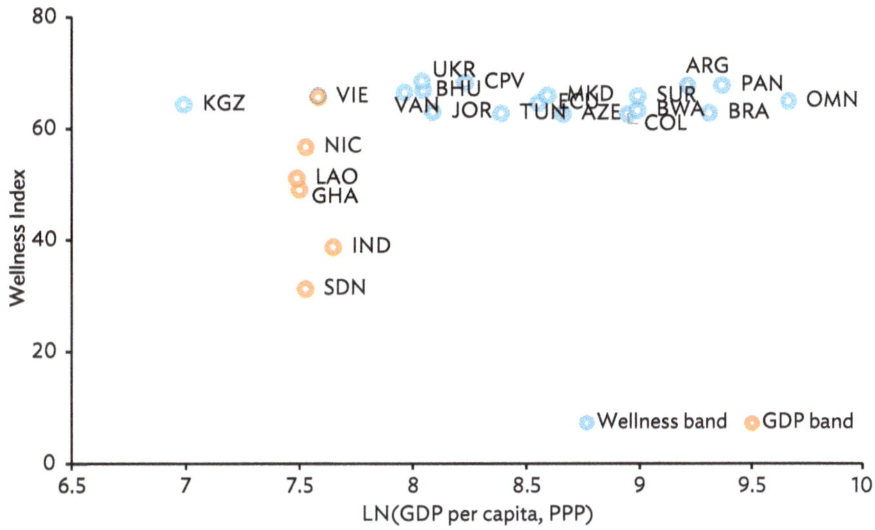

ARG = Argentina, AZE = Azerbaijan, BRA = Brazil, BHU = Bhutan, BWA = Botswana, COL = Colombia, CPV = Cabo Verde, ECU = Ecuador, GDP = gross domestic product, GHA = Ghana, IND = India, JOR = Jordan, KGZ = Kyrgyz Republic, LAO = Lao People's Democratic Republic, MKD = Republic of North Macedonia, NIC = Nicaragua, OMN = Oman, PAN = Panama, PPP = purchasing power parity, SDN = Sudan, SUR = Suriname, TUN = Tunisia, UKR = Ukraine, VAN = Vanuatu, VIE = Viet Nam.

Source: Authors' estimates.

Figure 3.7 **Variation in Performance of Countries with Similar Levels of Gross Domestic Product**

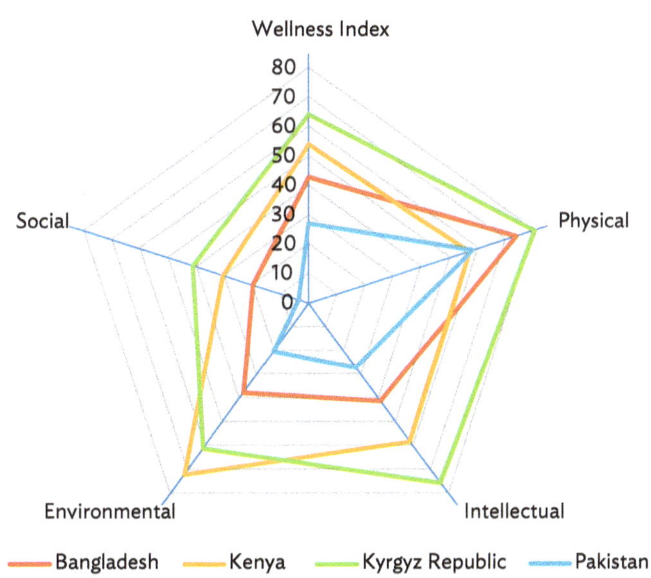

Source: Authors' estimates.

Concluding Remarks

The Wellness Index takes a grassroots approach to measure the average level of wellness of citizens in each country. It joins a expanding list of measures that seek to enrich policy beyond a focus on growth. It is the first measure that takes an individual-level approach and builds a country-level index through the use of multiple proxies for each of the four pillars of wellness.

The Wellness Index provides policy makers with an easy-to-use benchmark of their performance on each of four dimensions of wellness. The methodology employed allows us to leverage currently available data in order to identify areas of strength and weakness. The index's reliance on open data also allows for easy replication and lets users to easily add and subtract indicators to best suit their needs. Finally, it joins the growing chorus of work aimed at highlighting the need for measures of wellness, and the index's weakness, that is, its reliance on preexisting indicators, highlights the need for regional-level cooperation to realign data collection activities to more wellness-centric instruments.

In summation, given current data limitations, the Wellness Index provides the first step toward a comprehensive measure of individual wellness. It can in its current form already be used to benchmark country performance, and it highlights exciting new areas for future research in wellness, in particular the need for more wellness-focused data collection.

CHAPTER 4

Tracing the Production and Employment Linkages in Developing Asia's Wellness Economies

Rafael Martin Consing III, Michael John Barsabal, Julian Thomas Alvarez, and Mahinthan Mariasingham

This chapter serves as an expansion to the background note on wellness economy estimation prepared for the Asian Development Outlook 2020 Update. Procedures are discussed for using the system of national accounts framework to derive the wellness economy's contribution to overall production and employment in a country by employing input–output analysis to trace the production and employment linkages between wellness and non-wellness sectors. Estimates based on these procedures then are provided for nine countries in developing Asia that together provide a proxy for the region (Asia-9) across two time periods, along with a discussion on how these wellness economies have grown between the two periods.

Wellness Activities as Economic Activities

People have a natural preference for wellness, and this goes beyond the desire to avoid physical illness. Often, this means thriving holistically and leading well-rounded lives, and so people engage in diverse activities to help themselves feel and become well. While many of these activities, such as meditation and social interaction, do not necessarily involve monetary transactions, there are wellness-related activities that are also economic in nature, such as the consumption of health, personal care, and sporting goods and services. In a developing country, the volume and economic value of these activities are expected to increase as people become increasingly conscious of and able to meet their need for wellness.

Therefore, it is becoming increasingly important to be able to measure the *wellness economy*, defined here as "the linkages of an economy attributable to the production of wellness goods and services with monetary transactions attached to them." From a policy perspective, this gives a better understanding of how relevant wellness activities have become to the economy, which ones are the biggest economic contributors, and which ones are potentially underdeveloped in the context of country-specific unmet social needs. For policy makers interested in maximizing the wellness of their constituents, a measure of the wellness economy becomes another analytical tool for socioeconomic development.

This chapter contributes to the literature by showing how the system of national accounts (SNA) framework can be used to estimate the production and employment linkages of an economy's wellness sector, and then demonstrates this for selected developing member countries (DMCs) of the Asian Development Bank (ADB) over two time periods. The main advantage of this approach is that most countries follow the SNA framework when preparing their national accounts, and so theoretically this allows any country to estimate its own wellness economy.

What Is Wellness?

As an object of natural preference, wellness has been around potentially as long as humanity has. The desire for a better life is fundamentally a desire for wellness. As is common with such concepts, the term "wellness" can seem nebulous and imprecise, often grasped intuitively rather than scholastically. For the wellness economy to be measured, however, wellness must be defined explicitly.

In the modern academe, numerous definitions for wellness have been proposed, with one of the earliest coming from Dunn, who defines it as "a health condition which includes general well-being of body, mind, and spirit."[1] A review by Roscoe[2] indicates similarities in definitions across wellness literature in the decades following Dunn but with more dimensions added, the most prevalent being those related to social, emotional, physical, intellectual, and spiritual well-being. The multidimensionality of wellness trends into the next century, with Miller and Foster stating that the broadening scope of wellness is meant to create a "theoretical framework that views individuals within a holistic perspective and consists of many dimensions."[3] Wellness is also commonly viewed as both a state and the active pursuit of that state, and this appears in the Global Wellness Institute's (GWI's) definition of wellness as "the active pursuit of activities, choices, and lifestyles that lead to a state of holistic health."[4]

The World Health Organization (WHO) takes a broader view:

> Wellness is the optimal state of health of individuals and groups. There are two focal concerns: the realization of the fullest potential of an individual physically, psychologically, socially, spiritually, and economically, and the fulfillment of one's role expectations in the family, community, place of worship, workplace and other settings.[5]

This definition is the most explicitly comprehensive so far as it includes an economic dimension of wellness in addition to the other commonly cited dimensions and recognizes wellness as both a state and an activity. As this definition shares similarities with and encompasses many others covered, it is the definition for wellness that is primarily being referred to in this chapter. In the endeavor to estimate how much of an economy can systematically be attributed to the production of wellness goods and services, the most inclusive definition is correspondingly adopted.

1 H.L. Dunn. 1959. High-Level Wellness for Man and Society. *American Journal of Public Health*. 49 (6). pp. 786–792.
2 L.J. Roscoe. 2009. Wellness: A Review of Theory and Measurement for Counselors. *Journal of Counselling and Development*. 87 (2). pp. 216–226.
3 G. Miller. and L. Foster. 2010. *Critical Synthesis of Wellness Literature*. University of Victoria Faculty of Human and Social Development and Department of Geography.
4 GWI. 2018. *Global Wellness Economy Monitor 2018*.
5 WHO. 2006. *Health Promotion Glossary Update*. Geneva.

What Is the Wellness Economy?

Given the established multidimensionality of wellness, economic activities that fall under wellness cannot be limited to just the consumption of medical services and pharmaceutical goods. Potentially, wellness includes all economic activities and industries that help people feel and become well, such as those relating to travel, recreational, outdoor, sporting, and personal care activities. The specific economic activities considered as wellness are described further in the methodology and enumerated in Appendix 6. In this chapter, industries engaged in the production of such wellness goods and services are referred to collectively as the *wellness sector*.[6] As economies are complex systems with interconnected sectors, the wellness sector is itself supported by activities in other sectors of the economy.

In the context of economic productivity, the wellness economy is measured in terms of gross value added (GVA).[7] Therefore, the objective in this chapter is to show how much of a country's GVA is attributable to those wellness goods and services with monetary transactions attached to them. This refers to two main components: (i) the GVA from the wellness sector itself, such as the GVA from hospitals; and (ii) the contribution from supporting non-wellness sectors, such as the GVA from the energy sector used to produce hospital services.

It is important to emphasize that measuring the wellness economy is not the same as measuring the welfare, wellness, or well-being of people in a country. For example, a pandemic might increase spending on hospital activities, which might, holding other factors constant, mean a larger measurement of the wellness economy, yet a population's well-being could actually decline as more people fall ill or into anxiety and poverty because of the pandemic. Similarly, a wellness economy might be growing because of the high production of wellness goods and services, yet the population's welfare may remain low if only a wealthy minority of the population is able to consume these goods and services. This chapter focuses only on using input–output analysis to measure wellness economies and not welfare.

Besides measuring the wellness economy in GVA terms, another way to measure the relevance of the wellness sector to the overall economy under the SNA framework would be to estimate *wellness employment*, defined here as "the employment linkages attributable to the production of wellness goods and services with monetary transactions attached to them." In terms of production and employment, the wellness economy can be estimated using input–output analysis, and so they neatly relate to each other and are discussed as such in the methodology. Estimates for the wellness economy and wellness employment are then produced for selected countries in developing Asia, with available data over two time periods to show a practical application of this framework.

Methodology

Identifying the Wellness Sector

The first step is to identify which economic industries produce wellness goods and services. Using the fourth revision of the International Standard Industrial Classification of All Economic Activities (ISIC), 35 industrial codes were identified as composing the wellness sector. These codes were selected to be as inclusive as

6 In this context, wellness industries and wellness subsectors may be treated synonymously.

7 There is a small difference between a country's GVA and its gross domestic product (GDP). A country's GDP is equal to its GVA plus nonrefundable product or sales taxes. These taxes constitute a very small percentage of GDP and are a function of product-specific value added. Therefore, for all analytical purposes, this paper assumes that GVA is almost equal to GDP and uses the terms interchangeably. R.M. Consing et al. 2020. *Using the System of National Accounts to Estimate a Country's Wellness Economy*. Manila: ADB.

reasonably possible of the various dimensions of wellness embodied in WHO's definition. These are likewise consistent with wellness activities discussed in the literature, such as in Kickbusch and Payne, Pilzer, and GWI.[8]

Some codes are included to expand the scope of commonly recognized wellness activities. For example, these ISIC codes include hospital activities for ill patients (excluded in some definitions of wellness, such as that of GWI), under the assumption that ill patients engage in hospital activities with the intention of becoming well. As in Consing et al.,[9] these ISIC codes capture a variety of wellness goods and services from various industries, such as human health, residential care, social work, tourism, amusement, recreational, sports, creative, arts, entertainment, culture, and personal care activities, as well as the construction of wellness-related structures, such as health and sports facilities and the manufacture and retail trade of wellness goods such as pharmaceutical, beauty, and sports products. The list of ISIC codes covering the wellness sector is provided in Appendix 6.

Data

The main data source used in computing the contribution of the wellness sector to gross domestic product (GDP) is national input–output tables (IOTs). Symmetric IOTs summarize the flow of transactions across industries operating in the economy. These contain information on intermediate consumption, gross output, and GVA for each production sector. When IOTs are not readily available, supply and use tables (SUTs) from various national statistical offices are converted into industry-by-industry IOTs using the transformation model prescribed by Eurostat.[10] Inherent in the transformation of SUTs into IOTs is the assumption that, without any regard to the producing industry, each product has its own sale-specific structure (footnote 10).

While a country's IOT provides the information that is necessary for computing sectoral GVA, the industries of the wellness sector are often grouped into various sectoral aggregates, making the identification and computation of the GDP attributable to the wellness sector difficult. This is resolved by disaggregating or breaking down the IOT industries. With several methods available, this chapter uses information that is extrapolated from supply tables, administrative data, and secondary data. The several methods used in disaggregation are explained in Box 4.1.

Tracing the Production Linkages of the Wellness Sector

Given that a country's IOT is disaggregated following the procedure described in Box 4.1, the size of the wellness economy can now be estimated using the processed IOT. In particular, we use Leontief's insight[11] to derive the economic contributions of the wellness sector and its supporting non-wellness industries.

To trace the production linkages of the wellness sector, the disaggregated $n \times n$ IOT is converted into a table with $n\text{-}(q\text{-}1) \times n\text{-}(q\text{-}1)$ dimensions, where n is the total number of sectors in the economy and q the number of which are wellness industries. This ensures that there is only a single account dedicated to the wellness

8 I. Kickbusch and L. Payne. 2003. *Twenty-First Century Health Promotion: The Public Health Revolution Meets the Wellness Revolution*. Health Promotion International. 18 (4). pp. 275–278; P.Z. Pilzer. 2007. *The New Wellness Revolution: How to Make a Fortune in the Next Trillion Dollar Industry*. 2nd ed. Hoboken, NJ: John Wiley and Sons, Inc; and GWI. 2018. *Global Wellness Economy Monitor 2018*.

9 R.M. Consing et al. 2020. *Using the System of National Accounts to Estimate a Country's Wellness Economy*. Manila: ADB.

10 Eurostat. 2008. *The Eurostat Manual of Supply, Use and Input–Output Tables*. Luxembourg: Office for Official Publications of the European Communities.

11 W. Leontief. 1936. Quantitative Input and Output Relations in the Economic System of the United States. *Review of Economics and Statistics*. 18. pp. 105–125.

Box 4.1 Disaggregating Input–Output Tables

The first method of disaggregating an input–output table (IOT) involves the use of the supply table, which is the preferred method because it involves the use of system of national accounts components as a basis for disaggregation. This entails the identification of wellness products and the total amount of wellness products that are supplied by the sector to be broken down. The total amount of wellness products that are supplied by the aggregated industry is then divided by the total output of the aggregated sector to obtain the disaggregator. This ratio is then multiplied to the relevant gross value added in the IOT. This process is repeated to generate a set of disaggregators that are used to break down the aggregated sectors of interest. Once the wellness components have been separated, these are summed up to create a separate account for the wellness sector in the IOT.

Underlying the first method is the need for a highly disaggregated row of accounts in the supply table. That is, for the first method to be viable, the supply table must include numerous products. If a country's supply table is not detailed enough to produce disaggregators, an alternative method of disaggregation is to use firm-level data coming from a secondary source. Here, firm-level data from the Orbis database was used. After applying the methods on filtering firms in the database as prescribed in Kalemli-Ozcan et al., data on the operating revenue of each firm for each country is collected. The operating revenues are aggregated at the four-digit International Standard Industrial Classification of All Economic Activities (ISIC) level[a] and on the basis of the sectoral groupings in the IOT. The set of disaggregators are then computed by taking the ratio of the operating revenue of ISIC industry codes for wellness industries to the operating revenue of the sector being disaggregated. If a detailed supply table is unavailable and data from secondary sources are limited for disaggregation, the donor imputation method for deriving disaggregators is employed. The objective is to use the disaggregators from a donor country. The donor country is chosen based on the expectation that the economic structure of the imputed country closely resembles that of the donor.[b] Economic factors such as similarity in market structure; share of agriculture, industry, and services to gross domestic product; income group; and major commodities produced are the main considerations in choosing a donor for a recipient country.

Once disaggregators are estimated using the methods described above, these are further verified with available administrative data for each country of interest to ensure that the disaggregators are reliable and intuitive. The disaggregators are then used to dissect the aggregated sectors in each country's IOT. Since IOTs are characteristically symmetric, these disaggregators are multiplied to both the rows and columns corresponding to the industries in the IOT that contain the wellness activities of interest.

In effect, the symmetric IOT is expanded for each disaggregator that is being applied as the corresponding industry being disaggregated is split into the part of it that contains wellness activities and the part of it that contains non-wellness activities. For example, an IOT containing a single entry encompassing all ISIC codes starting with 47 (retail trade, except motor vehicles and motorcycles) would be split row-wise and column-wise, using a relevant disaggregator to create a separate entry just for ISIC code 4763 (retail sale of sporting equipment in specialized stores), which is considered part of wellness.

[a] Since firms in the Orbis database are classified according to the European Classification of Economic Activities (NACE) Rev. 2, a concordance table was used to convert these codes into ISIC Rev. 4 industry codes.

[b] The requirement is that the sector aggregation in the IOTs of the donor and imputed economies should be the same.

Sources: R.M. Consing et al. 2020. *The Wellness Economy: A Comprehensive System of National Accounts Approach*. Manila: Asian Development Bank; and S. Kalemli-Ozcan et al. 2019. How to Construct Nationally Representative Firm Level Data from the Orbis Global Database: New Facts and Aggregate Implications. *NBER Working Paper Series* No. 21558. Cambridge, MA: National Bureau of Economic Research.

sector and there is no double-counting that comes from the interaction of wellness industries with each other. Resizing the IOT entails that each entry of the wellness industry in the disaggregated IOT is added to a single account.[12]

Once the values for each wellness industry are aggregated into a single account, the matrix of technical coefficients, $\mathbf{A} = [a_{ij}]$, which gives the share of inputs to total output, is obtained. This matrix is derived by post-multiplying the matrix of intermediate consumption, $\mathbf{Z} = [z_{ij}]$, with the inverse of a diagonalized matrix of gross output, $\hat{\mathbf{X}}^{-1}$.[13] Subtracting **A** to an identity matrix and taking its inverse yields Equation 1, the Leontief Inverse.

$$\mathbf{B} = (\mathbf{I} - \mathbf{A})^{-1} = [b_{ij}] \tag{1}$$

The Leontief Inverse summarizes the output requirements from each sector to meet final demand, given a specific time period. Similarly, we also construct the direct value-added coefficient matrix $\hat{\mathbf{V}}$ by placing the elements of a vector of direct value-added coefficients, $v = [va_j / x_j]_{n-(q-1)\times 1}$, into the diagonal entries. Pre-multiplying **B** to $\hat{\mathbf{V}}$ gives us $\hat{\mathbf{V}}\mathbf{B}$, the total value-added matrix. This matrix indicates the value added each sector directly and indirectly required to produce a unit of its final demand. Thus, when $\hat{\mathbf{Y}}$, a diagonal matrix of the final demand, is post-multiplied to $\hat{\mathbf{V}}\mathbf{B}$, Equation 2 is derived.

$$\hat{\mathbf{V}}\mathbf{B}\hat{\mathbf{Y}} = \begin{bmatrix} v_1 b_{11} y_1 & \cdots & v_1 b_{1,n-(q-1)}, y_{n-(q-1)} \\ \vdots & \ddots & \vdots \\ v_{n-(q-1)} b_{n-(q-1),1} y_1 & \cdots & v_{n-(q-1)} b_{n-(q-1),n-(q-1)} y_{n-(q-1)} \end{bmatrix}_{n-(q-1)\times n-(q-1)} \tag{2}$$

Equation 2 traces the production linkages of each sector in the economy by decomposing the value added made by each sector in the economy.[14] Each element in the matrix is interpreted as the value added from each sector that is directly or indirectly used in the production of final goods and services of a specific sector.[15] Therefore, the sum of each entry of the $\hat{\mathbf{V}}\mathbf{B}\hat{\mathbf{Y}}$ matrix gives the total GDP of the entire economy.

To measure the wellness economy, the value-added contribution attributable to the wellness sector from Equation 2 is estimated. This is done by including the sum of all entries in the row for the wellness sector in Equation 2. The row sum, $\mathbf{i}'\hat{\mathbf{V}}\mathbf{B}\hat{\mathbf{Y}}\boldsymbol{\varepsilon}$, can be easily obtained by pre-multiplying a unit row vector and post-multiplying $\boldsymbol{\varepsilon}$ to Equation 2. The vector $\boldsymbol{\varepsilon}$ is an indicator vector for the wellness sector where each element of the vector is 0 except for the row corresponding to the wellness sector with a value of 1. This term captures the value-added contributions from the wellness sector that enable production in all sectors in the economy. The term $\mathbf{i}'\hat{\mathbf{V}}\mathbf{B}\hat{\mathbf{Y}}\boldsymbol{\varepsilon}$ also encapsulates the forward linkages of the wellness sector across all downstream sectors. Further, this term describes the GVA of the wellness sector that is consistent with the SNA framework.

12 Another way of aggregating values in each wellness industry is through the multiplication of an aggregator matrix to the components of the IOT. For a detailed exposition on the aggregator matrix, see C. Torelli. and A.J. Lumba. 2020. *The Core of the Digital Economy: A Proposed Framework*. Unpublished.

13 For notational purposes, a hat (i.e.: $\hat{\mathbf{X}}$) represents a diagonal matrix with elements of vector x on the diagonal.

14 This decomposition that is performed in this framework is based on the work of Wang, Wei, and Zhu and Wang, Wei, Yu, and Zhu, which decomposes the value added into various components in a multiregional input–output model. Z. Wang, S. Wei, and K. Zhu. 2013. Quantifying International Production Sharing at the Bilateral and Sector Levels. *NBER Working Paper Series* No. 19677. Cambridge, MA: National Bureau of Economic Research; and Z. Wang, S. Wei, X. Yu, and K. Zhu. 2017. Measures of Participation in Global Value Chains and Global Business Cycles. *NBER Working Paper Series* No. 23222. Cambridge, MA: National Bureau of Economic Research.

15 Z. Wang, S. Wei, and K. Zhu. 2013. Quantifying International Production Sharing at the Bilateral and Sector Levels. *NBER Working Paper Series* No. 19677. Cambridge, MA: National Bureau of Economic Research; and Z. Wang, S. Wei, X. Yu, and K. Zhu. 2017. Measures of Participation in Global Value Chains and Global Business Cycles. *NBER Working Paper Series* No. 23222. Cambridge, MA: National Bureau of Economic Research.

The measure for the size of the wellness economy also includes the backward linkages of the wellness sector. This is computed by taking the sum of the column dedicated for the wellness sector in Equation 4. Operationally, the value for the backward linkage is derived by post-multiplying $\boldsymbol{\varepsilon}$ to $\mathbf{i}'\,(\hat{\mathbf{V}}\mathbf{B}\hat{\mathbf{Y}})'$. With the inclusion of $\mathbf{i}'\,(\hat{\mathbf{V}}\mathbf{B}\hat{\mathbf{Y}})'\boldsymbol{\varepsilon}$ to the new estimate of wellness GDP, the value-added contribution from supporting non-wellness sectors that enables the production of the wellness sector is accounted.

Adding these two terms while adjusting for the intersection term, $\left[\text{diag}\,(\hat{\mathbf{V}}\mathbf{B}\hat{\mathbf{Y}})\right]'$, which is double counted, gives a GDP measure of the wellness economy based on its production linkages as shown in Equation 3.

$$\text{Wellness GDP} = \mathbf{i}'\,\hat{\mathbf{V}}\mathbf{B}\hat{\mathbf{Y}}\boldsymbol{\varepsilon} + \mathbf{i}'\,(\hat{\mathbf{V}}\mathbf{B}\hat{\mathbf{Y}})'\boldsymbol{\varepsilon} - \left[\text{diag}\,(\hat{\mathbf{V}}\mathbf{B}\hat{\mathbf{Y}})\right]'\boldsymbol{\varepsilon} \tag{3}$$

where $\left[\text{diag}\,(\hat{\mathbf{V}}\mathbf{B}\hat{\mathbf{Y}})\right]'$ is a n-(q-1) x 1 vector with the diagonal elements of Equation 2 as its entries.

Integration of Gross Fixed Capital Formation in Wellness Gross Domestic Product

While the wellness GDP stated in Equation 3 captures all contemporaneous input–output transactions with respect to the exogenous final demand, it does not include capital goods purchased by the wellness sector for future production. To account for the gross fixed capital formation (GFCF) attributable to the wellness sector but distributed in other industries, Equation 3 is adjusted as follows:

$$\text{Adjusted Wellness GDP} = \mathbf{i}'\,\hat{\mathbf{V}}\mathbf{B}\hat{\mathbf{Y}}\boldsymbol{\varepsilon} + \mathbf{i}'\,(\hat{\mathbf{V}}\mathbf{B}\hat{\mathbf{Y}})'\boldsymbol{\varepsilon} - \left[\text{diag}\,(\hat{\mathbf{V}}\mathbf{B}\hat{\mathbf{Y}})\right]'\boldsymbol{\varepsilon} + (\mathbf{i} - \boldsymbol{\varepsilon})'\,\hat{\mathbf{V}}\mathbf{B}\hat{\mathbf{Y}}\hat{\mathbf{R}}\boldsymbol{\Lambda}'\boldsymbol{\varepsilon}\,(\mathbf{i} - \boldsymbol{\varepsilon}) \tag{4}$$

Equation 4 is almost identical to Equation 3 except that a fourth term was added, where the $\hat{\mathbf{V}}\mathbf{B}\hat{\mathbf{Y}}$. matrix is post-multiplied with $\hat{\mathbf{R}}$. The post-multiplied matrix is a n-(q-1) x n-(q-1) diagonal matrix of the ratio of use of wellness GFCF to the total final use of each sector in the economy. Each ratio is computed by dividing the sum of each row in the wellness GFCF matrix[16] by the corresponding total final demand.

The matrix product $\hat{\mathbf{V}}\mathbf{B}\hat{\mathbf{Y}}\hat{\mathbf{R}}$ is again post-multiplied with a filter matrix, $\boldsymbol{\Lambda} = \hat{\boldsymbol{\alpha}}$. The diagonalized vector $\boldsymbol{\alpha}$ is an indicator vector whose value is 1 if the same industry in a donor country[17] uses wellness GFCF products and 0 otherwise. The post-multiplication of $\boldsymbol{\Lambda}$ to the matrix product $\hat{\mathbf{V}}\mathbf{B}\hat{\mathbf{Y}}\hat{\mathbf{R}}$ effectively filters out industries that might be providing wellness GFCF, but whose counterparts in the donor economy do not.

The sum of all entries in the resulting matrix less the entries corresponding to the wellness sector itself is the term representing the part of GDP attributable to the wellness sector's purchase of capital goods from other sectors in the economy. Thus, Equation 4 is the key equation in measuring the size of the wellness economy.

Measuring the Employment Attributable to the Wellness Economy

Besides measuring the economy attributable to wellness in terms of GVA, the economic relevance of wellness can be characterized through its contribution to total employment. The key step in performing this analysis is the collection and processing of sector employment data from official sources. Since sources of labor data are likely to release employment figures at an aggregated level, different techniques are applied to further disentangle the number of jobs attributable to each sector in the economy.

---

16 The wellness GFCF matrix (W) is extrapolated from the GFCF vector in the IOT by multiplying the corresponding ratio of the gross output of each wellness industry to total output with the row entry in the GFCF vector. In matrix notation, $\mathbf{W} = \mathbf{gt'}$, where g is a n-(q-1) x 1 GFCF vector and t is a qx1 vector of gross output ratios.

17 In the application of this estimation procedure, the donor country is Canada because of data limitations. However, another economy with available data can be used as a donor country. Consequently, if the matrix product is not filtered out, $\boldsymbol{\Lambda}$ becomes an identity matrix.

The first method in disaggregating employment data uses the unit labor cost (ULC) approach in which the sector ULC is defined as "the ratio of total labor cost to real output by sector."[18] Since the total labor cost is the product of real wages and the total number of employees in each sector, the sector ULC can be multiplied to the inverse of the wage-to-output ratio to recover total employment by industry. This step is operationalized in Equation 5.

$$\text{Employment}_j = \text{ULC}_j \times \frac{\text{Total Output}_j}{\text{Real Wage}_j} = \frac{\text{Real Wage}_j \times \text{Employment}_j}{\text{Total Output}_j} \times \frac{\text{Total Output}_j}{\text{Real Wage}_j} \tag{5}$$

Given that the ULC approach requires data that might not be readily available from official sources, another method in deriving sectoral employment is to use the distribution of compensation of employees (COE) by sector. Often, COE is provided in the SUT of a particular country. If COE is not available, the distribution of GVA can be an alternative in further dividing aggregated employment figures.

Once data on employment are processed to the desired sector disaggregation, the effect of the sector on jobs is determined by executing a procedure analogous to the method described for Equation 2. Unlike in Equation 2 where $\hat{\mathbf{V}}$ is pre-multiplied to $\mathbf{B}\hat{\mathbf{Y}}$, $\hat{\mathbf{V}}$ is replaced with an employment matrix, $\hat{\mathbf{E}}$, which is a n-(q-1) × n-(q-1) diagonal matrix with labor coefficients as its diagonal entries. Labor coefficients represent the total number of persons needed to produce a unit of output and are computed by dividing the total number of jobs for each sector to the gross output of the corresponding sector (i.e.: $e_j = \text{jobs}_j / x_j$). Pre-multiplying $\hat{\mathbf{E}}$ with $\mathbf{B}\hat{\mathbf{Y}}$ yields to the matrix equation below.

$$\hat{\mathbf{E}}\mathbf{B}\hat{\mathbf{Y}} = \begin{bmatrix} e_1 b_{11} y_1 & \cdots & e_1 b_{1,n-(q-1)} y_{n-(q-1)} \\ \vdots & \ddots & \vdots \\ e_{n-(q-1)} b_{n-(q-1),1} y_1 & \cdots & e_{n-(q-1)} b_{n-(q-1),n-(q-1)} y_{n-(q-1)} \end{bmatrix}_{n-(q-1) \times n-(q-1)} \tag{6}$$

Equation 6 shows the number of jobs created in each sector because of final demand. Particularly, $e_i b_{ij} y_j$ is the number of jobs created in Sector *i* because of the final demand of Sector *j*. Thus, summing up all entries in Equation 6 results in the total number of jobs in the economy.

To derive the employment attributable to the wellness economy, entries in the column and row vectors of Equation 6 corresponding to the wellness sector are added together. This procedure is summarized in Equation 7.

$$\text{Wellness Employment} = \mathbf{i}' \hat{\mathbf{E}}\mathbf{B}\hat{\mathbf{Y}}\boldsymbol{\varepsilon} + \mathbf{i}' (\hat{\mathbf{E}}\mathbf{B}\hat{\mathbf{Y}})'\boldsymbol{\varepsilon} - \left[\text{diag}\,(\hat{\mathbf{E}}\mathbf{B}\hat{\mathbf{Y}})\right]'\boldsymbol{\varepsilon} \tag{7}$$

The first term of Equation 7 shows the total number of jobs created in the wellness sector because of the demand of all sectors in the economy. Similarly, the difference between the second and third terms of the preceding equation indicates the number of jobs induced by the final demand for wellness goods and services in all other sectors in the domestic economy.

Results and Discussion

The Wellness Economy

Based on data for the previous decade, the wellness economy's prospects in developing Asia have been generally positive, demonstrating potential for high growth. Wellness traditions in the region have their roots in centuries-old practices and have deeply embedded themselves in its people's lives and cultures.

[18] C. Ernst and M. Sarabia. 2015. The Role of Construction as an Employment Provider: A World-Wide Input–Output *Analysis. ILO Employment Working Paper* No. 186. Geneva: International Labour Organization.

Asian economies have successfully assimilated some of these practices even in contemporary markets, notwithstanding significant changes in their economic structure. The wellness economy itself witnessed drastic changes in recent periods, resulting from changes in technology and changes in demographic composition. For example, advancements in technology have enabled greater volumes of wellness products to be more accessible to a wide array of consumers. At the same time, the aging population in several economies in developing Asia has also influenced wellness consumption patterns, as societies divert more resources toward meeting the demands of the elderly population.

The sharp increases in per capita income in developing Asia has been accompanied by a rapidly growing middle class.[19] As a consequence, large segments of the population have been able to integrate wellness goods and services into their daily consumption pattern. Moreover, there is an increasing recognition that wellness-oriented policies are needed to complement people's transitions toward improved and healthier lifestyles.[20] Given these developments, there is also growing demand for a framework by which to measure the wellness economy and to trace its evolution across countries and over time.

This section presents and discusses estimates of the wellness economy in selected countries in developing Asia using the procedures described in the previous section. The discussion in this section is outlined as follows: the first part discusses the size of the wellness economy in aggregate and in per capita terms. The second part decomposes the wellness economy into forward and backward linkages, and the wellness GFCF component. Similarly, the last part focuses on the wellness sector's employment linkages for each of the selected countries in developing Asia.

Size of the Wellness Economy

Table 4.1 shows the estimates of the wellness economy in nine of ADB's DMCs, as measured in million US dollars at constant 2010 prices. The wellness economies are calculated using Equation 4. The estimates are presented for two periods for each country, and the annualized growth rate for each wellness economy is also shown in the last column. Breaking down of national IOTs to disaggregate the wellness sector from the other sectors is implemented using Orbis firm-level data for the People's Republic of China (PRC), the Philippines, Thailand, and Viet Nam. Supply tables are used for Kazakhstan and Malaysia as these two countries have detailed products in their SUTs. When the other two sources are insufficient, the donor country structure is used to approximate the disaggregation for another country. The choice is based on the similarity in economic structure (i.e., share of agriculture, industry, and services to GDP); level of development (i.e., income classification, Human Development Index); geographic proximity; and historical context. Malaysia is used as the donor country for both Fiji and Sri Lanka, while the structure of the PRC is used for Mongolia.

Countries in developing Asia have made significant strides in the expansion of the wellness economy. In absolute terms, the PRC experienced the most significant expansion of the wellness economy, doubling its size from $585.5 billion to $1.2 trillion in just 7 years. This is equivalent to an average annual growth rate of about 10.5%. The annualized growth rate of the wellness economy has also been double-digit for Malaysia (13.2%), Viet Nam (11.8%), and Fiji (10.2%). If these growth rates are sustained, these countries' wellness economies can be expected to double in size in less than 7 years. Mongolia and the Philippines also experienced a significant increase in the size of the wellness economy, growing annually at an average rate of 9.3% and 8.6%, respectively.

[19] ADB. 2019. *Key Indicators for Asia and the Pacific 2019*. Manila; and H. Kharas. 2017. The Unprecedented Expansion of the Global Middle Class: An Update. *Global Economy and Development Working Paper* 100. Washington, DC: Brookings Institution.

[20] ADB. 2020. *Asian Development Outlook 2020 Update: Wellness in Worrying Times*. Manila.

Table 4.1 **Size of the Wellness Economy for Selected Asian Economies**
($ million, constant 2010 prices)

Country	Period 1	Period 2	Real Wellness GDP Growth Rate (annualized, %)	Real GDP Growth Rate (annualized, %)
Fiji	105	171	10.2	4.6
Kazakhstan	8,811	9,237	1.2	2.6
Malaysia	11,044	20,545	13.2	5.3
Mongolia	333	622	9.3	8.2
People's Republic of China	585,508	1,176,330	10.5	7.6
Philippines	14,410	21,802	8.6	6.6
Sri Lanka	8,783	9,351	1.3	4.3
Thailand	29,118	37,437	5.2	2.8
Viet Nam	7,786	13,601	11.8	6.2
Asia-9	665,898	1,289,097	10.2	7.2

GDP = gross domestic product.

Periods: Fiji (2012, 2017); Kazakhstan (2013, 2017); Malaysia (2010, 2015); Mongolia (2010, 2017); People's Republic of China (2010, 2017); Philippines (2012, 2017); Sri Lanka (2012, 2017); Thailand (2012, 2017); Viet Nam (2012, 2017).

Note: Real GDP data are derived from World Bank data. The growth rate for Asia-9 is the average growth rate of all countries' wellness economies weighted by each one's real GDP in the second period.

Source: Authors' calculations.

Together, these nine economies demonstrate rapid growth, from an estimated $665.9 billion in the first period to $1.3 trillion in the second period in constant 2010 prices.[21]

Except for Kazakhstan and Sri Lanka, the estimated annual growth rate of the wellness economy is much higher than the growth rate of the entire economy. This implies that the expansion of the wellness economy generally outpaced the other sectors. In Malaysia, for example, the annualized growth rate of the wellness economy is 7.9 percentage points higher than the average annual growth of its real GDP. The same pattern is observed in the cases of Fiji and Viet Nam, where the estimated growth of the wellness economy is at least 5.6 percentage points higher relative to the entire economy. For Mongolia, Thailand, the PRC, and the Philippines, the difference is between 1.0 percentage point and 3.0 percentage points. Collectively for Asia-9, wellness GVA has expanded in recent years at an estimated average of 10.2% annually, which is 3.0 percentage points higher than the 7.2% annual expansion of its overall GDP in constant prices. These estimates are consistent with earlier findings from GWI,[22] which suggests that the expansion of the wellness economy is relatively faster than the expansion of the overall economy.

Table 4.2 shows the size of the wellness economy in per capita terms, expressed in US dollars at constant 2010 prices. In this table, wellness is measured to take into account differences in population. These estimates can be

[21] The two periods estimated for each country are not necessarily the same because of data limitations. However, looking at these figures together as a proxy for developing Asia can provide an idea of how big the region's wellness economy has become. This is done by summing the GVA attributable to wellness for all countries and dividing by the sum of their total GVA in each of the two periods. R.M. Consing et al. 2020. *Using the System of National Accounts to Estimate a Country's Wellness Economy*. Manila: ADB.

[22] GWI. 2018. *Global Wellness Economy Monitor 2018*.

Table 4.2 Size of the Wellness Economy in per Capita Terms for Selected Asian Economies ($, constant 2010 prices)

Country	Period 1	Period 2	Real Wellness GDP per Capita Growth Rate (annualized, %)	Real GDP per Capita Growth Rate (annualized, %)
Fiji	122	195	9.9	4.3
Kazakhstan	517	512	(0.2)	1.2
Malaysia	392	679	11.6	3.8
Mongolia	122	200	7.2	6.1
People's Republic of China	438	848	9.9	7.1
Philippines	148	207	6.9	5.0
Sri Lanka	430	436	0.3	3.3
Thailand	429	541	4.7	2.4
Viet Nam	87	144	10.6	5.1
Asia-9	401	746	6.7	3.9

() = negative, GDP = gross domestic product.

Periods: Fiji (2012, 2017); Kazakhstan (2013, 2017); Malaysia (2010, 2015); Mongolia (2010, 2017); People's Republic of China (2010, 2017); Philippines (2012, 2017); Sri Lanka (2012, 2017); Thailand (2012, 2017); Viet Nam (2012, 2017).

Note: Population and real GDP per capita are derived from World Bank data. The wellness economy in per capita terms for Asia-9 is the average in each period weighted by each country's total population. The growth rate for Asia-9 is the average growth rate of all countries' wellness economies per capita weighted by each one's real GDP per capita in the second period.

Source: Authors' calculations.

interpreted as the annual spending on wellness per individual. While the aggregate size of the wellness economy, shown in Table 4.1, is comparable for Malaysia and the Philippines in period 2, the corresponding estimates in per capita terms differ significantly. Malaysia's wellness per capita in 2015 is 3.3 times the wellness per capita in the Philippines in 2017, and the latter's estimate is much closer to that of Mongolia ($200) and Fiji ($195) in the more recent period.

Notably, wellness per capita spending is comparable for the PRC ($438 in 2010), Sri Lanka ($430 in 2012), and Thailand ($429 in 2012) in period 1. However, stark differences are observed between their annual growth rates thereafter. Table 4.2 indicates that wellness per capita in Thailand grew at 4.7% annually, which is less than half the annual growth rate of wellness per capita in the PRC. In Sri Lanka, wellness per capita barely increased by $6 for a period of 5 years, while Kazakhstan experienced a $5 decline in wellness per capita between 2013 and 2017. In contrast, the double-digit annual growth rate in Malaysia and Viet Nam increased wellness per capita by $287 (73%) and by $57 (65%) in 2010 prices, respectively, and each expansion occurred within a span of 5 years.

Production Linkages of the Wellness Economy

As discussed in the methodology, the production of the wellness sector is interconnected with other sectors in the economy through its forward and backward linkages. Here, the forward linkage refers to the GVA from wellness industries used in the production of all goods and services, and this corresponds to the first term in Equation 4. Intuitively, production in the wellness sector and the demand for wellness goods and services used in the production of other goods and services (including within the wellness sector itself) move together. The length of the forward linkage of the wellness sector measures its relative significance in terms of the overall productive activities that the wellness sector could support.[23]

On the other hand, the backward linkage refers to the GVA from all industries used in the production of wellness goods and services, and this corresponds to the second term in Equation 4. Intuitively, a rise in production in the wellness sector is associated with an increase in demand for goods and services used in the production of wellness goods and services. The length of the wellness sector's backward linkage can be interpreted as its relative importance in the economy in terms of the overall productive activities that it generates (foonote 23). The total linkage of the wellness sector is the sum of the sector's forward and backward linkages less their intersection (to remove the double-count). Figure 4.1 presents the estimates for these linkages in terms of their percentage share of the country's total GVA, as indicated by the bars of different colors.

The orange bars represent the pure backward linkage, while the green bars represent the pure forward linkage. The blue bars indicate the intersection between forward and backward linkages, which is equivalent to the double-count. Hence, the pure backward linkage together with the intersection represents the total backward linkage. In the same manner, the pure forward linkage together with the intersection indicate the total forward linkage. Finally, yellow bars represent the GFCF that is relevant to the wellness sector. Wellness GFCF represents the investments made by the economy for future production of wellness goods and services, and this could be in the form of construction of buildings and infrastructure, purchase of machinery and equipment, or procurement of intellectual property rights. The total height of the bars indicates the size of the wellness economy as a percentage of total GVA, corresponding to Equation 4.

Figure 4.1 shows these estimates for nine of ADB's DMCs. With the exception of Sri Lanka and Kazakhstan, the share of the wellness economy increased between the two time periods for each country. This translates to a wellness economy that generally expands faster than the total economy, as shown in Table 4.1. Notice that the wellness economy's share in Sri Lanka and Kazakhstan actually decreased between the two time periods and, correspondingly, the wellness economy grew slowly relative to the total economy. In the PRC, the share of the wellness economy increased from 9.9% (2010) to 11.5% (2017). Considering that the PRC has a population of more than 1.3 billion and is one of the largest economies in the world, this rapid growth translates to a huge leap in the productive activities that constitute the wellness economy.

For the four Southeast Asian economies included, the share of the wellness economy is at least 6% in the latter period. In Thailand, the share of wellness GVA increased from 8.6% (2012) to 9.3% (2017), while in the Philippines, the share of the wellness economy grew from 6.5% (2012) to 7.3% (2017). Viet Nam and Malaysia experienced sharp increases in the size of the wellness economy. In Viet Nam, this share increased from 6.3% (2012) to 8.4% (2017), while in Malaysia, the share of the wellness economy grew from 4.4% (2010) to 6.4% (2015).

Mongolia's share of wellness GVA moderately increased by 0.2 percentage points, from 5.2% in 2010 to 5.4% in 2017. Likewise, the share of wellness GVA in Fiji increased from 4.0% in 2012 to 5.3% in 2017. In Sri Lanka, the share of wellness GVA was 13.9% in 2012. This share had moderately declined by 1.5 percentage points in 2017. The same trend is observed in the case of Kazakhstan, where the share of the wellness economy moderately shrank by 0.4 percentage points, from 5.6% in 2013 to 5.2% in 2017. However, the decrease in the share of the wellness economy for these two countries does not imply that the levels of wellness GDP decreased over time. Rather, this trend only indicates that the rest of the economy grew faster than the wellness economy.

Results indicate that the backward linkage of the wellness sector is longer than its forward linkage for all countries for both periods. In the context of input–output analysis, a strong backward linkage is indicative of heavy

[23] R. Miller and P. Blair. 2009. *Input–Output Analysis: Foundations and Extensions*. Cambridge: Cambridge University Press.

Figure 4.1 **Disaggregation of the Wellness Economy by Country and by Period**
(% of gross domestic product)

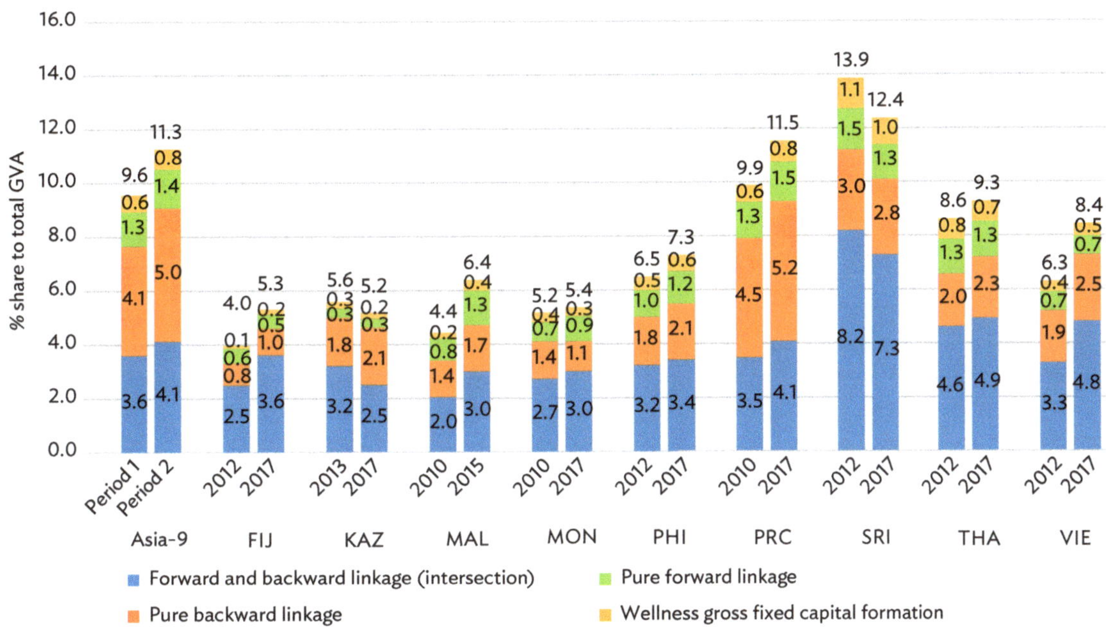

FIJ = Fiji, GVA = gross value added, KAZ = Kazakhstan, MAL = Malaysia, MON = Mongolia, PHI = Philippines, PRC = People's Republic of China, SRI = Sri Lanka, THA = Thailand, VIE = Viet Nam.

Note: The estimates for Asia-9 are the average gross value added share to total gross value added of each country weighted by each country's real gross domestic product in the second period.

Source: Authors' calculations.

reliance on interindustry supply. This is usually evident in the case of the services sector, where inputs from other industries are required for its production. Since a huge proportion of the wellness economy is comprised of services, as in health care, amusement and entertainment, and tourism activities, the interconnection with the upstream sectors is also expected to be much more significant compared with the downstream sectors. The gap between the backward linkage and the forward linkage is largest in the case of the PRC for both periods, between which it increased. This reflects the "rebalancing of the economy" in the PRC, where the services sector now comprises a bigger share of the economy than industry.[24]

Finally, wellness GFCF as a percentage of GVA is largest in Sri Lanka (1.1% in 2012 and 1.0% in 2017). This reflects the economic boost driven by public investment to rebuild after ending its 3-decade conflict in 2009. However, this source of growth is not sustainable in the long run,[25] which could also explain the declining share of wellness GFCF in the latter period. In the other economies, the share of wellness GFCF is less than 1%. The PRC's wellness GFCF stands at $95.1 billion in 2017, and this is more than 12 times higher than the wellness GFCF of the other eight economies combined.

[24] World Bank. 2017. *China: Systematic Country Diagnostic, Towards a More Inclusive and Sustainable Development*. Washington, DC.
[25] World Bank. 2015. *Sri Lanka: Ending Poverty and Promoting Shared Prosperity, a Systematic Country Diagnostic*. Washington, DC.

Wellness Employment

As discussed in the previous section, the wellness economy makes a sizable contribution to the GDP of developing economies in Asia. Hence, it should also be expected that the wellness economy generates and supports a significant portion of the overall employment. This section delves into this empirical inquiry by quantifying the size of wellness employment in terms of the number of jobs attributable to the wellness economy. This section also presents the decomposition of wellness employment into forward and backward linkages to quantify the relative size of employment that is directly or indirectly generated by the wellness sector.

Size of Wellness Employment

Table 4.3 shows the estimated wellness employment for each country and time period, including the jobs that are both directly and indirectly attributable to the production of wellness goods and services. The annualized growth rate of wellness employment is included in the third column, where it can be compared with the growth rate of total employment for each country. Further insights on the wellness sector's economic relevance may be derived from this. Malaysia's wellness employment had the largest increase, from 595,000 in 2010 to 1.6 million in 2015, and this is followed by the PRC, where wellness employment grew from 58.7 million in 2010 to 118.5 million in 2017. Both countries experienced double-digit wellness employment growth rates of 21.9% and 10.5%, respectively. Generally, the economies of Asia-9 have experienced a positive growth in wellness employment across the two time periods estimated. Collectively, wellness employment in Asia-9 expanded from 66.9 million to 128.8 million between the two periods estimated, increasing at an annual growth rate of 9.5%.

Except for Malaysia and the PRC, the growth of wellness GVA is generally faster than the growth of wellness employment. Collectively for Asia-9, the weighted average annual growth rate of wellness GVA is 0.7 percentage points higher than the weighted average annual growth rate of wellness employment. This indicates growth

Table 4.3 Wellness Employment for Selected Asian Economies ('000)

Country	Period 1	Period 2	Wellness Employment Growth Rate (annualized, %)	Employment Growth Rate (annualized, %)
Fiji	10	13	5.4	2.9
Kazakhstan	634	654	0.8	0.0
Malaysia	595	1,600	21.9	3.4
Mongolia	63	91	5.4	2.6
People's Republic of China	58,742	118,536	10.5	0.3
Philippines	1,959	2,292	3.2	1.4
Sri Lanka	487	495	0.3	1.5
Thailand	2,049	2,327	2.6	(0.8)
Viet Nam	2,381	2,774	3.1	1.1
Asia-9	66,920	128,782	9.5	0.4

( ) = negative.

Periods: Fiji (2012, 2017); Kazakhstan (2013, 2017); Malaysia (2010, 2015); Mongolia (2010, 2017); People's Republic of China (2010, 2017); Philippines (2012, 2017); Sri Lanka (2012, 2017); Thailand (2012, 2017); Viet Nam (2012, 2017).

Note: Real gross domestic product data are derived from World Bank data. The growth rate for Asia-9 is the average growth rate of all countries' wellness employment weighted by each one's real total employment in the second period.

Source: Authors' calculations.

in labor productivity within the wellness economy in recent years, consistent with what is shown in Table 4.3 for most of ADB's DMCs. Labor productivity in the wellness economy increased from $8,594 to $9,160 for Asia-9, ranging from $4,903 (Viet Nam) to as high as $18,891 (Sri Lanka) in period 2. The structure of the wellness sector may explain the variation in labor productivity across countries. For example, industries such as the manufacturing of pharmaceutical goods may be more productive than retail trade services.

Wellness Employment: Forward and Backward Linkages

Figure 4.2 shows the disaggregation of wellness employment in terms of its forward and backward linkages. Forward linkage captures the number of jobs that are directly generated by the wellness sector, while backward linkage captures the employment that is indirectly attributed to the wellness industries, as these jobs are generated by other sectors that support wellness industries. The blue bars represent the intersection between forward and backward linkages (equivalent to what is double-counted applying the methodology). The orange bars represent the pure backward linkage, while the green bars represent the pure forward linkage. The cumulative height of the three bars is the percentage share of wellness employment to the country's total employment.

In general, the percentage share of wellness employment to total employment increased for each country over the two time periods estimated. The sharpest rise is seen in the case of the PRC, increasing by 7.6 percentage points, and Malaysia, increasing by 6.4 percentage points. For other countries in Asia-9, wellness employment varies between 3.6% and 7.6% of total employment by the second period. Collectively, Asia-9's share of wellness employment increased rapidly between the two periods, from 7.3% to 13.7% of total employment in the region,

Figure 4.2 Disaggregation of Wellness Employment by Country and by Period
(% of gross domestic product)

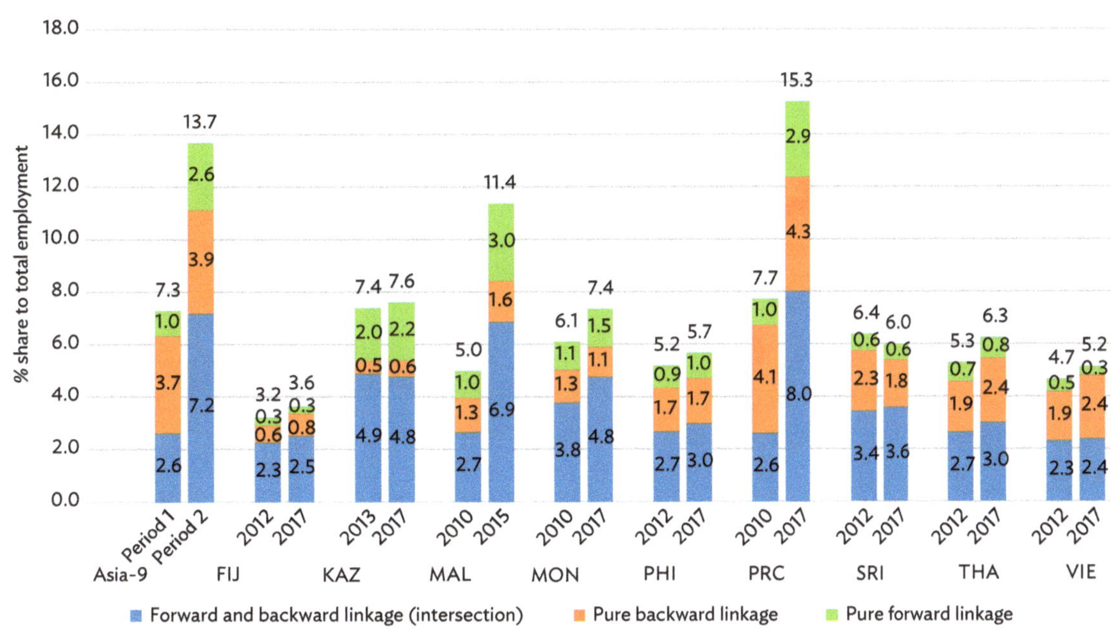

FIJ = Fiji, KAZ = Kazakhstan, MAL = Malaysia, MON = Mongolia, PHI = Philippines, PRC = People's Republic of China, SRI = Sri Lanka, THA = Thailand, VIE = Viet Nam.

Note: The estimates for Asia-9 are the average wellness employment share of each country weighted by each one's total employment in the second period.

Source: Authors' calculations.

primarily driven by the steep increase in wellness employment in the PRC. It is also observed that the backward linkage is generally higher than the forward linkage, indicating that much of the employment attributable to wellness comes from the industries supporting the wellness sector. Generally, this is consistent with the results shown in Figure 4.1, where wellness-supporting industries are shown to account for a larger share of the wellness economy relative to the wellness sector itself.

Conclusion

This chapter contributes to the literature on wellness economics and national accounting by showing how the system of national accounts (SNA) framework can be used to estimate the economy attributable to the production of wellness goods and services, and then applying this methodology to selected countries in developing Asia. Through input–output analysis, it is possible to derive the production and employment linkages between the wellness sector and the non-wellness sector. Theoretically, this means that any country whose economic accounting is consistent with the SNA framework can estimate the economic relevance of its wellness sector. This creates fertile new ground in the field of wellness economics as new data create new possibilities for research and, eventually, policies to promote wellness. As estimates for more countries are produced over time, it becomes feasible to generate reliable figures at regional and, eventually, global levels.

Nevertheless, there are ways to improve the quality of wellness economy estimation within the SNA framework. The main challenges are data-related. First, there would be no need for disaggregation if each country's input–output table (IOT) were highly detailed, ideally with rows and columns for all four-digit ISIC rev. 4 codes. In practice, however, a balanced IOT of such a size would be costly to produce. A second-best scenario would be for each country's IOT to contain rows and columns corresponding to at least the four-digit codes covering the production of wellness goods and services, such as those listed in Appendix 6. A similar prescription applies when estimating wellness employment, as employment numbers are needed for each industry in the IOT in order to estimate the wellness economy's contribution to overall employment.

Second, while the selected ISIC codes provide a basis for estimating the wellness economy, the process of drawing out the corresponding GVA from available SNA components often differs in practice between countries because of non-uniformity in the level of detail and aggregation. Access to highly detailed supply tables and nationally representative firm-level data on output would allow for more reliable disaggregation of IOTs when needed, and uniformity in the level of aggregation across countries would allow for better comparisons in wellness economy estimates among countries and across time.

Fortunately, uniformity can be achieved through the use of national IOTs derived from regional IOTs, such as the World Input–Output Tables and ADB's Multi-Regional Input–Output Tables, which provide annual national accounts data at a uniform level of detail for a multitude of countries across time. While the level of detail per country is highly aggregated under these regional IOTs, the fact that they are uniform in detail means that they may be subjected to a uniform process of disaggregation and allow for more reliable cross-country analyses.

PART 3

Holistic Pathways to Physical Wellness

CHAPTER 5

The Physical Activity Economy in Asia—Market Size, Participation, Barriers, and Options to Increase Movement

Ophelia Yeung and Katherine Johnston

Across countries, including in Asia, low or declining physical activity levels tend to be associated with high or rising national income levels. This chapter examines the economy of physical activity in Asia (including its three main segments: sports and active recreation, fitness, and mindful movement); the rates of participation in recreational physical activities across the region; and industry size and trends, using recent data on the global physical activity sector developed by the authors for the Global Wellness Institute (GWI). It also examines the main barriers to physical activity participation, and it highlights options that can encourage and support all populations to be more physically active, including the elderly, youth, and marginalized groups.

The Rise of Physical Inactivity in Asia

Physical Inactivity: A Rising Global Crisis

Physical activity is intrinsic to wellness. As advocated by physicians and public health authorities around the world, a regular and adequate level of physical activity is vital to our health in all aspects: muscular and cardiorespiratory fitness; bone and functional health; energy, balance, and weight control; and lowering the risks of depression and many chronic diseases (hypertension, coronary heart disease, stroke, diabetes, and various types of cancer). Yet in recent decades there has been an alarming trend of declining physical activity in countries around the world.[1] Recent data indicate that as many as 27.5%[2]–31%[3] of adults may be physically inactive. Across countries, including in Asia, low or declining physical activity levels tend to be associated with high or rising national income levels. Research also shows that women and girls tend to be more inactive than men and boys.[4]

[1] S.W. Ng and B.M. Popkin. 2012. Time Use and Physical Activity: A Shift away from Movement across the Globe. *Obesity Reviews*. 13 (8). pp. 659–680. https://doi.org/10.1111/j.1467-789X.2011.00982.x.

[2] R. Guthold et al. 2018. Worldwide Trends in Insufficient Physical Activity from 2001 to 2016: A Pooled Analysis of 358 Population-Based Surveys with 1.9 Million Participants. *The Lancet Global Health*. 6 (10). pp. e1077–1086. https://doi.org/10.1016/S2214-109X(18)30357-7.

[3] P.C. Hallal et al. 2012. Global Physical Activity Levels: Surveillance Progress, Pitfalls, and Prospects. *The Lancet*. 380 (9838). pp. 247–257. https://doi.org/10.1016/S0140-6736(12)60646-1.

[4] R. Guthold et al. 2018. Worldwide Trends in Insufficient Physical Activity from 2001 to 2016: A Pooled Analysis of 358 Population-Based Surveys with 1.9 Million Participants. *The Lancet Global Health*. 6 (10). pp. e1077–1086. https://doi.org/10.1016/S2214-109X(18)30357-7; P.C. Hallal et al. 2012. Global Physical Activity Levels: Surveillance Progress, Pitfalls, and Prospects. *The Lancet*. 380 (9838). pp. 247–257. https://doi.org/10.1016/S0140-6736(12)60646-1; and World Health Organization (WHO). 2014. *Global Status Report on Noncommunicable Diseases*. https://www.who.int/nmh/publications/ncd-status-report-2014/en.

These trends are occurring at a time when we need physical activity more than ever to mitigate the rise of chronic disease and the impacts of population aging. *The Lancet* has described the rise of physical inactivity as "pandemic, with far-reaching health, economic, environmental, and social consequences."[5] Obesity, which is linked with physical inactivity, has nearly tripled worldwide since 1975; 39% of adults are now overweight.[6] Physical inactivity and obesity are key lifestyle risk factors that directly contribute to the rise of chronic or noncommunicable diseases (including heart disease, stroke, cancer, diabetes, and chronic lung disease), which are collectively responsible for 71% of deaths worldwide every year.[7] Physical inactivity is the fourth leading cause of death in the world, responsible for more than 5 million preventable deaths annually.[8] The global economic burden of physical inactivity was estimated at INT$67.5 billion in 2013 ($53.8 billion in direct health care costs and $13.7 billion in productivity losses).[9]

What Is Physical Activity?

The World Health Organization (WHO) defines physical activity as "any bodily movement produced by skeletal muscles that requires energy expenditure—including activities undertaken while working, playing, carrying out household chores, travelling, and engaging in recreational pursuit." According to WHO, in order to maintain good health, children and adolescents need 60 minutes of moderate- to vigorous-intensity physical activity daily, and adults need 150 minutes of moderate-intensity physical activity, or 75 minutes of vigorous-intensity physical activity, on a weekly basis.[10] The benefits of physical activity are varied, widely proven, and well-known, including preventing chronic disease, reducing stress, managing weight, strengthening functional mobility, improving sleep, alleviating depression, and improving cognitive function. To receive these benefits, our engagement in physical activity needs to be regular, consistent, and sustained—not intermittent, only during holidays, or only when we want to lose weight or can find the time.

Physical activities can be broadly divided into natural movement and recreational physical activity.

(i) Natural movement encompasses the physical activities that are essential to our daily lives, including transportation (e.g., walking and cycling as transportation); occupational (e.g., work that requires manual labor); and domestic movement (e.g., household chores and gardening). These kinds of activities have been the core of physical activity for humankind for millennia. Unfortunately, as discussed below, natural movement is now on the decline around the world, progressively discouraged by our modern lifestyles and built environments.

(ii) We also engage in optional and intentional movement as part of our hobbies and leisure time. Recreational physical activity can include going to the gym, playing sports, taking a walk or cycling for fun, dancing, and children playing on a playground. As natural movement declines, recreational physical activity is becoming essential for a growing number of people in order to stay healthy.

[5] H.W. Kohl et al. 2012. The Pandemic of Physical Inactivity: Global Action for Public Health. *The Lancet*. 380 (9838). pp. 294–305. https://doi.org/10.1016/S0140-6736(12)60898-8.

[6] WHO. 2018. *Obesity and Overweight Fact Sheet*. http://www.who.int/mediacentre/factsheets/fs311/en.

[7] WHO. 2018. *Fact Sheet: Noncommunicable diseases*. http://www.who.int/en/news-room/fact-sheets/detail/noncommunicable-diseases.

[8] H.W. Kohl et al. 2012. The Pandemic of Physical Inactivity: Global Action for Public Health. *The Lancet*. 380 (9838). pp. 294–305. https://doi.org/10.1016/S0140-6736(12)60898-8.

[9] INT=International dollars, which means that the values in each country are converted to dollars at a purchasing power parity rate that accounts for differentials in the prices of goods and services across countries (https://datahelpdesk.worldbank.org/knowledgebase/articles/114944-what-is-an-international-dollar). D. Ding et al. 2016. The Economic Burden of Physical Inactivity: A Global Analysis of Major Non-communicable Diseases. *The Lancet*. 388 (10051). pp. 1311–1324. https://doi.org/10.1016/S0140-6736(16)30383-X.

[10] WHO. 2018. Physical Activity: Key Facts. *WHO Fact Sheet*. https://www.who.int/news-room/fact-sheets/detail/physical-activity.

The Current State of Physical Inactivity in Asia

The most recent country-level data on physical activity (compiled by *The Lancet*) show that about 27.5% of the world's adult population has insufficient levels of physical activity (i.e., not meeting the WHO standards described above).[11] As shown in Table 5.1, physical inactivity varies widely across Asia.

(i) In general, inactivity is higher than the global average in high-income Asian countries and South Asia, but lower than the global average in East Asia, Southeast Asia, and the Pacific. The disparities in inactivity rates between men and women are generally less stark in East Asia and Southeast Asia than in other regions across Asia.

(ii) Countries with the largest inactive populations include the Philippines, Malaysia, Singapore, Japan, the Republic of Korea (ROK), India, and Pakistan, as well as a number of Pacific nations (American Samoa, the Marshall Islands, Nauru, Palau, Kiribati, and Micronesia).

(iii) Countries with the lowest levels of inactivity in Asia include Cambodia, Myanmar, Nepal, the People's Republic of China (PRC), and many Pacific nations (Niue, Vanuatu, Tokelau, Samoa, and Papua New Guinea).

(iv) Countries with the least amount of disparity in inactivity rates between men and women include the PRC, Indonesia, Niue, Cambodia, Vanuatu, Nepal, Japan, and Singapore. Conversely, in many countries across the region, women are far more inactive than men, including Palau, Bangladesh, Tuvalu, India, the Philippines, Pakistan, the Cook Islands, Tonga, Sri Lanka, and Timor-Leste.

Table 5.1 Prevalence of Insufficient Physical Activity in Asia and the Pacific, 2016

	Overall % of Population with Insufficient Physical Activity	% of Men	% of Women
High-Income Asia and the Pacific	**35.7**	**33.0**	**38.3**
Japan	35.5	33.8	37.0
Republic of Korea	35.4	29.5	41.0
Singapore	36.5	34.3	38.6
East and Southeast Asia	**17.3**	**17.6**	**16.9**
Brunei Darussalam	27.3	21.2	33.9
Cambodia	10.5	9.8	11.1
Indonesia	22.6	23.5	21.7
Lao People's Democratic Republic	16.3	11.7	20.6
Malaysia	38.8	34.6	42.8
Maldives	30.3	25.8	34.8
Myanmar	10.7	8.1	13.1
People's Republic of China	14.1	16.0	12.2
Philippines	39.7	30.1	49.1
Sri Lanka	28.9	20.2	36.7
Thailand	24.6	21.8	27.2

continued on next page

[11] R. Guthold et al. 2018. Worldwide Trends in Insufficient Physical Activity from 2001 to 2016: A Pooled Analysis of 358 Population-Based Surveys with 1.9 Million Participants. *The Lancet Global Health*. 6 (10). pp. e1077–1086. https://doi.org/10.1016/S2214-109X(18)30357-7.

Table 5.1 *(continued)*

	Overall % of Population with Insufficient Physical Activity	% of Men	% of Women
Timor-Leste	17.8	10.3	25.5
Viet Nam	25.4	19.9	30.6
South Asia	**33.0**	**23.5**	**43.0**
Bangladesh	27.8	16.1	39.5
Bhutan	23.0	17.7	29.5
India	34.0	24.7	43.9
Nepal	13.4	12.0	14.6
Pakistan	33.7	24.4	43.3
Oceania	**16.3**	**12.3**	**20.3**
American Samoa	53.4	49.3	57.5
Cook Islands	18.5	9.8	27.2
Fiji	17.4	10.8	24.1
French Polynesia	17.9	13.5	22.5
Kiribati	40.4	34.5	45.8
Marshall Islands	43.5	37.0	50.0
Micronesia	36.6	32.9	40.5
Nauru	42.1	34.9	49.4
Niue	6.9	7.8	6.0
Palau	40.9	28.3	53.5
Papua New Guinea	14.8	11.4	18.2
Samoa	12.6	8.2	17.2
Solomon Islands	18.2	13.3	23.2
Tokelau	11.1	4.5	17.7
Tonga	17.4	8.5	25.9
Tuvalu	27.3	17.5	37.2
Vanuatu	8.0	7.2	8.8

Source: R. Guthold et al. 2018. Worldwide Trends in Insufficient Physical Activity from 2001 to 2016: A Pooled Analysis of 358 Population-Based Surveys with 1.9 Million Participants—Supplementary Appendix. *The Lancet Global Health*. 6 (10). https://doi.org/10.1016/S2214-109X(18)30357-7. This study pooled data from 358 population-based surveys across 168 countries, including 1.9 million participants.

Why Is Physical Inactivity Rising?

There is no question that our modern lifestyles and livelihoods require much less physical exertion than those of previous generations of farmers, fisherman, herders, tradesmen, and industrial workers. All aspects of our daily lives have become more sedentary. Across Asia, urbanization, technological developments, and growing service economies have drawn more people into sedentary jobs. For the growing middle class and for people who live in middle-income and high-income countries, household chores such as cooking and cleaning have been greatly eased by modern appliances and industrialized food production. Meanwhile, the digital revolution has enabled us to shop, socialize, and consume news and entertainment without leaving our homes or even our sofas.

The trend is equally alarming for youth. Studies have found a long-term decline in cardiovascular fitness levels among children and adolescents, especially in upper-income and middle-income countries.[12] In many countries, fewer children are walking or biking to school.[13] Across cities and suburbs, the spontaneous and unsupervised outdoor play of past generations has been replaced with scheduled playdates, structured lessons, and sports leagues—activities to which children are often transported by vehicles. Similar to adults, teens now have less motivation to be active when they are glued to their mobile devices for social media, gaming, and entertainment.

As essential physical tasks steadily disappear from our daily lives, they have not been replaced by other types of built-in movement. Our modern built environment—both urban and suburban—is often described as obesogenic, with many factors interacting and conspiring against a physically active lifestyle.

(i) The design of modern neighborhoods and buildings often prioritizes the speed and convenience of vehicular traffic, with the unintended result of making walking or cycling an unpleasant, inconvenient, or even dangerous way to travel.
(ii) Density, overcrowding, and sprawling are becoming the norm for people who live in the largest and rapidly growing metropolises. Lack of sidewalks or crosswalks, wide lanes, heavy traffic, and auto-centric planning have made walking or biking less viable as a transportation option across many cities.
(iii) Many people do not have adequate access to parks, green space, or sports and recreational facilities near their homes. Some people live in areas where crime and safety concerns discourage them from being outdoors. Some stay indoors because of poor air quality and pollution.
(iv) Similarly, most modern buildings have been designed for efficiency and comfort, rather than to encourage movement—for example, placing elevators prominently in lobbies, while hiding narrow and dark stairways.

All those missed opportunities to move in our daily lives, such as short distances not walked and flights of stairs eschewed, have now become the "steps" that we need to make up each day to meet our daily requirements for physical activity. Not surprisingly, in just a generation or two, physical activity has become less natural and more structured and intentional. To stay active, many people now have to schedule time to exercise. Increasingly, people also have to spend money for the opportunity to exercise. This is giving rise to the physical activity economy.

[12] G.R. Tomkinson, J.J. Lang, and M.S. Tremblay. 2019. Temporal Trends in the Cardiorespiratory Fitness of Children and Adolescents Representing 19 High-Income and Upper Middle-Income Countries between 1981 and 2014. *British Journal of Sports Medicine*. 53 (8). pp. 478–486. https://doi.org/10.1136/bjsports-2017-097982; G.R. Tomkinson et al. 2012. Temporal Changes in Long-Distance Running Performance of Asian Children between 1964 and 2009. *Sports Medicine*. 42 (4). pp. 267–279. https://doi.org/10.2165/11599160-000000000-00000; and D.J. Macfarlane and G.R. Tomkinson. 2007. Evolution and Variability in Fitness Test Performance of Asian Children and Adolescents. *Medicine & Sport Science*. 50. pp. 143–167. https://doi.org/10.1159/000101358.

[13] R. Uddin et al. 2019. Active Commuting to and from School among 106,605 Adolescents in 27 Asia-Pacific Countries. *Journal of Transport & Health*. 15. https://doi.org/10.1016/j.jth.2019.100637; and W. Lu et al. 2014. Perceived Barriers to Children's Active Commuting to School: A Systematic Review of Empirical, Methodological and Theoretical Evidence. *International Journal of Behavioral Nutrition & Physical Activity*. 11 (140). https://doi.org/10.1186/s12966-014-0140-x.

The Physical Activity Economy in Asia

What Is the Physical Activity Economy?

Physical activity generates significant economic activities, both around the world and in Asia. As leisure-time fitness, exercise, and active recreation become more popular, these pursuits represent an important private household spending line item. Government spending also plays a substantial role in supporting physical activity.

(i) **Private expenditures** are primarily on intentional recreational physical activities, which individuals and families increasingly choose to do during their leisure time. These expenditures include the fees to join a gym or YMCA, attend a fitness class or yoga class, join a recreational sports team or club, swim laps at a pool, and run a marathon. Individuals also spend money on clothing, shoes, equipment, sporting goods, and technology devices or services that support their participation in recreational physical activities (and which might also support walking and biking as transit, or natural movement physical activity).

(ii) **Public expenditures** support both natural movement and recreational physical activities, primarily in the form of infrastructure investments and youth and education spending, and often at the municipal or city level of government. In most countries, governments support recreational physical activities and sports in a variety of ways, including building and maintaining public sports fields, swimming pools, tennis courts, and running paths and trails, as well as providing funding for youth and community sports leagues and training programs. A smaller number of governments build and/or subsidize community fitness centers and gyms. Governments fund physical education classes in schools, which provide children with early exposure to a variety of sports and physical activities and help instill lifelong healthy habits. Public expenditures are also critical for facilitating natural movement physical activity, especially via urban planning and public transit investments that create the infrastructure for people to walk and ride bicycles as part of their commute or daily activities.

Figure 5.1 Private and Public Expenditures on Physical Activity

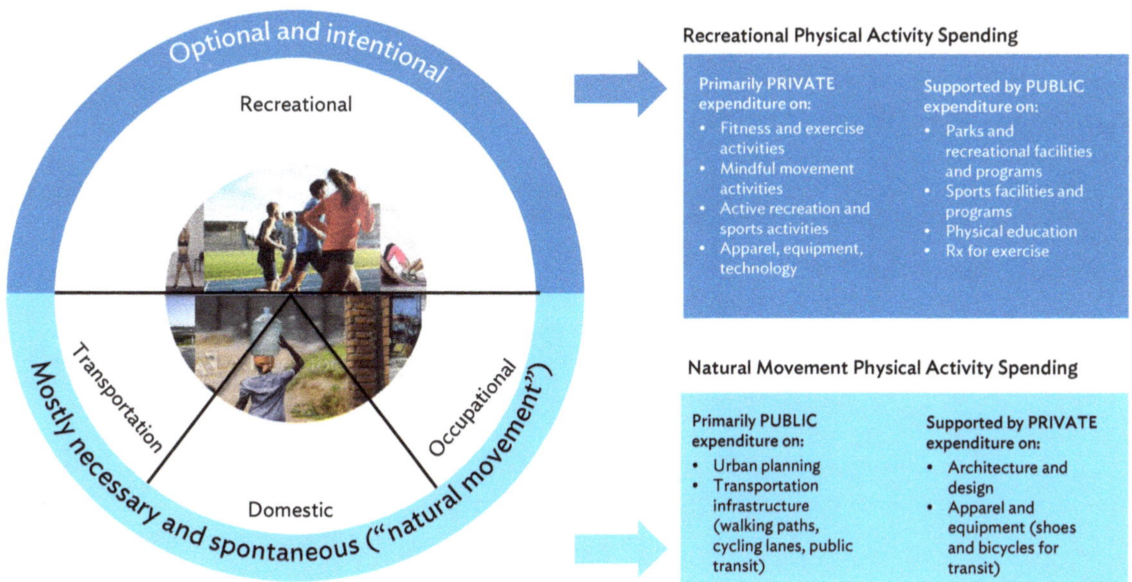

Source: Global Wellness Institute.

In 2019, the authors estimated the size of the global physical activity market, focusing on private spending on recreational physical activity.[14] In our study, we defined the global physical activity market as consumer spending associated with intentional physical activities performed during leisure and recreation. The core of the market is the services that allow consumers to participate in three categories of recreational physical activities: fitness, sports and active recreation, and mindful movement. The market also includes three supporting sectors that enable and facilitate consumer participation in these activities: technology, equipment and supplies, and apparel and footwear.[15]

Box 5.1 Different Ways of Measuring Physical Activity

The physical activity participation and market size data developed by the authors and presented in this section are not the same as the "physical inactivity" statistics presented in the first section of this chapter.

The first section of this chapter, "The Rise of Physical Inactivity in Asia," presents global and country-level physical inactivity statistics compiled by *The Lancet*. These figures measure physical activity and inactivity, defined as the share of the population that is or is not meeting the World Health Organization (WHO) recommendations to maintain good health (e.g., adults need 150 minutes of moderate-intensity physical activity, or 75 minutes of vigorous-intensity physical activity, on a weekly basis). In this definition, WHO guidelines may be met by any type of physical activity, whether from recreational activities or natural movement (occupational, transport, or domestic). *The Lancet* dataset draws upon studies and surveys developed by researchers and public health experts across countries, such as the WHO STEPwise approach to surveillance (STEPS).[a]

The second section of this chapter, "The Physical Activity Economy in Asia," presents the data developed by the authors that measures the share of the population participating in recreational physical activities. Here, participation is defined as doing any kind of recreational physical activity at least once a month or with some regularity. These data do not measure the intensity of recreational physical activities or whether they are sufficient to meet WHO physical activity guidelines. In fact, the minimum threshold used to define "participation" in the authors' dataset (at least once a month) is certainly not sufficient to meet WHO guidelines or stay healthy. In addition, the focus is solely on participation in recreational physical activities and not on other types of physical activity via natural movement (occupational, transport, and domestic).

With this dataset, the authors aim to capture the share of each domestic population that is part of the discretionary consumer marketplace for various types of recreational physical activities. Based on participation rates, the authors then estimate the direct, out-of-pocket expenditures made by consumers each year in order to participate in various types of recreational physical activities. In some instances, fees for participation may be subsidized (e.g., in fitness facilities run by governments), and in these instances the authors still count consumer participation in the activity although out-of-pocket expenditures would be reduced or possibly zero. Likewise, for some activities there is no service provider or participation fee (e.g., running in the park or playing a pickup basketball game with friends), and in these instances the authors count consumer participation in the activity although the expenditures are zero.

[a] WHO. No date. *STEPwise Approach to Surveillance (STEPS)*. http://www.who.int/ncds/surveillance/steps/en; and L. Riley et al. 2016. The World Health Organization STEPwise Approach to Noncommunicable Disease Risk-Factor Surveillance: Methods, Challenges, and Opportunities. *American Journal of Public Health*. 106 (1). pp. 74–78. https://doi.org/10.2105/AJPH.2015.302962.

Source: Authors.

[14] GWI. 2019. *Move to Be Well: The Global Economy of Physical Activity*. https://globalwellnessinstitute.org/industry-research/global-economy-physical-activity.

[15] For definitions of each of these subsectors, see GWI. 2019. *Move to Be Well: The Global Economy of Physical Activity*. https://globalwellnessinstitute.org/industry-research/global-economy-physical-activity.

While public expenditures are an important component of the physical activity economy (as elaborated above), they are not estimated as part of the data presented in this chapter. There is not sufficient data to make a credible estimate of government expenditures in this sector because this spending occurs at multiple levels of government (local, regional, and national) and across multiple agencies and budgetary items (such as transportation and infrastructure, parks and recreation, and sports). The focus of the authors' data-gathering is on private spending, which is the best gauge for the rising consumer interest in intentional recreational physical activities and related services. Public spending, public initiatives, and public policies that support physical activities are addressed qualitatively in the final section of this chapter.

Asia's Physical Activity Economy in 2018

Valued at $240.4 billion in 2018, the physical activity market in Asia and the Pacific is large, diverse, and dynamic. It accounts for 29% of the total global economy for physical activity ($828.2 billion). Asia and the Pacific is the second-largest regional market in the world for physical activity, after North America. Within the Asian physical activity market, $116.6 billion (48%) represents direct consumer expenditures on participating in a variety of recreational physical activities—primarily sports and active recreation, as well as fitness and mindful movement. The remaining 52%, or $125.5 billion, represents expenditures on a variety of enabling and supporting sectors—primarily clothing and footwear, along with fitness equipment, sporting goods, and related supplies, and fitness- and exercise-related technologies.

Physical activity spending averages about $176 per participant per year in Asia and the Pacific, divided into $85 spent on participating in recreational physical activities and $92 spent on associated apparel, footwear, equipment, sporting goods, and technology devices and services. Per participant expenditures in Asia are quite a bit lower than the global average ($176 in Asia versus $306 globally). In Asia's most developed economies, and in its largest metropolitan areas, middle-class and upper-class consumers have access to a well-developed industry of fitness and sporting facilities (e.g., gyms and health clubs, yoga studios, sporting clubs, swimming pools, and dance studios). In these places, participant spending levels are higher, not only because average incomes are higher, but also because there is a wider variety of fitness and recreational physical activities that people can pay for. However, for the majority of people living in Asia, the market and infrastructure for fitness and sports are simply not well-developed. In these places, people who engage in recreational physical activities do so with little to no spending—for example, playing soccer in a local league or with friends, going for a run outside, or doing tai chi in a park. For this reason, average spending per participant can vary widely across Asia, with annual averages of $622 in the ROK, $495 in Japan, and $460 in Singapore, compared with $66 in India, $55 in the Philippines, and $29 in Indonesia and Viet Nam.

The percentage of the population participating in recreational physical activities in Asia is estimated at 33.2%, which is just below the global average of 35.5%. A high level of *spending* on recreational physical activities does not always equate to a higher level of participation in these activities (and vice versa). For example, as a region, the Asia and Pacific region has a lower participation rate than Latin America and the Caribbean, although its per participant spending is quite a bit higher. Similarly, the Asia and Pacific region's participation rate is just slightly higher than that of sub-Saharan Africa, even though its per participant spending is more than seven times higher.

Across Asia, recreational physical activity participation varies widely, from a high of 84% in Australia and Taipei,China to a low of 13%–15% in India and Pakistan (Table 5.3). Importantly, many people in Asia conduct their leisure time physical activity in public places with little or no spending. In the lower-income countries, people participate in sports and other recreational activities in a variety of public and free venues (e.g., in

Figure 5.2 **Physical Activity Economy by Region, 2018**

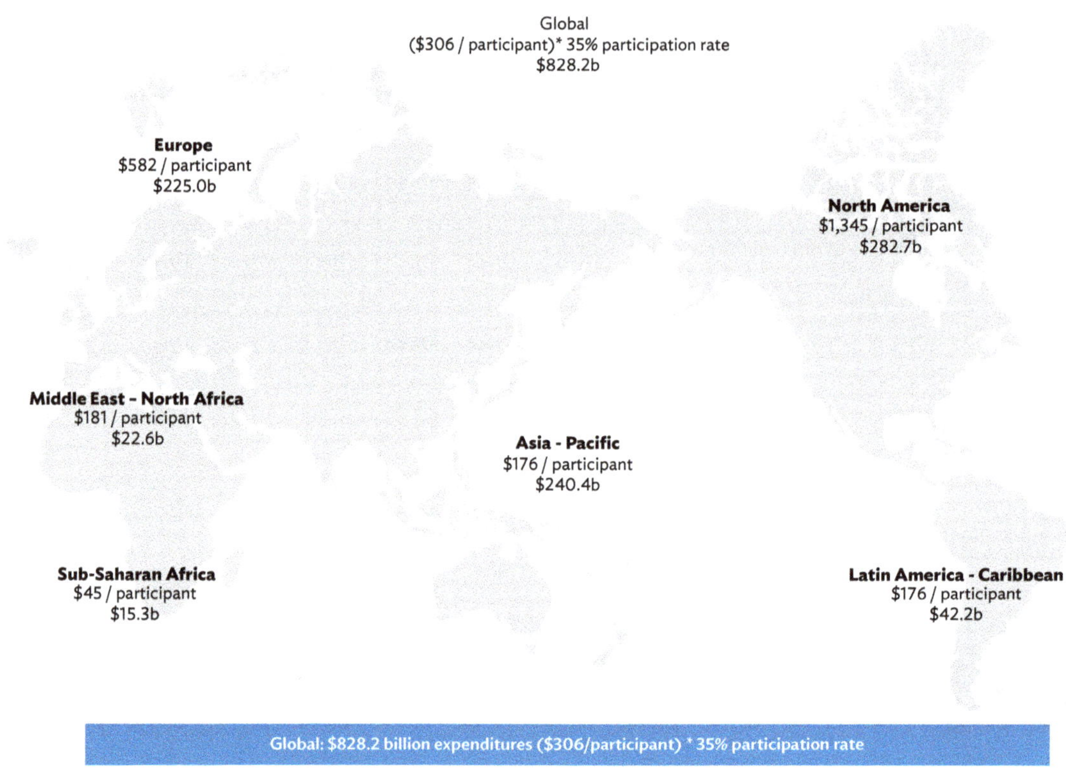

b = billion.

Source: Global Wellness Institute.

public parks and plazas; in free sporting facilities, such as neighborhood basketball courts or ball fields, in vacant lots, in the streets; and at home). Their out-of-pocket spending is lower (or zero) because private fitness and recreation businesses, facilities, and infrastructure are less developed. For example, no-cost individual and group exercises in public outdoor gyms, plaza dancing, and tai chi in parks are very popular in the PRC, especially among seniors. "Plaza dancing" (*guangchang wu*) has become a major exercise phenomenon, practiced by an estimated 100 million Chinese women (and some men)—who are mostly middle-aged and seniors—in public squares, parks, parking lots, and other public venues.

Even in higher-income markets, many people pay nothing to participate in sports and other recreational physical activities. For example, national survey data show that 67% of adult participants in Japan,[16] 25% in the ROK,[17]

[16] Japan Sports Agency. 2017. スポーツの実施状況等に関する世論調査 *(Public Opinion Survey on the Implementation Status of Sport).* http://www.mext.go.jp/prev_sports/comp/b_menu/other/__icsFiles/afieldfile/2018/03/30/142346_77_1.pdf.

[17] Government of the Republic of Korea, Ministry of Culture, Sports, and Tourism. 2017. 국민생활체육참여실태조사 *(National Sports Participation Survey 2017).* https://www.sports.re.kr/front/board/boardFileUseDown.do?board_seq=74&con_seq=2848&file_seq=1606.

Table 5.2 Physical Activity Economy in Asia and the Pacific, 2018

	Participation Rate[a]	Market Size[a] ($ billion)	Average Spending per Participant
Recreational Physical Activities	**33.2%**	**$116.6**	**$85**
Sports and active recreation	30.4%	$83.0	$66
Fitness	1.1%	$22.7	$494
Mindful movement	4.5%	$10.9	$58
Enabling Sectors	**$125.5**		**$92**
Apparel and footwear	$87.5		$8
Equipment and supplies	$27.6		$20
Technology	$10.8		$64
Total Physical Activity Economy in Asia and the Pacific	**$240.4**		**$176**

[a] Market size measures consumer expenditures on classes, memberships, entry fees, trainers, and related services and methods of participation. Participation rate measures the share of the total population who participate in one or more of the three physical activity categories on a regular basis (at least monthly).

Note: Numbers may not sum precisely because of overlap between segments and rounding.

Source: Global Wellness Institute.

and 41% in Australia[18] spend no money on participating in these activities, and yet participation rates across all three nations are quite high. In addition to their well-developed private sector fitness markets, the governments in all three of these countries have invested in widespread publicly subsidized fitness and sports facilities and infrastructure, which allow their populations to participate with very low out-of-pocket expenditures.

Recognizing the growing public health crisis associated with inadequate levels of physical activity, a number of governments across Asia have committed to increasing participation rates through greater public investment in exercise and sports facilities and infrastructure.

(i) Japan's high participation rates are supported by government investment in affordable public facilities. Public and community facilities account for half of the nation's gyms. There are at least 5,000 public gyms across the country, and these are supplemented with facilities in schools and universities that are accessible to the public, which mean that nearly every city in Japan has access to public or community fitness clubs that offer basic and affordable workout equipment and services (typically costing less than $4 per visit). Most small parks and gardens have some outdoor fitness apparatus, and sports and recreational facilities are ample in larger parks (e.g., tennis and basketball courts and playgrounds).

(ii) Singapore's high participation rate is also buoyed by extensive government investment in exercise, sports, and recreational facilities and infrastructure that are affordable and accessible for the entire population. Sport Singapore's ActiveSG initiative manages over 180 community gyms and recreational centers with classes and programs for all ages, 27 swimming complexes, and dozens of sporting fields, and there are also over 1,200 free outdoor gyms throughout the city. ActiveSG and the Singapore Health Promotion Board (HPB) run a number of national challenges and events to encourage residents to walk and get

[18] Australian Sports Commission Clearinghouse for Sport and Physical Activity. *AusPlay National Data Tables—July 2018 to June 2019 Data*. https://www.clearinghouseforsport.gov.au/research/smi/ausplay/results/national.

Figure 5.3 **Recreational Physical Activity Participation Rates and Average Spending per Participant, by Region, 2018**

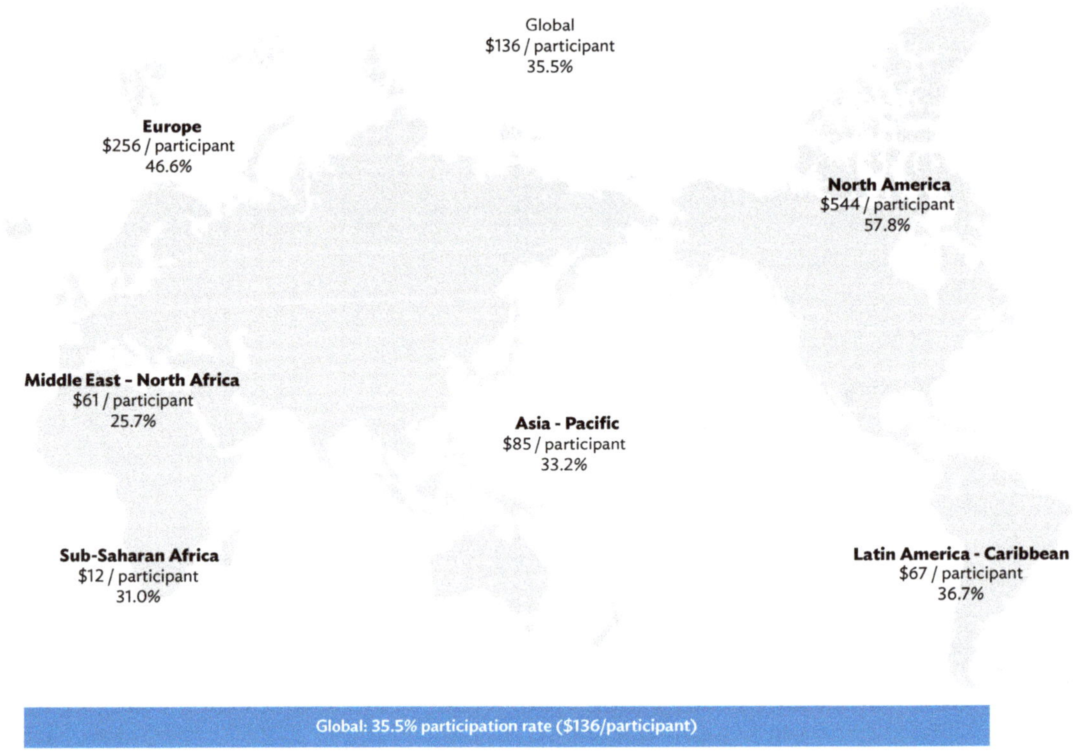

Note: In this figure, spending participant figures include only participation in recreational physical activities, but not enabling sectors.

Source: Global Wellness Institute.

more exercise, and some of these offer cash incentives and prizes (as well as free fitness trackers).[19] In 2019, the HPB announced a new "comprehensive digital health platform" based on the use of wearables (in partnership with Fitbit), as part of its national "Live Healthy SG" initiative to encourage physical activity, healthy eating, and better sleep.[20]

(iii) In the ROK; Hong Kong, China; and Taipei,China outdoor recreational activities such as running, walking, hiking, and exercising in parks and squares are popular, and these activities rely on ongoing investments in public infrastructure. Facing similar demographic trends of rapidly aging populations, governments are putting increased attention on engaging and serving an aging population, partly to mitigate concern

[19] GetActive! Singapore. 2019. https://events.myactivesg.com/getactive2019; National University of Singapore Bicentennial Challenge. https://www.myactivesg.com/whats-on/event/2019/9/nus-sg-bicentennial-challenge; and National Steps Challenge. https://www.healthhub.sg/programmes/37/NSC.

[20] J. Somauroo. 2019. Fitbit Partners with Singapore Government to Offer Trackers to 5.6 Million People. *Forbes*. https://www.forbes.com/sites/jamessomauroo/2019/08/22/fitbit-partners-with-singapore-government-to-offer-trackers-to-56m-people/#176c8d7a2031; and K. Kwang. 2019. HPB Partners Fitbit to Encourage Singaporeans to Adopt Healthier Habits. *Channel News Asia*. https://www.channelnewsasia.com/news/singapore/hpb-fitbit-encourage-singaporeans-adopt-healthier-habits-11828980.

Table 5.3 **Recreational Physical Activity Participation Rates in Asia and the Pacific, 2018**

	Participation Rate[a]	Rank		Participation Rate[a]	Rank
Australia	84.1%	1	Viet Nam	35.7%	14
Taipei,China	84.0%	2	Indonesia	34.2%	15
New Zealand	83.8%	3	Philippines	32.7%	16
Mongolia	75.0%	4	Thailand	27.8%	17
Republic of Korea	73.7%	5	Timor-Leste	26.3%	18
Japan	69.6%	6	Bangladesh	25.2%	19
Singapore	64.9%	7	Cambodia	21.4%	20
Hong Kong, China	58.2%	8	Myanmar	21.3%	21
Macau, China	51.1%	9	Nepal	20.0%	22
People's Republic of China	48.6%	10	Sri Lanka	19.2%	23
Papua New Guinea	46.4%	11	India	15.0%	24
Malaysia	41.1%	12	Pakistan	13.2%	25
Lao People's Democratic Republic	39.8%	13			

[a] Participation rate measures the share of the total population who participate in one or more of the three physical activity categories on a regular basis (at least monthly).

Source: Global Wellness Institute.

over rising health care costs. For example, in Taipei,China, the government has built a large-scale sports and recreational center in each of the capital city's 12 districts since 2003. Exercise for Health was launched in the city in 2016; the project dispatches instructors to community centers in each of the city's 29 districts, targeting seniors and residents with reduced mobility who may not be able to access the existing civic sports complexes. As part of the program, the city government signed a 2-year cooperation agreement with Exercise Is Medicine, an initiative launched by the American Medical Association and the American College of Sports Medicine in 2007 to integrate physical activity into medical treatment plans.[21]

(iv) In the PRC, the government has made significant efforts to raise awareness about the importance of physical activity, and to reduce the disparity of access across regions. In 2016, the PRC announced a National Fitness Plan, which lays out ambitious goals of having 700 million people engage in exercise at least once a week, and 435 million exercising regularly. In support of this aim, the government has made substantial investments in public sports and recreational facilities, outdoor gyms, and running paths, as well as in sports programs and promotional campaigns.[22] These efforts have greatly increased the awareness and interest of the Chinese public in physical activity, and they have contributed to rising participation in running, walking, hiking, community sports, and fitness training in the past few years.

[21] Based on an article published via the online news portal in Taipei,China on 29 March 2019.

[22] S. Wu, Y. Luo, and M. Bao. 2017. Building a Healthy China by Enhancing Physical Activity: Priorities, Challenges, and Strategies. *Journal of Sport and Health Science*. 6 (1). pp. 125–126. https://doi.org/10.1016/j.jshs.2016.10.003; and International Health, Racquet & Sportsclub Association (IHRSA). 2018. *Asia-Pacific Health Club Report*. 2nd ed. https://www.ihrsa.org/publications/ihrsa-asia-pacific-health-club-report-second-edition.

(v) In Southeast Asia, countries such as Indonesia, Malaysia, the Philippines, and Thailand typically have lower levels of recreational physical activity participation than in East Asia. The urban infrastructure in these countries for an active lifestyle (e.g., public parks, jogging trails, bike paths, and public recreational facilities) is not well-developed. Outside major cities, the infrastructure for recreational physical activity, both public and private facilities, is even more limited. Overall, the vast majority of the population lacks access to sports and recreational facilities and has limited knowledge about the importance of exercise. To the extent that physical activity is supported in schools, the emphasis is often on preparing the best athletes for competition rather than encouraging physical activity for all. Several governments have launched events and media campaigns (e.g., Fit Malaysia)[23] to encourage physical activity, while also making investments to improve public infrastructure and facilities. The Government of the Philippines was especially motivated to improve public awareness of sports and fitness before it hosted the 2019 Southeast Asian Games.

(vi) Across Asia, recreational physical activity participation rates are typically lowest in South Asia. India lacks physical activity infrastructure, especially outdoor active recreation venues in cities. But this is changing. Since 2016, members of Parliament have used local development funds to install 1,700 open-air gyms in parks throughout New Delhi (at about $10,000 each), and hundreds more are being planned.[24] In Pakistan, there are also very low levels of participation, limited public awareness about the health benefits of exercise, and an undeveloped infrastructure throughout the country. In both markets, female participation in physical activity, especially in sports and active recreation, has been hampered by cultural and religious beliefs; however, attitudes are changing, especially among the urban and educated elites, and participation of women and girls in recreational physical activity is growing.

Three Subsegments of Recreational Physical Activities: Sports and Active Recreation, Fitness, and Mindful Movement

Recreational physical activities are the core of the global physical activity market. The authors estimate that Asian consumers spent $117 billion out-of-pocket on these activities in 2018. By far, sports and active recreation is the largest category of expenditures ($83 billion) and participation (30%) across Asia, followed by fitness ($22.7 billion) and mindful movement ($10.9 billion), as shown in Table 5.2.

Sports and Active Recreation

By far, sports and active recreation is the most popular way for people to engage in recreational physical activities, both across Asia and globally. An estimated 30% of Asia's population participates on a regular basis (and 33% of the population globally). Asian consumers spent about $66 per participant annually on sports and active recreation, or $83.0 billion in 2018, accounting for 71% of all recreational physical activity spending in the region.

Sports and active recreation comprises the largest category of recreational physical activity because it is the most diverse, accessible, affordable, and prevalent way to be physically active, across every region and population group, rich or poor, young or old, urban or rural, developed or underdeveloped.

23 Y.A. Kamil. 2014. Nationwide Campaign to Get Fit. *The Star*. https://www.thestar.com.my/news/community/2014/09/05/nationwide-campaign-to-get-fit-movement-aims-to-highlight-benefits-of-active-lifestyle; K. Michael. 2019. Healthy Turnout for Fitness Campaign. *The Star*. https://www.thestar.com.my/metro/metro-news/2019/03/27/healthy-turnout-for-fitness-campaign; and H.A. Suffian. 2018. *FIT Malaysia: Examining Health Related Campaign on Social Media*. https://expert.taylors.edu.my/file/rems/publication/100975_4483_3.pdf.

24 M. Manohar and P. Singh. 2018. New Delhi: Open Gyms Make Fitness a Mass Exercise. *Times of India*. https://timesofindia.indiatimes.com/city/delhi/open-gyms-make-fitness-a-mass-exercise/articleshow/65507526.cms; and A. Mishra and R. Chitlangia. 2019. Why Open-Air Gyms Topped Delhi MPs' List of Development Projects. *Hindustan Times*. https://www.hindustantimes.com/delhi-news/why-open-air-gyms-topped-delhi-mps-list-of-development-projects/story-uVwa3VLjcn8de5flfcROxJ.html.

By type of activity. In Asia and in nearly every economy around the world, walking for exercise or recreation is by far the most popular activity. Participation in walking appears to range from 20% to 60% in Asian economies, while an estimated 7%–25% participate in running or jogging.[25] It is challenging to analyze the popularity of playing various team sports because the types of sports played (and included in survey questions) vary so widely across borders; soccer is the most "universal" sport and appears in nearly every sports participation survey. Other popular activities in Asia include cycling (5%–25%), swimming (8%–12%), dancing (1%–7%), and martial arts (1%–8%).

By population segment. Almost across the board, participation rates in sports and active recreational activities are lower for women than for men (the exceptions are for a few activities such as dancing). Sports and active recreation is also the predominant way in which children and youth participate in physical activities. These kinds of activities are critical for introducing children to a lifelong habit of staying active. Out of the 1.3 billion people in Asia who participate in sports and active recreation, an estimated 0.5 billion are children (under age 18). The share of children who participate in sports and active recreation (45%) is higher than the participation rate for adults (24%), because participation tends to taper off as people enter adulthood and face the responsibilities and time constraints of jobs, families, and housework. It should be noted that participation rates measure people doing at least one activity on a regular basis, but many participants in sports and active recreation often do more than one type of activity. An adult participant may swim laps and play on a volleyball team, while a child may play soccer and take karate or dance lessons.

Fitness

Just over 1% of the population in Asia are members of gyms, health clubs, and fitness studios, and/or participate in structured or independent fitness activities or classes on a regular basis. Participants in Asia spent $22.7 billion, or an average of $494 per participant, on fitness activities in 2018. These figures are much broader than just the number of paying members at commercial gyms and health clubs, who only represent a portion of the market. We include membership and participation in a variety of other types of gyms and fitness classes in public, nonprofit, university, hotel, outdoor, home, and other settings, both free and paid (see more details below).

Per participant average spending of $494 in Asia is quite high relative to other regions around the world (e.g., $383 in North America and $400 in Europe). This is likely because the fitness market is generally less advanced across most of Asia, and the existing facilities tend to be concentrated in wealthier cities and serve the higher end of the market. Budget or low-frills gym concepts are generally newer and less prevalent outside of major metropolises, and public gyms and subsidized or free fitness classes and programs are also less common in Asia (except in a few key economies, such as Australia, Japan, New Zealand, and Singapore).

People do fitness activities in a wide range of venues. The authors estimate that more than 25 million people are members of private or commercial gyms and fitness facilities in Asia, across more than 61,000 locations. This is what most studies generally consider to be the extent of the "fitness market." However, there are many other ways to participate in fitness, and not all of them require monetary expenditures.

(i) An additional 6.5 million people in Asia utilize public, nonprofit (YMCA), and public–private gyms and fitness facilities, across 7,600 locations (primarily in Australia; New Zealand; Japan; Singapore; the ROK; and Hong Kong, China), typically with low or subsidized membership fees.
(ii) There are an estimated 7,500 free outdoor gyms across Asia (primarily in the PRC, India, and Singapore).

[25] Across much of Asia, survey data that assess the popularity of various types of activities are incomplete. The participation estimates, as shown here, are very rough estimates made by the authors, and are based on a scan of participation surveys from 10–12 Asian markets.

(iii) About 3.7 million people in Asia (mostly students and young adults) access gyms and fitness facilities on nearly 4,500 university campuses.

(iv) An estimated 1,600 hotels in Asia offer public memberships to their fitness centers, serving about 1.2 million members.

(v) An estimated 24.4 million people in Asia work out independently or at home. A significant portion of this number overlaps with other categories above, because many gym members also do workouts at home. Among those doing at-home workouts, an estimated 12.4 million in Asia subscribe to on-demand and streaming fitness services (via online platforms and mobile apps).

While these estimates for the fitness segment primarily focus on gym memberships across different types of facilities, this is not necessarily the best way to assess participation in fitness activities (although it is the most common and feasible measurement, given the availability of data across borders). Paying for a gym membership does not necessarily mean that a person is actually going to the gym frequently or participating in classes. According to the 2018 United States (US) consumer study of the International Health, Racquet & Sportsclub Association (IHRSA), more than 12% of Americans with health club memberships use them less than once a month.[26] Another recent study in the US found that 6.3% of Americans who have gym memberships do not use them at all.[27] It is likely that the same trend or development can be found in Asia. In fact, many gyms build their business models around a certain portion of members having low usage rates or not using the gym at all.

Mindful Movement

Mindful movement is the smallest category of recreational physical activities (both in Asia and globally), with $10.9 billion in consumer expenditures in Asia in 2018. An estimated 4.5% of Asia's population participates in mindful movement activities on a regular basis (which is higher than the global average of 3.8%). Yoga is the predominant activity, followed by tai chi and qigong, Pilates, barre, and a range of other niche activities (e.g., Gyrotonic and Feldenkrais).

The mindful movement market in Asia is a juxtaposition of the old and the new, as traditional spiritual and meditative practices have become coopted as modern exercise trends.

(i) **Yoga** has deep and ancient roots in India and has been practiced as part of the Hindu religion. However, its current and most popularized form was born in the US, where yoga was coopted into the fitness industry as a flexible (from mild to rigorous) form of exercise that includes a mindful component. The agnostic and often athletic forms of yoga have become a global phenomenon that is generating its own fitness subsector and related fashion, while influencing food, décor, jewelry, and lifestyle. Asian consumers, including a growing number in India, have largely embraced the Western style of practicing yoga at gyms, boutique studios, community centers, parks, and other outdoor venues, and using online sources. Although this style of yoga is still dominated by younger, more educated, and affluent women, men and older exercisers have begun to join in. Over the past few years, India has reasserted its dominance as the birthplace of yoga. The Government of India has instituted yoga practice among children and youth at schools, and it proposed an International Day of Yoga (June 21), which was adopted by the United Nations General Assembly in 2014. Although yoga data for India are sparse, the authors estimate that more than 53 million people in India practice yoga, mostly in its traditional form and with very low expenditures, although Western-style, commercialized, exercise-focused yoga

[26] IHRSA. 2018. *2018 IHRSA Health Club Consumer Report*. https://www.ihrsa.org/publications/the-2018-ihrsa-health-clubconsumer-report.

[27] *Finder.com*. 2019. Americans Spending $1.8 Billion on Unused Gym Memberships Annually. 1 April. https://www.finder.com/unused-gym-memberships.

offerings also exist in India's urban areas and tourism-focused establishments, and yoga has seen rapid growth and resurgence in India partly in response to its popularity and media attention in the West.[28]

(ii) **Tai chi** is an ancient form of martial arts in the PRC that was codified into a structured exercise by various martial arts schools and later by the Government of the PRC (Chinese Sports Committee) in the 1950s. Tai chi has long been practiced by the Chinese people in public places, and is often taught informally when groups gather to exercise in parks or public squares as an early morning ritual. Because the movements are slow, gentle, and deliberate, with a focus on breathing and balance, it is often favored by the elderly. In the PRC, the traditional art of tai chi remains popular—practiced in parks by millions of elderly Chinese—and is now promoted by the government as an important health and cultural practice.[29] Data on tai chi in the PRC are also sparse, but the authors estimate that about 80 million people in the PRC practice tai chi, mostly with very low expenditures. Although less ubiquitous than yoga, tai chi has spread around the world with the Chinese diaspora and is rising in popularity globally among younger participants alongside other mindful, stress-reducing practices and martial arts.

Across Asia, access to formal, Western-style mindful movement classes and studios remains concentrated in the wealthiest and most-developed urban areas. Fees for a single yoga or barre class can range from $10 to $30 in many specialized studios and full-service gyms, and the cost of equipment-based Pilates training is even higher. However, it is important to keep in mind that the rapidly rising popularity of mindful movement practices has been accompanied by a proliferation of ways in which to participate. In addition to the thousands of chain and independent yoga and barre studios, and classes in comprehensive gyms, there are now classes in YMCAs and community centers, streaming apps, books, and instructional DVDs.

A significant portion of the growth in yoga practice across Asia and worldwide is now in online, at home, and low-cost methods of participation, which are expanding access and lowering cost barriers to participation. In addition, scientific evidence of the efficacy of yoga for mental and physical wellness has led to its introduction in a variety of settings and populations outside the mainstream (and higher-priced) fitness market, such as in prisons, in programs for refugees and former soldiers, and in inner-city schools.

Overcoming Barriers to Physical Activity

While the physical activity sector Asia is sizable, it is currently engaging only about one-third of the region's population (with a 33.2% participation rate in recreational physical activities). As noted earlier, between 16% and 36% the adults across different regions within Asia are not getting sufficient physical activity by any method (via natural movement or recreational activities).[30] The large and growing share of the region's population with insufficient physical activity represents a major ongoing public health challenge, especially alongside rising rates of obesity and chronic disease. The solution lies in addressing the major barriers to physical activity across all spheres of life—from leisure and recreation options to increasing the natural movement embedded in daily life (i.e., transportation, domestic, and occupational physical activity).

[28] A. Tripathi. 2016. Number of Yoga Practitioners Increases by 30% across Metros: Assocham Survey. *Times of India*. https://timesofindia.indiatimes.com/city/lucknow/Number-of-yoga-practitioners-increases-by-30-acrossmetros-Assocham-survey/articleshow/52832153.cms; and ASSOCHAM. 2015. *Demand for Yoga Instructors Likely to Increase by 35%: ASSOCHAM. http://www.assocham.org/newsdetail.php?id=5030.*

[29] R. Zhang. 2019. *China Launches New Integrated Tai Chi Platform*. China Internet Information Center. http://www.china.org.cn/sports/2019-04/03/content_74641794.htm.

[30] R. Guthold et al. 2018. Worldwide Trends in Insufficient Physical Activity from 2001 to 2016: A Pooled Analysis of 358 Population-Based Surveys with 1.9 Million Participants. *The Lancet Global Health*. 6 (10). pp. e1077–1086. https://doi.org/10.1016/S2214-109X(18)30357-7.

Key Barriers to Increasing Physical Activity

To explore how to engage more people in physical activity, the authors reviewed more than a dozen national surveys and studies[31] that collect information on the motivations for and barriers to participation in physical activities. While these studies employed different methodologies, were conducted in different languages, and differed in the way they framed questions and responses, in aggregate they reveal important findings about physical activity motivations and barriers.

(i) **Motivations.** When people were asked why they engage in regular physical activity, by far the most cited reason is for maintaining good health (also "physical well-being," "to feel good," "to be fit," and other similar responses). The next most cited reasons are related to stress reduction ("to relax," "for emotional well-being," and "for mental health"). Other motivations include being with friends and family, building muscle strength, to look good, weight loss, to be out in nature, and to feel challenged or fulfilled, or for self-improvement.

(ii) **Barriers.** For those who do not engage in regular physical activity, the most significant barrier for adults is lack of time, followed by health problems, lack of energy (or too tired), and too lazy. For children and youth, the most frequently mentioned barrier is lack of time because of schoolwork. Other reasons cited by youth include the lack of interest or lack of opportunity.

It is not a surprise that those who are physically active cite health as their main motivation. It is also not surprising that time constraints are the most significant barrier for those who are inactive, especially in higher-income economies. More surprising is that physical conditions (e.g., health-related reasons, illness, age, or the perceived inability to engage in physical activity) are frequently mentioned as a barrier, more so than cost or money constraints or access to facilities. Outside of Asia, women and girls have mentioned personal safety and being uncomfortable at a gym as a concern, particularly in countries where gender and social norms discourage female participation in sports and outdoor recreation, in co-ed settings, or in certain types of physical activity. While these questions were not included in the surveys in Asian economies reviewed by the authors, it is very likely that similar barriers exist for women and girls in some parts of Asia.

Business Innovations and Public Initiatives Can Help Overcome Barriers and Close the Physical Activity Gap

While substantial barriers exist, it is possible to address them. This section provides examples of innovations, business models, and public policy initiatives that can help overcome barriers to physical activity, increase participation, and extend the many benefits of movement to more people around the world.

Business-Led Innovations

Leveraging technology. The most important barrier to participating in physical activity is time constraints. While most people are aware of the benefits of physical activity, their busy lives (work, school, and family obligations) deplete energy and preclude many people from exercising when it competes with other priorities. In the last 5 to 10 years, ubiquitous broadband and WiFi services and ownership of mobile devices have enabled the proliferation of exercise apps and streaming services that help people fit exercise into their busy schedules. The options are increasingly diverse and abundant, from free YouTube videos and mobile apps to fitness video games (or "exergaming") to paid monthly subscription services and sophisticated networked equipment. Workouts can be accessed via livestreamed classes or downloadable pre-recorded videos, and

[31] These studies cover Hong Kong, China; Japan; Malaysia; New Zealand; the Philippines; the ROK; Singapore; Taipei,China; Thailand; and Viet Nam. The studies reviewed are listed in GWI. 2019. *Move to Be Well: The Global Economy of Physical Activity*. https://globalwellnessinstitute.org/industry-research/global-economy-physical-activity.

through computers, mobile devices, wearables, and gaming systems. These services now enable people to exercise at home or in any other convenient location, at any time of day, at any intensity, and for any length of time. They are particularly important in markets where the infrastructure, facilities, and programming for physical recreation are limited.

Technology is also being used to make physical activities more fun and rewarding, especially by tapping into the competitive spirit and social aspect of exercising (virtually) with peers. "Gamification" has become one of the most popular trends and buzzwords in the fitness industry. The latest fitness equipment often incorporates high-tech functions (e.g., high-resolution video displays, biometric sensors, and cameras) that allow participants to track their metrics and compare or compete with peers virtually and in real time. Fitness games, which have engaged children, teens, and families since the 1980s, have progressed from home-based video gaming systems (e.g., *Dance Dance Revolution* and Wii Fit) to employing augmented reality and global position system or GPS technologies that take exercise gaming outdoors (e.g., *Pokémon Go*, *Ingress*, and *Zombies, Run!*). Exergaming and health games are now attracting broad attention, even from the medical and research communities, for their potential to leverage gaming's appeal to encourage exercise and change behaviors, from young children to aging seniors.[32]

Some governments are recognizing the potential of consumer-based technologies to support public health priorities. In 2019, Singapore's Health Promotion Board established a partnership with Fitbit to launch Live Healthy SG—a healthy population initiative built on a digital health platform.[33] The aim is to enroll 1 million Singaporeans by offering them free wearable devices (i.e., Fitbits) if they commit to a 1-year service agreement, which will provide personalized programs, health and fitness guidance, and behavioral insights that support healthy lifestyle habits, including physical activity, sleep, nutrition, and emotional well-being. The integration of personal health data will also support the development of health analytics on a national level. This represents the first major integration of fitness wearables into a national public health program anywhere in the world.[34]

Physical activity in the workday. Work is a key reason that adults do not have time for regular physical activity. Yet physical activity during the workday is more important than ever given our stressful, fast-paced, but increasingly sedentary work lives. A growing number of employers are aware that unhealthy employees can be bad for the bottom line because of reduced productivity, higher health-care costs, higher absentee rates, and other costs. Many workplace wellness programs now provide amenities and "perks" that encourage employees to be more active, such as employer-subsidized gym memberships, corporate gyms, free on-site fitness and yoga classes, free fitness bands, workplace running clubs, and employee fitness challenges. Employers can also proactively incorporate movement directly into their employees' work days—for example, by conducting walking meetings, providing daily stretching and activity breaks, allowing for exercise during paid work hours, providing flextime for workers to participate in fitness and outdoor recreation, encouraging casual attire that is conducive for movement, installing banks of treadmill and stationary bike desks, and designing movement-friendly workplaces (e.g., open and attractive stairwells).

---

[32] S.G. Parker. 2015. Health Games Research: Advancing Effectiveness of Interactive Games for Health. *Robert Wood Johnson Foundation Program Results Report*. https://www.rwjf.org/en/library/research/2011/03/advancing-the-field-of-health-games.html.

[33] C. Farr. 2019. Fitbit Wins Contract with Singapore to Supply Trackers to Potentially Hundreds of Thousands of Citizens. *Consumer News and Business Channel*. https://www.cnbc.com/2019/08/21/fitbit-to-supply-trackers-to-hundreds-of-thousands-in-singapore.html.

[34] J. Somauroo. 2019. Fitbit Partners with Singapore Government to Offer Trackers to 5.6 Million People. *Forbes*. https://www.forbes.com/sites/jamessomauroo/2019/08/22/fitbit-partners-with-singapore-government-to-offer-trackers-to-56m-people/#176c8d7a2031; K. Kwang. 2019. HPB Partners Fitbit to Encourage Singaporeans to Adopt Healthier Habits. *Channel News Asia*. https://www.channelnewsasia.com/news/singapore/hpb-fitbit-encourage-singaporeans-adopt-healthier-habits-11828980; and C. Farr. 2019. Fitbit Wins Contract with Singapore to Supply Trackers to Potentially Hundreds of Thousands of Citizens. *CNBC*. https://www.cnbc.com/2019/08/21/fitbit-to-supply-trackers-to-hundreds-of-thousands-in-singapore.html.

Fitness for seniors. Rising life expectancies, chronic disease, unsustainable health-care costs, and the ample leisure time of the senior population are converging in the growing need and opportunity for "silver fitness." In Japan, seniors (age 60 and above) now make up a substantial portion of fitness club membership and spend more on fitness and sports facilities than any other segment of the population.[35] In 2018, Australia's first Club W opened as a boutique fitness and wellness lifestyle space, aimed at providing an intimate, social "third place" that serves women over 55, who may otherwise be uninterested in, or intimidated by, mainstream gyms and fitness studios.[36] However, many seniors do not have the means to pay for private exercise facilities. In the PRC, more than 600,000 pieces of outdoor gym equipment (including jungle gyms, pull-up bars, ping pong tables, metal bikes, elliptical machines, and exercise pavilions) have been installed in neighborhood parks to facilitate outdoor exercise among the senior population. In fact, parks across the PRC are primarily used by seniors, and their design and equipment often target older users rather than youth. This concept of "senior playgrounds" first originated in the PRC in the 1990s, but quickly spread in Asia (Japan; Taipei,China), Europe, and North America. In Europe and North America, senior playground facilities tend to be co-located with children's playgrounds (so seniors can exercise while minding their grandchildren) or designed as multigenerational spaces.[37] Exercising in public spaces also provides other important benefits, such as regular social interactions for seniors who are susceptible to loneliness and social isolation.

Public Policy–Led Innovations

Governments can enable, encourage, and widen participation in recreational physical activity through multiple avenues. These are discussed in more detail in Chapter 13, "Policy Options to Promote Wellness in Asia," and include the following.

Prescribing exercise. The majority of exercise facilities and classes serve people who are already active or capable of physical activities, leaving out many people whose medical or physical conditions make it difficult for them to exercise, even though they would benefit greatly from it. Having a physician prescribe exercise as part of a treatment plan can give patients a powerful nudge.

Publicly funded infrastructure, facilities, and programs. It does not have to cost anything to be physically active, if people can access public infrastructure, parks, green spaces, running and biking paths, outdoor gyms, and recreational facilities and programs. As governments across Asia and around the world increasingly turn to physical activity as a way to keep their populations healthy and to prevent disease, they are investing in the necessary infrastructure to support these aims, including free outdoor gyms and subsidized and low-cost fitness centers (as elaborated in the second section of this chapter, "The Physical Activity Economy in Asia"). As more nations implement "national fitness and exercise" and "sport for all" plans, public investments in such infrastructure, programs, and activities will likely increase.

Physical activity in schools. To cultivate a lifelong habit of staying active, it is important to start at an early age. Physical education classes in schools are recognized as essential for helping children build awareness, skills, and lifelong habits of physical activity; they also contribute to better mental wellness, social development, academic performance, and school outcomes. Given that many children and teens do not have access to private sports clubs and activities, prioritizing physical education at school may be one of the highest-impact ways to increase physical activity participation. Outside of physical education classes, it is also important to incorporate movement throughout the school day, especially as the amount of time allotted

[35] *Australasian Leisure Management*. 2018. Japan's Fitness Industry Adapts to Ageing Demographics. 28 June. https://www.ausleisure.com.au/news/japans-fitness-industry-adapts-to-ageing-demographics.

[36] K. Cracknell. 2018. New Concept: Tony de Leede's Club W. *Health Club Management*. Issue 7. https://www.healthclubmanagement.co.uk/health-club-management-features/Tony-de-Leedes-Club-W/32858.

[37] L. Abbit. 2015. Playgrounds for Seniors Coming Your Way. *Senior Planet*. https://seniorplanet.org/playgrounds-for-seniors.

to physical education each week (averaging 84 minutes per week in Asian primary schools) falls short of the 1 hour of activity per day recommended for children by WHO.[38] Some schools (mostly outside of Asia) are experimenting with ways to incorporate movement and play into the classroom and the school day, such as play-based lessons, movement breaks, and activity-based equipment and active seating (e.g., balance balls, pedal desks, yoga mats, and balance boards), departing from the tradition of having children sitting quietly at desks all day.

Putting "play" back in sports. Outside of formal physical education in schools, sports are the most important access point for children to learn physical skills and build a lifelong habit and love of being active. Sports used to be a fun, informal activity that children did in their free time, and they remain so in many less-developed and lower-income regions. However, over the past few decades (along with urbanization, rising incomes, and the growth of the middle class), youth sports have become formalized, more expensive, and competitively focused around the world (often following the US model), including in Asia. Unfortunately, the trajectory that youth sports have taken tends to discourage youth from staying in sports if they are not playing at a competitive level. When they are simply considered "play" or recreation, and not an opportunity for achievement, sports are often not valued by Asian parents, especially when compared with the importance of studying and doing well on exams.

Embedding physical activity in the built environment. As natural movement has progressively diminished in our modern lives, many people cannot find the time to replace it with intentional, recreational physical activities. An important way to keep people physically active is by making movement a default in daily life, through infrastructure, design, and convenient amenities. In recent years, advocates for new urbanism, active design, and sustainability have promoted planning and design approaches that encourage natural movement, including attractive and accessible stairways; walkways and pedestrian paths within and between buildings; access to public transit; creating sidewalks, dedicated bike lanes, and bike parking and storage areas; and vibrant streetscapes. These design and infrastructure features help make human-powered movement the easy, convenient, attractive, and default or preferred way to go from place to place and can go a long way in helping people meet the daily requirement of moderate physical activity.[39]

Safe and comfortable public spaces for women. Social and religious norms and government regulations can be significant barriers to women being physically active. In some countries, the fear of harassment and even violence can greatly discourage women and girls from engaging in outdoor physical activities. In recent years, a number of countries have created women's parks to provide "safe" places for women to get outdoor recreation and fresh air. For example, in 2012, the first "women only" park opened in Lahore, Pakistan, a 4-acre space secured behind 7-foot-high walls, with its own jogging track, gymnasium, and badminton court.[40] Women-only parks have also been opened in Afghanistan so that women can enjoy the outdoors and engage in physical activity without being accompanied by male family members.[41] Other strategies to provide women with safe spaces include setting aside hours in parks and gyms for use exclusively by women. Outside Asia, new policies in Saudi Arabia that grant business licenses to female-only gyms have spurred the opening of many private fitness facilities that cater to growing demand from female customers.

[38] UNESCO. 2014. *World-Wide Survey of School Physical Education*. Paris. https://en.unesco.org/inclusivepolicylab/e-teams/quality-physical-education-qpe-policy-project/documents/world-wide-survey-school-physical.

[39] For more information on active design: Center for Active Design. 2010. *Active Design Guidelines: Promoting Physical Activity and Health in Design*. https://centerforactivedesign.org/guidelines.

[40] S. Ali. 2012. Are Women-Only Parks the Answer to Street Harassment in Pakistan. *Independent*. https://www.independent.co.uk/voices/comment/are-women-only-parks-the-answer-to-street-harassment-in-pakistan-8223147.html; and R. Khan. 2012. Six Women's-Only Parks Being Developed. *Tribune*. https://tribune.com.pk/story/434063/harassment-protection-six-womens-only-parks-being-developed.

[41] Institute for War & Peace Reporting (IWPR) Afghanistan. 2016. Afghanistan's Women-Only Parks. *Global Voices Asia*. https://iwpr.net/global-voices/afghanistans-women-only-parks.

CHAPTER 6

Improving Workplace Wellness in Asia—Business Case, Approaches, and Successful Practices

Ophelia Yeung and Katherine Johnston

Every day, more than 1.9 billion people in Asia go to work. In a lifetime, the average person will spend at least 90,000 hours working.[1] Some lucky slice of the population may find meaningful purpose through work, but for the majority of people, work is a necessity to survive. Asia's workforce is increasingly unwell, and the region can scarcely afford it. The chapter looks at the state of workplace wellness in Asia and discusses a comprehensive framework for workplace wellness.

Asia's Unwell Workforce

Globalization has brought rapid economic growth to Asia over the past 2 decades, pulling millions of workers into the formal economy, lifting their families out of poverty, rapidly expanding the ranks of the middle class, and creating megacities across the region. Yet the health and wellness of Asian workers is far from optimal, considering that a compelling business case already exists showing companies that care for and respect their employees are more competitive and successful in the marketplace. The issues vary across countries and industries—from the investment banker who is perpetually exhausted by working 14-hour days, to the small business employee who receives no benefits or sick leave, to the manufacturing worker who receives no break and is forced to work overtime, and to the miner who toils in life-threatening conditions.

Work-Related Illnesses, Injuries, and Deaths

In 2015, an estimated 1.8 million people died from occupational injuries or work-related diseases in Asia (accounting for more than two-thirds of all work-related mortality globally). In 2014, an additional 267 million persons suffered from nonfatal occupational accidents that resulted in at least 4 days of absence from work.[2] The most vulnerable workers are typically the poorest, least informed, least trained, and least protected, including women, children, disabled workers, migrant workers, and ethnic minorities. Not only do these injuries, diseases, and fatalities bring immense suffering to workers and their families, they also represent massive

---

1 J. Pryce-Jones. 2010. *Happiness at Work: Maximizing Your Psychological Capital for Success*. Chichester, United Kingdom: John Wiley & Sons Ltd.

2 P. Hämäläinen, J. Takala, and T.B. Kiat. 2017. *Global Estimates of Occupational Accidents and Work-Related Illnesses 2017*. Singapore: Workplace Safety and Health Institute. http://www.icohweb.org/site/images/news/pdf/Report%20Global%20Estimates%20of%20Occupational%20Accidents%20and%20Work-related%20Illnesses%202017%20rev1.pdf.

economic losses to businesses, communities, and the overall economy.[3] Globally, the economic costs of work-related illness and injury have been estimated at between 1.8% and 6.0% of gross domestic product (GDP) across various countries, including 3.2% of Singapore's GDP in 2011, and 4.8% of Australia's GDP in 2008–2009.[4] One alarming trend is the global shifting of hazardous industries (e.g., manufacturing, construction, mining, and agriculture) to the rapidly industrializing countries in Asia, which is likely linked to the declining trend of occupational injuries in higher-income countries, and the increase in occupational injury fatalities across Asia. In 2015, among the 1.8 million occupational fatalities in Asia, the biggest killers were work-related circulatory and cardiovascular diseases and stroke (31%), work-related cancers (24%), work-related respiratory diseases (21%), and occupational injuries (15%).[5]

An Aging Workforce and the Rise of Chronic Disease

Asia's population is rapidly aging, and so is Asia's workforce. Globally, the share of people over age 60 is expected to nearly double, from 12% to 22%, between 2015 and 2050.[6] Much of this aging will take place in Asia, where the share of the population over age 60 is projected to increase to more than 24% (or about 1.3 billion people) by 2050.[7] The aging of the workforce has profound implications for businesses across Asia, particularly because older employers are more likely to carry the burden of chronic diseases into their working lives.

Noncommunicable diseases (NCDs) are on the rise throughout Asia, not just among older demographics, but across all segments of the population. NCDs, also known as chronic diseases, refer to diseases or medical conditions that are not caused by any infectious agents, including cardiovascular diseases, chronic respiratory diseases, cancer, and diabetes. In Asia, NCDs accounted for 76% of all deaths in 2016, and this percentage is on the rise across the region, in developed and developing countries alike.[8] A recent study has put the total macroeconomic losses from chronic disease at $16 trillion in the People's Republic of China (PRC), $5.7 trillion in Japan, and $1.5 trillion in the Republic of Korea (ROK), over the period 2010–2030 (measured in real US dollars with base year 2010).[9] Chronic disease affects all employers and the overall economy because it reduces the quantity and quality of human capital across all age groups. Beyond direct health-care expenses, the indirect or hidden costs of chronic disease to employers include lost productivity because of absenteeism (e.g., sick leave, disability, and time off for medical care) and presenteeism (i.e., when a person at work is unable to perform at full capacity because of illness, stress, or other issues). A 2017 global benefits survey found that employees in poor health have twice as many absences, more than 25% higher presenteeism, and are twice as likely to be disengaged at work as employees in good health.[10] Workers and their families also face the threats of lost income, job insecurity, and possible unemployment.

---

3 ILO. n.d. *Occupational Safety and Health in Asia and the Pacific*. https://www.ilo.org/asia/projects/WCMS_099347/lang--en/index.htm (accessed 29 October 2019).

4 J. Takala et al. 2014. Global Estimates of the Burden of Injury and Illness at Work in 2012. *Journal of Occupational and Environmental Hygiene*. 11 (5). pp. 326–337. http://dx.doi.org/10.1080/15459624.2013.863131.

5 P. Hämäläinen, J. Takala, and T.B. Kiat. 2017. *Global Estimates of Occupational Accidents and Work-Related Illnesses 2017*. Singapore: Workplace Safety and Health Institute. http://www.icohweb.org/site/images/news/pdf/Report%20Global%20Estimates%20of%20Occupational%20Accidents%20and%20Work-related%20Illnesses%202017%20rev1.pdf.

6 World Health Organization (WHO). 2018. *WHO Fact Sheet: Ageing and Health*. https://www.who.int/news-room/fact-sheets/detail/ageing-and-health.

7 United Nations, Department of Economic and Social Affairs, Population Division. 2019. *World Population Prospects 2019*. https://population.un.org/wpp (accessed 30 October 2019).

8 WHO. 2018. *Global Health Estimates 2016: Deaths by Cause, Age, Sex, by Country and by Region, 2000–2016*. Geneva. https://www.who.int/healthinfo/global_burden_disease/estimates/en.

9 D. Bloom, et al. 2017. The Economic Burden of Chronic Diseases: Estimates and Projections for China, Japan, and South Korea. Program on the Global Demography of Aging at Harvard University, *PGDA Working Paper* No. 140. https://cdn1.sph.harvard.edu/wp-content/uploads/sites/1288/2012/11/The-Economic-Burden-of-Chronic-Diseases-Estimates-and-Projections-for-China-Japan-and-South-Korea-Bloom_etal_2017-FINAL.pdf.

10 Willis Tower Watson. 2017. *2017 Global Benefits Attitudes Survey*. https://www.willistowerswatson.com/en-US/Insights/2017/11/2017-global-benefits-attitudes-survey-health-and-well-being.

Job Insecurity and Financial Stress

Along with globalization, a confluence of business, technology, and demographic trends has brought great changes among Asian economies, transforming work and work life for many people. In today's fast-paced, hypercompetitive, and globalized business environment, company life cycles have become shorter, as have employees' tenures with specific employers, bringing greater insecurity for many workers. The Great Recession of 2008 led to widespread downsizing and a reduction in real wages, benefits, and retirement security in many developed countries. Contingent, part-time, temporary, irregular, informal, and unpaid work arrangements are rising around the world, while only one-quarter of all workers have a permanent, stable, and formal relationship with an employer.[11] According to Gallup World Polls conducted from 2014 to 2016, only 32% of working-age adults across 155 countries work at least 30 hours a week for an employer who provides a regular paycheck—what Gallup calls a "good job."[12] The share of "good jobs" varies across Asia, from 34% in East Asia, to 28% in South Asia and 25% in Southeast Asia. The gender gap in the percentage of residents with a "good job" is especially large in South Asia, where 43% of male workers have "good jobs" versus only 14% of female workers.

More than 68% of workers across Asia work in the informal economy. Informal employment is predominant especially in developing and emerging Asian nations (with more than 71% of jobs informal), in rural areas, and among younger workers.[13] A job in the formal economy is no guarantee of good working conditions, either. According to the International Labour Organization (ILO), 40%–60% of wage workers across Asia have no formal written contract of employment. In addition to financial insecurity, workers in informal, temporary, and contingent jobs face immense challenges to their health and well-being, such as a lack of health insurance and social protections, as well as a lack of oversight for working hours and workplace health and safety risks. These workers have a limited capacity to save, invest in housing, or consume goods and services, which has broader impacts on economic growth.[14]

Financial insecurity and informal employment are not limited to developing nations. The rise of the "gig economy" in developed economies has brought additional stress for workers, many of whom have to work irregular and long hours, or multiple "gigs," to compensate for their lack of a stable job and income. In a 2017 global benefits survey, many people reported that they live paycheck to paycheck, including 32% in the PRC and India; 31% in Japan; 28% in Australia; 27% in Singapore; and 19% in Hong Kong, China. Employees who are worried about their finances reported higher stress levels, more absences and presenteeism, and lower levels of work engagement than those who are financially secure. With rising longevity and health-care costs, alongside the decline of traditional retirement benefits, many more workers will have to work into their later years to make ends meet, which leads to higher numbers of disengaged, financially insecure, and unhealthy older workers. In the same survey, 45% of respondents in Japan; 17% in Hong Kong, China; and 15% in Singapore reported that they expect to work to age 70 or later (footnote 11). In many developing economies, modernization has been accompanied by the erosion of the traditional safety nets that were provided by families and communities in the past (e.g., health care, education, and childcare).

[11] United Nations. 2015. Most Workers Now Employed in Part-Time or Temporary Jobs—UN Labour Agency. *UN Sustainable Development Goals Blog*. https://www.un.org/sustainabledevelopment/blog/2015/05/most-workers-now-employed-in-part-time-or-temporary-jobs-un-labour-agency.

[12] Gallup. 2017. *State of the Global Workplace*. New York: Gallup Press. https://www.gallup.com/workplace/238079/state-global-workplace-2017.aspx.

[13] ILO. 2018. *Women and Men in the Informal Economy: A Statistical Picture*. 3rd ed. Geneva: ILO. https://www.ilo.org/global/publications/books/WCMS_626831/lang--en/index.htm.

[14] ILO. 2018. *Asia-Pacific Employment and Social Outlook 2018: Advancing Decent Work for Sustainable Development*. Geneva. https://www.ilo.org/wcmsp5/groups/public/---asia/---ro-bangkok/---sro-bangkok/documents/publication/wcms_649885.pdf.

Rampant Mental Stress and Burnout

Technology increases freedom, autonomy, and flexibility for many workers, while allowing work to constantly intrude on private lives, removing the boundaries between work and life. Collaboration among globalized teams also means that more people are working across different time zones and calendars, creating more intrusions on evenings, weekends, and holidays. The inability to "unplug" has become a fact of life for many workers in many fields, and it has become one of the biggest sources of stress in modern work life. In a recent global well-being survey conducted by the health-care firm Cigna (covering many Asian economies, including Hong Kong, China; India; Indonesia; the PRC; the ROK; Singapore; Taipei,China; and Thailand; as well as Australia and New Zealand), 87% of workers said they are stressed in their workplace, and 12% felt their stress is unmanageable, with 64% claiming to work in an "always on" environment. While 46% of workers reported that they receive support from employers to deal with stress, only 28% felt this support was adequate, and 38% claimed that no stress management support was provided by their employer at all.[15]

The physical and mental impacts, as well as the costs, of the 24/7 work culture and the resulting worker exhaustion are increasingly gaining the attention of workers, employers, researchers, and public health authorities. In May 2019, the World Health Organization (WHO) expanded its definition of "burnout" in the International Classification of Diseases as an "occupational phenomenon:" "Burn-out is a syndrome conceptualized as resulting from chronic workplace stress that has not been successfully managed." It is characterized by feelings of exhaustion; negativism, cynicism, and increased mental distance from one's job; and reduced professional efficacy.[16]

A culture of overwork and burnout seems to be particularly rampant in East Asia. In Japan, 60+ hour work weeks have been commonplace for decades. In Taipei,China, a survey reported that more than 60% of salaried employees worry about health issues stemming from overwork, while 75% of them have considered quitting their jobs because of work-related exhaustion.[17] In the PRC, the grueling work schedules for workers in technology fields have inspired an "anti-996" campaign to shame offending employers and combat the norm of working from 9 a.m. to 9 p.m., 6 days a week—a work system and culture that is often glorified by business leaders.[18] Death by overwork is a term in East Asia: *karoshi* in Japan, *guolaosi* in the PRC, and *gwarosa* in the ROK. A 2016 Japanese paper on *karoshi* found that working more than 60 hours per week significantly increases the risk of *karoshi* for males, while the threshold for females is about 45 hours. Because Japanese women tend to bear more of the burden of housework, when housework is added to working time, women face a serious risk of *karoshi*.[19]

Asia's overtime culture could be aggravated by the traditional respect for authority and hierarchy, which makes workers feel that they should not leave the office before their managers. Some managers may conflate long hours (i.e., inputs) with performance (i.e., outputs), and frown upon those who leave early. Further, some managers may think that they will look lazy or set a bad example if they leave before their employees, thus creating a vicious cycle of staying at work beyond the point where it is harmful to workers and unproductive for employers. Experts at Singapore's Institute of Mental Health have described poor organizational culture,

[15] Cigna. 2019. *2019 Cigna 360 Well-Being Survey: Well & Beyond.* https://wellbeing.cigna.com/360Survey_Report.pdf.

[16] WHO. 2019. *Mental Health: Burn-out an "Occupational Phenomenon": International Classification of Diseases.* https://www.who.int/mental_health/evidence/burn-out/en.

[17] Based on an article by T. Huang published via the online news portal in Taipei,China on 23 April 2018.

[18] L. Qiqing and R. Zhong. 2019. "996" Is China's Version of Hustle Culture. Tech Workers Are Sick of It. *New York Times.* https://www.nytimes.com/2019/04/29/technology/china-996-jack-ma.html.

[19] A. Kamesaka and T. Tamura. 2016. 労働時間と過労死不安 (Working hours and karoshi risk assessment). *ESRI Discussion Paper Series* No. 325. http://www.esri.go.jp/jp/archive/e_dis/e_dis325/e_dis325.pdf.

unrealistic expectations of workers' productivity, role ambiguity, and lack of recognition as chief reasons that drive the vicious cycle of burnout in the country, where two out of three workers report above-average to high levels of stress.[20]

Widespread Workforce Disengagement and Disenfranchisement

Engaged employees are happy employees. They are highly involved in and enthusiastic about their work and workplace. They are psychological "owners," driving performance and innovation, and moving their organization forward. However, worker engagement has been persistently low since Gallup began measuring employee engagement in the late 1990s.[21] The most recent Gallup World Poll across 155 countries found that only 15% of employees worldwide are engaged in their job, that is, psychologically invested in their work and motivated to be highly productive. In Asia, the level of employee engagement varies widely—from the highest in Southeast Asia at 19%, to very low in East Asia at 6%. Meanwhile, the level of active disengagement is alarmingly high. Actively disengaged employees are not just unhappy at work; they are resentful of and dissatisfied with work, and are acting out their unhappiness. Studies have found that actively disengaged employees are less productive, have more on-the-job accidents, miss more workdays, and quit at a higher rate than engaged employees. They are also more likely to steal from their company, negatively influence their coworkers, and drive customers away. Globally, Gallup found that 18% of employees surveyed were actively disengaged, including 11% in Southeast Asia, 21% in South Asia, and 20% in East Asia.[22]

Key factors that drive the varying rates of employee engagement around the world include economic uncertainties (e.g., people feel that they are stuck in jobs they do not like); management styles (e.g., top–down or "command-and-control" management); and poor workplace cultures (e.g., high stress or people gaining advancement at work through personal relationships rather than good performance). The persistently low rates of employee engagement and high rates of active disengagement in East Asia suggest that cultural norms are at work—in particular, the collectivist mindset in which individual needs and desires concede to organizational goals, breeding a culture of overwork that is harmful to employee health and well-being.

The State of Workplace Wellness in Asia

A Brief History of Workplace Wellness

Unwellness at work is not a new phenomenon, although the challenges have changed over time alongside economic transformations and the evolving nature of work. Historically, the health, safety, and well-being of workers have been shaped by the labor–capital relationship—the extent to which labor is an essential and valued factor of production, the costs and risks faced by employers, and the "voice" of employees to advocate for their rights. Many of today's laws, policies, and programs that support workplace wellness originate from labor movements that sought to protect worker safety and health amid the difficult and unsafe working conditions that arose during the Industrial Revolution. For example, the first occupational safety and health

[20] C. Chan and S. Fan. 2019. Commentary: What's Behind Burnout? Confusing Long Hours and Face Time for Work Performance. *ChannelNewsAsia*. https://www.channelnewsasia.com/news/commentary/behind-burnout-long-hours-face-time-work-performance-fatigue-11579678.

[21] Gallup. n.d. *Gallup's Employee Engagement Science*. https://q12.gallup.com/help/en-us/about (accessed 6 November 2019).

[22] Gallup. 2017. *State of the Global Workplace*. New York: Gallup Press. https://www.gallup.com/workplace/238079/state-global-workplace-2017.aspx.

legislation enacted in the mid-19th century in the US and the United Kingdom (UK) mainly had railroad, mine, and mill workers in mind.

Early workplace wellness programs, focusing on fitness for executives, were introduced in the US in the 1940s and proliferated and broadened their focus in the 1970s alongside the growth of the modern wellness movement.[23] Concern for workers' health also extended to their emotional and mental health. The first employee assistance programs (EAPs) were launched in the US in the 1940s to combat widespread alcoholism. By the 1970s, these programs expanded to include mental health, addiction, and family issues, and they were adopted more widely by large companies.

The proliferation of workplace wellness programs and approaches in Asia tends to track industrialization, globalization, and the expansion of multinational companies. For example, Japan established its first workplace health measures in 1972 with its Industrial Safety and Health Law, which mandated that employers provide periodic physical checkups for all employees.[24] Australia adopted the EAP model in the early 1980s, and its modern occupational safety and health system was adopted around the same time.[25] In the PRC, the first formal EAP was introduced in 1997 and, by 2012, there were more than 20 foreign and local providers of EAPs in the country.[26]

Size and Coverage of the Existing Workplace Wellness Sector in Asia

In recent research for the Global Wellness Institute, the authors have defined the workplace wellness market as "employer expenditures on programs, services, activities, and equipment, aimed at improving their employees' health and wellness."[27] These expenditures typically seek to raise awareness, provide education, and offer incentives that encourage employees to adopt healthier lifestyles. Workplace wellness programs target a wide range of employee behaviors (e.g., lack of exercise, poor eating habits, smoking, and lack of sleep) and risk factors (e.g., chronic illness, obesity, addiction, depression, and stress). Programs can encompass a variety of services, products, and platforms, including health screening assessments; diagnostic testing; in-house amenities or subsidized memberships for fitness clubs and exercise classes; healthy food offerings at company cafeterias; wearable fitness trackers; health fairs, educational programming, and counseling services for wellness; and incentives for participation in wellness activities. While some companies may design and administer their own wellness programs, there is now a sizable industry of third-party service providers who can administer these programs for companies (e.g., Optum, Virgin Pulse, ComPsych Corporation, Bupa Wellness, ConneXionsAsia, and WellteQ). Many private insurance companies also administer wellness programs for the companies whose employees they insure.

The workplace wellness market in Asia is estimated by the authors at $9.3 billion in 2017, representing about 20% of global workplace wellness expenditures ($47.5 billion). Asia's workplace wellness expenditures grew by 5.1% annually

[23] For a more detailed history of workplace wellness: Global Wellness Institute. 2016. *The Future of Wellness at Work*. https://globalwellnessinstitute.org/industry-research/the-future-of-wellness-at-work. For a detailed history of the wellness movement: SRI International. 2010. *Spas and the Global Wellness Market: Synergies and Opportunities*. https://globalwellnessinstitute.org/industry-research/spas-global-wellness-market.

[24] M.P. O'Donnell. 2002. *Health Promotion in the Workplace*, 3rd edition. Albany, New York: Thomson Learning.

[25] R.F. Peters and T. Firth. 1990. *Employee Assistance Programs: Their Development and Benefit*. http://www.heas.com.au/publications/eap.htm; and C. Chu et al. 2000. Health-Promoting Workplaces—International Settings Development. *Health Promotion International*. 15 (2). pp. 155–167. http://heapro.oxfordjournals.org/content/15/2/155.full.

[26] X. Zhu, Z. Wang, and T. Buon. 2012. Trauma Counseling and Psychological Support in the People's Republic of China (PRC). In R. Hughes, C. Cooper, and A. Kinder, eds. *International Handbook of Workplace Trauma Support*, First Edition. Chichester, United Kingdom: John Wiley & Sons, Ltd. pp. 436–446. https://doi.org/10.1002/9781119943242.ch27.

[27] Global Wellness Institute. 2018. *Global Wellness Economy Monitor*. https://globalwellnessinstitute.org/industry-research/2018-global-wellness-economy-monitor; and Global Wellness Institute. 2016. *The Future of Wellness at Work*. https://globalwellnessinstitute.org/industry-research/the-future-of-wellness-at-work.

from 2015 to 2017.[28] Worker well-being is gaining attention in Asia, motivated by growing concerns about managing health-care costs; improving employee morale, recruitment, and retention; and increasing productivity and competitiveness. A recent survey of office-based companies in Asia and the Pacific found that about 60% of the companies surveyed either had or intended to start some type of workplace wellness program in the near future.[29]

The current level of workplace wellness expenditures in Asia (and globally) is low when viewed from the perspective of employee coverage. The authors estimate that about 97.8 million workers in Asia benefit from some form of workplace wellness program, representing only 5.2% of all employed workers in the region (Table 6.1). Workplace wellness is still not a widespread concept in Asia, benefiting only a small slice of workers who mostly work for multinational corporations and in knowledge-intensive industries (e.g., finance, investment, consulting, information technology, high-tech, higher education, and creative industries), and those living in the region's wealthiest economies and cities.

Table 6.1 **Top 20 Workplace Wellness Markets in Asia and the Pacific, 2017**

	Number of Workers Covered (million)	Expenditures ($ million)
Japan	21.39	3,915.2
Republic of Korea	8.33	1,524.8
Australia	5.85	1,112.1
Taipei,China	3.47	634.6
People's Republic of China	33.11	496.7
Indonesia	2.54	222.6
Hong Kong, China	1.20	220.4
New Zealand	1.16	212.5
Singapore	1.02	186.5
India	9.21	184.2
Thailand	1.55	130.5
Viet Nam	1.47	119.9
Philippines	1.41	115.9
Malaysia	0.57	47.7
Bangladesh	2.03	40.6
Pakistan	1.81	36.3
Macau, China	0.12	20.1
Myanmar	0.91	18.3
Sri Lanka	0.22	17.6
Brunei Darussalam	0.05	7.5

Source: Global Wellness Institute. 2018. *Global Wellness Economy Monitor*. https://globalwellnessinstitute.org/industry-research/2018-global-wellness-economy-monitor.

[28] Global Wellness Institute. 2018. *Global Wellness Economy Monitor*. https://globalwellnessinstitute.org/industry-research/2018-global-wellness-economy-monitor.

[29] CBRE Group. 2017. *Workplace Wellness Gains Traction in Asia Pacific*. https://www.cbre.com.au/about/media-center/workplace-wellness-gains-traction-in-asia-pacific0.

As workplace wellness programs and spending expand in Asia, work-related wellness challenges are also rampant and growing (as elaborated in the previous section). A 2018 AIA Vitality workplace survey in Australia; Hong Kong, China; Malaysia; and Thailand found that 51% of employees suffer from at least one dimension of work-related stress, 83% have at least one musculoskeletal condition, and health-related productivity loss ranged from 48 days to 78 days per year.[30] In a 2017 GSK Consumer Healthcare study, more than 67% of workers in the PRC, India, Indonesia, and the Philippines felt that their work environment caused their body pain, and more than 60% said their work environment caused them head pain—human suffering that also translates into significant productivity loss.[31] Workplace wellness concerns vary widely across locations and economic conditions. In wealthier economies, the issues typically revolve around preventable and chronic disease, mitigating stress, improving work–life balance, enhancing engagement, and improving workplace culture and management structures. In lower-income countries, a large share of the workforce suffers from dire and often life-threatening issues related to exploitation, workplace safety or health threats, and the lack of living wages or a secure job—challenges that are not within the purview of typical workplace wellness programs.

Toward a Holistic Framework for Workplace Wellness

Like it or not, our work and our wellness are locked in an interdependent relationship. We all bring our underlying state of wellness to work with us—our physical and mental health, family life and relationships, personal motivations, values, and experiences—and these factors affect our job performance. At the same time, what we do at work and how we work have a profound impact on our personal wellness, from our financial stability and social status, to our physical health and stress, and even our self-esteem and sense of purpose. Our personal wellness is optimized when both our working lives and our personal lives are positive and mutually reinforcing. A comprehensive framework to improve workplace wellness should first look inward, to mitigate the unwellness that work and workplaces bring into the lives of workers, in addition to addressing the non-work-related issues that may have an impact on workers' health and well-being (and resulting job performance and productivity).

Ensure Physically Safe Working Conditions and Healthy Environments

Everyone works within a specific physical environment or space, be it indoors, outdoors, on the road (in an airplane or vehicle), at home, in spaces provided by employers or clients, or in a combination of sites. Work also places many demands on our bodies—whether we sit at a desk all day or stand on our feet, whether we lift patients or heavy boxes, or whether we operate heavy equipment or handle dangerous chemicals. The physical environment and the physical demands of our work can greatly affect our health and well-being. Regardless of where we work, every worker has a basic human right to a safe and healthy working environment.[32] Adherence to existing standards and regulations and application of safe and healthy practices should be the baselines for every employer. However, basic physical health and safety are not enough to meet the demands of the next economic era. Employers need to go further, proactively infusing health and wellness-enhancing features into physical work environments in order to encourage motivated, happy, and productive workers.

Reduce Hazards and Prioritize Safe and Healthy Work Conditions

Every job or workplace brings with it different types of physical health hazards and risks—for example, nurses risking back injuries from lifting heavy patients; office workers with carpal tunnel syndrome; truck drivers facing road accidents; professional athletes suffering concussions; and factory workers dealing with hazardous

---

[30] AIA Vitality. 2019. *Healthiest Workplace Survey 2018*. https://healthiestworkplace.aia.com/regional/eng/ .

[31] GSK Consumer Healthcare. 2017. *GSK Global Pain Index 2017, Global Research Report*. https://www.gsk.com/media/3814/global-pain-index-2017-report.pdf.

[32] ILO. 2009. *Health and Life at Work: A Basic Human Right—World Day for Safety and Health at Work 2009*. Geneva, Switzerland: ILO. https://www.ilo.org/safework/WCMS_108590/lang--en/index.htm.

chemicals, heavy equipment, or loud noises. Despite the proliferation of government regulations on workplace and occupational safety and health, work is unhealthy and unsafe for many workers across Asia. As noted earlier, an estimated 1.8 million people died from occupational injuries or work-related diseases in Asia in 2015 (accounting for more than two-thirds of all work-related mortality globally). An additional 267 million persons suffered from nonfatal occupational accidents that resulted in at least 4 days of absence from work in 2014.[33] Physical safety and health at work is a dual responsibility of both the public and private sectors. Industry associations, labor unions, and nongovernment organizations can play an important advocacy role in informing policies that protect the health and safety of workers, especially as changing technologies and new modes of work in each occupation bring different risks and potential hazards.[34] Meanwhile, individual workers need to be informed about the risks they face in their job, and empowered to advocate for improvements.

Create Healthy and Wellness-Enhancing Work Environments

Scientists are only beginning to understand how synthetic and natural materials, light, sound, and other features in the built environment affect human health. Modern construction techniques, building materials, and products expose workers to numerous potentially harmful substances in their workplaces, such as polyvinyl chloride and phthalates, flame retardants, volatile organic compounds, antimicrobials, bisphenol A, and nanomaterials. Indoor air quality and "sick building syndrome" were identified as major concerns by WHO more than 30 years ago,[35] yet these issues have not received adequate attention, and they continue to threaten the health of workers in offices and other buildings around the world. Ongoing and expanded research is needed in both the public and private sectors to understand and ameliorate these impacts, while policy makers need to keep up with the latest research and clinical studies in order to update building standards.

At a minimum, workplace built environments should not make their inhabitants sick. However, recent developments in architecture, management science, organizational psychology, and environmental science are providing new insights into how working environments can actually increase workers' productivity, happiness, and wellness at work. For example, a study in the UK showed that "high performance" office buildings can improve productivity by 12.5%, while the worst buildings can reduce productivity by 17.5%.[36] The environmental and sustainability movements have advanced design and construction techniques that enhance the wellness of both the planet and individuals, such as access to fresh air (windows that open or access to outdoor spaces); access to daylight and other natural elements indoors (windows with views or greenery and plants inside); thermal control and good air quality; and the use of environment-friendly, natural, healthy, and "toxin-free" materials. Major green building certifications, such as Leadership in Energy and Environmental Design (LEED) and Building Research Establishment Environmental Assessment Method (BREEAM), now include criteria related to indoor environments and occupant health and

[33] P. Hämäläinen, J. Takala, and T.B. Kiat. 2017. *Global Estimates of Occupational Accidents and Work-Related Illnesses 2017*. Singapore: Workplace Safety and Health Institute. http://www.icohweb.org/site/images/news/pdf/Report%20Global%20Estimates%20of%20Occupational%20Accidents%20and%20Work-related%20Illnesses%202017%20rev1.pdf.

[34] S. Li and M. Wang. 2017. International Experience of Co-governance in Occupational Safety. *Journal of Contemporary East Asia Studies*. 6 (2). pp. 170–186. https://doi.org/10.1080/24761028.2017.1391622; J.K. Park and T.T. Kjai. 2015. Occupational Safety and Health Activities Conducted across Countries in Asia. *Safety and Health at Work*. 6 (2). pp. 143–145. https://doi.org/10.1016/j.shaw.2015.03.001; and K. Kazutaka. 2012. Roles of Participatory Action-Oriented Programs in Promoting Safety and Health at Work. *Safety and Health at Work*. 3 (3). pp. 155–165. https://doi.org/10.5491/SHAW.2012.3.3.155.

[35] US Environmental Protection Agency. 1991. *Indoor Air Facts No. 4 (revised): Sick Building Syndrome*. http://www2.epa.gov/sites/production/files/2014-08/documents/sick_building_factsheet.pdf; and WHO. *WHO Guidelines for Indoor Air Quality*. http://www.euro.who.int/en/health-topics/environment-and-health/air-quality/policy/who-guidelines-for-indoor-air-quality (accessed 6 November 2019).

[36] A. Leaman. 2000. The Productive Workplace: Themes and Variations. *Building Services Journal*. https://www.usablebuildings.co.uk/UsableBuildings/Unprotected/ProductivityBSJ2000paper.pdf; A. Leaman and B. Bordass. 2016. *Productivity in Buildings: The Killer Variables Twenty Years On*. https://www.researchgate.net/publication/313553225_Productivity_in_Buildings_The_Killer_Variables; A. Leaman. 2005. *Productivity in Buildings: The Killer Variables Updated*. http://www.usablebuildings.co.uk/Pages/Unprotected/KVChicagoApr05.pdf; and A. Leaman and B. Bordass. 1998. Probe 15: Productivity the Killer Variables. *Building Services Journal*. E19–E21. http://www.usablebuildings.co.uk/Probe/ProbePDFs/Probe15.pdf.

well-being.[37] In Japan, the government has worked with the Institute for Building Environment and Energy Conservation (IBEC) to develop a health and wellness certification for offices as part of the country's Comprehensive Assessment System for Built Environment Efficiency (CASBEE) certification system with the first project evaluations taking place in 2019.[38] Over the last decade, new health-focused building certifications, such as WELL and Fitwel,[39] have also been introduced, which provide guidelines, road maps, and standards for companies to design wellness-enhancing built environments for their employees. To date, there are 16 Fitwel-certified projects and 45 WELL-certified projects across Asia (primarily in Australia and the PRC, as well as Taipei,China; Japan; India; the Philippines; Singapore; and Viet Nam).[40] These certifications are still new and evolving, and more research is needed to validate the impact of various workplace environmental features on worker health, well-being, and productivity, and to prioritize the most effective approaches. Clearly, not every company has the resources to achieve these kinds of certifications or to create new, purpose-built wellness-enhancing campuses, but many of these improvements can be made incrementally and over time with more modest investments.

Promote Healthy Behaviors at Work

Health researchers have identified five major determinants of people's health (genetics, behavior, social circumstances, environmental and physical influences, and medical care), and recent research has placed heavy emphasis on the influences of our social and physical environment (that is, the conditions in which we are born, live, work, and age).[41] Since many of us spend up to half our waking hours at work, the working environment (both physical and social) can have a profound influence on our lifestyles and health behaviors. As individuals, we are responsible for making good choices about how to live and take care of ourselves. However, our workplaces play an important role in supporting or hindering us in this personal endeavor.

Use Design and Amenities to Drive Healthy Behaviors during the Workday

While employers may have little direct influence over how their employees behave at home or during their daily lives, they can and do have significant influence on employee behavior within the workplace. Many companies are making incremental changes in workplaces and workspaces to promote employee wellness and encourage healthy choices and behaviors. These include a variety of design features and amenities, such as ergonomic workstations and equipment, standing and treadmill desks, private spaces for personal needs (e.g., nap or meditation rooms, lactation rooms), cafeterias with healthy food options, on-site fitness facilities, bike sharing or parking, outdoor walking paths, rooftop gardens, accessible and attractive stairways, and other features, which help employees to be active, exercise, eat better, take breaks, meditate, be exposed to nature, and do other positive things for their personal wellness during the workday.

However, employers must be careful to ensure that redesigned workspaces and amenities are not just superficial changes, but rather an intentional component of a company's culture and employees' needs and work styles. For example, wellness-focused amenities like on-site gyms or gardens are much more likely to affect health behaviors if employees are allowed and encouraged to utilize them during the workday. In Japan, many companies are starting to encourage workers to take nap breaks at work, supported by health ministry recommendations emphasizing the importance of sleep and taking a 30-minute nap every afternoon, as well as the cultural

[37] For more information, see T. Taylor and H. Pineo. 2015. Health and wellbeing in BREEAM. *Briefing paper*. https://tools.breeam.com/filelibrary/Briefing%20Papers/99427-BREEAM-Health---Wellbeing-Briefing.pdf; and U.S. Green Building Council. *Human health and well-being through LEED*. https://www.usgbc.org/articles/human-health-and-wellbeing-through-leed.

[38] *Nikkei Asian Review*. 2017. Japan Readies Certification for Healthier Office Buildings. 15 August. https://asia.nikkei.com/Politics/Japan-readies-certification-for-healthier-office-buildings2; and CASBEE Wellness Office Evaluation Certification. *IBEC*. http://www.ibec.or.jp/CASBEE/certification/WO_certification.html.

[39] For more information, see https://www.fitwel.org/ and http://www.wellcertified.com.

[40] Authors' analysis of Fitwel and WELL online project databases as of November 2019. https://www.fitwel.org/project-directory and https://www.wellcertified.com/directories/projects.

[41] L. McGovern, G. Miller, and P. Hughes-Cromwick. 2014. Health Policy Brief: The Relative Contributions of Multiple Determinants to Health Outcomes. *Health Affairs*. https://doi.org/10.1377/hpb20140821.404487.

concept of *inemuri* ("sleeping while present").[42] In several Asian economies (Japan; the PRC; and Taipei,China), workplace-based group exercise is popular, and even sometimes required. In Japan, more than 27 million workers across all industries—from banking to construction to factories—take mandatory exercise breaks during their workdays to do a short workout routine together. In Beijing, the government reinstituted mandatory exercise breaks at state-owned companies in 2010, also supported by radio-based programming, and sent 5,000 trained instructors into companies to teach workers the exercise routines.[43]

Cultivate Healthy Relationships and Encourage Friendships among Colleagues

With a few exceptions, most of us work with people: customers, colleagues, managers, subordinates, and sometimes even our families. The quality of these interactions and relationships has a profound impact on our own mental wellness and that of the people around us. Advances in neuroscience and imaging technology and the rise of interdisciplinary studies in biological, social, behavioral, and management sciences have led to major breakthroughs in our understanding of the connections among human interactions, our emotions, our motor and cognitive abilities, and our physical health and mental resilience. Interactions that are characterized by kindness, respect, collegiality, openness, teamwork, and a shared purpose increase our sense of well-being.

Over many years of survey research on organizational performance and personal well-being, Gallup has identified having "a best friend at work" as one of the key traits for productive work groups and high employee retention.[44] We all need healthy relationships in our lives to be mentally and emotionally well. Because friendship is based on trust, its impact in a work setting is manifold. Research has shown that friendships within a workplace can increase collaboration, communication, and honest feedback; drive a sense of loyalty (i.e., the need to have your friend's back and a commitment to shared success); reduce misunderstanding and friction; and help to increase retention.[45] Clearly, friendships at work can increase productivity and benefit employers, but the main beneficiaries are the people who get to work with others they can trust and respect and who care about their well-being. For example, Gallup observed that employees who reported having a best friend at work were 43% more likely to report having received praise or recognition for their work in the last 7 days, and were 37% more likely to report that someone at work encourages their development.[46]

Cultivate a Healthy Work Culture

Many factors in our workplaces, from organizational culture to management styles to compensation and benefits, go far beyond the scope of traditional "wellness programs" and can be improved to ensure that the relationship between work and personal wellness is a positive one. Glassdoor's research on companies that consistently rate as "best places to work" found that these companies have several common traits, including a well-defined mission that motivates employees, a culture of engaged employees, and a people-oriented culture that values

[42] J. McCurry. 2014. Japanese Firms Encourage Their Dozy Workers to Sleep on the Job. *The Guardian*. https://www.theguardian.com/world/2014/aug/18/japanese-firms-encourage-workers-sleep-on-job; and M. Shibata. 2019. Why Overtired Japan Is Turning to Office Siestas. *BBC*. https://www.bbc.com/worklife/article/20190809-why-overtired-japan-is-turning-to-office-siestas.

[43] J. McCurry. 2019. Listen, Bend and Stretch: How Japan Fell in Love with Exercise on the Radio. *The Guardian*. https://www.theguardian.com/world/2019/jul/20/japan-love-mass-radio-exercise-rajio-taiso; J.M. Glionna. 2010. China's State-Mandated Lunge Break. *Los Angeles Times*. https://www.latimes.com/archives/la-xpm-2010-aug-31-la-fg-china-exercise-20100901-story.html; C. Bas-Wohlert. 2018. Mandatory Exercise at the Office, Sweden's Latest Craze. *The Jakarta Post*. https://www.thejakartapost.com/life/2018/02/28/mandatory-exercise-at-the-office-swedens-latest-craze.html; and *British Broadcasting Corporation*. 2017. Should Exercise Be Compulsory at Work? 5 April. https://www.bbc.com/news/health-39490607.

[44] *Gallup Business Journal*. 1999. Item 10: I Have a Best Friend at Work. 26 May. http://www.gallup.com/businessjournal/511/item-10-best-friend-work.aspx.

[45] R. Friedman. 2014. *The Best Place to Work: The Art and Science of Creating an Extraordinary Workplace*. New York: Perigee Books.

[46] *Gallup Business Journal*. 1999. Item 10: I Have a Best Friend at Work. 26 May. http://www.gallup.com/businessjournal/511/item-10-best-friend-work.aspx.

employees.[47] Both research and anecdotal evidence suggest that the most effective employee wellness initiatives are implemented within the context of a broader organizational culture of wellness, which treats employees as key assets and proactively addresses all aspects of their well-being. Wellness-oriented work cultures must address and mitigate the stress and work-life balance issues that are major factors in employee's mental and physical wellness, and may even help employees enhance their sense of purpose at work. In addition, the best initiatives originate top-down from executive management and are often led by a wellness "evangelist" who is passionate about wellness and leads by example.[48]

Recognize and Mitigate Overwork and Stress

Stress and work–life balance are universal concerns of workers and employers around the world. A Willis Towers Watson survey found that stress was the number one workforce risk faced by employers globally and the number two risk among employers in Asia.[49] A growing number of companies are trying to address employee stress and its health impacts via their workplace wellness programs, typically offering classes (e.g., yoga, meditation or mindfulness, time management, and stress management); counseling; or perks and on-site amenities (e.g., nap pods, quiet rooms, free massages, and games or activities). To promote work–life balance, some employers may also offer options such as part-time, flextime, and off-site work, as well as family leave, assistance or subsidies for childcare, and other services. These kinds of benefits are highly desired by most employees. However, the challenge is that these benefits are only useful if the company culture supports employees to take advantage of them. What is the use of lunchtime yoga or a free massage if workers have no time to take part? Can workers take paternity leave if it would affect their prospect for advancement? How does flextime help if workers are expected to answer e-mails late into the night?

Further, workplace wellness programs do little to address the work culture and organizational issues that are often the primary cause of employee stress: that employers are often making more demands than their employees can handle, that the 24/7 nature of work communications does not allow for rest and rejuvenation, and that work can relentlessly intrude on our lives in an unhealthy way. Some types of working arrangements that companies tout for their flexibility (e.g., gig work for companies like Uber or Grab) can significantly increase stress for many workers (as elaborated in the second section of this chapter, "The State of Workplace Wellness in Asia"). Many managers are part of the problem, addicted to their devices and perpetuating a culture of manufactured urgency and the expectation of instantaneous responses. Executives, managers and supervisors, and individual workers can all play a role in balancing expectations, reshaping organizational cultures, and reorganizing work tasks and hierarchies in a way that allows for downtime and proactively prevents stress and burnout. In Japan, a country known for its entrenched culture of overwork, the government is attempting to address these issues through "work-style reform" legislation that caps overtime work hours and requires workers to take paid leave time each year.[50] Some Japanese companies (e.g., Microsoft Japan, Fast Retailing/UNIQLO, Yahoo Japan, and NEC Corporation) are experimenting with shortened or flexible work weeks and finding that employees are both happier and more productive. In the Philippines (and other countries such as France), the government is pushing

[47] Glassdoor. 2016. What Do All the 2017 Best Places to Work Have in Common? *Glassdoor.com blog*. https://www.glassdoor.com/employers/blog/2017-best-places-work-common.

[48] For an example of Aetna, see *CBS News*. 2015. How Aetna CEO Brings Health and Healing to Workplace. 26 March. http://www.cbsnews.com/news/aetna-ceo-mark-bertolini-healthy-workplace-healing-meditation-yoga.

[49] Willis Towers Watson. 2016. *2015/2016 Staying@Work™—Asia Findings*. https://www.willistowerswatson.com/en-ID/insights/2016/03/2015-2016-Staying-at-Work-Asia-findings.

[50] K. Paul. 2019. Microsoft Japan Tested a Four-Day Work Week and Productivity Jumped by 40%. *The Guardian*. https://www.theguardian.com/technology/2019/nov/04/microsoft-japan-four-day-work-week-productivity; M. Koizumi. 2019. Japanese Companies Warming Up—Slowly—to Four-Day Workweek. *The Japan Times*. https://www.japantimes.co.jp/news/2019/02/12/reference/japanese-companies-warming-slowly-four-day-workweek; and D. Demetriou. 2019. New Labour Law Puts Limits on Japan's Overworking Culture. *The Telegraph*. https://www.telegraph.co.uk/news/2019/04/02/new-labour-law-puts-limits-japans-overworking-culture.

companies to address work–life balance with "right to disconnect" laws that prohibit electronic communications outside of regular work hours.[51]

Integrate Well-Being into Leadership

Leaders have an outsized role in establishing the workplace culture, which in turn shapes social interactions at work. If the message from the top is that profit must be sustained and increased every quarter at all costs, human and even ethical considerations may be pushed aside. If a leader believes that human capital is the organization's most important asset and demonstrates this commitment through his or her actions and decisions, the message will filter down to all levels of the organization, influencing its culture and its employees' relationships with one another. People yearn for positive role models and leadership at work. Studies have shown that, when managers are fair to their team members in an interpersonal way, team members become more committed and effective and will show more citizenship behavior.[52] Leading by example, managers can promote positive behaviors, such as fair praise, regular and constructive feedback, empathy and understanding, honesty, and openness.[53] When management fosters a culture of wellness at all levels, there are greater possibilities for harnessing human energies toward new innovations, more productive collaborations, and better partnerships that benefit the organization as a whole.

Align Work with Personal Values, Intrinsic Motivations, and Purpose

Work is always going to be experienced and filtered through our individual values and motivations. Are my tasks interesting or boring? Does my job advance or thwart my ambitions? Do I feel valued or exploited? Am I growing as a person? Am I am contributing something to the world? Do I like the people with whom I spend my days? Does my employer respect and support my life outside of work? Honest answers to these questions determine whether we are filled with a sense of joy or loaded with misery after a day of work.

For most employers, aligning work with employees' personal values and intrinsic motivations may not be a foremost concern. Yet if a worker is unmotivated, he or she will most likely become disengaged and unproductive. Indeed, businesses are taking heed, as leadership, culture, and employee engagement have become management buzzwords in recent years. Some organizations have deliberately abandoned the traditional hierarchical management structure and are empowering employees to seek their passions, define their roles, elect their own leaders, perform their work with more autonomy and purpose, and even set their own compensation.[54] While many of these practices are still emerging, most organizations, whether they are for-profit or mission-driven, can do better in explicitly linking their objectives with employees' motivations and sense of purpose, such as articulating how customers' lives are made better or the impact of their work on the community.

Recognizing this intrinsic motivation, some business leaders have even begun to frame their business missions and visions in terms of customer, social, and community impacts, moving toward a purpose-driven mission rather than a profit-driven one. The concept of corporate social responsibility has been around for decades, and it broadly translates into practices that promote ethical business behavior, environmental sustainability, fair labor practices, and social impact in the community. In recent years, new business philosophies have emerged that expand and/or redirect a purely profit-seeking business model toward

[51] M. Vardeleon. 2017. Workers Have Right to "Disconnect"—DOLE. *The Manila Times*. https://www.manilatimes.net/2017/02/01/news/latest-stories/workers-right-disconnect-dole/310057; and E.C. Collins et al. 2019. More Countries Consider Implementing a "Right to Disconnect." *The National Law Review*. https://www.natlawreview.com/article/more-countries-consider-implementing-right-to-disconnect.

[52] T. Qiu et al. 2009. The Effect of Interactional Fairness on the Performance of Cross-Functional Product Development Teams: A Multilevel Mediated Model. *Journal of Product Innovation Management*. 26 (2). pp. 173–187. https://doi.org/10.1111/j.1540-5885.2009.00344.x.

[53] E. Seppälä. 2014. The Hard Data on Being a Nice Boss. *Harvard Business Review*. https://hbr.org/2014/11/the-hard-data-on-being-a-nice-boss.

[54] For some of the new organizational concepts and examples, see F. Laloux. 2014. *Reinventing Organizations*. Brussels, Belgium: Nelson Parker; and J. Ritchit-Dunham and B. Pruitt. 2014. *Ecosynomics, The Science of Abundance*. Belchertown, Massachusetts: Vibrancy Publishing.

social good. For example, a new type of corporate entity, the "B Corp" or "for-benefit corporation," explicitly recognizes social benefits as a core corporate mission.[55] Some companies have adopted the *triple bottom line* to measure their performance using financial, social, and environmental metrics, while others have added "treating employees well" to create the quadruple bottom line measurement.[56] The concept of "net-positive" or "positive handprints"[57] has also emerged, which seeks to capture the intangible value of making a positive contribution to the world, rather than only minimizing the negative impacts of business. The spread of environmental, social, and governance (ESG) reporting, the development of ESG guidelines, and the growth of socially responsible investing and impact investing are helping to encourage companies to consider their business practices and impacts.[58] These examples point to the many ways that business and organizational leaders can incorporate the notion of "purpose" in work as a source of motivation and wellness for their employees.

Support Healthy Habits outside Work

As elaborated above, typical workplace wellness programs provide a suite of programs and services that address employees' general health and wellness issues related to lifestyle, behavior, and disease management. These programs tend to be disconnected from what may be happening within the workplace, and they are filling widespread gaps in the provision of preventive health services. While employer provision of preventive health and lifestyle services will not fix the systematic failures of the world's health-care systems, these programs are expected to grow in the near term because companies can see the negative impact of chronic disease and rising health costs on their bottom lines. Research on workplace wellness programs points toward approaches that can make them more effective. For example, the most effective wellness programs provide tailored options and allow employees to choose what works for their individual, unique needs. With a growing recognition of how much our environments shape our behaviors, some companies are also extending programs to include families and address broader community factors that affect wellness.

Address Diverse Employee Needs and Cultural Contexts

A major shortcoming of typical wellness programs is that, too often, they are cookie-cutter or off-the-shelf packages that do not provide meaningful services for employees. In most wellness programs, a health risk assessment questionnaire or biometric screening tool is used as a starting point to assess employee health risks. From there, employees may be channeled into an online educational program or seminar to address their individual health risks or issues, and often that is the full extent of the wellness program. Some companies may go a step further—for example, providing employees with lifestyle-related services or benefits to encourage healthy behaviors (e.g., subsidized gym memberships, free wearable trackers, "step challenges," on-site immunization clinics or health fairs, nutrition counseling, and smoking cessation program) or enrolling employees in programs to manage chronic conditions or diseases (e.g., weight management program or competition, diabetes management, etc.).

These kinds of programs are most effective when they are tailored to the specific demographics, lifestyles, and needs of employees. Clearly, the health and wellness concerns of a twentysomething tech worker would be

[55] Fourth Sector Network. No date. *For-Benefit Corporations*. http://www.fourthsector.net/learn/for-benefit-corporations (accessed 6 November 2019).

[56] E.E. Lawler. 2014. The Quadruple Bottom Line Has Come. *Forbes*. http://www.forbes.com/sites/edwardlawler/2014/05/07/the-quadruple-bottom-line-its-time-has-come.

[57] G. Norris. 2015. *Handprint-Based NetPositive Assessment*. Harvard T.H. Chan School of Public Health and SHINE. http://hwpi.harvard.edu/files/chge/files/handprint-based_netpositive_assessment.pdf; and NetPositive Project. https://www.netpositiveproject.org.

[58] For more information on ESG in Asia and globally, see CFA Institute and PRI. 2019. *ESG Integration in Asia Pacific: Markets, Practices, and Data*. https://www.cfainstitute.org/-/media/documents/survey/esg-integration-apac.ashx; A. Holt. 2019. Asian Companies Get Serious about ESG. *IR Magazine*. https://www.irmagazine.com/reporting/asian-companies-get-serious-about-esg; and R.G. Eccles and S. Klimenko. 2019. The Investor Revolution. *Harvard Business Review*. https://hbr.org/2019/05/the-investor-revolution.

very different than those of a 40-year-old single mother working in a retail environment, or a 50-plus factory worker. For companies operating across different regions and countries, or in multiethnic communities, it is also important to incorporate cultural sensitivities (such as to mental illness) and local wellness traditions (e.g., Ayurveda and traditional Chinese medicine), as well as awareness of unique health needs across different cultural and ethnic groups (such as local diet and disease prevalence), in order to engage employees in a meaningful way.[59]

Extend Wellness Benefits to Families and Community Issues

Behavioral science and psychology show that our household, socioeconomic, and physical environments have a massive influence on our lifestyles and behaviors.[60] Recognizing that delivering wellness services just to employees is not enough to influence lifestyle and behavior change, a growing number of companies are extending workplace wellness benefits to include family members (spouses and children). Including families in wellness programs can expand participation, improve outcomes, and also help address health costs in places where employers are providing health insurance coverage for employees and their families.[61]

While it is admirable when employers provide gym memberships, free health screenings, or yoga classes, these benefits are not particularly helpful if the most basic employee wellness issues are ignored. Employees' needs vary widely across locations, demographics, industries, and socioeconomic environments. In some developing countries, the most pressing health priority for workers could be clean air or safe drinking water in their communities, and perhaps not massage tables or Fitbits. It could be transportation and safety for female employees working night shifts, or childcare for single mothers, or it could be a matter of earning a living wage or improving work–life balance. Some of these issues may require creative solutions within the workplace, while others may require working with governments or local authorities. These types of programs are often pursued as part of corporate social responsibility initiatives, but they also have wide-ranging impacts on employee wellness and retention, as well as company productivity and bottom lines. For example, a study by the ILO on companies in developing countries that provide nutritious on-site meals or food vouchers for undernourished low-income employees found widespread positive impacts, including reduced illnesses and medical costs, reduced absenteeism, higher morale, and increased productivity.[62] Efforts to address the issues that are most important and appropriate for employees communicate a real sense of caring that slickly packaged wellness programs will not.

[59] Global Wellness Institute. 2015. *2015 Roundtable Report, Redefining Workplace Wellness*. New York: Global Wellness Institute. http://www.globalwellnessinstitute.org/re-defining-workplace-wellness-roundtable; and R. Sims. A Failure to Communicate: How Cultural Incompetence Leaves Many Wellness Programs Incomplete. *Corporate Wellness Magazine*. https://www.corporatewellnessmagazine.com/article/a-failure-to-communicate (accessed 6 November 2019).

[60] S.E. Jackson, A. Steptoe, and J. Wardle. 2015. The Influence of Partner's Behavior on Health Behavior Change: The English Longitudinal Study of Ageing. *JAMA Internal Medicine*. 175 (3). pp. 385–392. https://doi.org/10.1001/jamainternmed.2014.7554; M. Kelly and M. Barker. 2016. Why Is Changing Health-Related Behavior So Difficult? *Public Health*. 136. pp. 109–116. https://doi.org/10.1016/j.puhe.2016.03.030; B. Stulburg. 2014. The Key to Changing Individual Health Behaviors: Change the Environments That Give Rise to Them. *Harvard Public Health Review*. 2. http://harvardpublichealthreview.org/wp-content/uploads/2014/10/HPHRv2-Stulberg.pdf; and S. Kahan et al. 2014. *Health Behavior Change in Populations*. Baltimore, Maryland: Johns Hopkins University Press. https://jhupbooks.press.jhu.edu/title/health-behavior-change-populations.

[61] D. Tobenkin. 2013. Wellness Agenda: Stay Well Together. *SHRM Magazine*. https://www.shrm.org/hr-today/news/hr-magazine/pages/0213-family-wellness-benefits.aspx; V. Bolden-Barrett. 2017. Wellness Programs Involving Employee Spouses More Likely to See Engagement. *HR Dive Brief*. https://www.hrdive.com/news/wellness-programs-involving-employee-spouses-more-likely-to-see-engagement/449127; and K. Moseley. 2017. Why Employers Should Include Spouses in Well-being Programs. *EBN Benefit News*. https://www.benefitnews.com/opinion/why-employers-should-include-spouses-in-well-being-programs.

[62] C. Wanjek. 2005. *Food at Work: Workplace Solutions for Malnutrition, Obesity and Chronic Diseases*. Geneva: International Labour Office. https://www.ilo.org/wcmsp5/groups/public/---dgreports/---dcomm/---publ/documents/publication/wcms_publ_9221170152_en.pdf.

Workplace Wellness: A Business Case

As elaborated in the first section of this chapter, "Asia's Unwell Workforce," the impacts of an unwell workforce are enormous in terms of both economic costs and human suffering. It is relatively simple to quantify the monetary costs of a physically unwell workforce, since illness, injury, and chronic disease have direct, measurable impacts on health-care spending, missed work days, lost wages, and productivity loss. For example, the global economic costs of work-related illness and injury have been estimated at between 1.8% and 6.0% of GDP across various countries, including 3.2% of Singapore's GDP in 2011, and 4.8% of Australia's GDP in 2008–2009.[63] Less tangible and quantifiable are the nonphysical aspects of workforce unwellness, such as financial stress and job insecurity, stress and burnout, and disengagement and disenfranchisement at work. Gallup has estimated that the economic costs of employee disengagement are about $7 trillion in lost productivity globally, which represents over 8% of global GDP.[64]

There is a strong business case to invest in the wellness of the workforce and workplace, especially in the context of the so-called Fourth Industrial Revolution, whereby a range of new technologies are "fusing the physical, digital and biological worlds, impacting all disciplines, economies and industries, and even challenging ideas about what it means to be human."[65] Technology has already had wide-ranging impacts on work, productivity, and competitiveness. Not only are humans increasingly replaced by robots and computers for routine, computational, and repetitive tasks, even jobs in high-skilled professions such as law, medicine, and consulting are being threatened by rapidly advancing computing power and artificial intelligence. To compete with machines and add value, workers need to be creative, innovative, perceptive, intuitive, and adaptive. This requires workers to bring high levels of motivation and energy to work—qualities that most strongly manifest when an individual is healthy and intrinsically motivated, rather than lured by external rewards. In other words, organizations need workers with a high level of well-being—supported by a wellness-oriented work culture and environment—in order to survive and thrive in the future of work.

However, we do not need to look to the future for evidence. Already, there is a compelling business case that companies who care for and respect their employees are more competitive and successful in the marketplace.

Stock market performance. A study published in the *Journal of Occupational and Environmental Medicine* showed that companies recognized by the C. Everett Koop National Health Awards for nurturing a culture of health, by specifically focusing on the well-being and safety of their workers, have outperformed the stock market by a factor of three from 2000 to 2014.[66] Companies that rate highly for their employee-focused cultures show similar results. For example, the Great Place to Work® Institute, which recognizes the 100 top companies in the United States for workplace culture, found that "great workplaces" have stock market returns that were nearly three times higher than industry peers from 1998 to 2016.[67] Companies appearing on Glassdoor's "best places to work" list (based on ratings derived directly from employee feedback) outperformed the S&P 500 by 115.6% from 2009 to 2014; conversely, companies with the lowest employee ratings on Glassdoor significantly

[63] J. Takala et al. 2014. Global Estimates of the Burden of Injury and Illness at Work in 2012. *Journal of Occupational and Environmental Hygiene*. 11 (5). pp. 326–337. http://dx.doi.org/10.1080/15459624.2013.863131.

[64] J. Harter. 2017. GDP Data from the International Monetary Fund, *World Economic Outlook Database*, July 2019 edition. https://www.imf.org/external/pubs/ft/weo/2019/01/weodata/index.aspx.

[65] K. Schwab. 2016. *The Fourth Industrial Revolution*. Geneva: World Economic Forum. https://www.weforum.org/about/the-fourth-industrial-revolution-by-klaus-schwab.

[66] R. Goetzel et al. 2016. The Stock Performance of C. Everett Koop Award Winners Compared with the Standard & Poor's 500 Index. *Journal of Occupational and Environmental Medicine*. 58 (1). pp. 9–15. https://doi.org/10.1097/JOM.0000000000000632.

[67] Great Place to Work®. 2017. *Three Predictions for the Workplace Culture of the Future*. https://www.greatplacetowork.com/images/reports/Fortune_100_Report_2017_FINAL.pdf; and A. Edmans. 2011. Does the Stock Market Fully Value Intangibles? Employee Satisfaction and Equity Prices. *Journal of Financial Economics*. 101. pp. 621–640. http://faculty.london.edu/aedmans/Rowe.pdf.

underperformed the market.[68] While most of the few existing studies on the impact of employee wellness on stock market performance have been centered in the United States, one study in India found similarly positive results, with India's "best companies to work for" outperforming key stock market indices by a factor of four from 2008 to 2016, yielding five times the return on an initial investment.[69]

Key business performance metrics. A wealth of research has shown that employee engagement has a strong positive impact on companies' bottom lines. Gallup, which has collected primary data and studied this topic for more than 40 years, has conducted several large-scale, global meta-analyses that demonstrate a strong correlation between employee attitudes (satisfaction and engagement) and overall business outcomes. The latest 2016 study[70] aggregates data from 339 independent research studies (encompassing all available Gallup studies) across 230 organizations, including more than 1.8 million employees in 73 countries, and it examines the relationship between employee engagement and nine business performance outcomes. Business units scoring in the top quartile for employee engagement outperformed those in the bottom quartile by 70% in safety incidents (fewer), 40% in quality defects (fewer), 41% in employee absenteeism (lower), 24%–59% in employee turnover (lower), 21% in profitability (higher), 20% in sales production (higher), and 10% in customer satisfaction (higher).

A separate study in the *2019 Global Happiness and Wellbeing Policy Report* has taken the same set of Gallup research data and conducted a meta-analysis on the relationship between employee satisfaction and business outcomes.[71] It also found positive correlations between employee satisfaction with the organization as a place to work and key metrics such as customer satisfaction, productivity, and higher profitability, as well as a substantial negative correlation with staff turnover. While a large number of the studies included in the analysis were based in the United States, it also covered enterprises in a number of Asian economies, including Bangladesh; Cambodia; Hong Kong, China; India; Indonesia; Japan; Malaysia; Nepal; Pakistan; the PRC; the Philippines; the ROK; Singapore; Sri Lanka; Taipei,China; and Thailand. To look at differences between United States and non-United States regions, the researchers conducted another meta-analysis by region and found evidence that employee satisfaction tends to be more important for performance outcomes in non-United States regions, with the exception of staff turnover, for which it is the opposite. Overall, 95% confidence intervals for United States and non-United States regions are highly overlapping, which the authors interpreted as a negligible degree of true regional differences in correlation (footnote 71).

[68] A. Chamberlain. 2015. *Does Company Culture Pay Off? Analyzing Stock Performance of "Best Places to Work" Companies.* Mill Valley, California: Glassdoor.com. https://research-content.glassdoor.com/app/uploads/ sites/2/2015/05/GD_Report_1.pdf.

[69] RSM India. 2017. *Study on Shareholder Returns of Great Workplaces—2017, Identified by Great Place to Work® Institute.* Mumbai: RSM Astute Consulting Group. https://www.rsm.global/india/sites/default/files/media/RSM%20India/Publications/2017/study_on_shareholder_returns_of_great_workplaces_-2017_-_by_rsm_india.pdf.

[70] J.K. Harter et al. 2016. *The Relationship between Engagement at Work and Organizational Outcomes—2016 Q12 Meta-Analysis: Ninth Edition.* Washington, DC: Gallup. https://news.gallup.com/reports/191489/q12-meta-analysis-report-2016.aspx.

[71] C. Krekel et al. 2019. Employee Well-being, Productivity, and Firm Performance: Evidence and Case Studies. In Global Council for Happiness and Wellbeing. *Global Happiness and Wellbeing Policy Report 2019.* pp. 73–94. New York: Sustainable Development Solutions Network. https://s3.amazonaws.com/ghwbpr-2019/UAE/GHWPR19.pdf.

CHAPTER 7

Eating in Developing Asia—Trends, Consequences, and Policies

Anne Marie Thow, Penny Farrell, Matthias Helble, and Cut Novianti Rachmi

This chapter reviews the changing diets, food supply, and food environments in the Asia and Pacific region. It then describes the prevalence and nature of undernutrition across the region, including anthropometric measures of undernutrition such as stunting, wasting and underweight, "hidden hunger" resulting from micronutrient deficiencies, and dietary caloric deficiencies relating to food security. It also examines the rising prevalence of diet-related risks for noncommunicable diseases (NCDs), such as dietary patterns high in salt, fat, and sugar, and low in health-protective foods, such as fruits and vegetables; and trends in overweight and obesity. The range of forms that malnutrition takes is often referred to as the "double burden of malnutrition" (DBM) or the "triple burden of malnutrition," to emphasize the diversity encompassed within the concept of nutrition. The chapter concludes by examining the policy response to the burden of malnutrition in Asia and the Pacific and identifying opportunities to strengthen action.

Introduction

Recognition of the importance of good nutrition as critical to human flourishing, as well as to sustainable development, is growing. The estimated annual impact of malnutrition on the global economy is $3.5 trillion in direct economic costs and lost productivity, with direct treatment costs up to $2 trillion per year.[1] Undernutrition, particularly in early life, is associated with increased risk of infection as well as reduced cognition and educational achievement, and subsequent reduced economic productivity.[2] In Asia and the Pacific, many populations continue to experience high rates of undernutrition. Two-thirds of the 49.5 million children globally under 5 years of age who are wasted (low weight-for-height) live in Asia, and more than 50% of pregnant women in South Asia are anemic (deficient in iron).[3] Annual economic losses from low weight, poor childhood growth, and micronutrient deficiencies in Asia average 11% of gross domestic product (GDP).[4]

Early childhood nutrition has been identified as a critical contributor to human capital (the aggregate levels of education, training, skills, and health in a population), which is associated with higher GDP and faster economic

1 Food and Agriculture Organization (FAO). 2013. *The State of Food and Agriculture: Food Systems for Better Nutrition*. Rome: Food and Agriculture Organization of the United Nations.

2 D.S. Madjdian et al. 2018. Socio-Cultural and Economic Determinants and Consequences of Adolescent Undernutrition and Micronutrient Deficiencies in LLMICs: A Systematic Narrative Review. *Annals of the New York Academy of Sciences*. 1416 (1). pp. 117–139.

3 FAO et al. 2019. *The State of Food Insecurity in the World: Safeguarding against Economic Slowdowns and Downturns*. Rome: UN Food and Agriculture Organization, International Fund for Agricultural Development, United Nations Children's Fund, World Health Organization and World Food Programme.

4 UNICEF. 2019. *The State of the World's Children 2019. Children, Food and Nutrition: Growing Well in a Changing World*. New York: UNICEF. p. 62.

growth.[5] A critical time period for maintaining good nutrition is the introduction of food for infants and young children up to 3 years of age, known as complementary feeding (as it is recommended that it coexist with breastfeeding). Consumption of diverse energy- and nutrient-dense foods is important for young children to obtain all the nutrients necessary for adequate nutrition. Complementary feeding has been a long-term concern in Asia and the Pacific, where rice-based weaning foods are heavily relied upon, which has contributed to low dietary diversity in many countries.[6]

At the same time, overweight and diet-related noncommunicable diseases (NCDs) are increasing rapidly, leading to a double burden of malnutrition (DBM). Dietary patterns high in fruits, vegetables, whole grains, legumes, seeds, nuts, fish, and dairy; and low in processed meat, sweets, and salty foods have been shown to reduce the risk of NCDs, particularly diabetes; cardiovascular disease (CVD); and some cancers (including colon, pancreatic, and breast cancers).[7] Overweight and obesity in Asia and the Pacific generate significant economic costs; the annual burden of direct medical costs has been estimated at 0.78% of GDP.[8] Diets in Asia and the Pacific have changed rapidly with modernization and globalization. Consumption of fruits and vegetables remains low in many countries, and consumption of refined staple carbohydrates, such as white rice, dominates many diets. Consumption of highly processed foods has risen dramatically over the past 20 years.[9]

The influences on diets are complex, and include person-level considerations such as income, taste, preference, and culture (Figure 7.1). They also include external or "food environment" influences, including prices, marketing, retail availability, and food safety, with major influences on these identified as trade and urbanization. Nutritional status is also affected by factors other than diet, including access to clean water, sanitation, and infant feeding; and obesity is affected by physical activity. However, in this chapter we will focus on diets, food environments, and nutrition: "Eating in Developing Asia."

Inequalities in dietary consumption have been found across the region, in part because of inequalities in access to nutritious foods at the household and community levels. The major determinants of access include gender, socioeconomic status, geography, land ownership, and cultural factors.[10] Socioeconomic status has a major influence on dietary intakes, with low socioeconomic status households across the region experiencing higher levels of food insecurity and reduced access to nutritious foods (footnote 10). In addition, the well-being and education of women is also positively associated with dietary diversity and intakes across the region.[11]

---

5 S.S. Lim et al. 2018. Measuring Human Capital: A Systematic Analysis of 195 Countries and Territories, 1990–2016. *The Lancet*. 392 (10154). pp. 1217–1234.

6 M. Inoue and C.W. Binns. 2014. Introducing Solid Foods to Infants in the Asia Pacific Region. *Nutrients*. 6 (1). pp. 276–288; and V.M. Aguayo. 2017. Complementary Feeding Practices for Infants and Young Children in South Asia. A Review of Evidence for Action Post-2015. *Maternal and Child Nutrition*. 13.

7 R.N. Ndanuko et al. 2016. Dietary Patterns and Blood Pressure in Adults: A Systematic Review and Meta-Analysis of Randomized Controlled Trials. *Advances in Nutrition*. 7 (1). pp. 76–89; and Z. Maghsoudi, R. Ghiasvand, and A. Salehi-Abargouei. 2016. Empirically Derived Dietary Patterns and Incident Type 2 Diabetes Mellitus: A Systematic Review and Meta-analysis on Prospective Observational Studies. *Public Health Nutrition*. 19 (2). pp. 230–241.

8 M. Helble and K. Francisco. 2018. Chapter 8: The Imminent Obesity Crisis in Asia and the Pacific: First Cost Estimates. In *Wealthy but Unhealthy: Overweight and Obesity in Asia and the Pacific: Trends, Costs, and Policies for Better Health*. Tokyo: Asian Development Bank Institute.

9 P. Baker and S. Friel. 2016. Food Systems Transformations, Ultra-processed Food Markets and the Nutrition Transition in Asia. *Globalization and Health*. 12 (1): 80; and K. Sievert et al. 2019. Processed Foods and Nutrition Transition in the Pacific: Regional Trends, Patterns and Food System Drivers. *Nutrients*. 11 (6): 1328.

10 FAO. 2019. *Europe and Central Asia Regional Overview of Food Security and Nutrition: Structural Transformations of Agriculture for Improved Food Security, Nutrition and Environment*. Budapest: Food and Agriculture Organization of the United Nations; and FAO, UNICEF, World Food Programme, and World Health Organization (WHO). 2019. *Placing Nutrition at the Centre of Social Protection. Asia and the Pacific Regional Overview of Food Security and Nutrition 2019*. Bangkok.

11 E. Sraboni and A. Quisumbing. 2018. Women's Empowerment in Agriculture and Dietary Quality across the Life Course: Evidence from Bangladesh. *Food Policy*. 81. pp. 21–36; and H. Torlesse and V.M. Aguayo. 2018. Aiming Higher for Maternal and Child Nutrition in South Asia. *Maternal & Child Nutrition*. 14 (S4): e12739.

In this chapter, we review changing diets, food supply, and food environments in Asia and the Pacific. We then describe the prevalence and nature of undernutrition across the region, including measures of undernutrition such as stunting, wasting and underweight, "hidden hunger" resulting from micronutrient deficiencies, and dietary caloric deficiencies relating to food security. We also examine the rising prevalence of diet-related risks for NCDs (sometimes called "overnutrition"), such as dietary patterns high in salt, fat, and sugar, and low in health-protective foods, such as fruits and vegetables; and anthropometric measures of overweight and obesity. The range of forms that malnutrition takes is often referred to as the "double burden of malnutrition" (the term we will use throughout this chapter) or the "triple burden of malnutrition," in order to emphasize the diversity encompassed within the concept of nutrition.

We conclude by examining the policy response to the DBM in Asia and the Pacific and identifying opportunities to strengthen action. Nutrition features in six of the United Nations Sustainable Development Goals and is important for the achievement of at least 12,[12] including those related to economic growth, education, and health. Governments across Asia and the Pacific have committed to addressing the DBM.[13] There is widespread recognition that it is essential to have multisector policy approaches that address both the consumer side (such as nutrition education, food skills, and access to healthy food) and the supply side in ways that create food environments that support availability, convenience, attractiveness, and affordability of healthy foods.

Figure 7.1 **Overview of Diets and Other Factors as Influences on the Double Burden of Malnutrition**

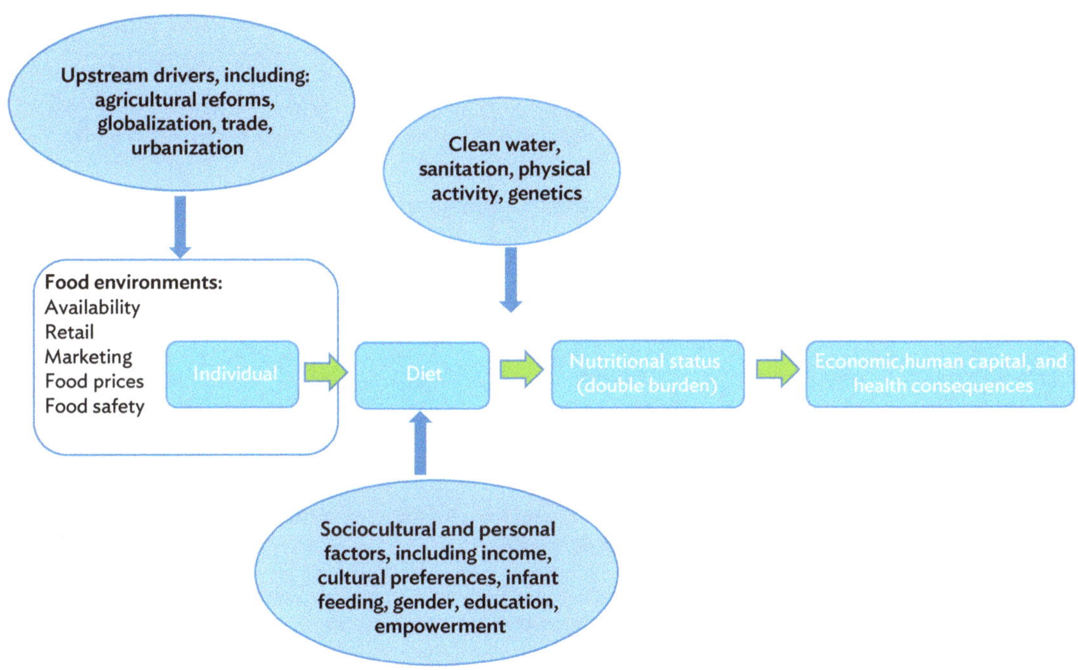

Source: Authors' analysis.

[12] United Nations. 2015. *Sustainable Development Goals*. https://sustainabledevelopment.un.org/?menu=1300.

[13] R. Dodd et al. 2020. The Politics of Food in the Pacific: Coherence and Tension in Regional Policies on Nutrition, the Food Environment and Non-communicable Diseases. *Public Health Nutrition*. 23 (1). pp. 168–180; and Association of Southeast Asian Nations (ASEAN). 2017. ASEAN Leaders' Declaration on Ending All Forms of Malnutrition. https://asean.org/wp-content/uploads/2017/11/2.-ADOPTION_2017_ALD-on-Ending-All-Forms-of-Malnutrition_Endorsed-by-the-AHMM.pdf (accessed 12 March 2020).

Food Environments and Drivers of Dietary Change

The food environment reflects external influences—such as prices, retail availability, marketing, and food safety, with major influences on these including trade and urbanization—that interact with person-level determinants of diet, such as income, taste, preference, and culture.[14] Food environments describe the context in which people make decisions about what they eat, where, and when, and are an important factor to consider in seeking to promote good nutrition. For example, the school food environment is critical for promoting good nutrition in the early years of habit formation. In this section, we examine key indicators of the food environment in Asia and the Pacific, and the influence of major drivers (urbanization and trade) on food environments.

Food Availability

Food availability has increased across Asia and the Pacific over the past 40 years, with concomitant reductions in food insecurity. However, dietary changes have also been associated with the "nutrition transition," in which traditional diets are replaced by higher-energy diets with increased dietary risk factors for diet-related NCDs. Per capita calorie availability has risen across the region in the past 40 years. Among the 34 developing member economies of the Asian Development Bank (ADB) for which food balance sheet data[15] are available, the supply of calories now exceeds 2,500 calories per capita per day in all except Cambodia, Timor-Leste, Maldives, Solomon Islands, Mongolia, Afghanistan, Tajikistan, and Pakistan (Figure 7.2).

The predominant staples in the region are rice and wheat, except in the Pacific islands, where starchy root crops remain significant (Figure 7.2). Diets have diversified away from staples in many countries, which reflects rising affluence and urbanization across the region.[16] For example, in the People's Republic of China (PRC), diet quality improved between 1991 and 2011 in all sociodemographic groups,[17] including for children,[18] and the contribution of staple foods to calorie intake declined by 10 percentage points (Figure 7.2). Across the region, consumption of highly polished rice and refined wheat flour is becoming increasingly the norm,[19] with consumption of fiber declining.

Since 2000, diets in Central and West Asia and Southeast Asia have seen the greatest diversification away from staple foods. Diversification has included the increasing consumption of animal source foods, including meat consumption, particularly poultry and pork, which has risen across the region.[20] With this diversification has come increased availability of animal and vegetable fats, which contribute more than 15% of available calories in Pakistan; Kazakhstan; Taipei,China; the Republic of Korea (ROK); Fiji; and Malaysia (Figure 7.2). Sales of vegetable oils (i.e., palm, coconut, and blended vegetable oil) are rapidly increasing in the Pacific,[21] as

---

[14] C. Turner et al. 2018. Concepts and Critical Perspectives for Food Environment Research: A Global Framework with Implications for Action in Low- and Middle-Income Countries. *Global Food Security*. 18. pp. 93–101.

[15] Food availability data provides an indication of the food supply, although it may underestimate the availability of processed (particularly imported processed) foods, which contribute significantly to fat, salt, and sugar intakes. It is also likely to be higher than actual consumption, because of losses and wastage at the point of consumption. Generally, food balance sheets are constructed for primary crops, livestock, and fish commodities up to the first stage of processing in the case of crops and to the second (and sometimes the third) stage of processing in the case of livestock and fish products. See FAO. http://www.fao.org/economic/ess/fbs/ess-fbs02/en (accessed 6 April 2020).

[16] C.P. Timmer 2014. Food Security in Asia and the Pacific: The Rapidly Changing Role of Rice. *Asia & the Pacific Policy Studies*. 1 (1). pp. 73–90.

[17] Z. Wang et al. 2017. Sociodemographic Disparity in the Diet Quality Transition among Chinese Adults from 1991 to 2011. *European Journal of Clinical Nutrition*. 71 (4). pp. 486–493.

[18] G. Cheng et al. 2016. Development of a Dietary Index to Assess Overall Diet Quality for Chinese School-Aged Children: The Chinese Children Dietary Index. *Journal of the Academy of Nutrition and Dietetics*. 116 (4). pp. 608–617.

[19] J.M. Awika. 2011. Major Cereal Grains Production and Use around the World, in *Advances in Cereal Science: Implications to Food Processing and Health Promotion*. ACS Publications.

[20] J. Jakobsen and A. Hansen. 2020. Geographies of Meatification: An Emerging Asian Meat Complex. *Globalizations*. 17 (1). pp. 93–109; and A.B. Milford et al. 2019. Drivers of Meat Consumption. *Appetite*. 141: 104313.

[21] K. Sievert et al. 2019. Processed Foods and Nutrition Transition in the Pacific: Regional Trends, Patterns and Food System Drivers. *Nutrients*. 11 (6).

well as in Asia,[22] with Malaysia being a country of particular concern (footnote 22). Consumption of sugar has also risen across the region, particularly in South Asia, Southeast Asia, and the Pacific.[23] Diets high in sugar are associated with an increased risk of dental cavities, which is also creating a significant health burden across the region.[24] Since 2000, sugar intake has risen in all populations, mainly in line with overall increases in calorie intakes, although a notable increase of 4% in the contribution of sugar to calorie intake occurred in Thailand, Cambodia, and Fiji (Figure 7.2). Consumption of processed and fast food, particularly foods high in salt, fat, and sugar, has increased across the region. Euromonitor data indicate that processed food sales have increased

Figure 7.2 **Total Calorie Availability by Subregion, 2000 and 2017**
(calories per capita per day)

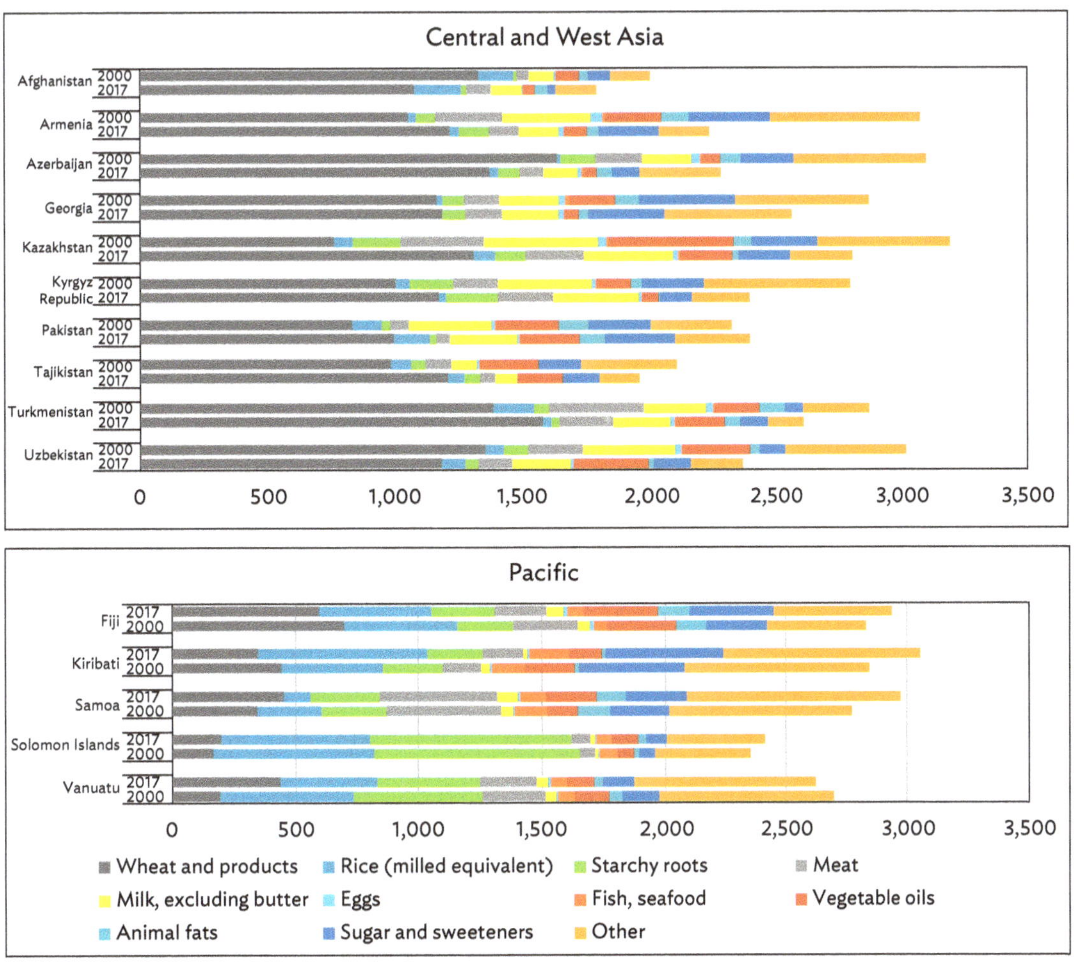

(Continued)

[22] P. Baker and S. Friel. 2016. Food Systems Transformations, Ultra-processed Food Markets and the Nutrition Transition in Asia. *Globalization and Health*. 12 (1): 80.

[23] N.I. Lipoeto, K. Geok Lin, and I. Angeles-Agdeppa. 2013. Food Consumption Patterns and Nutrition Transition in South-East Asia. *Public Health Nutrition*. 16 (9). pp. 1637–1643; and J.A. Santos et al. 2019. Contribution of Fat, Sugar and Salt to Diets in the Pacific Islands: A Systematic Review. *Public Health Nutrition*. 22 (10). pp. 1858–1871.

[24] M.M. Almoudi et al. 2019. Dental Caries and Vitamin D Status in Children in Asia. *Pediatrics International*. 61 (4). pp. 327–338.

Figure 7.2 *(Continued)*

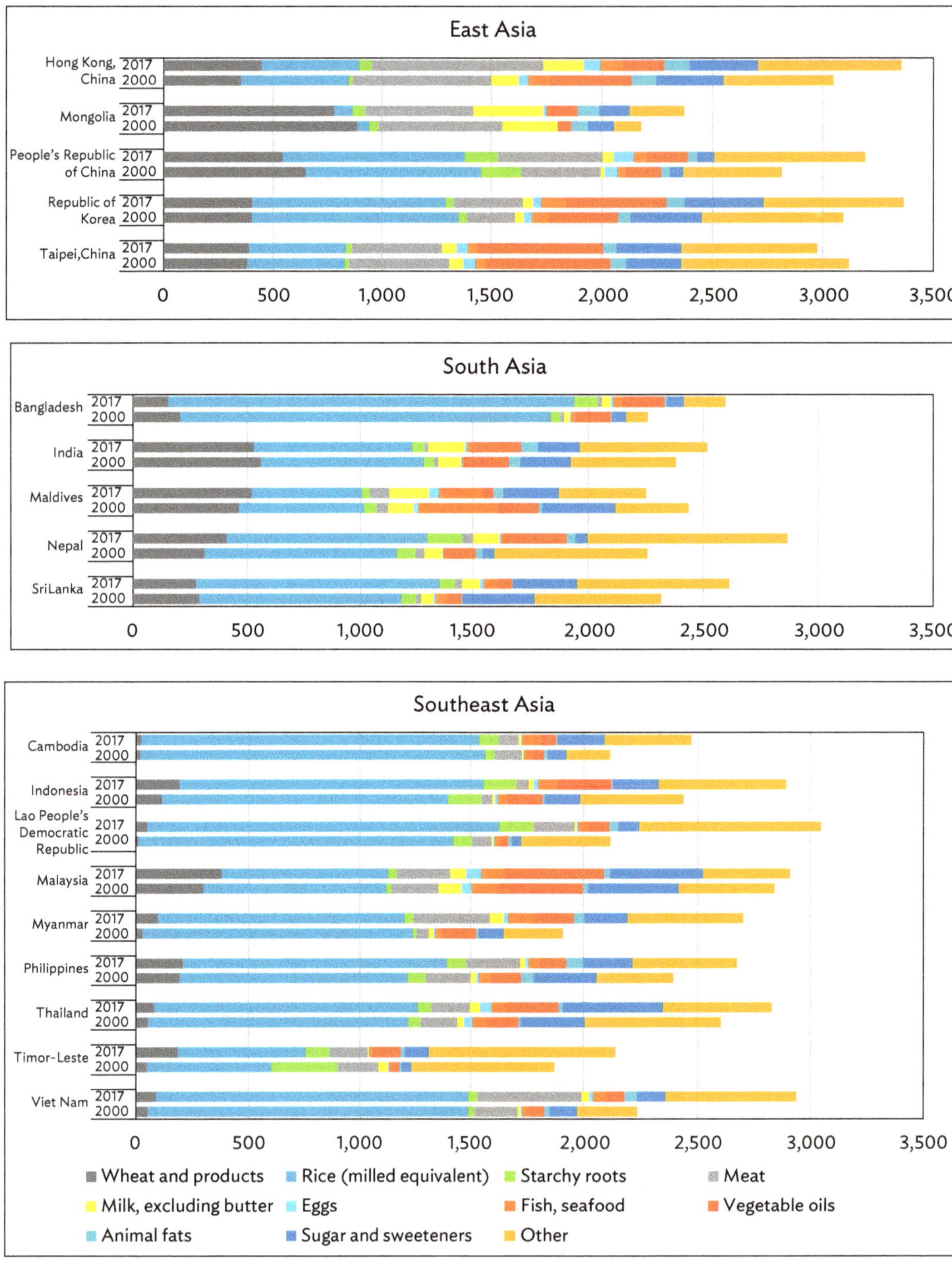

Source: Food and Agriculture Organization of the United Nations. FAOSTAT data. http://www.fao.org/faostat/en/#data (accessed 10 March 2020).

Note: The economies included are those in the region for which 2017 Food and Agriculture Organization Food Balance Sheet data are available.

rapidly throughout Asia and the Pacific, particularly in middle-income countries. Major types of processed foods consumed in Asia include instant noodles and soft drinks (footnote 22).

The Global Burden of Disease (GBD) study in 2017 found low intake of all types of healthy food in all 21 GBD regions. However, two exceptions were high intakes of vegetables in Central Asia and legumes in South Asia.[25]

Figure 7.3 **Fruit, Vegetable, and Pulse Availability, by Subregion, 2000 and 2017**
(kilograms per capita per year)

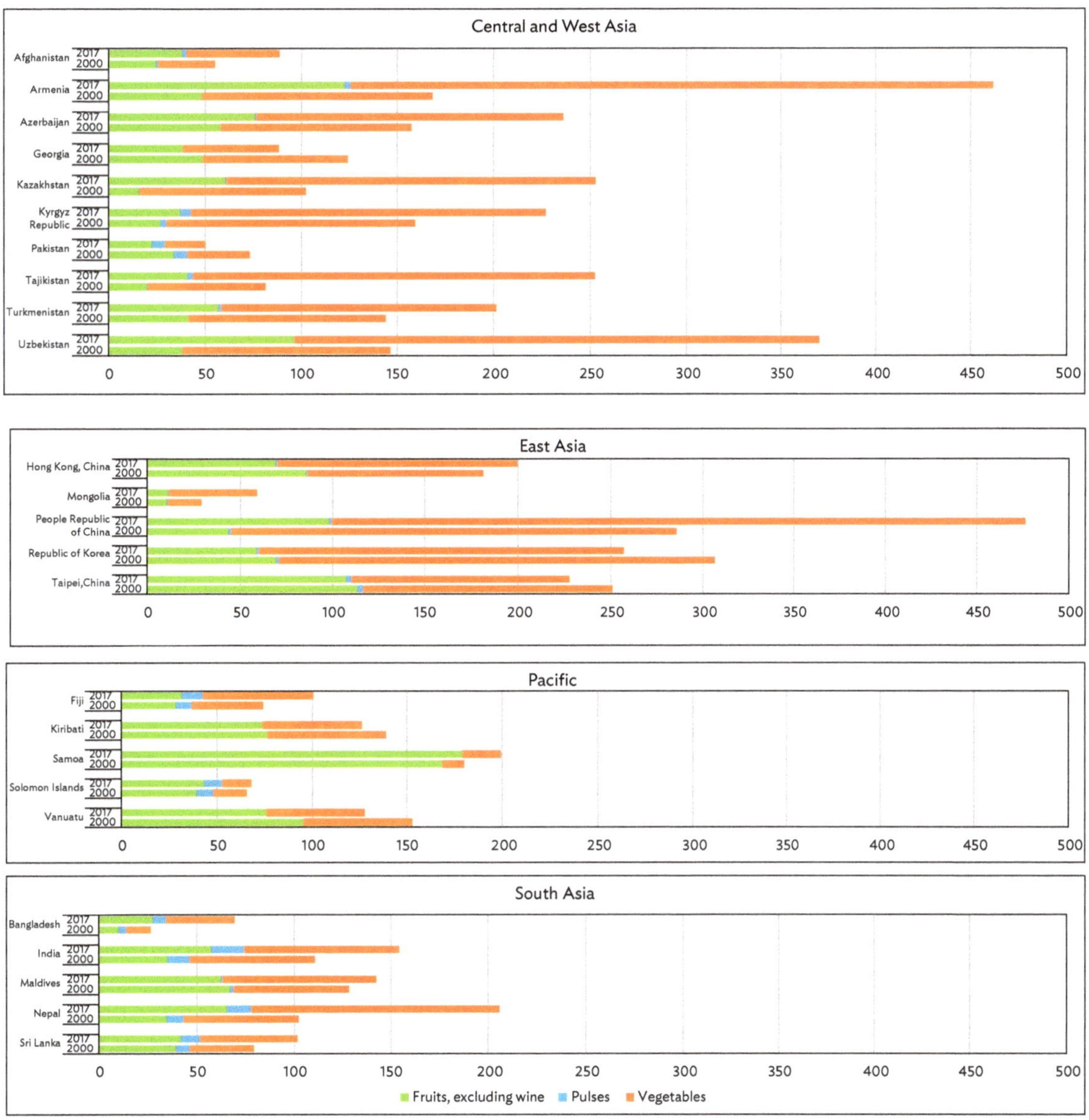

(Continued)

[25] A. Afshin et al. 2019. Health Effects of Dietary Risks in 195 Countries, 1990–2017: A Systematic Analysis for the Global Burden of Disease Study 2017. *The Lancet*. 393 (10184). pp. 1958–1972.

Figure 7.3 *(Continued)*

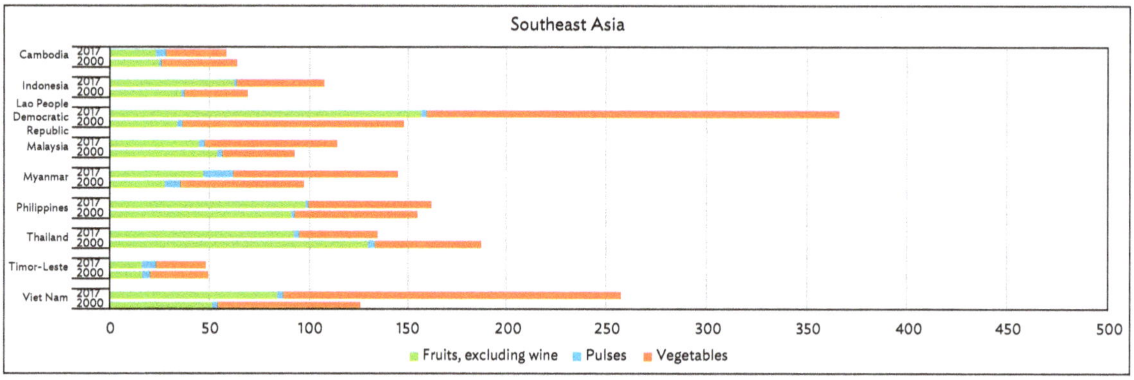

Note: The economies included are those in the region for which 2017 Food and Agriculture Organization Food Balance Sheet Data are available.

Source: Food and Agriculture Organization of the United Nations. FAOSTAT data. http://www.fao.org/faostat/en/#data (accessed 10 March 2020).

Food availability data show that availability of fruits, vegetables, and pulses varies widely, but availability is particularly high in Central and West Asia, as well as East Asia (Figure 7.3). Since 2000, availability has increased for all economies except Pakistan; Georgia; Taipei,China; Timor-Leste; and Cambodia. This low availability is supported by evidence that shows insufficient consumption across the region.[26] In the PRC, 60% of children in a 2009 survey consumed inadequate amounts of fruits and vegetables according to the Chinese Dietary Guidelines.[27] Fruit and vegetable consumption has also been reported as low in adolescents in Southeast Asia.[28]

Price Trends

The price of food in Asia and the Pacific is intimately linked to food security and nutrition, particularly for low-income populations in the region.[29] Food is a major contributor to the consumer price index, and it comprises a significant component of expenditure for poor households.[30] ADB has estimated that a 10% rise in domestic food prices in developing Asia would result in a 1.9 percentage point increase in poverty incidence, translating to an additional 64.4 million people living below the $1.25-a-day poverty line.[31] In low-income countries, stable prices for staple foods benefit not only consumers but also farmers, by reducing risk and stabilizing livelihoods.[32] Economic crises can have a significant impact on food security and nutrition through their dual impacts on food prices and on incomes.[33]

[26] K.K. Aryal et al. 2015. The Burden and Determinants of Non Communicable Diseases Risk Factors in Nepal: Findings from a Nationwide STEPS Survey. *PLOS ONE*. 10 (8).

[27] G. Cheng et al. 2016. Development of a Dietary Index to Assess Overall Diet Quality for Chinese School-Aged Children: The Chinese Children Dietary Index. *Journal of the Academy of Nutrition and Dietetics*. 116 (4). pp. 608–617.

[28] K. Peltzer and S. Pengpid. 2012. Fruits and Vegetables Consumption and Associated Factors among In-School Adolescents in Five Southeast Asian Countries. *International Journal of Environmental Research and Public Health*. 9 (10). pp. 3575–3587.

[29] FAO. 2018. *Asia and the Pacific Regional Overview of Food Security and Nutrition 2018—Accelerating Progress towards the SDGs*. Bangkok, Thailand; and ADB. 2011. *Global Food Price Inflation and Developing Asia*. Manila.

[30] F.F. Dizon and A. Herforth. 2018. *The Cost of Nutritious Food in South Asia*. Policy Research Working Paper 8557. Washington DC: World Bank.

[31] ADB. 2011. *Global Food Price Inflation and Developing Asia*. Manila.

[32] D. Dawe and P. Timmer. 2012. Why Stable Food Prices Are a Good Thing: Lessons from Stabilizing Rice Prices in Asia. *Global Food Security*. 1 (2). pp. 127–133.

[33] H.J. Brinkman et al. 2009. High Food Prices and the Global Financial Crisis Have Reduced Access to Nutritious Food and Worsened Nutritional Status and Health. *The Journal of Nutrition*. 140 (1). pp. 153S–161S.

Although the prices of rice and wheat have risen since 2010 in the region, the inflation-adjusted prices have remained fairly constant over this time, indicating minimal real price increases.[34] However, it is important to note that price and market shocks often have a greater impact on urban households than on rural households in the region because urban households rely more on the market for food and other services (footnote 29). A recent World Bank analysis found that the nutritious food price index increases faster than the consumer price index, and that this can be exacerbated during lean or "hungry" seasons.[35] Historical analyses suggest that, as the cost of staple food in the region declined following the green revolution, some populations experienced decreased dietary diversity as production of traditional crops, leafy vegetables, and fish declined, and they became relatively more expensive.[36]

Food Safety

In 2019, the emergence of a novel coronavirus in a wet market in the PRC drew global attention to potential human risks associated with food safety and informal food markets. There is widespread recognition of an increased risk of infectious human diseases originating from animals as a result of expanding human habitation and climate change; 60%–70% of newly emerged diseases have come from animals.[37] Food safety principles of water, sanitation, and hygiene are key underlying drivers of nutrition and are pivotal to reversing malnutrition (footnote 29). Most Asia and Pacific countries are members of the Codex Alimentarius Commission (the United Nations body that develops food safety standards) and have developed national food safety standards—for example, India's Food Safety and Standards Act 2006 and the Food Safety Act 2013 of the Philippines. Adoption of food standards has also been encouraged by increasing trade; the World Trade Organization Agreement on Sanitary and Phytosanitary Measures references the Codex Alimentarius.[38]

However, the burden of foodborne disease in Asia and the Pacific remains high. Despite rising awareness among consumers and adoption of food safety standards by governments, capacity for enforcement remains low in many countries.[39] Together with sub-Saharan Africa, Asia has the highest incidence of foodborne disease and resultant deaths, leading to productivity loss estimated at $63.1 billion.[40] Food-borne diseases in Asia are primarily due to microbial hazards during food preparation and food storage; primary sources include animal products, fruits, and vegetables, including fish in some parts of Asia (for example, raw or partially cooked fish is common in Southeast Asia and the PRC) (footnote 40). Another source of concern is the informal food retail sector, particularly wet markets, where hygiene and waste disposal can be challenging (footnote 29).

---

34 FAO. 2016. *Asia Pacific Food Price and Policy Monitor Issue 33*. FAO Regional Office for Asia and the Pacific.

35 F.F. Dizon and A. Herforth. 2018. *The Cost of Nutritious Food in South Asia*. Policy Research Working Paper 8557. Washington DC: World Bank.

36 D. Glover and N. Poole. 2019. Principles of Innovation to Build Nutrition-Sensitive Food Systems in South Asia. *Food Policy*. 82. pp. 63–73.

37 FAO Regional Office for Asia and the Pacific. 2014. *Improving Food Safety Standards in Asia Requires Parallel Action on Improving Regional Food Security*.

38 S. Kathuria. 2018. *A Glass Half Full: The Promise of Regional Trade in South Asia*. Washington DC: World Bank.

39 D.L. Ortega and D.L. Tschirley. 2017. Demand for Food Safety in Emerging and Developing Countries. *Journal of Agribusiness in Developing and Emerging Economies*; and WHO. 2018. *Codex Standards in the WHO South-East Asia Region*. New Delhi: World Health Organization, Regional Office for South-East Asia.

40 S. Jaffee et al. 2019. *The Safe Food Imperative: Accelerating Progress in Low- and Middle-Income Countries*. Agriculture and Food Series. Washington, DC: World Bank.

Urbanization

More than half of the global population now live in cities, and this is expected to reach two-thirds by 2050, with the majority of the increase in low- and middle-income countries (LMICs).[41] Asia has the highest rate of urbanization in the world, and it is estimated that India and the PRC alone will account for 28% of the world's urban population growth by 2050.[42] Urban food environments in the region have several prominent features, which have both strengths and limitations from a nutritional point of view. These include a diverse food market; high availability of processed foods high in fat, salt, and sugar; and an abundance of pre-prepared food (both healthy and unhealthy) to be purchased outside of the home.

In urban areas, a diverse range of places to acquire food is on offer. These include supermarkets, open-market vendors, informal street vendors, and restaurants.[43] Wet markets selling fresh food are a vital food source. For example, in Thailand, shopping in fresh markets is associated with increased vegetable consumption.[44] However, income affects where and how food is sourced. The urban poor are especially vulnerable to challenges in consuming a nutritious diet because of lack of access to cash to purchase adequate food. Those with very low incomes tend to acquire food from smaller retail spaces such as local shops, and often source food from fairs, street vendors, and hawkers, which are usually part of the informal food market. The urban poor often need to travel long distances, incurring additional expenses, to overcrowded retail markets or street stalls where hygiene, drainage, clean water, and waste disposal are often insufficient. In contrast, consumers with middle or high incomes often shop at modern supermarkets, which tend to be conveniently located and offer a diverse range of foods. Often these stores offer foods in bulk for a lower price than smaller stores, and those with suitable transportation can access this source of affordable food. Those with higher incomes also purchase a significant amount of pre-prepared foods such as those from convenience stores, restaurants, and street vendors (footnote 44).

Urban diets in the region tend to contain more calorie-dense, low-nutrient foods, which are often higher in salt, fat, and sugar than rural diets.[45] Many factors contribute to this, including convenience and affordability, and more intense marketing in urban areas. Busy urban lifestyles and long working hours mean urban households tend to seek pre-prepared foods from sources including convenience stores and street vendors (footnote 44). There has been a "supermarket revolution" in the region over recent decades. The types of foods available in supermarkets also have a strong influence on urban diets: on the positive side, they offer a diverse range of nutritious foods; however, they are also a strong contributor to selling and promoting unhealthy foods.[46]

[41] J. Graziano da Silva and S. Fan. 2017. Smallholders and Urbanization: Strengthening Rural-Urban Linkages to End Hunger and Malnutrition. In *2017 Global Food Policy Report*. Washington, DC: International Food Policy Research Institute. pp. 14–23. https://doi.org/10.2499/9780896292529_02.

[42] UN DESA. 2019. *2018 Revision of the World Urbanization Prospects*. New York: Population Division of the United Nations Department of Economic and Social Affairs.

[43] FAO. 2018. *Asia and the Pacific Regional Overview of Food Security and Nutrition 2018—Accelerating Progress towards the SDGs*. Bangkok, Thailand; M.T. Ruel, J.L. Garrett, and S. Yosef. 2017. Food Security and Nutrition: Growing Cities, New Challenges. In *2017 Global Food Policy Report*. Washington, DC: International Food Policy Research Institute. pp. 24–33. https://doi.org/10.2499/9780896292529_03; and H. Liu et al. 2015. Household Composition, Income, and Food-Away-from-Home Expenditure in Urban China. *Food Policy*. 51. pp. 97–103.

[44] C. Hawkes, J. Harris, and S. Gillespie. 2017. Changing Diets: Urbanization and the Nutrition Transition. In *2017 Global Food Policy Report*. Washington, DC: International Food Policy Research Institute. pp. 34–41. https://doi.org/10.2499/9780896292529_04.

[45] FAO. 2018. *Asia and the Pacific Regional Overview of Food Security and Nutrition 2018—Accelerating Progress towards the SDGs*. Bangkok, Thailand; M.T. Ruel, J.L. Garrett, and S. Yosef. 2017. Food Security and Nutrition: Growing Cities, New Challenges. In *2017 Global Food Policy Report*. Washington, DC: International Food Policy Research Institute. https://doi.org/10.2499/9780896292529_03. pp. 24–33; and C. Hawkes, J. Harris, and S. Gillespie. 2017. Changing Diets: Urbanization and the Nutrition Transition. In *2017 Global Food Policy Report*. Washington, DC: International Food Policy Research Institute. pp. 34–41. https://doi.org/10.2499/9780896292529_04.

[46] P. Baker and S. Friel. 2016. Food Systems Transformations, Ultra-Processed Food Markets and the Nutrition Transition in Asia. *Globalization and Health*. 12 (1): 80.

Schools

The school food environment consists of all the areas and places where food is acquired (including canteens or cafeterias, kiosks, informal food vendors, and vending machines) and consumed in schools and their immediate environment. It also takes into account the nutritional content of foods sourced from the school environment. The school food environment also encompasses all food promotion and consumer information made available, such as marketing and promotions, food labeling, and food pricing.[47] School food environments provide a critical opportunity for teaching and fostering healthy food consumption behaviors for students, for advancing nutrition and sustainable development, and for interaction with the broader community. They also provide an opportunity to provide nutritious food and clean drinking water to students.[48]

Evidence from several countries in Asia shows high availability and accessibility of unhealthy foods in school canteens and indicates that school communities (school teaching and leadership staff, parents, and students) have limited awareness about healthy food environments.[49]

Trade in Foods

Trade in foods is recognized as an upstream influence on food security and nutrition. Food production is typically more volatile than consumer demand, and trade in foods therefore can be critical to ensure food security. Domestic fluctuations in production, e.g., because of adverse weather events, can be balanced by importation of food.[50] Further, a more open trade regime allows for the cheaper importation of agricultural inputs, thereby increasing agricultural productivity. Evidence from Asia indicates that trade has contributed to food security in the region.[51] Trade data show that imports into ADB developing member countries have risen dramatically since the mid-1990s, with a greater increase in imports from the rest of the world compared with regional trade since 2011 (Figure 7.4).

Opening food trade typically allows consumers to have access to a larger variety of foods and to cheaper calories. Existing evidence suggests that trade in foods indeed has helped to improve dietary quality and reduce undernutrition.[52] For example, rising incomes and trade openness helped to increase dietary diversity in 26 post-Communist countries of Eastern Europe and Central Asia for the period 1996–2013, during which time trade reforms triggered growth in trade flows and foreign direct investment, which in turn affected food systems in these countries.[53] Analysis of "indicator" commodity imports into the region shows that all subregions had an increase in imports of healthy foods (Figure 7.5). The greatest increase occurred in Central Asia, with a sevenfold increase between 2003 and 2018, and with concomitant increases in the value of healthy food imports. Unhealthy food imports also increased in all subregions (Figure 7.5). The increase was particularly strong in South Asia and Southeast Asia. In Central Asia, unhealthy food imports almost

---

[47] FAO. *Health*[y] *Food Environment and School Food*. 2020. http://www.fao.org/school-food/areas-work/food-environment/en; and FAO. 2019. *School Food and Nutrition Framework*.

[48] FAO. 2019. *School Food and Nutrition Framework*.

[49] P. Sharma, S.S. Yadav, and K. Menon. 2019. A Review of the Nutritional Quality of School Canteen Foods in South Asia. *Indian Journal of Public Health Research & Development*. 10 (7). pp. 1600–1606.

[50] As Burgess and Donaldson show, in the case of India, connecting a district to the national railway network almost completely eliminated famines in that region. R. Burgess and D. Donaldson. 2010. Can Openness Mitigate the Effects of Weather Shocks? *American Economic Review: Papers & Proceedings*. 100. pp. 449–453.

[51] K. Anderson et al. 2013. Re-examining Policies for Food Security in Asia. *Food Security*. 5 (2). pp. 195–215.

[52] S.C. García-Dorado et al. 2019. Economic Globalization, Nutrition and Health: A Review of Quantitative Evidence. *Globalization and Health*. 15 (1): 15.

[53] E. Krivonos and L. Kuhn. 2019. Trade and Dietary Diversity in Eastern Europe and Central Asia. *Food Policy*. 88: 101767.

Figure 7.4 Imports of Food by ADB Developing Member Countries from Other ADB Developing Member Countries and Rest of the World

(1996–2018, value of imports in current United States dollar)

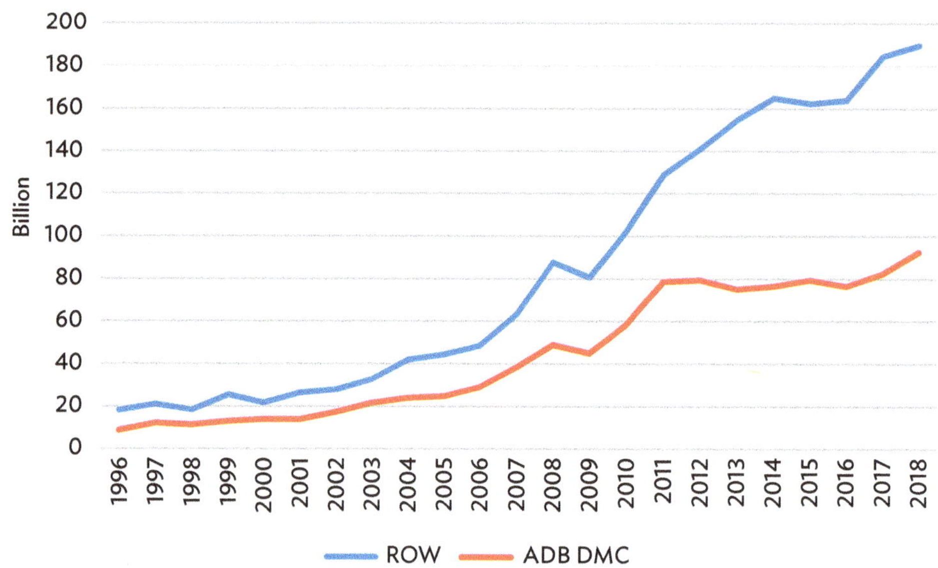

ADB = Asian Development Bank, DMC = developing member country, ROW = rest of the world.

Note: Definition of food in Harmonised System (HS) chapter (two-digit): HS 02–04, 07–12, and 15–21.

Sources: United Nations Comtrade database; authors' calculations.

stagnated, and their value steadily declined as a proportion of total imports. Staple foods (rice and flour) witnessed the least dynamic development.

Consequences: The Double Burden of Malnutrition

The double burden of malnutrition (DBM) is defined as concurrent manifestation of undernutrition (stunting, wasting, underweight, or micronutrient deficiency) with overweight or obesity (indicators of an unhealthy diet). The DBM can manifest at (i) the national level, where countries have both undernutrition and unhealthy diets prevalent among their population; (ii) the household level, where households have members with different forms of malnutrition; and (iii) the individual level, where an individual experiences multiple forms of malnutrition either concurrently (e.g., being overweight and anemic) or at different points in life.[54] There are four most known types of the DBM within the same household: (i) overweight and stunted child, (ii) overweight mother and wasted under-5 child, (iii) overweight mother and stunted under-5 child, and (iv) thin mother and overweight child.[55]

[54] A. Abdullah. 2015. The Double Burden of Undernutrition and Overnutrition in Developing Countries: An Update. *Current Obesity Reports*. 4 (3). pp. 337–349; and WHO. 2017. *The Double Burden of Malnutrition: Policy Brief*. Geneva: World Health Organization.

[55] B.M. Popkin, C. Corvalan, and L.M. Grummer-Strawn. 2019. Dynamics of the Double Burden of Malnutrition and the Changing Nutrition Reality. *The Lancet*. 395 (10217). pp. 65–74.

Figure 7.5 **Imports of Indicator Foods, Volume, and Value, by ADB Subregion**

Note: Indicator foods defined according S. Friel et al. 2013. Monitoring the Impacts of Trade Agreements on Food Environments. *Obesity Reviews*. 14. pp. 120–134. Healthy foods include fresh fruits and vegetables, including staple root crops, pulses, nuts, seeds, and staple whole-grain cereal. Unhealthy foods include fatty meat, energy-dense beverages, savory ready-to-eat snacks and meals, sweet snacks, sugars, and other caloric sweeteners.

Sources: United Nations Comtrade database; authors' calculations.

In the Marshall Islands, for example, a quarter of households have a stunted child with an overweight or obese mother (footnote 29). In India, the proportion of households with an underweight child and an overweight mother increased from 4% to 5% in rural India and from 6% to 8% in urban India between 2004 and 2012.[56] In this section of the chapter, we will focus on the DBM at the national level within the region.

Child Nutrition

Underweight (low weight-for-age), stunting (low height-for-age), and wasting (low weight-for-height) are the main measures of child undernutrition, and all have serious health consequences. There have been some reductions in undernutrition in the region, but it remains a significant challenge.[57] Major drivers of stunting in the region have been identified as poor dietary quality and quantity for children under 2 years of age, and poor maternal nutrition (before and during pregnancy) (footnote 61). Data from the Global Health Observatory for the region indicate that the highest prevalence of stunting, wasting, and underweight was found in South Asia, closely followed by Southeast Asia (Figure 7.6 and Figure 7.7). In some countries with high levels of stunting, including Bhutan, Pakistan, and Timor-Leste, it has also been found that up to half of overweight children are also stunted (footnote 29).

All subregions were observed to have a higher prevalence of stunting in children under 5 years, compared with wasting (Figure 7.6).

In almost all countries in the region for which data are available, the prevalence of child underweight and overweight indicates the presence of a DBM (Figure 7.7). In South Asia and Southeast Asia, the prevalence of underweight in children under 5 years is higher than the prevalence of overweight[58] (Figure 7.7). Among older children aged 5–9, overweight has risen across the region (Figure 7.8). The highest prevalence of child overweight is observed in the Pacific, as well as the most substantial increases between 2010 and 2016. The three individual countries showing the highest prevalence are from the Pacific: Nauru (67%), followed by Palau and the Cook Islands (66%). Southeast Asia also experienced a substantial increase in prevalence between 2010 and 2016, and is the second leading subregion.

Overweight and Obesity among Adults

Data from the Global Health Observatory indicate that overweight among adults (defined as a body mass index greater than 25, and greater than 30 for obesity) has increased across the region since 2010 (Figure 7.9). The highest prevalence is observed in the Pacific, followed by Central and West Asia. Countries with the highest prevalence are in the Pacific: Nauru (89%), followed by Palau (85%) and the Cook Islands (85%). However, the prevalence of overweight is also more than 50% in all other Pacific island countries for which data are available, as well as Mongolia, Armenia, Georgia, Azerbaijan, Turkmenistan, and Kazakhstan (Figure 7.9). South Asian countries show the lowest prevalence of overweight, ranging from 20% to 31% in 2016. Across Asia and the Pacific, those in urban

[56] A. Dang and J.V. Meenakshi. 2018. Chapter 1: The Nutrition Transition and the Intra-Household Double Burden of Malnutrition in India. In *Wealthy but Unhealthy: Overweight and Obesity in Asia and the Pacific: Trends, Costs, and Policies for Better Health*. Tokyo: Asian Development Bank Institute.

[57] H. Torlesse and V.M. Aguayo. 2018. Aiming Higher for Maternal and Child Nutrition in South Asia. *Maternal & Child Nutrition*. 14 (S4): e12739; and FAO. 2018. *Asia and the Pacific Regional Overview of Food Security and Nutrition 2018—Accelerating Progress towards the SDGs*. Bangkok, Thailand.

[58] Overweight for children and adolescents is defined according to WHO growth reference.

Figure 7.6 **Prevalence of Stunting and Wasting in Children under 5, by Subregion**

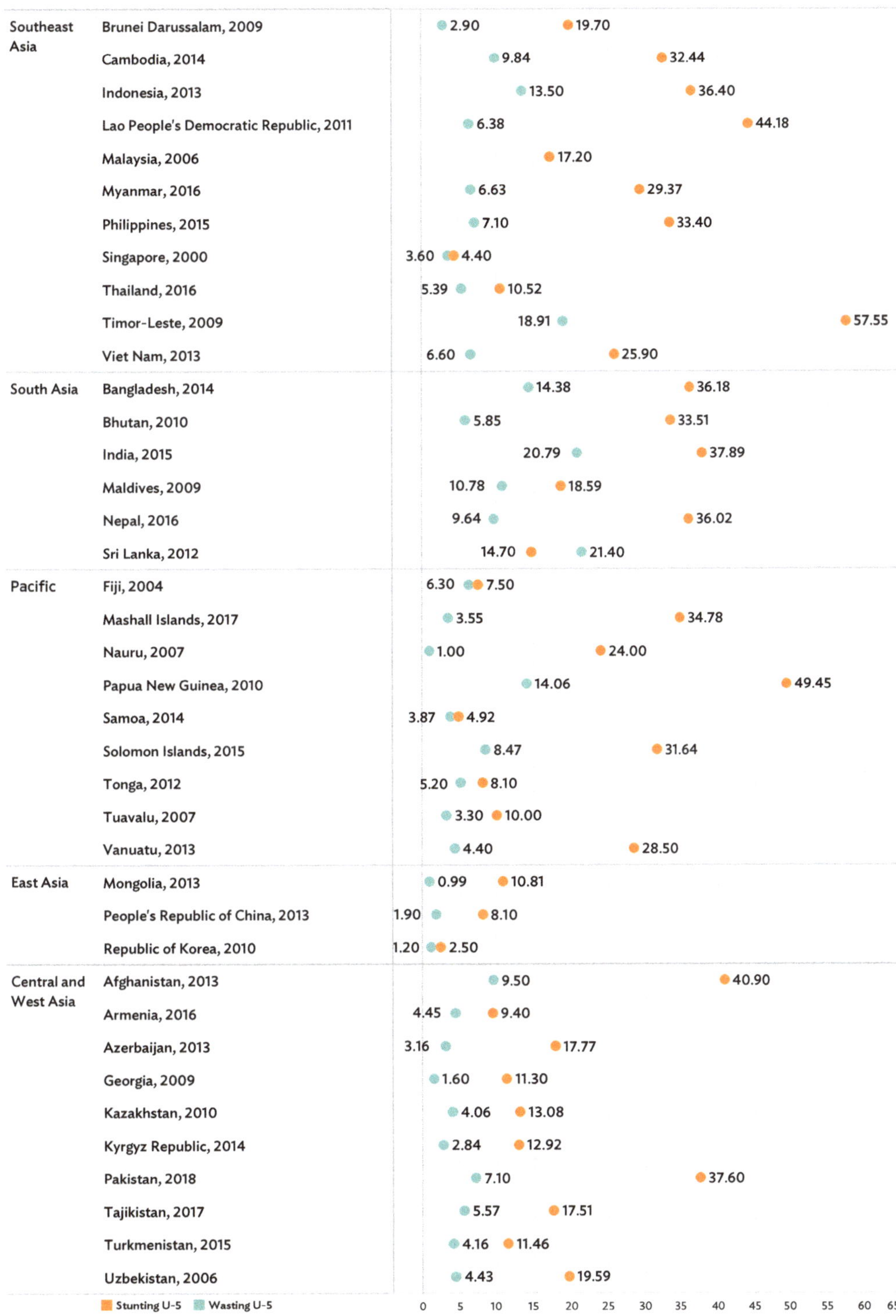

U-5 = under 5.

Source: Global Health Observatory.

Figure 7.7 Prevalence of Overweight and Underweight in Children under 5, by Subregion

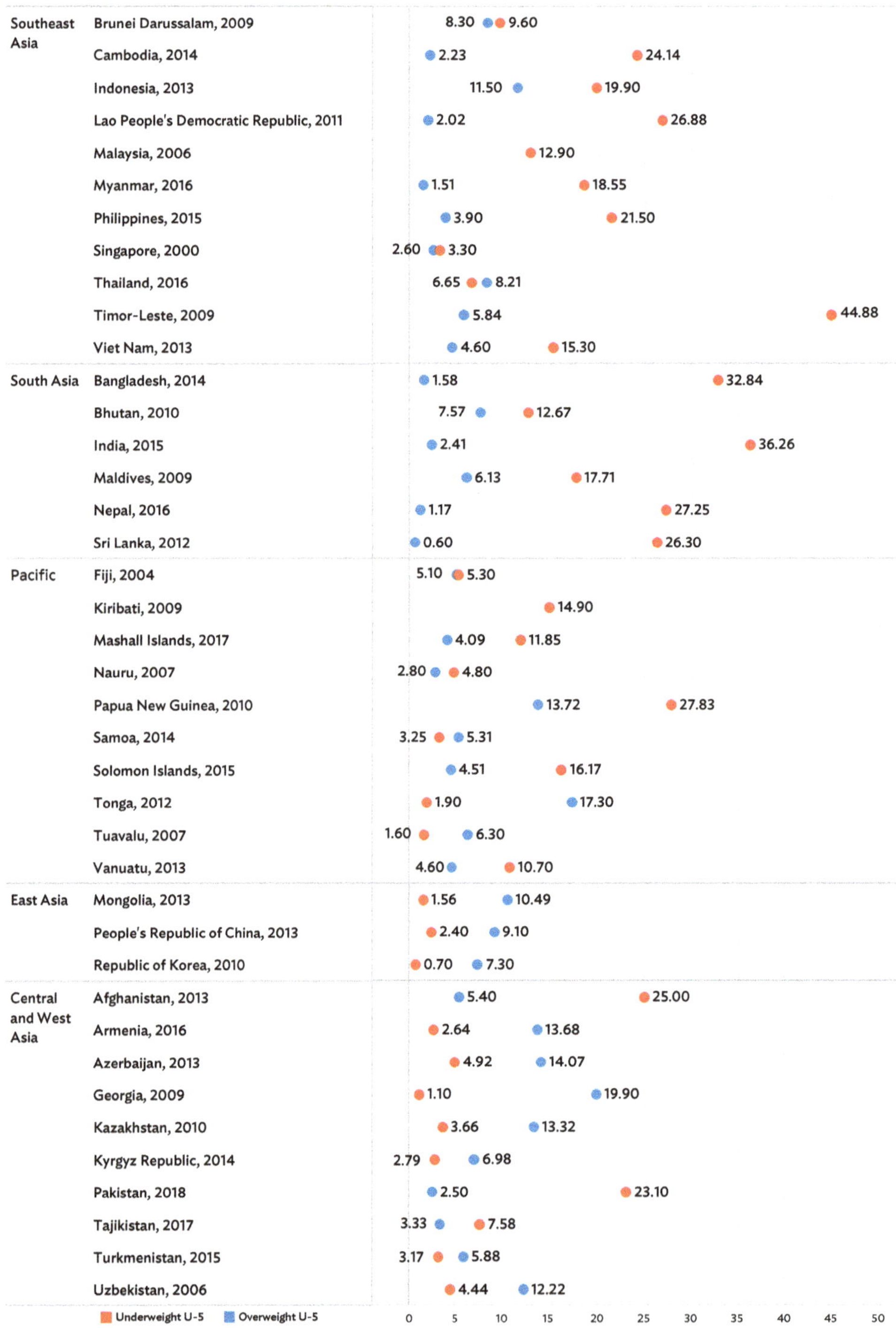

U-5 = under 5.

Source: Global Health Observatory.

Figure 7.8 **Prevalence of Overweight (Including Obesity) in Children Ages 5–9, by Subregion**

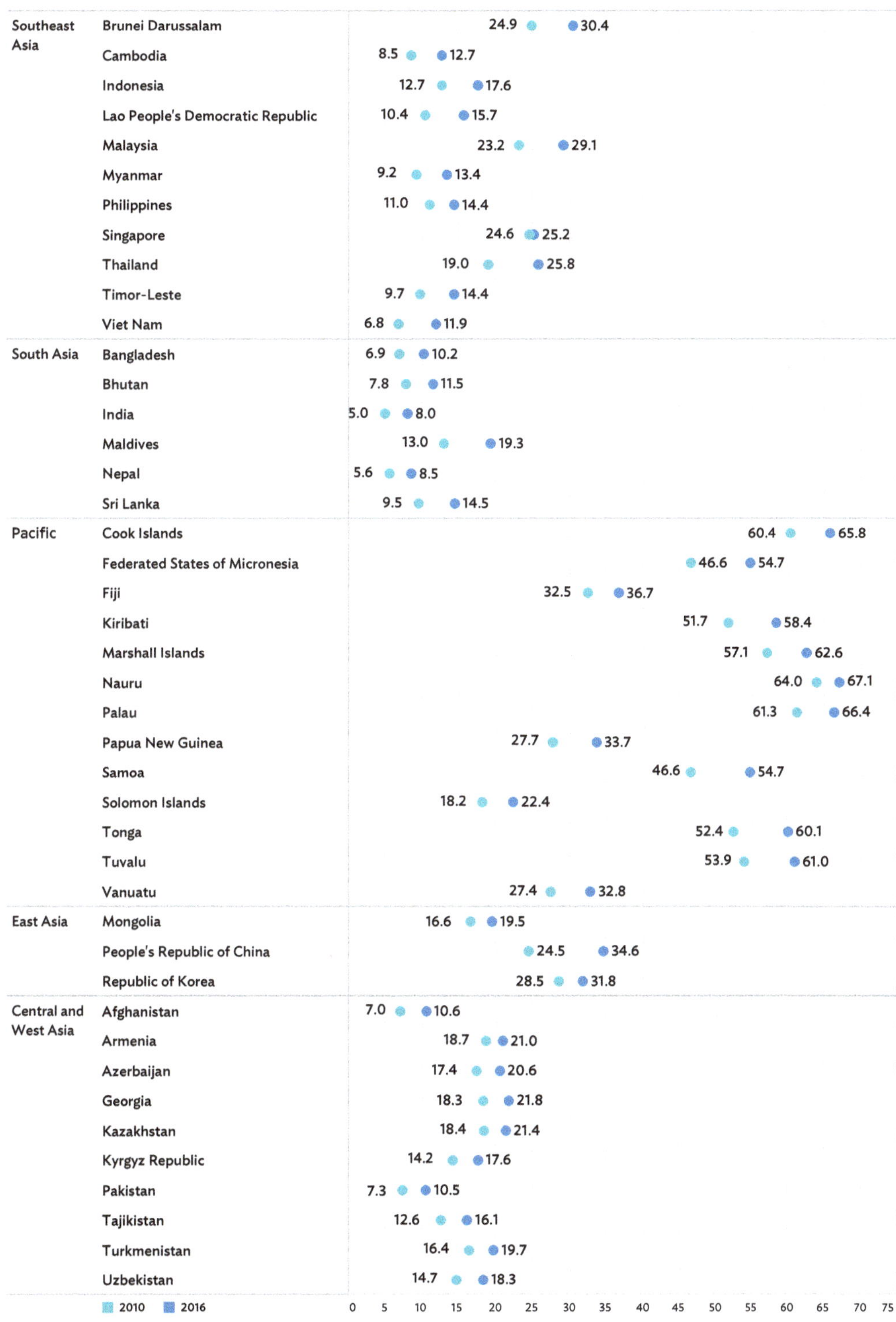

Source: Global Health Observatory.

Figure 7.9 Prevalence of Overweight (Including Obesity) among Adults in 2010 and 2016, by Subregion

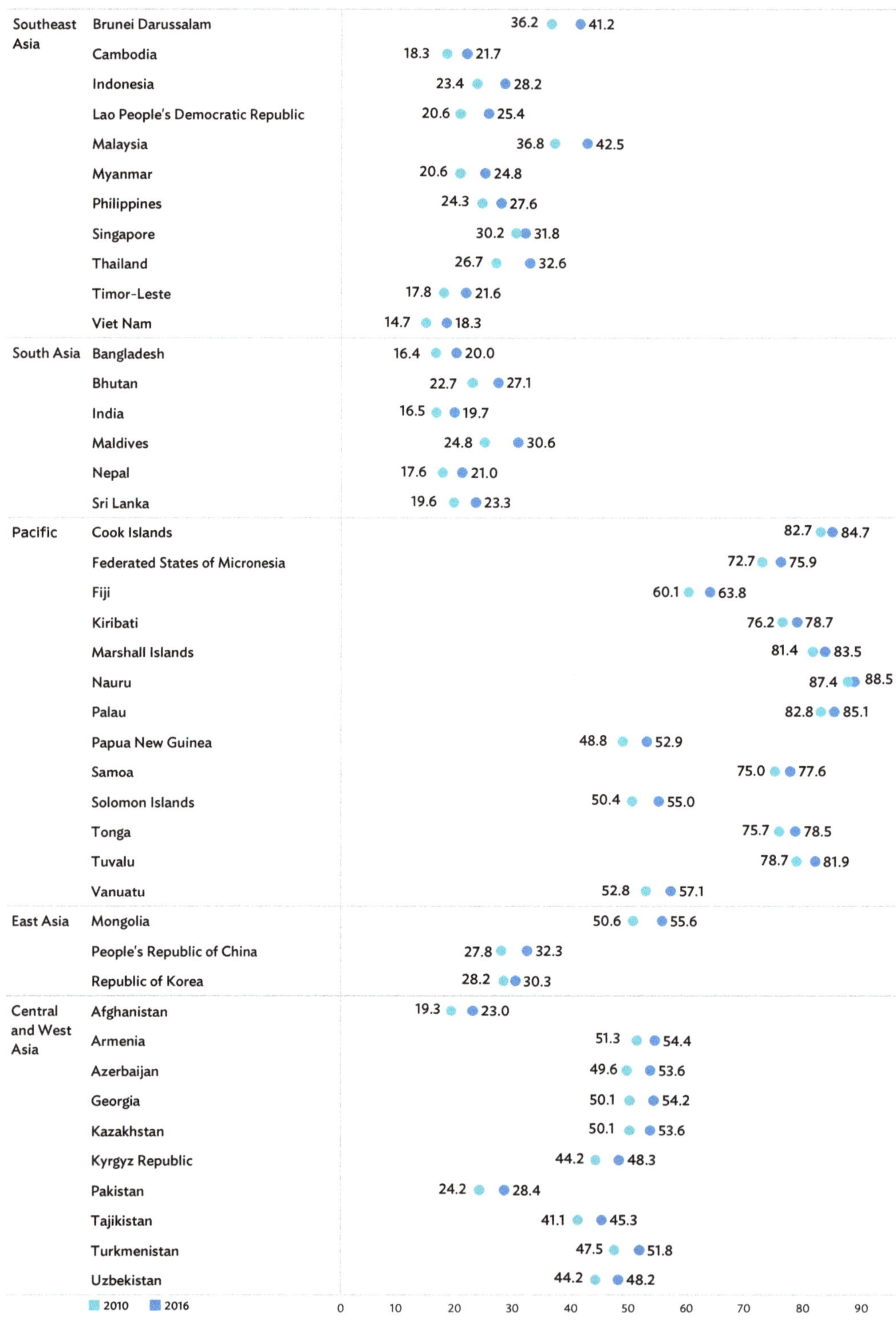

Source: Global Health Observatory.

areas are more likely to be overweight or obese than those in rural areas.[59] Gender and socioeconomic status are also associated with differential rates of overweight and obesity. Women in the region are especially at risk of overweight and obesity.[60] Across the region, higher socioeconomic status is associated with a greater likelihood of being overweight and obese. However, recent evidence shows that those with relatively low incomes are also affected. In Indonesia, a higher (and rising) prevalence of overweight and obesity has been consistently observed in higher-income households between 1993 and 2014. However, the rate of increase of obesity among disadvantaged groups was higher compared with higher-income households throughout this period.[61]

Micronutrient Deficiencies

Micronutrient deficiencies are a significant concern in the region because they are associated with poor birth outcomes for both mothers and babies, as well as impaired physical and cognitive development (footnote 29). The prevalence of micronutrient deficiencies has risen in most countries, and the region is unlikely to meet WHO 2025 targets. In Asia and the Pacific, it has been estimated that about 400 million women of reproductive age are anemic. Data from the global health observatory show that countries in Southeast Asia experienced the most substantial increase in prevalence of anemia between 2010 and 2016 (Figure 7.10). However, countries in South Asia and Central and West Asia have the highest prevalence of anemia overall. Some improvements are also evident. Bangladesh, Bhutan, India, Nepal, the Philippines, Sri Lanka, and Uzbekistan experienced decreases in prevalence of anemia between 2010 and 2016.

Vitamin deficiencies are also highly prevalent in the region. Inadequate intakes of vitamin A, riboflavin, and vitamin B_{12} are significant in South Asia, particularly for Bangladesh, India, and Sri Lanka.[62] These vitamins are critical for immune function, vision, and healthy pregnancy.

Health Consequences of Malnutrition

Undernutrition, either in children or adults, has serious consequences. In adults, underweight might lead to complications in pregnancy, intrauterine growth retardation, and death.[63] Children affected by wasting tend to have low-immune-system functioning and are more prone to developmental delays, with a heightened risk of morbidity and mortality.[64] Stunted children have higher rates of morbidity and mortality, are more prone to infectious diseases, and have less optimal development of their cognitive, motor, and language functioning.[65]

---

59 NCD Risk Factor Collaboration. 2019. Rising Rural Body-Mass Index Is the Main Driver of the Global Obesity Epidemic in Adults. *Nature*. 569 (7755): 260.

60 T. Biswas et al. 2017. Increasing Prevalence of Overweight and Obesity in Bangladeshi Women of Reproductive Age: Findings from 2004 to 2014. *PLOS ONE*. 12 (7).

61 T. Aizawa and M. Helble. 2017. Socioeconomic Inequality in Excessive Body Weight in Indonesia. *Economics & Human Biology*. 27. pp. 315–327.

62 H.E. Mark et al. 2016. Estimating Dietary Micronutrient Supply and the Prevalence of Inadequate Intakes from National Food Balance Sheets in the South Asia Region. *Asia Pacific Journal of Clinical Nutrition*. 25 (2). pp. 368–376.

63 R.E. Black et al. 2013. Maternal and Child Undernutrition and Overweight in Low-Income and Middle-Income Countries. *The Lancet*. 382 (9890). pp. 427–451.

64 WHO. 2020. *UNICEF/WHO/The World Bank Group Joint Child Malnutrition Estimates: Levels and Trends in Child Malnutrition: Key Findings of the 2020 Edition*.

65 R.E. Black et al. 2013. Maternal and Child Undernutrition and Overweight in Low-Income and Middle-Income Countries. *The Lancet*. 382 (9890). pp. 427–451; and A.L. Sawaya et al. 1998. Mild Stunting Is Associated with Higher Susceptibility to the Effects of High Fat Diets: Studies in a Shantytown Population in Sao Paulo, Brazil. *The Journal of Nutrition*. 128 (2). pp. 415S–420S.

Figure 7.10 **Prevalence of Anemia among Women of Reproductive Age (15–49), by Subregion**

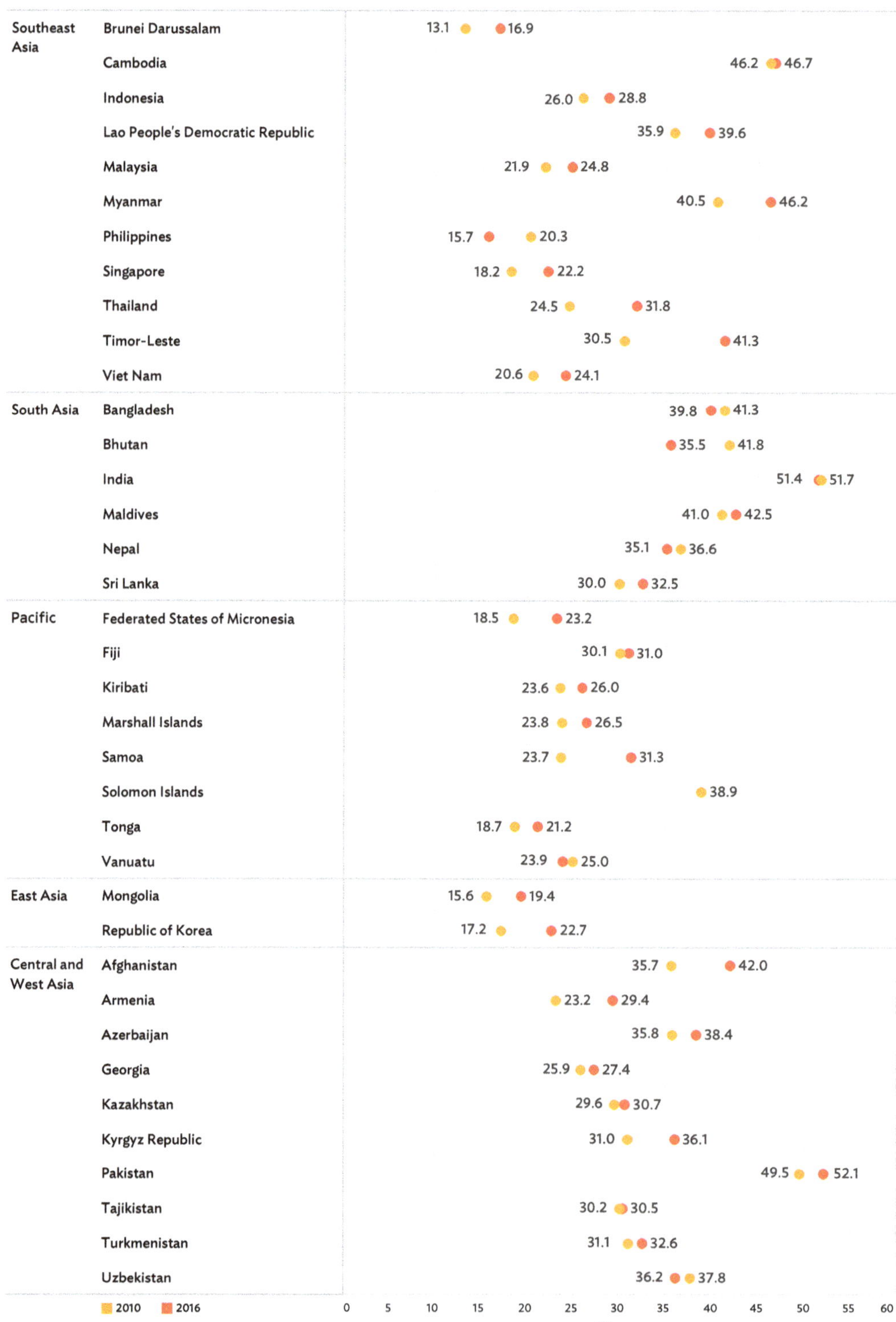

Source: Global Health Observatory, years 2010 and 2016.

Unhealthy diets are associated with increased risk of major diet-related NCDs, including type 2 diabetes mellitus (diabetes) and cardiovascular disease (CVD). Unhealthy dietary patterns, together with overweight and obesity, are major risk factors for the development of type 2 diabetes.[66] Evidence is also mounting for the increased risk arising from intrauterine undernutrition and overnutrition (i.e., during pregnancy) for development of NCDs in later life.[67] For example, fetal exposure to malnutrition during the 1959–1961 Great Chinese Famine had long-lasting impacts on physical health, including the risks of suffering a stroke, as well as physical disabilities in speech, walking, and vision.[68]

In 2017, the Global Burden of Disease (GBD) study indicated that 64% of disability-adjusted life years lost in East Asia were because of NCDs as a result of CVD.[69] In South Asia, ischemic heart disease is the leading cause of death in India, Pakistan, Nepal, and Sri Lanka. In Bangladesh, NCDs caused 59% of total deaths in 2014, with CVD the leading contributor at 17%,[70] and stroke is the leading single cause of death.[71] In 2017, stroke and ischemic heart disease were also the leading causes of death at the national level in the PRC.[72] Hypertension is the leading modifiable risk factor for CVD and premature death worldwide. Diets high in salt are one of the major contributors to hypertension.[73] Globally, the highest prevalence of hypertension among men is in Central Asia, at 39%.

Nutrition is also important for brain function and mental health. In particular, low intakes of omega-3 fatty acids are associated with an increased risk of depression, as are deficiencies in folate, vitamin B_{12}, iron, zinc, and selenium; the effects on the brain can result in apathy and depression.[74] Analysis of the effects of the 1959–1961 Great Chinese Famine found that fetal exposure to malnutrition reduced measures of mental acuity even half a century after the tragic event (footnote 73). Childhood undernutrition and maternal malnutrition also impair immune development,[75] and are associated with an increased risk of infection, particularly in developing countries.[76] Studies in developed countries suggest that infection risk is also increased in obese children and adolescents. In addition, this immune dysfunction also contributes to higher morbidity and mortality associated with malnutrition (footnote 80).

Economic Consequences of Unhealthy Diets and Malnutrition

In addition to the consequences that malnutrition has for populations in terms of health, it also impacts the health-care system, education, and human capital. In Asia and the Pacific, of particular concern are the costs of the high stunting prevalence among children, which is associated with "increased mortality, increased morbidity (in childhood and later as adults), decreased cognitive ability, poor educational outcomes, lost earnings and

[66] A.P. Hills et al. 2018. Epidemiology and Determinants of Type 2 Diabetes in South Asia. *The Lancet Diabetes & Endocrinology*.

[67] A.P. Hills et al. 2018. Epidemiology and Determinants of Type 2 Diabetes in South Asia. *The Lancet Diabetes & Endocrinology*; and J.C. Wells, et al. 2019. The Double Burden of Malnutrition: Aetiological Pathways and Consequences for Health. *The Lancet*. 395 (10217). pp. 75–88.

[68] S. Kim, B. Fleisher, and J.Y. Sun. 2017. The Long-term Health Effects of Fetal Malnutrition: Evidence from the 1959–1961 China Great Leap Forward Famine. *Health Economics*. 26 (10). pp. 1264–1277.

[69] A. Afshin et al. 2019. Health Effects of Dietary Risks in 195 Countries, 1990–2017: A Systematic Analysis for the Global Burden of Disease Study 2017. *The Lancet*. 393 (10184). pp. 1958–1972.

[70] A.M. Islam, A. Mohibullah, and T. Paul. 2016. Cardiovascular Disease in Bangladesh: A Review. *Bangladesh Heart Journal*. 31 (2). pp. 80–99.

[71] A. Misra et al. 2017. Diabetes, Cardiovascular Disease, and Chronic Kidney Disease in South Asia: Current Status and Future Directions. *BMJ*. 357: j1420.

[72] M. Zhou et al. 2017. Mortality, Morbidity, and Risk Factors in China and Its Provinces, 1990–2017: A Systematic Analysis for the Global Burden of Disease Study 2017. *The Lancet*. 394 (10204). pp. 1145–1158.

[73] K.T. Mills, A. Stefanescu, and J. He. 2020. The Global Epidemiology of Hypertension. *Nature Reviews Nephrology*. 2020. pp. 1–15.

[74] L.M. Bodnar and K.L. Wisner. 2005. Nutrition and Depression: Implications for Improving Mental Health among Childbearing-Aged Women. *Biological Psychiatry*. 58 (9). pp. 679–685.

[75] C.D. Bourke, J.A. Berkley, and A.J. Prendergast. 2016. Immune Dysfunction as a Cause and Consequence of Malnutrition. *Trends in Immunology*. 37 (6). pp. 386–398.

[76] J. Dobner and S. Kaser. 2018. Body Mass Index and the Risk of Infection—from Underweight to Obesity. *Clinical Microbiology and Infection*. 24 (1). pp. 24–28.

losses to national economic productivity."[77] Investing in nutrition can benefit communities through poverty reduction and economic growth.

The economic consequences and costs of undernutrition are mainly indirect: lost productivity as a result of reduced capacity, illness, and death. In Asia and the Pacific, the economic burden of underweight has been estimated at 3%–4% of economies' total GDP. Research from low- and middle-income countries (LMICs) shows that the first 2 years of life (the first 1,000 days from conception to the second birthday) are a critical period during which good nutrition has a strong association with subsequent schooling.[78] Evidence from the region also demonstrates the relationship between poor nutrition and educational outcomes. A study conducted in Malaysia, Indonesia, Thailand, and Viet Nam found that undernourishment was associated with significantly lower nonverbal IQ (intelligence quotient) in 6–12-year-old children.[79]

The World Bank Human Capital Project includes stunting as a key indicator because of the significant contribution that malnutrition makes to reduced productivity: "baseline estimates suggest that a reduction in stunting rates of 10% raises worker productivity by 3.5%."[80] A review of the evidence from South Asia found that low productivity was associated with malnutrition, particularly micronutrient deficiency.[81] There is also evidence from the PRC that increasing human capital is related to improvements in nutrition.[82]

The direct and indirect costs of malnutrition in the form of obesity and diet-related disease are also significant. A recent review for Asia and the Pacific found that overweight and/or obesity accounted for an estimated 2%–10% of countries' total health-care expenditure. The additional health-care costs for overweight individuals were estimated at more than 7%, and these increased for obese individuals to about 20%.[83] Including productivity losses from obesity, recent estimates suggest that overweight and obesity cost countries in Asia and the Pacific 0.78% of their GDP or $166 billion annually.[84] The cost of diet-related chronic diseases is similarly substantial. A review of direct health-care costs in South Asia found that annual medical costs for CVD were about $500, and for diabetes were closer to $1,000, and these costs were mainly borne by households.[85] The International Diabetes Foundation has estimated that medical costs related to diabetes in 2014 were about $6.9 billion in South Asia (footnote 90). A recent global review found estimates of annual costs (converted to 2015 prices), because of CVD-related productivity costs, of $0.5 billion–$2 billion in the Republic of Korea (ROK).[86] The cost of absenteeism because of stroke was estimated at $147 (35 days annually, per person) in Indonesia and $981 (early retirement, per person) in the PRC.[87]

[77] M. Shekar, J. Dayton Eberwein, and J. Kakietek. 2016. The Costs of Stunting in South Asia and the Benefits of Public Investments in Nutrition. *Maternal & Child Nutrition*. 12. pp. 186–195.

[78] R. Martorell et al. 2009. Weight Gain in the First Two Years of Life Is an Important Predictor of Schooling Outcomes in Pooled Analyses from Five Birth Cohorts from Low- and Middle-Income Countries. *The Journal of Nutrition*. 140 (2). pp. 348–354.

[79] Sandjaja et al. 2013. Relationship between Anthropometric Indicators and Cognitive Performance in Southeast Asian School-Aged Children. *British Journal of Nutrition*. 110 (S3). pp. S57–S64.

[80] A. Kraay. 2018. *Methodology for a World Bank Human Capital Index*. Washington DC: World Bank.

[81] S. Akhtar. 2016. Malnutrition in South Asia—a Critical Reappraisal. *Critical Reviews in Food Science and Nutrition*. 56 (14). pp. 2320–2330.

[82] H. Li et al. 2017. Human Capital and China's Future Growth. *Journal of Economic Perspectives*. 31 (1). pp. 25–48.

[83] M.E. Hoque et al. 2016. Economic Burden of Underweight and Overweight among Adults in the Asia-Pacific Region: A Systematic Review. *Tropical Medicine & International Health*. 21 (4). pp. 458–469.

[84] M. Helble and K. Francisco. 2018. Chapter 8: The Imminent Obesity Crisis in Asia and the Pacific: First Cost Estimates. In *Wealthy but Unhealthy: Overweight and Obesity in Asia and the Pacific: Trends, Costs, and Policies for Better Health*. Tokyo: Asian Development Bank Institute.

[85] I.F. Walker et al. 2018. The Economic Costs of Cardiovascular Disease, Diabetes Mellitus, and Associated Complications in South Asia: A Systematic Review. *Value in Health Regional Issues*. 15. pp. 12–26.

[86] A.L. Gordois et al. 2016. Productivity Losses Associated with Cardiovascular Disease: A Systematic Review. *Expert Review of Pharmacoeconomics & Outcomes Research*. 16 (6). pp. 759–769.

[87] T.R. Hird et al. 2019. The Impact of Diabetes on Productivity in China. *Diabetologia*. 62 (7). pp. 1195–1203.

Policies for Healthy Eating

Significant progress has been made on nutrition in Asia and the Pacific. However, development continues to be hampered by food insecurity, undernutrition, and diet-related NCDs. In this section, we identify five key areas for policy action to promote healthy eating to combat the DBM in Asia and the Pacific. The first, double-duty nutrition intervention, extends the increasingly effective interventions for undernutrition in the region to address risk factors for diet-related NCDs. The second element is the important role of nutrition-sensitive social welfare interventions in facilitating household access to healthy food and supplemental nutrition. Such demand-oriented interventions so far have been the main approach to nutrition taken in many countries in the region.[88]

A combination of demand- and supply-oriented approaches is needed to effectively improve nutrition in the region. Thus, the third element is investment in agriculture and supply chains to enhance the supply of healthy foods. The fourth element addresses the food environment as a key interface between people and these supply chains. The external food environment includes the availability, price, marketing, and retail of foods, and recent research in developing countries highlights its critical nature in influencing food choice and behaviors.[89] The fifth element of comprehensive policy for nutrition addresses the need for continued innovation and new technology in improving access to healthy foods.

Double-Duty Nutrition Interventions

Specific nutrition interventions in health-care settings, schools, and communities are critical points at which nutrition education and supplemental nutrition can be delivered, to address both undernutrition and NCD prevention.[90] WHO has recommended that countries adopt "double duty" actions where possible: nutrition interventions that take an integrated approach to improve both undernutrition and diet-related NCD prevention.[91] Community-based nutrition programs that include nutrition education as part of health services, and sometimes direct provision of healthy food, have been found to be effective in the region. A recent community nutrition program in India found improved knowledge regarding healthy diets among children aged 8–11.[92] Supplementation is also a common and effective nutrition-specific intervention to address micronutrient deficiencies, particularly in South Asia and Southeast Asia.[93] These health sector–led interventions could be strengthened with the inclusion of education and behavior change measures to promote healthy diets that are low in salt, sugar, and processed foods to address the DBM.

Success has also been seen with nutrition education regarding the DBM in parenting training and pregnancy- and infant-related health services,[94] as well as in community-based programs, particularly for rural areas where health

[88] ASEAN. 2017. *ASEAN Leaders' Declaration on Ending All Forms of Malnutrition. Association of South East Asian Nations.* https://asean.org/wp-content/uploads/2017/11/2.-ADOPTION_2017_ALD-on-Ending-All-Forms-of-Malnutrition_Endorsed-by-the-AHMM.pdf (accessed 12 Mar 2020).

[89] C. Turner et al. 2018. Concepts and Critical Perspectives for Food Environment Research: A Global Framework with Implications for Action in Low- and Middle-Income Countries. *Global Food Security*. 18. pp. 93–101.

[90] WHO. 2013. *Follow-up to the Political Declaration of the High-Level Meeting of the General Assembly on the Prevention and Control of Non-communicable Diseases. SIXTY-SIXTH WORLD HEALTH ASSEMBLY WHA66.10 Agenda item 13.1, 13.2, 27 May 2013. Annex: Global Action Plan for the Prevention and Control of Noncommunicable diseases 2013–2020*. Geneva: World Health Organization; and WHO. 2015. *Action Plan to Reduce the Double Burden of Malnutrition in the Western Pacific Region (2015–2020)*. Manila: WHO Regional Office for the Western Pacific.

[91] WHO. 2017. Double-Duty Actions for Nutrition: Policy Brief. Geneva: World Health Organization.

[92] W.Y. Low, Y.K. Lee, and A.L. Samy. 2015. Non-communicable Diseases in the Asia-Pacific Region: Prevalence, Risk Factors and Community-Based Prevention. *International Journal of Occupational Medicine and Environmental Health*. 28 (1). pp. 20–26.

[93] M.A. Dijkhuizen et al. 2019. Interventions to Improve Micronutrient Status of Women of Reproductive Age in Southeast Asia: A Narrative Review on What Works, What Might Work, and What Doesn't Work. *Maternal and Child Health Journal*. 23. pp. 18–28.

[94] H. Li et al. 2017. Human Capital and China's Future Growth. *Journal of Economic Perspectives*. 31 (1). pp. 25–48.

system contact is limited.[95] School-based nutrition education interventions to promote healthy diets are also effective strategies; they are critical to promote good nutrition preconception among adolescent girls because of the importance of good maternal nutrition for birth outcomes.[96] School-feeding programs, in which food is provided to children directly at low cost or free, are a key public health nutrition strategy across the world. In Asia, school-feeding programs have been introduced in most countries, and the PRC and India have particularly large-scale programs that use nutrient-based standards that have been associated with improvements in nutrition indicators.[97]

Nutrition-Sensitive Social Welfare

Addressing the poverty–health nexus will be critical to lasting improvements in nutrition in the region.[98] A recent review commissioned by the United Nations Children's Fund (UNICEF) in South Asia highlighted the importance of a coordinated approach involving social protection systems for improving nutrition in the region, particularly among women and children.[99] Cash transfers are particularly important for low-income households in the region, which are unable to afford a diversified healthy diet (footnote 29).

Cash transfers can improve nutrition by increasing the resources available for household food security. If the cash transfer goes to the primary caregiver, it can increase control over more resources for children and decrease poverty-related stress.[100] Combining cash transfers with nutrition education has been found to be feasible and acceptable to communities in the region, and to lead to improvements in diet.[101]

Improving nutrition through social welfare policies can also be achieved through interventions to promote the empowerment of women. Two reviews from South Asia have highlighted the importance of measures for empowerment of women, such as health services for women, prevention of early marriage, completion of secondary education, enhancement of purchasing power, secure employment opportunities, and elimination of domestic violence (footnote 111).

Investment in Diverse and Resilient Agricultural Production and Supply

Agriculture policy in many countries in the region remains focused on food insecurity, and in particular the adequate supply of calories.[102] This is understandable, given the persistently high rates of food insecurity and undernutrition in the region. However, there is a significant opportunity for the agriculture sector to increase investment in diverse nutrient-rich foods, such as fruits and vegetables, which are also often economically

95 V.M. Aguayo and K. Paintal. 2017. Nutrition in Adolescent Girls in South Asia. *BMJ*. 357: j1309.

96 S.C. Vir. 2016. Improving Women's Nutrition Imperative for Rapid Reduction of Childhood Stunting in South Asia: Coupling of Nutrition Specific Interventions with Nutrition Sensitive Measures Essential. *Maternal and Child Nutrition*. 12. pp. 72–90.

97 L. Drake et al. 2017. School Feeding Programs in Middle Childhood and Adolescence. In D. Bundy et al, eds. *Disease Control Priorities, 3rd ed: Child and Adolescent Health and Development*. USA: World Bank Publications.

98 L. Allen et al. 2017. Socioeconomic Status and Non-communicable Disease Behavioural Risk Factors in Low-Income and Lower-Middle-Income Countries: A Systematic Review. *The Lancet Global Health*. 5 (3). pp. e277–e289.

99 H. Torlesse and V.M. Aguayo. 2018. Aiming Higher for Maternal and Child Nutrition in South Asia. *Maternal & Child Nutrition*. 14 (S4): e12739.

100 R. de Groot et al. 2017. Cash Transfers and Child Nutrition: Pathways and Impacts. *Development Policy Review*. 35 (5). pp. 621–643.

101 A. Alam et al. 2019. Feasibility of Integrating Agriculture and Nutrition Behavior Change Interventions with Cash Transfers in Rural Bangladesh: A Mixed-Methods Assessment (P10-126-19). *Current Developments in Nutrition*. 3 (Supplement 1).

102 S. Gillespie, M. van den Bold, and J. Hodge. 2019. Nutrition and the Governance of Agri-Food Systems in South Asia: A Systematic Review. *Food Policy*. 82. pp. 13–27.

high-value as well.[103] In many countries, this could be achieved by increasing agricultural investment in healthy, traditional foods, including staples (such as millets, local rice, and root crops); fruits; and vegetables. These foods are rich in nutrients and are generally appropriate to the ecosystems, making them resilient. Investment in research and development can improve cultivation techniques and help to increase yields, as well as improving post-harvest storage and transport.

There is increasing evidence for the importance of agriculture and other food systems interventions in increasing access to diverse nutritious foods, as well as improving livelihoods and food security for rural households. In particular, evidence from South Asia indicates that interventions, such as seed, plant, and/or poultry provision; home garden training; and nutrition education can increase dietary quality and diversity.[104] Efforts to improve agriculture productivity and resilience through access to inputs and credit, insurance to reduce risks, improvement of rural and marketing infrastructure, and micro financing initiatives can also improve diets, particularly when combined with direct nutrition interventions.[105] Diverse peri-urban farming (e.g., including chickens and leafy greens) was associated with improved food security and healthier diets in Nepal.[106]

Creating Healthy Food Environments

WHO and the Food and Agriculture Organization of the United Nations (FAO) have recommended a range of policies to address the DBM through improved food environments. These include school food policies, labeling, restrictions on marketing of unhealthy foods to children, and fiscal interventions (such as taxes on unhealthy foods and subsidies for healthy foods).[107] There has been limited uptake of many of these food environment policies in the region, and thus there is significant scope to develop and adopt contextually relevant policies to promote healthy food environments.

School food policies are a key mechanism through which governments can create healthy school food environments by directly influencing the availability, marketing, and prices of foods that children are exposed to in this setting.[108] Within the region, the Ministry of Education in Malaysia has developed the *Guide for Healthy School Canteen Management* (2012) as a mandatory requirement for public schools.[109] Similarly, the Government of the ROK prohibited the sale of sugary drinks and other energy-dense and nutrient-poor foods within school premises, as an action of a Special Presidential Committee in 2007 (footnote 115).

[103] A.M. Thow et al. 2018. How Can Health, Agriculture and Economic Policy Actors Work Together to Enhance the External Food Environment for Fruit and Vegetables? A Qualitative Policy Analysis in India. *Food Policy*. 77. pp. 143–151.

[104] F.A. Bird et al. 2019. Interventions in Agriculture for Nutrition Outcomes: A Systematic Review Focused on South Asia. *Food Policy*. 82. pp. 39–49.

[105] S.C. Vir. 2016. Improving Women's Nutrition Imperative for Rapid Reduction of Childhood Stunting in South Asia: Coupling of Nutrition Specific Interventions with Nutrition Sensitive Measures Essential. *Maternal and Child Nutrition*. 12. pp. 72–90; and V.L. Pandey, S. Mahendra Dev, and U. Jayachandran. 2016. Impact of Agricultural Interventions on the Nutritional Status in South Asia: A Review. *Food Policy*. 62. pp. 28–40.

[106] C. Moucheraud et al. 2018. Engagement in Agriculture Protects AGAINST Food Insecurity and Malnutrition in Peri-Urban Nepal. *Current Developments in Nutrition*. 3 (1).

[107] FAO and WHO. 2014. *Second International Conference on Nutrition. Conference Outcome Document: Rome Declaration on Nutrition*. ICN2 2014/2. Rome: Food and Agriculture Organization of the United Nations and World Health Organization.

[108] FAO. *Healthy Food Environment and School Food*. 2020. http://www.fao.org/school-food/areas-work/food-environment/en.

[109] World Cancer Research Fund. 2017. *WCRF International Food Policy Framework for Healthy Diets: NOURISHING*. http://www.wcrf.org/int/policy/nourishing-framework.

Governments across the region have adopted "back-of-pack" nutrition labeling in line with the FAO's Codex Alimentarius guidelines, usually in the form of nutrition information panels. However, as evidence emerges regarding the difficulty that consumers have in interpreting this information, particularly in developing countries, WHO has begun to support countries to consider interpretive front-of-pack labeling.[110] Examples of an interpretive approach include the voluntary Healthier Choices logo in Thailand.

Fiscal policy initiatives to disincentivize unhealthy food consumption and incentivize healthier foods have been recommended by WHO to address price-related incentives. As of April 2019, 16 countries and territories in Asia and the Pacific had taxes on sugar-sweetened beverages, which are associated with poor diet quality, weight gain, and diabetes.[111] In the Philippines and Tonga, early evaluation of the taxes on sugar-sweetened beverages suggest that they are likely to be effective in reducing consumption and averting deaths.[112] A critical opportunity for many countries is raising the rate of taxes on unhealthy foods and beverages, which are often below the WHO recommended rate of 20%–50%.[113]

Restrictions on marketing to children have been recommended to limit the volume and the appeal of advertising to children. Such restrictions have been found to be effective in reducing exposure to advertising among children.[114] However, within the region, there has been limited implementation of restrictions on advertising. Taipei,China is one of the few economies to have implemented strong restrictions on marketing to children under 12 years of age.

Technology, Innovation, and Healthy Diets

The final element of a strong policy response to the DBM in the region will entail innovation and engagement with new technologies to support healthy diets. This includes making better use of new communication technology to promote nutrition education and healthy behaviors. Global studies indicate that mobile apps show promise in allowing nutrition education to reach populations who may not have access to traditional clinical services.[115] Mobile phone approaches have been successfully used to communicate information about nutrition for young children in the region.[116]

New technologies in the food and agriculture space also have the potential to improve food systems and nutrition. However, it is imperative that such technologies are considered in context, such that improvements in productivity, yields, and processing are not detrimental to nutritional quality.[117] New opportunities arising from food and agricultural technology include crop varieties and processing techniques that enhance nutritional

[110] WHO. 2015. *Technical Meeting on Nutrition Labelling for Promoting Healthy Diets.* 9–11 December 2015, Lisbon, Portugal. http://www.who.int/nutrition/events/2015_meeting_nutrition_labelling_diet_9to11dec/en.

[111] FAO, UNICEF, World Food Programme, and WHO. 2019. *Placing Nutrition at the Centre of Social Protection. Asia and the Pacific Regional Overview of Food Security and Nutrition 2019.* Bangkok.

[112] A. Saxena et al. 2019. Modelling the Impact of a Tax on Sweetened Beverages in the Philippines: An Extended Cost–Effectiveness Analysis. *Bulletin of the World Health Organization.* 97 (2): 97; and World Bank. 2019. *Using Taxation to Address Noncommunicable Diseases: Lessons from Tonga.* Nuku'alofa, Tonga: World Bank.

[113] WHO. 2016. *Fiscal Policies for Diet and Prevention of Noncommunicable Diseases; Technical Meeting Report.* 5–6 May 2015, Geneva, Switzerland. Geneva: World Health Organization.

[114] T. Correa et al. 2019. Responses to the Chilean Law of Food Labeling and Advertising: Exploring Knowledge, Perceptions and Behaviors of Mothers of Young Children. *International Journal of Behavioral Nutrition and Physical Activity.* 16 (1): 21.

[115] M. Hingle and H. Patrick. 2016. There Are Thousands of Apps for That: Navigating Mobile Technology for Nutrition Education and Behavior. *Journal of Nutrition Education and Behavior.* 48 (3). pp. 213–218.e1.

[116] A. Alam et al. 2019. Feasibility of Integrating Agriculture and Nutrition Behavior Change Interventions with Cash Transfers in Rural Bangladesh: A Mixed-Methods Assessment (P10-126-19). *Current Developments in Nutrition.* 3 (Supplement 1).

[117] D. Glover and N. Poole. 2019. Principles of Innovation to Build Nutrition-Sensitive Food Systems in South Asia. *Food Policy.* 82. pp. 63–73.

quality, and new approaches to post-harvest processing to reduce losses, particularly for perishable produce such as fruits.[118] New sources of protein are also being investigated, such as edible insects.[119]

Conclusion and Key Messages

Food environments are improving across Asia and the Pacific. While diets have improved in terms of diversity and the sufficiency of caloric intake in most locations, particular challenges remain for countries with very low incomes. As caloric intakes improve, the region faces the emerging challenge of unhealthy diets, as consumption of fats, sugars, and highly processed foods rises. Food prices are fairly stable, but high prices for nutritious foods are contributing to both undernutrition and unhealthy diets. Despite improvements in food safety standards, food safety remains a challenge across the region, particularly in informal settings. Urbanization and globalization have contributed to changing diets through impacts on food availability, retail, and marketing. Increased openness to trade has made food supply chains more resilient and enabled access to similar foods all year-round, but can also increase vulnerability to global price shocks and increase the availability and affordability of unhealthy processed food.

In line with these changes in diets and food environments, there have been improvements in undernutrition prevalence, but there is evidence of the DBM at household, community, and national levels across the region. Undernutrition remains pervasive, and obesity rates are increasing in all countries. Obesity increased across all income groups, especially among lower-income groups. Higher obesity rates translate into higher risk of developing diabetes and a number of cancers, which are associated with substantial health-care system costs. Further, the high prevalence of childhood obesity predicts further increase in obesity rates. All forms of malnutrition also hamper educational attainment and productivity in the region, leading to significant economic costs.

Flanking policies to support supply and demand for healthy foods, such as fiscal policies and education, will help to ensure that consumers make informed decisions and minimize negative externalities for the public health-care system. Efforts to improve policies addressing the DBM should focus on integrated nutrition interventions for preventing undernutrition and obesity or diet-related NCDs, nutrition-sensitive social welfare, agriculture and supply chains for healthy foods, food environment policies, and innovation.

[118] K. Njogu et al. 2016. *Tree Crops Development in Africa and Asia to Benefit the Poor-Fruit Component*. Nairobi, Kenya: The World Agroforesty Centre.

[119] G. Ssepuuya, I.M. Mukisa, and D. Nakimbugwe. 2017. Nutritional Composition, Quality, and Shelf Stability of Processed Ruspolia nitidula (Edible Grasshoppers). *Food Science & Nutrition*. 5 (1). pp. 103–112.

PART 4

Leveraging Asian Traditions for Mental Wellness

CHAPTER 8

Mental Wellness

Gerard Bodeker

"There is no health without mental health." —World Health Organization

This chapter focuses on individual and community approaches that reduce the burden of mental illness by promoting the adoption of evidence-based pathways that are culturally familiar within Asia and can prevent stress, reduce depression and anxiety, and promote mental well-being throughout the life span. The chapter presents new directions for improving mental wellness across Asia in accordance with the principles of de-institutionalization, patient-centered care, personal responsibility for mental and physical health, community support systems, and evidence as the basis for strengthening the widespread adoption of culturally familiar pathways to mental wellness.

Mental Health: Global Trends

In 2017, the World Health Organization (WHO) produced its *Mental Health Atlas 2017* with data from questionnaires completed by 177 of WHO's 194 member states,[1] and used to monitor the development and implementation of WHO's Mental Health Action Plan 2013–2020.

The WHO atlas reported that the level of public expenditure on mental health in low-income and middle-income countries was meager, and more than 80% of funds went to mental hospitals. The allocation for human resources for mental health services has extreme variation between low-income and high-income countries (1 in low-income countries to 72 in high-income countries, per 100,000 population), while globally, the median number of mental health workers is 9 per 100,000 population (footnote 1). The number of mental health beds per 100,000 population is less than 8 in low and lower middle-income countries, but more than 50 in high-income countries (footnote 1). In the sector of mental health promotion and prevention, only 63% of WHO member economies have a minimum of two functioning multisector mental health promotion and prevention programs at the national level, even though 72% of member economies have a dedicated policy or plan for mental health and 57% have a stand-alone mental health law (footnote 1).

[1] WHO. 2018. *WHO Mental Health.*

WHO has taken the position that mental health leads to mental and psychological well-being. With mental health given its due importance in the United Nations Sustainable Development Goals, for the first time, leaders of the world have acknowledged that mental health promotion and well-being and the prevention and treatment of substance abuse are likely to have a positive impact on communities and countries where millions of people require much-needed help. The focus on ensuring healthy lives and promoting well-being for everyone and at all ages lies in Goal 3 of the 17 Sustainable Development Goals. Goal 3, Target 3.4 calls on countries to reduce premature mortality from noncommunicable diseases by a third, through prevention, treatment, and mental health and well-being promotion. Target 3.5 calls on governments to reinforce and increase efforts in the prevention and treatment of substance abuse, including narcotic drug abuse and the use of alcohol at harmful levels.

The 2018 Lancet Commission on global mental health and sustainable development reported: "Despite substantial research advances showing what can be done to prevent and treat mental disorders and to promote mental health, translation into real-world effects has been painfully slow. The global burden of disease attributable to mental disorders has risen in all countries in the context of major demographic, environmental, and sociopolitical transitions."[2]

The Committee on Ethical Issues of the European Psychiatric Association has proposed a new definition of mental health: *"Mental health is a dynamic state of internal equilibrium which enables individuals to use their abilities in harmony with universal values of society. Basic cognitive and social skills; ability to recognize, express and modulate one's own emotions, as well as empathize with others; flexibility and ability to cope with adverse life events and function in social roles; and harmonious relationship between body and mind represent important components of mental health which contribute, to varying degrees, to the state of internal equilibrium."*[3]

A Life Span Approach to Understanding Mental Health

WHO has taken a life span approach to understanding the risk factors and influencers on mental health and noted that these vary significantly for an individual as they move through the course of life. The following are the risk factors for a given stage of life identified by WHO:

Preconception and Prenatal Period

A given individual's mental health and well-being can be influenced by factors present prior to conception or birth, including maternal tobacco, alcohol and drug use, malnutrition, low birth weight, and micronutrient deficiency (for example, iodine deficiency).

Infancy and Early Childhood

Emotional attachment in early childhood has a considerable impact on later vulnerability to mental health and well-being. As a result, particular risk factors include separation from the primary caregiver, in some cases post-natal depression in mothers (which can result in sub-optimal attachment), and parents for whom communication and social interaction is challenging. Child maltreatment and neglect has been found to have a significant impact on vulnerabilities to mental well-being. Malnutrition, poor access to basic services, and disease and parasites are also important contributors.

Childhood

Childhood conditions form a critical component of health and well-being later in life. Negative experiences, either at home or outside of the home (for example, bullying in school), can have lifelong impacts on the

[2] V. Patel et al. 2018. Lancet Commission on Global Mental Health and Sustainable Development. *The Lancet*. 392 (10157). p. 1553. https://doi.org/10.1016/S0140-6736(18)31612-X.
[3] S. Galderisi et al. 2015. Toward a New Definition of Mental Health. *World Psychiatry*. 14 (2). pp. 231–233. doi: 10.1002/wps.20231.

development of core cognitive and emotional skills. Poor socioeconomic conditions also have a significant effect on vulnerability to mental health disorders. Children with a parent who has a mental illness or substance use disorder have a higher risk of psychiatric problems themselves.

Adolescence

Adolescence is typically the stage of life where mental health disorders tend to become more apparent. The risk factors and contributors to well-being in childhood apply equally to those in adolescence. In addition, several other contributing factors appear. It is in the years of adolescence when the use of substances, including alcohol and drugs, first appear.

Adulthood

Experiences and emotional capabilities that were developed through childhood and adolescence are important factors in the effect that particular events and scenarios in adulthood have on mental health outcomes.

Older Age

Older-age individuals have notably high risk of poorer mental health and well-being. Typically, this results from notable changes in life conditions (such as a cease in employment that affects both the feeling of contribution and economic freedom), higher social exclusion, and loneliness. This is particularly true when an older individual begins to lose close family and friends. Bereavement in general is an important predictor of mental health disorders such as depression. A decline in physical health can have major impacts on life capabilities by affecting an individual's mobility and freedom. Older individuals are also at higher risk of abuse or neglect from caregivers and, in some cases, family members.[4]

Economics and Mental Wellness

Depression affects at least 322 million people globally, or approximately 4.4% of the world's population, and is rated by WHO as the leading cause of disability worldwide.

A systematic review of more than 100 research studies on mental health outcome in times of economic recession has found that periods of economic recession are associated with a higher prevalence of mental health problems, including common mental disorders, substance disorders, and ultimately suicidal behavior.[5]

In asking whether the same factors misery as life satisfaction, one survey used by the World Happiness Report team examined how much misery, in principle, could be avoided by eliminating either poverty, low education, unemployment, living alone, physical illness, or mental illness.[6]

They found that, in all countries, the most powerful effect would come from the elimination of depression and anxiety disorders, which are the main forms of mental illness. This turns out to be the least costly way of reducing misery. As can be seen from the many bodies of evidence referenced in this section, depression and anxiety respond readily to the many paths to mental wellness available today—paths that can be self-managed and are of low cost or no cost.

4 WHO. 2013. *Mental Health Action Plan 2013–2020*.

5 D. Frasquilho et al. 2016. Mental Health Outcomes in Times of Economic Recession: A Systematic Literature Review. *BMC Public Health*. 16: 115. doi: 10.1186/s12889-016-2720-y.

6 J. Helliwell, R. Layard, and J. Sachs. 2017. *World Happiness Report 2017*. New York: Sustainable Development Solutions Network.

Rising Mental Illness in Asia

Data from WHO and the Organisation for Economic Co-operation and Development (OECD) have identified the five leading mental health problems in Asia and the Pacific: (i) depression, (ii) anxiety, (iii) post-traumatic stress disorder, (iv) suicidal behavior, and (v) substance-abuse disorder.

For example, a cross-section study on major depressive disorder showed a prevalence of 20.0% in Thailand; 19.9% in Taipei,China; 19.4% in the Republic of Korea; 17.5% in Malaysia; and 16.5% in the People's Republic of China (PRC). Few of these conditions are adequately addressed in Asia and the Pacific.[7]

Wide Regional Variation

Lower middle-income countries, such as India, Indonesia, Pakistan, the Philippines, and Viet Nam, face many challenges, including little available medical treatment, inadequate investment, lack of capacity to spend funds effectively, dilapidated facilities, and critically low numbers of mental health professionals.

A common goal across the region is de-institutionalization—changing the focus of mental health management from secondary care to integrated community-based care with multidisciplinary input. Yet, while global models of mental health prioritize the individual, more family-oriented cultures prevail in Asia and the Pacific. This family orientation to mental health may, on the one hand, complicate moves to expand community-based services and access to professional care, especially if lack of funding obliges families to accommodate patients. On the other hand, it opens new opportunities for preventive and supportive care that are more in line with the shift toward patient-centered and integrated mental health care, specifically around the potential for mental wellness pathways to impact anxiety and depression—the leading causes of mental health problems in Asia and the largest economic burden of mental health problems in the region.

Youth and Digital Media

The United Nations *World Happiness Report 2019* cites a number of studies in the United States that have found that adolescents and young adults who spend more time on digital media are lower in well-being.[8] For example, girls who spend 5 or more hours a day on social media are three times more likely to be depressed than non-users.[9] Heavy internet users (versus light users) are twice as likely to be unhappy.[10]

Mental Wellness: Definition

A collaboration of interdisciplinary researchers and practitioners from the Mental Wellness Initiative of the Global Wellness Institute has produced a white paper that conceptualizes wellness in terms of general sense of well-being in the physical, social, occupational, spiritual, financial, and environmental aspects of our lives. The process of maintaining mental wellness is viewed as lifelong and involves developing the skills and knowledge

7 M. Srisurapanont et al. 2013. Clinical Features of Depression in Asia: Results of a Large Prospective, Cross-sectional Study. *Asia-Pacific Psychiatry*. 5 (4). pp. 259–67. doi: 10.1111/appy.12104.

8 For example, C. Booker et al. 2015. Media Use, Sports Participation, and Well-Being in Adolescence: Cross-sectional Findings from the UK Household Longitudinal Study. *American Journal of Public Health*. 105. pp. 173–179. https://doi.org/10.2105/AJPH.2013.301783; L.Y. Lin et al. 2016. Association between Social Media Use and Depression among US Young Adults. *Depression and Anxiety*. 33 (4). pp. 323–331. doi: 10.1002/da.22466; and J.M. Twenge, G.N. Martin, and W.K. Campbell. 2018. Decreases in Psychological Well-being among American Adolescents after 2012 and Links to Screen Time during the Rise of Smartphone Technology. *Emotion*. 18 (6). pp. 765–780. http://dx.doi.org/10.1037/emo0000403.

9 Y. Kelly et al. 2019. *Social Media Use and Adolescent Mental Health: Findings from the UK Millennium Cohort Study*. https://doi.org/10.1016/j.eclinm.2018.12.005.

10 J.M. Twenge, G.N. Martin, and W.K. Campbell. 2018. Decreases in Psychological Well-being among American Adolescents after 2012 and Links to Screen Time during the Rise of Smartphone Technology. *Emotion*. 18 (6). pp. 765–780.

to make conscious and intentional choices toward living a healthy, purposeful, and fulfilling life. This lifelong process enables individuals to realize their potential; cope with daily stresses; work productively; and contribute meaningfully to family, community, and society.[11] The definition of mental wellness has subsequently been developed further in a chapter on "Well-Being and Mental Wellness" in the *Oxford Research Encyclopedia of Global Public Health*.[12]

Emotional well-being. The stream of research that defines well-being by the degree of positive feelings experienced, such as happiness, and the perception of one's overall life, whether the individual is satisfied or not, is known as emotional well-being.[13]

Psychological well-being. The next stream of research, known as psychological well-being, includes modalities of positive functioning where the individual realizes their potential in terms of autonomy and personal growth. Those who are high in emotional well-being feel good about life, while those who have high psychological well-being or social well-being function well in daily routine and are resilient.[14]

Resilience and balance. In a 2019 scoping review[15] on the definition of youth resilience, mental health is seen as "a state of wellbeing in which an individual realizes his or her own abilities, can cope with the normal stresses of life, can work productively and is able to make a contribution to his or her community." The notion of "normal stresses of life" stands in contrast to the definition of resilience provided by Tusaie et al. in Christmas and Khanlou,[16] where good mental health or resilience is the capability to adapt better than expected in the face of significant adversity or risk. A more recent definition of well-being is "the balance point between an individual's resource pool and the challenges faced."[17]

Flourishing. A multidimensional construct of well-being, using the term "flourishing" or "optimal functioning," is now a common approach in well-being research. The pioneering work of positive psychology founder Marten Seligman has aligned the definition of wellness to endeavors that strive to capture the complex nature of human flourishing (through positive emotion, engagement, relationships, meaning, and accomplishment) instead of preventing or ameliorating "mental illness."[18]

---

11 G. Bodeker, ed. 2018. *White Paper on Mental Wellness: Pathways, Evidence and Horizons*. Global Wellness Institute.

12 G. Bodeker et al. 2020. Well-Being and Mental Wellness. In D. McQueen and P. Buss, eds. *Oxford Research Encyclopedia of Global Public Health*. Oxford University Press. DOI: 10.1093/acrefore/9780190632366.013.162.

13 E. Diener et al. 1999. Subjective Well-being: Three Decades of Progress. *Psychological Bulletin*. 125 (2). pp. 276–302. http://dx.doi.org/10.1037/0033-2909.125.2.276.

14 Patel et al. 2018. Lancet Commission on Global Mental Health and Sustainable Development. *The Lancet*. 392 (10157). pp. 1553–1598. https://doi.org/10.1016/S0140-6736(18)31612-X; and J.L. Magyar, and C.L.M. Keyes. 2019. Defining, Measuring, and Applying Subjective Well-being. In *M.W. Gallagher* and *S.J. Lopez, eds. Positive Psychological Assessment: A Handbook of Models and Measures*. 2nd ed. Washington DC: American Psychological Association. pp. 389–415.

15 C.M. Christmas and N. Khanlou. 2019. Defining Your Resilience: A Scoping Review. *International Journal of Mental Health and Addiction*. 17 (3). pp. 731–742. https://psycnet.apa.org/doi/10.1007/s11469-018-0002-x.

16 K. Tusaie, K. Puskar, and S.M. Sereika. 2007. A Predictive and Moderating Model of Psychosocial Resilience in Adolescents. *Journal of Nursing Scholarship*. 39 (1). pp. 54–60. http://dx.doi.org/10.1111/j.1547-5069.2 007; and C.M. Christmas and N. Khanlou. 2019. Defining Your Resilience: A Scoping Review. *International Journal of Mental Health and Addiction*. 17 (3). pp. 731–742. https://psycnet.apa.org/doi/10.1007/s11469-018-0002-x.

17 M. Hanc, C. McAndrew, and M. Ucci. 2018. Conceptual Approaches to Wellbeing in Buildings: A Scoping Review. *Building Research and Information*. p 230. 10.1080/09613218.2018.1513695.

18 M.E. Seligman, A.C. Parks, and T. Steen. 2004. A Balanced Psychology and a Full Life. *Philosophical Transactions of the Royal Society of London*. Series B, Biological Sciences. 359 (1449). pp. 1379–1381; and M. Hanc, C. McAndrew, and M. Ucci. 2018. *Conceptual Approaches to Wellbeing in Buildings: A Scoping Review*. Building Research and Information. 10.1080/09613218.2018.1513695.

Mental wellness, in the view of the Lancet Commission, can be "defined as an asset or resource that enables positive states of wellbeing and provides the capability for people to achieve their full potential."[19] The challenge to demarcate the differences between mental wellness and disorder is such that an individual could struggle with symptoms of mental disorder, but at the same time be able also to maintain a degree of mental health parallel to their expectations of life satisfaction, flourishing, and achieving their potential. According to the authors of the Lancet Commission report, the association between mental health and disorder is not linear, even though it may seem that they exist on a continuum.[20]

Social foundations of well-being. The United Nations *World Happiness Report 2017* (footnote 6) identifies four factors as best representing different aspects of the social foundations of well-being. These are social support, freedom to make life choices, generosity, and absence of corruption in government and business.

Among the many findings cited, two key social variables—social support and volunteering—are consistently associated with better self-reported health status. Positive mental health, well-being, and flourishing refer to the presence of high levels of positive functioning—primarily in the mental health domain (inclusive of social health). However, in its broadest sense, well-being encompasses physical, mental, and social domains.

Mental Wellness Strategy

The mental wellness strategy is to focus on what everyone can do in a self-managed and self-empowering way to enhance their own mental well-being by using evidence-based pathways that work for them. Evidence is of central importance because it offers wellness service providers a sound base from which to explain this approach of self-managed progress to mental well-being.

Mental wellness has been defined by the Government of the United Kingdom's Office for Science as "a dynamic state, in which the individual is able to:

(i) develop their potential,
(ii) work productively and creatively,
(iii) build strong and positive relationships with others, and
(iv) contribute to their community."[21]

This is a new approach to public health with mental health as an integral and complementary part of the proposed new direction. It places health improvement as everyone's responsibility. Factors of self-esteem, confidence, and resilience are seen as key to health behavior change.[22]

The Global Wellness Institute's *White Paper on Mental Wellness* has identified several evidence-based pathways for creating and maintaining mental wellness that are low-cost, effective, and easily implemented at the individual and community levels (footnote 11). These are explored in the "Overview of Wellness Modalities" section that follows. But first, important developments in neuroscience in the past decade or so have revealed that the brain can grow and create new connections across the adult life span, given the influence of suitable wellness methods, and that this, in turn, can contribute to actualizing fuller human potential and reducing mental health challenges.

[19] Footnote 2, p. 1562. https://doi.org/10.1016/S0140-6736(18)31612-X.
[20] Footnote 2,. pp. 1553–1598.
[21] Government of the United Kingdom, Office for Science. 2008. *Mental Capital and Wellbeing: Making the Most of Ourselves in the 21st Century*. p. 10.
[22] Government of the United Kingdom, Department of Health and Social Care. 2010. *Healthy Lives, Healthy People: Our Strategy for Public Health in England*. United Kingdom: The Stationery Office. pp. 1–96.

Brain Plasticity

Neuroplasticity is the ability of the nervous system to adapt, change, and rebuild, and it is the strongest during our first 5 years of life (footnote 12). The agile nature of neural cells occurs at multiple levels, ranging from microscopic to the observable and behavioral. Brain plasticity is also, however, vulnerable to harmful, dysfunctional, and undesirable adaptations and change, despite its ability to make favorable positive changes. During the developmentally sensitive "use it or lose it" periods, neural connections become stronger and more permanent through repeated use. Weak or unused neural connections may prune off. Hence, repetition is the key to learning and mastery.[23]

The impact of stress on a child or adolescent's developing brain can have a lifelong effect and is avoidable when the right wellness support is provided. Psychosocial stressors in childhood, such as poverty; parental separation and divorce; emotional neglect; psychological, physical, or sexual abuse; and mental illness and substance use in the home environment, are capable of negative rewiring of the development of our prefrontal cortex. The prefrontal context is the part of the higher-level brain region that benefits from wellness practices.

Wellness-based neuroplasticity enables us to achieve self-actualization and, ultimately, to undergo a transformation toward self-transcendence. Only when we realize this dimension of well-being are we able to set aside our own needs to help others fulfill theirs. To this end, we will be able to create a sustainable, integrated, and harmonious path toward personal and global wellness.

Overview of Wellness Modalities

Wellness modalities are a range of activities and programs that have positive effects on somatic, psycho, and emotional well-being. In this section, we provide a general introduction to a few modalities that have experienced a surge in research interest, the results of which are now translated to the broader population.

Nutrition

The International Society for Nutritional Psychiatry Research has reported: "A traditional whole-food diet, consisting of higher intakes of foods such as: vegetables, fruits, seafood, whole grains, lean meat, nuts, and legumes with avoidance of processed foods is more likely to provide the nutrients that afford resiliency against the pathogenesis of mental disorders."[24] The gut–brain axis (GBA) is emerging as a key pathway for modulating behavior.

The GBA is explained in a 2017 collection of articles published by *Nature*: "It is becoming increasingly evident that bidirectional signaling exists between the gastrointestinal tract and the brain, often involving the gut microbiota. This relationship, commonly dubbed the gut–brain axis (or the microbiota–gut–brain axis), involves various afferent and efferent pathways such as the vagus nerve and the hypothalamic-pituitary-adrenal pathway to regulate aspects of homeostasis such as satiety and hunger, and inflammation. Disruption of the gut–brain axis has been shown to be involved in the pathogenesis of a diverse range of diseases, including Parkinson's disease and irritable bowel syndrome. Key aspects of the gut–brain axis include immune, neuroendocrine and neural factors."[25]

[23] L. Choy. 2018. Neuroplasticity. In G. Bodeker, ed. *White Paper on Mental Wellness: Pathways, Evidence and Horizons*. Global Wellness Institute.

[24] J. Sarris et al. Nutritional Medicine as Mainstream in Psychiatry. *Lancet Psychiatry*. 2. pp. 271–74. http://dx.doi.org/10.1016/ 2215-0366(14)00051-0.

[25] *Nature*. http://www.nature.com/collections/dyhbndhpzv.

Research has found that gut disorders, known as functional gastrointestinal disorders (FGIDs), are associated with the prevalence of both depression and anxiety, and these increase with both the number of FGIDs and the frequency and severity of gastrointestinal disorders symptoms.[26]

Antibiotic use in neonates and in young infants has a severe impact on gut microbiota development. Repeated courses of antibiotics given during the first years of life affect children's gut microbiota and can make them predisposed to conditions such as allergies, asthma, obesity, or even type 2 diabetes. This is because antibiotics profoundly alter gut microbiota. In turn, this has implications for the health of the GBA and, in turn, the developing child's physiological, behavioral, and cognitive functions.[27]

In a major review of stress and the GBA, researchers note that "The concept of psychobiotics, bacteria with positive effects on mental health, was coined in 2013 and has recently been expanded to include other microbiota-targeted interventions that can positively modify mental health including in healthy volunteers. (...) the relationship between diet and the microbiota-gut-brain axis is ripe for exploitation to develop therapeutic strategies for treating stress-related disorders."[28] Studies have shown that increases in the amount of good bacteria in the gut can curb inflammation and cortisol levels, reduce symptoms of depression and anxiety, lower stress reactivity, improve memory, and even lessen neuroticism and social anxiety. This shows that the beneficial gut bacteria or probiotics probably function mechanistically as delivery vehicles for neuroactive compounds. Thus, a psychobiotic is a live organism which, when ingested in adequate amounts, produces a health benefit in patients suffering from mental illness. Now researchers are of the opinion that study of a novel class of probiotics may open up the possibility of rearrangement of intestinal microbiota for effective management of various psychiatric disorders and mental health conditions.

There is now a substantial body of research examining the benefit of nutrient supplementation in people with mental disorders. Research has found strong evidence that certain supplements are an effective additional treatment for some mental disorders.[29] Clinical studies[30] have found omega-3 fatty acids to be beneficial in the treatment of bipolar depression, post-traumatic stress disorder, and major depression, as well as the prevention of psychosis.

In a study on cognitive functioning and brain aging, higher levels of B family vitamins, as well as vitamins C, D, and E, were all associated with higher scores on cognitive tests. The same positive relationship was found for omega-3 fatty acids, which have been linked previously to better brain health. But those with higher levels of trans fats, which are found in a variety of junk foods, performed more poorly in thinking and memory tests. Their magnetic resonance imaging scans also revealed more brain shrinkage than people who had lower trans fats levels. The study found that, overall, nutrition accounted for 37% of the variation in brain volume.[31]

[26] M.I. Pinto-Sanchez et al. 2015. Anxiety and Depression Increase in a Stepwise Manner in Parallel with Multiple FGIDs and Symptom Severity and Frequency. *The American Journal of Gastroenterology*. 110 (7). pp. 1038–1048.

[27] E. Van der Beek. 2018. Nutritional Programming and Later Life: The Role of Macronutrient Quality during the First 1,000 Days. *Sight and Life E-magazine*. 32 (1). pp. 46–52.

[28] J.A. Foster et al. 2017. Stress and the Gut-Brain Axis: Regulation by the Microbiome. *Neurobiology of Stress*. p. 9. http://dx.doi.org/10.1016/j.ynstr.2017.03.001.

[29] J. Firth et al. 2019. The Efficacy and Safety of Nutrient Supplements in the Treatment of Mental Disorders: A Meta-review of Meta-analyses of Randomized Controlled Trials. *World Psychiatry*. 18 (3). pp. 308–324. https://doi.org/10.1002/wps.20672.

[30] F. Jacka. 2017. Nutritional Psychiatry: Where to Next? *EBioMedicine*, doi: 10.1016/j.ebiom.2017.02.020; D. Mischoulon and M.P. Freeman. 2013. Omega-3 Fatty Acids in Psychiatry. *Psychiatric Clinics of North America*. 36. pp. 15–23; and J.D. Sarris, D. Mischoulon, and I. Schweitzer. 2012. Omega-3 for Bipolar Disorder: Meta-analyses of Use in Mania and Bipolar Depression. *The Journal of Clinical Psychiatry*. 73. pp. 81–86.

[31] G.L. Bowman et al. 2012. Nutrient Biomarker Patterns, Cognitive Function, and MRI Measures of Brain Aging. *Neurology*. 78 (4): 249. doi: 10.1212/WNL.0b013e3182436598.

A landmark study has found that inexpensive B vitamins stopped shrinkage in the area of the brain called the medial temporal lobe that defines Alzheimer's disease. The study, led by David Smith of the University of Oxford, gave a combination of vitamin B_6 (20 milligrams), B_{12} (500 micrograms), and folic acid (800 micrograms) or placebo pills to people with mild cognitive impairment, the stage before a diagnosis of dementia or Alzheimer's disease. In those with high homocysteine levels, the specific areas of the brain associated with Alzheimer's disease shrank eight times more slowly in those taking B vitamins than in those on the placebo. This is strongly indicative that the B vitamins may be substantially slowing down, or even potentially arresting, the disease process in those with early stage cognitive decline. This is the first treatment that has been shown to do this.[32]

Traditional Asian Foods That Utilize Microorganisms

While adding fermented foods and beverages to the diet has been proclaimed recently as the newest health movement in the United States, fermented foods are a well-established part of the daily diet in many Asian countries because there is a long tradition of fermented foods across Asian cultures.

In Japan, *Aspergillus* strains of bacteria provide the means to ferment rice wine (sake), soy sauce (shoyu), soybean paste (miso), and distilled spirits (shochu).[33] This species also contributes to the distinctive color, flavor, and aroma of traditionally fermented Asian foods.

Kimchi, a fermented food primarily eaten in the Republic of Korea, is made from pickled vegetables and involves another variety of microbes supplying the bacteria to ferment a food source. The microbial communities contributing to the fermentation process of kimchi were analyzed and found to come from three main sources. These types of analysis are difficult as the microbes in foods are rapidly changing as fermentation is a continual process in food products.[34]

Movement away from these traditional foods could contribute to a change in the amount and diversity of the intestinal microbiome and reduce exposure to beneficial microbes found in these foods.

Exercise and Mental Wellness

In addition to the well-documented effects of exercise on quality of life (QOL) and longevity, there is an emerging body of findings that show the benefits of exercise to mental well-being.[35]

The *Journal of Clinical Psychiatry* published a study about exercise as a secondary treatment for patients with major depressive disorder who had not achieved remission through drugs alone. The researchers evaluated two exercise doses: one group of patients burned 4 kilocalories per kilogram each week, while another burned 16 kilocalories per kilogram weekly. They found that both exercise protocols led to significant improvements, though the higher-dose exercise program was more effective for most patients.[36]

[32] G. Douaud et al. 2013. Preventing Alzheimer's Disease-Related Gray Matter Atrophy by B-vitamin Treatment. *Proceedings of the National Academy of Sciences of the United States of America*. 110 (23). pp. 9523–9528. doi: 10.1073/pnas.1301816110 PMCID: PMC3677457.

[33] Y. Zhu and J. Tramper. 2013. Koji—Where East Meets West in Fermentation. *Biotechnology Advances*. 31. pp. 1448–1457.

[34] Y.J. Jung et al. 2011. Metagenomic Analysis of Kimchi, a Traditional Korean Fermented Food. *Applied and Environmental Microbiology*. 77 (7). pp. 2264–2274.

[35] S.A. Lear et al. 2017. The Effect of Physical Activity on Mortality and Cardiovascular Disease in 130 000 People from 17 High-Income, Middle-Income, and Low-Income Countries: The PURE Study. *The Lancet*. doi: http://dx.doi.org/10.1016/S0140-6736(17)31634-3.

[36] M.H. Trivedi et al. 2011. Exercise as an Augmentation Treatment for Nonremitted Major Depressive Disorder: A Randomized, Parallel Dose Comparison. *The Journal of Clinical Psychiatry*. 72 (5). pp. 677–684. doi: 10.4088/JCP.10m06743.

In a study funded by the US National Institutes of Health, researchers looked at affective response to an initial exercise session as a predictor of the effectiveness of treatment for depressed patients. Noting that predicting treatment response very early in the course of treatment can avoid unnecessarily lengthy trials with ineffective treatments, the researchers looked at the same low- and high-dose exercise regimens. They found that response to the very first high-dose exercise session was a reliable predictor of treatment outcome for depression. However, this was not the case for low-dose exercise. Knowledge of initial response to high-dose exercise has clinical utility to predict treatment response to exercise in depression and enable clinicians to match the "right patient" with the "right treatment."[37]

The growing body of research findings on exercise and mood is now being translated into "how to" approaches. For example, in their book *Exercise for Mood and Anxiety*, authors Michael Otto and Jasper Smits translate scientific findings and principles of behavior change into accessible strategies for the general public. The focus is on helping to establish and maintain an exercise program by understanding the relationship between mood and motivation. The strategy includes worksheets and checklists to help record information on moods before and after a workout in order to improve motivation.[38]

In deprived neighborhoods, there are benefits to mental well-being from boosting physical activity among residents, especially those with particularly low general levels of mental well-being. A study of 3,854 adults from 30 neighborhoods in Glasgow, UK, found that adults who do more physical activity generally have better mental well-being.[39] Clearly, exercise is a major platform of wellness policy around the world, and the public in industrialized societies is engaging more with exercise.

Exercise in Asia and the Pacific

A review of surveillance systems for physical activity identified estimates for adult population physical activity in Asia and the Pacific and examined variation in trends and prevalence rates obtained using different physical activity measures. Data were obtained from a Medline search, the WHO's Global Health Infobase, government websites, and reference lists of relevant papers. In total, 56 population surveys from 29 Asia and Pacific economies were identified.

Of the 56 surveys reported, 11 (22%) were conducted more than once (Table 8.1). These provided trend information.

The study highlighted "an urgent need for standardization of physical activity measures and survey methods used ... in order to accurately document risk factor prevalence and population trends."[40]

While data collection in the region is inconsistent within and between economies, the importance of exercise for mental health and well-being is becoming increasingly clear in the face of robust evidence.

[37] A.M. Suterwala et al. 2016. Affect Following First Exercise Session as a Predictor of Treatment Response in Depression. *The Journal of Clinical Psychiatry*. 77 (8). pp. 1036–1042. doi: 10.4088/JCP.15m10104.
[38] M. Otto and J. Smits. 2011. *Exercise for Mood and Anxiety: Proven Strategies for Overcoming Depression and Enhancing Well-being*. Oxford University Press.
[39] P. Mason and A. Kearns. 2013. Physical Activity and Mental Wellbeing in Deprived Neighbourhoods. *Mental Health and Physical Activity*. 6 (2). pp. 111–17.
[40] R. Macniven, A. Bauman, and M. Abouzeid. 2012. A Review of Population-Based Prevalence Studies of Physical Activity in Adults in the Asia-Pacific Region. *BMC Public Health*. 12 (41). p. 39. doi: 10.1186/1471-2458-12-41.

Table 8.1 Results of a Review of Surveillance Systems for Physical Activity in Asia and the Pacific

Economies Surveyed	Results
Indonesia; New Zealand; Singapore; Taipei,China; and Thailand	Demonstrated increase in physical activity levels over time
Australia, Republic of Korea, and Japan	Demonstrated decrease in physical activity over time
Australia, Japan, and New Zealand	No significant changes in either direction were recorded over time (data not shown)

Source: R. Macniven, A. Bauman, and M. Abouzeid. 2012. A Review of Population-Based Prevalence Studies of Physical Activity in Adults in the Asia-Pacific Region. *BMC Public Health*. 12 (41). doi: 10.1186/1471-2458-12-41.

An important new body of research is examining the possibility that benefits from exercise can be inherited. Noting that epigenetics is the study of gene expression changes that occur in the absence of altered genotype, a 2017 review presented experimental evidence that indicates that environmentally induced alterations to epigenetic modifications lead to changes in health and disease across generations.[41]

Looking ahead, if the benefit of exercise can be established to confer benefits to successive generations, there is clearly a need for research on the many other wellness modalities referenced here and elsewhere to determine if these benefit not only the practitioner, but their descendants as well.

Yoga

In the sphere of mental wellness, some exercise modalities have been well studied and are growing rapidly in popularity both in Asia and globally—yoga is a case in point.[42]

Denise Rankin-Box explains:

> Yoga is an ancient practice; it has been associated with cultural, religious, and physical activity for more than 2,000 years. Its practitioners have asserted its effect on balancing emotional, physical, and spiritual health for decades, but only recently has there been a move to substantiate these claims through research. So far, the result has been definitive, significant evidence of the broad-ranging benefits of yoga, both as a treatment and as a preventative form of medicine and health care.[43]

For example, a 2016 study conducted in the United States found that about 31 million adults had used yoga, and about 21 million practiced yoga in the past 12 months (footnote 42).

A survey of yoga research reports that at least two studies have demonstrated significant increase in mindfulness, while several others have measured reduction in job stress in both office and fire station settings.[44] Studies of yoga's effects on anxiety are common, with significant series and single-session effects on measures of stress, anxiety, fatigue and depression, well-being, and vigor. The survey cites several studies in which measures of

---

[41] J. Denham. 2017. Exercise and Epigenetic Inheritance of Disease Risk. *Acta Physiologica*. doi:10.1111/apha.12881.

[42] H. Cramer et al. 2016. Prevalence, Patterns, and Predictors of Yoga Use: Results of a U.S. Nationally Representative Survey. *American Journal of Preventive Medicine*. 50 (2). pp. 230–235.

[43] D. Rankin-Box. 2015. The Science of Yoga—What Research Reveals. *Elsevier Connect*. https://www.elsevier.com/connect/the-science-of-yoga-what-new-research-reveals.

[44] E. Della Valle et al. 2020. Effectiveness of Workplace Yoga Interventions to Reduce Perceived Stress in Employees: A Systematic Review and Meta-Analysis. *Journal of Functional Morphology and Kinesiology*. 5 (2): 33. doi: 10.3390/jfmk5020033.

depression decreased after extended practice (around 2 months). In all studies, yoga was found to have increased sleep efficiency, total sleep time, number of awakenings, and sleep quality.

Tai Chi

The National Health Service of the UK describes the traditional Chinese movement traditions as follows: "Tai chi, also called tai chi chuan, combines deep breathing and relaxation with flowing movements. Originally developed as a martial art in 13th-century [PRC], tai chi is now practiced around the world as a health-promoting exercise."[45] It is a means of developing self-awareness.

A meta-analysis of studies on the effects of tai chi in preventing falling in the elderly found that tai chi exercise is effective for preventing falls in older adults. The preventive effect seems to increase with the frequency of tai chi practice. Interestingly, the study found a difference in effect with different styles of tai chi. Yang-style tai chi (created in the 19th century and the most widespread form of tai chi today) seemed to be more effective than Sun-style tai chi, the most recently created form of tai chi.[46]

Veterans with post-traumatic stress symptoms took part in a four-session introduction to tai chi in Boston. In addition to reporting a high degree of satisfaction with the program, participants reported feeling very engaged during the sessions, and found tai chi to be helpful in managing distressing symptoms (i.e., intrusive thoughts, concentration difficulties, and physiological arousal).[47]

Dance

The diverse cultures of Asia are prominent in the many dances that are influenced by the region's religion, rituals, and mythical stories. In the PRC, "every day, an estimated more than 100 million people—dubbed 'dancing aunties' as they are primarily older women—take over squares and parks to tango, waltz, and grind out everything from flamenco to Chinese traditional dance."[48]

A quarter of a century of research has underscored the benefits of dance and dance movement therapy on generalized mental well-being,[49] on brain development in adults and children,[50] on mood stabilization in adolescents,[51] and in reducing depression and anxiety across the age-span.[52] In short, dance has been shown to combine many different factors that contribute to improvement in the competence needed in everyday life.[53]

Research across the age span has highlighted the differing benefits of dance for different age groups. Children, especially girls, have been found to make significant physical advances as well as improvements in measures of

---

[45] National Health Service. *A Guide to Tai Chi*. http://www.nhs.uk/Livewell/fitness/Pages/taichi.aspx.

[46] Z. Huang et al. 2017. Systematic Review and Meta-analysis: Tai Chi for Preventing Falls in Older Adults. *BMJ Open*. (7) 2.

[47] B. Niles et al. 2016. Feasibility, Qualitative Findings and Satisfaction of a Brief Tai Chi Mind–Body Programme for Veterans with Post-traumatic Stress Symptoms. *BMJ Open*. (6) 11.

[48] *Newsgram*. 2018. "Dancing Aunties" Take Over Public Places in China. 7 October. https://www.newsgram.com/video-dancing-aunties-public-places-china.

[49] S. Koch et al. Effects of Dance Movement Therapy and Dance on Health-Related Psychological Outcomes: A Metaanalysis. *The Arts in Psychotherapy*. 41 (1). pp. 46–64.

[50] S. Brown and L. M. Parsons. 2008. The Neuroscience of Dance. *Scientific American*. 299 (1). pp. 78–83; and F.J. Karpati et al. 2015. Dance and the Brain: A Review. *Annals of the New York Academy of Sciences*. 1337 (1). pp. 140–46.

[51] A.N. Anderson et al. 2014. Dance Movement Therapy Impacts Mood States of Adolescents in a Psychiatric Hospital. *Arts in Psychotherapy*. 41 (3). pp. 257–262.

[52] I. Bräuninger. 2012. The Efficacy of Dance Movement Therapy Group on Improvement of Quality of Life: A Randomized Controlled Trial. *Arts in Psychotherapy*. 39 (5). pp. 443–450.

[53] M. Ritter and K.G. Lowe. 1996. The Effectiveness of Dance/Movement Therapy. *The Arts in Psychotherapy*. 23 (3). pp. 249–620.

psychological well-being through dance training.[54] Adults have been found to undergo structural brain changes associated with creativity and artistic expression (footnote 49). Older-aged dance participants with Parkinson's disease have shown improved mobility, reduced tremor, and improved social outreach.[55] There is an international program called Dance for Parkinson's Disease that began in New York and has spread to many countries. It offers dance as a means of enhancing QOL and improving symptoms in people with Parkinson's disease.[56]

A *New England Journal of Medicine* study examined physical and cognitive activities associated with reduced risk of developing Alzheimer's disease. The researchers found that cognitive activities such as reading, playing board games, and playing musical instruments were associated with a lower risk of dementia. However, of the 11 physical activities, "dancing was the only physical activity associated with a lower risk of dementia."[57]

Mental health conditions such as anxiety and depression have been reduced through participation in dance and dance movement therapy. A report in the online newsletter of the Harvard Mahoney Neuroscience Institute in the Harvard Medical School states that "Studies show that dance helps reduce stress, increases levels of the feel-good hormone serotonin, and helps develop new neural connections, especially in regions involved in executive function, long-term memory, and spatial recognition."[58]

Meditation

Meditation is like exercise for the brain and has been shown to assist in mental health maintenance and improve memory, empathy, and sense of self. A meta-analysis in the *Journal of the American Medical Association* identified almost 19,000 studies on different forms of meditation. Four decades of studies highlight the effects of meditation in enhancing immunity, reducing depression and anxiety, improving academic performance, reducing age-related cognitive decline, increasing happiness and QOL, and managing and reducing trauma.

Brain changes associated with the practice of meditation include enhanced neural plasticity and increased gray and white matter development in the brains of meditators. Studies on the Transcendental Meditation technique have found reductions in anxiety[59] and post-traumatic stress;[60] improvement in the mental health of caregivers;[61] and, in a study on survivors of the Japanese earthquake-tsunami of 2011, improvements in both mental and physical symptoms following instruction in this meditation technique.[62]

In research conducted at the Massachusetts General Hospital, magnetic resonance images were taken of the brain structure of 16 study participants 2 weeks before and after they took part in an 8-week mindfulness meditation program. The research team found increased gray matter density in the hippocampus, known to be important for learning and memory, and in structures associated with self-awareness, compassion, and

---

[54] Y.J. Jeong et al. 2005. Dance Movement Therapy Improves Emotional Responses and Modulates Neurohormones in Adolescents with Mild Depression. *International Journal of Neuroscience*. 115 (12). pp. 1711–1720.

[55] O. Westheimer et al. 2015. Dance for PD: A Preliminary Investigation of Effects on Motor Function and Quality of Life among Persons with Parkinson's Disease (PD). *Journal of Neural Transmission*. 122 (9). pp. 1263–1270.

[56] Dance for Parkinson's Disease. http://www.capturinggracefilm.com/about-dance-for-pd; and https://danceforparkinsons.org.

[57] J. Verghese et al. 2003. Leisure Activities and the Risk of Dementia in the Elderly. *New England Journal of Medicine*. 348 (25). pp. 2508–2516.

[58] S. Edwards. 2016. Dancing and the Brain. *On the Brain: The Harvard Mahoney Neuroscience Institute Newsletter*. http://neuro.hms.harvard.edu/harvard-mahoney-neuroscience-institute/brain-newsletter/and-brainseries/dancing-and-brain (accessed 21 September 2017); and L.J. Mills and J.C. Daniluk. 2002. Her Body Speaks: The Experience of Dance Therapy for Women Survivors of Child Sexual Abuse. *Journal of Counselling and Development*. 80 (1). pp. 77–85.

[59] H. Tomljenović, D. Begić, and Z. Maštrović. 2016. Changes in Trait Brainwave Power and Coherence, State and Trait Anxiety after Three-Month Transcendental Meditation (TM) Practice. *Psychiatria Danubina*. 28 (1). pp. 63–72.

[60] B. Rees et al. 2014. Significant Reductions in Posttraumatic Stress Symptoms in Congolese Refugees within 10 Days of Transcendental Meditation Practice. *Journal of Traumatic Stress*. 27. pp. 112–115.

[61] S. Nidich et al. 2015. Stress Reduction with the Transcendental Meditation Program in Caregivers: A Pilot Study. *International Archives of Nursing and Health Care*. 1 (2).

[62] M. Yoshimura et al. 2015. Disaster Relief for the Japanese Earthquake-Tsunami of 2011: Stress Reduction through the Transcendental Meditation® Technique. *Psychological Reports*. 117 (1). pp. 206–16. doi: 10.2466/02.13.PR0.117c11z6.

introspection. Participants' reports of reduced stress were correlated with decreased gray matter density in the amygdala, which is known to play an important role in anxiety and stress.[63]

With benefits ranging from enhanced mental well-being to the reduction of deeply traumatic stress, from changes in brain structure and functioning to changes in gene expression and telomere length, and reduced age-related decline, meditation stands as a primary pathway for lifelong enhancement of physical and mental wellness.

Massage

A meta-analysis of 37 studies of massage has found that multiple treatments reduced pain. Reductions in anxiety and depression were the largest effects, with a course of massage treatment providing benefits similar in magnitude to those of psychotherapy.

Researchers have studied the effects of massage on many conditions. These studies include the following:

- A 2010 meta-analysis of 17 clinical trials concluded that massage therapy may help to reduce depression.
- A 2012 clinical trial funded by the National Center for Complementary and Integrative Health showed that brief, twice-weekly yoga and massage sessions for 12 weeks were associated with a decrease in depression, anxiety, and back and leg pain in pregnant women with depression. Also, the women's babies weighed more than babies born to women who did not receive the therapy.
- A 2020 research review found that massage therapy might be more effective in reducing pregnant women's anxiety and depression than usual care, although the current results may be prone to bias.
- A 2010 review concluded that massage may help older people relax.[64]

Social Dimensions of Mental Wellness

In its broadest sense, well-being encompasses physical, mental, and social domains. By contrast, loneliness or social isolation is, in terms of mortality risk, comparable with established risk factors such as smoking.[65]

The *World Happiness Report 2017* addresses the social foundations of happiness: "To feel secure, people need to feel that others care for them and will come to their aid when needed. To some extent, being in such a network of usually mutual obligations sets limits on each person's freedom to make life choices freely, as the interests of others must always be borne in mind. It is apparent from our results that both features are important for a good life. It is also clear from the data that these different aspects need not conflict with each other, as the most successful societies are ones where both measures of the social fabric are strong. Indeed, some of the features of the social fabric that reflect its ability to care for people, in particular the health and education systems, also serve to level out the differences in life opportunities that affect the breadth and reality of the life choices open to each individual."[66]

Addressing the role of generosity as a social determinant of happiness, the report notes that "subjective well-being research is now showing that in all cultures, and even from infancy, people are drawn to pro-social behaviour, and that they are happier when they act pro-socially" (footnote 66).

[63] Hölzel et al. 2011. Mindfulness Practice Leads to Increases in Regional Brain Gray Matter Density. *Psychiatry Research Neuroimaging*. 191 (1). pp. 36-43. DOI: 10.1016/j.pscychresns.2010.08.006.

[64] H.G. Hall et al. 2020. The Effectiveness of Massage for Reducing Pregnant Women's Anxiety and Depression: Systematic Review and Meta-analysis. *Midwifery*. 90:102818. November. DOI: 10.1016/j.midw.2020.102818. Epub 14 August. PMID: 32827841.

[65] H.J. Lunstad, T.B. Smith, and J.B. Layton. 2010. Social Relationships and Mortality Risk: A Meta-analytic Review. *PLOS Medicine*. 7: e1000316.

[66] Footnote 6, p. 32.

Social Laughter

Laughter yoga (*Hasyayoga*) is a practice involving prolonged voluntary laughter. Laughter yoga is based on the belief that voluntary laughter provides the same physiological and psychological benefits as spontaneous laughter. Laughter yoga is done in groups, with eye contact, jokes, and playfulness between participants. Forced laughter soon turns into real and contagious laughter. In the mid-1990s, laughter yoga was practiced in the early mornings in open parks, primarily by groups of older people. Laughter yoga was made popular as an exercise routine developed by Indian physician Madan Kataria, who has written about the practice in his book *Laughter Yoga*.[67]

Some small-scale scientific studies indicate that laughter yoga may potentially have some medically beneficial effects on cardiovascular health and mood.[68]

As it is termed, social laughter seems to release endorphins associated with feelings of well-being and heightened mood. Oxford University researchers conducted a series of experiments and found that pain thresholds—an indicator for endorphin release—were significantly higher after laughter. The researchers suggest that "laughter, through an endorphin-mediated opiate effect, may play a crucial role in social bonding."[69]

In subsequent work, researchers found that social laughter "increased pleasurable sensations and triggered endogenous opioid release in thalamus, caudate nucleus, and anterior insula. In addition, baseline MOR [mu-opoid receptors] availability in the cingulate and orbitofrontal cortices was associated with the rate of social laughter."[70]

One research team paired laughter with physical exercise, noting that "despite the health benefits of physical activity and the risks of physical inactivity, many adults don't engage in sufficient physical activity to achieve health benefits. Maintaining the motivation to adhere to regular physical activity is a challenge for many older adults."[71]

The researchers consider that simulated laughter may be an ideal way for older adults with functional or cognitive impairment to achieve the health benefits of laughter, which include improved physiological and psychological functioning. Participants simply choose to laugh and initiate laughter as bodily exercise.

Nature

In a 2010 Japanese study of *shinrin-yoku* (defined as "taking in the forest atmosphere" or "forest bathing"), researchers found that elements of the environment, such as the odor of wood, the sound of running stream water, and the scenery of the forest, can provide relaxation and reduce stress. Those who took part in the study

[67] M. Kataria. 2020. *Laughter Yoga*. New York: Penguin, Random House.

[68] R. Dolgoff-Kaspar et al. 2012. Effect of Laughter Yoga on Mood and Heart Rate Variability in Patients Awaiting Organ Transplantation: A Pilot Study. *Alternative Therapies in Health and Medicine*. 18 (5). pp. 61–66; and M. Shahidi et al. 2011. Laughter Yoga Versus Group Exercise Program in Elderly Depressed Women: A Randomized Controlled Trial. *International Journal of Geriatric Psychiatry*. 26 (3). pp. 322–327. DOI:10.1002/gps.2545.

[69] R.I. Dunbar et al. 2012. Social Laughter Is Correlated with an Elevated Pain Threshold. *Proceedings of the Royal Society B: Biological Sciences*. 279 (1731). pp. 1161–1167. doi: 10.1098/rspb.2011.1373.

[70] S. Manninen et al. 2017. Social Laughter Triggers Endogenous Opioid Release in Humans. *Journal of Neuroscience*. 37 (25). pp. 6125–6131. doi: 10.1523/JNEUROSCI.0688-16.2017.

[71] C. Greene et al. 2016. Evaluation of a Laughter-Based Exercise Program on Health and Self-efficacy for Exercise. *The Gerontologist*. 57 (6). pp. 1051–1061. doi: 10.1093/geront/gnw105.

experienced lower levels of cortisol; lower pulse rate; lower blood pressure; strengthened immunity; and reduced stress, depression, and anxiety.[72]

A 2007 study from the University of Essex in the UK found that a walk in the country reduced depression in 71% of participants.

By contrast, research from the PRC, home to 16 of the cities on the United Nations' list of top 20 most polluted cities in the world, has found that bad air quality contributes to poor mental health and unhappiness. The study looked at the impact of air pollution on several key dimensions, including mental health status, depressive symptoms, moment-to-moment happiness, and evaluative happiness (i.e., overall life satisfaction). What researchers found was that air pollution reduces all forms of happiness and increases the rate of depressive symptoms over time.[73]

Data from more than 70,000 women in the United States Nurses' Health Study revealed that exposure to fine particulate matter was associated with high symptoms of anxiety. The Johns Hopkins team that carried out the research proposed that this may be because exposure to particulate matter air pollution induces or exacerbates anxiety through increased oxidative stress and systemic inflammation. It could also be through promotion or aggravation of chronic disease.[74]

A Swedish study investigated the mental health effects of air pollution on more than half a million children and adolescents. Using a national registry of medication, researchers found evidence for a link between exposure to air pollution and dispensed medications for certain psychiatric disorders in children and adolescents.[75]

A number of other studies replicate and expand these findings. What is clear from the perspective of mental wellness is that living with access to green space and nature enhances our mental well-being, and exposure to air pollution worsens it.

Clearly, air quality should be a key feature of wellness programs for urban dwellers and for offerings at urban wellness destinations, as should access to nature.

The quality of green space, including its richness in wildlife, may be more important to mental health benefits than its quantity.[76] People living near quality green space, full of wildlife and thriving habitats, were twice as likely to report low psychological distress as those living near low-quality open spaces.

People tend to live longer when they have access to green space, and perceived neighborhood greenness is strongly associated with better mental and physical health.[77] Those living in highly green areas are much more likely to have better physical and mental health than those living near open areas that are not highly green.[78]

[72] B.J. Park et al. 2010. The Physiological Effects of Shinrin-Yoku (Taking in the Forest Atmosphere or Forest Bathing): Evidence from Field Experiments in 24 Forests across Japan. *Environmental Health and Preventive Medicine.* 15 (1). pp. 18–26. doi: 10.1007/s12199-009-0086-9.

[73] X. Zhang, X. Zhang, and X. Chen. 2017. Happiness in the Air: How Does a Dirty Sky Affect Mental Health and Subjective Well-being? *Journal of Environmental Economics and Management.* (85). pp. 81–94.

[74] M.C. Power et al. 2015. The Relation between Past Exposure to Fine Particulate Air Pollution and Prevalent Anxiety: Observational Cohort Study. *BMJ.* 350:h1111. doi: 10.1136/bmj.h1111.

[75] A. Oudin et al. 2016. Association between Neighbourhood Air Pollution Concentrations and Dispensed Medication for Psychiatric Disorders in a Large Longitudinal Cohort of Swedish Children and Adolescents. *BMJ Open.* 6 (6).

[76] F.J. Wood, M. Knuiman, and B. Giles-Corti. 2012. Quality or Quantity? Exploring the Relationship between Public Open Space Attributes and Mental Health in Perth. *Western Australia. Social Science and Medicine.* 74. pp. 1570–1577.

[77] T. Tanako, K. Nakamura, and M. Watanabar. 2002. Urban Residential Environments and Senior Citizens Longevity in Megacity Areas: The Importance of Walkable Green Spaces. *Journal of Epidemiology and Community Health.* 56. pp. 913–918.

[78] T. Sugiyama et al. 2008. Associations of Neighbourhood Greenness with Physical and Mental Health: Do Walking, Social Coherence and Local Social Interaction Explain the Relationships? *Journal of Epidemiology and Community Health.* 62: e9.

Nature near home is important particularly for children because it increases their ability to cope with stressful life events, directed attention, and cognitive function.[79] Exposure and connectedness to nature have been found to be associated with body appreciation and self-esteem in women and men.[80]

New research has reported that gentle woodland sounds, such as birdsong and the breeze rustling leaves in the trees, are more relaxing than meditation recordings. Researchers exposed participants to three soundtracks: a woodland, a woman guiding a meditation session, and deep silence. When asked to listen to the woodland sounds for one minute, people felt 30% more relaxed, while stress and anxiety dropped. There was no change in the level of relaxation people felt after listening to the meditation or the silence.[81]

Climate Change: Effect on Mental Health

People who worry about the planet's animals and plants are more likely than others to experience stress, and even depression, related to climate change.

University of Arizona researchers studied how people's perception of the threat of global climate change affects their mental health. They found that, while some people have little anxiety about the planet's changing climate, others are experiencing high levels of stress, and even depression, based on their perception of the threat of global climate change. Specifically, psychological responses to climate change seem to vary based on what type of concern people show for the environment, with those highly concerned about the planet's animals and plants experiencing the most stress. By contrast, people higher in egoistic concern did not seem to perceive climate change threats as having a profound effect on their own or their family's life despite the reality that it will. The researchers emphasized that the impact of climate change on individuals seems to be growing slowly and needs to be taken very seriously.[82]

Conclusion

Asia is confronted with rising levels of mental illness due in part to pressures of life, poor nutrition, lack of exercise, increased time on digital media, social isolation, and lack of contact with nature. At the same time, numbers of mental health professionals are critically low across the region, and there is no realistic scenario where these would increase in the coming generation or two.

This raises the prospect of either increasing burdens of mental illness across Asia or the potential for new and innovative preventive and remediative strategies to be put in place across all levels of society and age groups that focus on self-managed and evidence-based pathways to mental well-being.

Depression and anxiety are the mental health issues that most impact national economies. They are also the mental health concerns that are most easily self-managed by way of the many evidence-based wellness modalities reviewed in this section.

[79] N.M. Wells. 2000. At Home with Nature: Effects of "Greenness" on Children's Cognitive Functioning. *Environment and Behaviour*. 32. pp. 775–795.

[80] V. Swami et al. 2016. Bodies in Nature: Associations between Exposure to Nature, Connectedness to Nature, and Body Image in U.S. Adults. *Body Image*. 18. pp. 153–161.

[81] National Trust. 2019. *Places That Make Us*. https://nt.global.ssl.fastly.net/documents/places-that-make-us-research-report.pdf.

[82] S. Helma et al. 2018. Differentiating Environmental Concern in the Context of Psychological Adaption to Climate Change. *Global Environmental Change*. 48. pp. 158–167.

Further Reading

G. Bodeker and A. Hernandez. 2018. Economic Factors Influencing Mental Wellness. In G. Bodeker, ed. *MWI White Paper on Mental Wellness.*

Centers for Disease Control and Prevention. 2017. Early Release of Selected Estimates Based on Data From the 2016 National Health Interview. Survey.https://www.cdc.gov/nchs/data/nhis/earlyrelease/earlyrelease201705.pdf.

Faculty of Public Health. http://www.fph.org.uk/concepts_of_mental_and_social_wellbeing.

J. Helliwell, R. Layard, and J. Sachs. 2019. *World Happiness Report 2019.* New York: Sustainable Development Solutions Network.

CHAPTER 9

Asian Traditions of Wellness

Gerard Bodeker

The World Health Organization (WHO) and national health administrations now recognize that lifestyle changes are the only effective way to reverse the rising trend of noncommunicable diseases (NCDs). With the evidence in support of the effectiveness of Asian wellness traditions in reducing NCD risk, reducing stress and mental health issues, and enhancing quality of life (QOL) and longevity, there is an opportunity for Asia to integrate its own cultural traditions into national and regional guidelines for NCD risk reduction and overall health promotion and mental wellness. This has cost-reduction implications for national health systems, economic opportunities for wellness tourism, and new possibilities for entrepreneurship. This chapter brings into focus Asia's wealth of health prevention and promotion strategies that are culturally relevant, evidence-based, self-managed, and low cost, as a means of enhancing health in the region and reducing the illness burden on national health budgets.

Introduction

Regional perspective. Asia's two major systems of traditional health knowledge—traditional Chinese medicine (TCM) and India's Ayurveda—are grounded in principles of living healthy and well throughout the human life span. Lifestyle is given primary emphasis over medicines in the classical texts.

East Asia and Viet Nam are strongly influenced by Chinese health knowledge, especially the knowledge in Sun Simiao's *Encyclopedia of Medicine* and in the *Huangdi Neijing*, the classic text of Chinese medicine. The health traditions of South Asia and most of Southeast Asia are grounded in Ayurvedic theory and practice, which have the *Charaka Samhita* of Ayurveda as their core text.

Core principles. Central to these Asian traditions of wellness is an understanding that people have different metabolic styles, and that understanding these is the basis for developing personalized preventive health and wellness routines. Also of primary importance in Asian wellness theories and practices is an individualized and balanced approach to nutrition based on body type and cultural food traditions.

Integrative exercise is given priority, along with stress-reducing and integrative breathing and meditative practice. Regular connection with nature is seen as a balancing influence on overall well-being.

Scientific evidence. Many practices from Asian wellness traditions have become popular in the West, generating a sizable global economy around yoga, tai chi, Asian massage traditions, and Asian herbal supplements. In turn, this has led to a surge in research investigating the health benefits of Asian health and wellness practices. Scientific journals now exist for studies on Chinese medicine, Japanese medicine (Kampo), Korean medicine, and Ayurvedic medicine. This has resulted in a large body of evidence that is now available, not only on the medicines from Asian health traditions but on the lifestyle practices and preventive strategies from Asia's wellness traditions, including integrative exercise programs such as yoga and tai chi and the untapped potential of Asia's vast diversity of martial arts practices.

Potential. WHO and national health administrations now recognize that lifestyle changes are the only effective way to reverse the rising trend of NCDs. With the evidence in support of the effectiveness of Asian wellness traditions in reducing NCD risk, reducing stress and mental health issues, and enhancing QOL and longevity, there is an opportunity for Asia to integrate its own cultural traditions into national and regional guidelines for NCD risk reduction and overall health promotion and mental wellness. This has cost-reduction implications for national health systems, economic opportunities for wellness tourism, and new possibilities for entrepreneurship.

New Economics Focuses on Quality of Life

Relevant to the understanding of well-being in Asia in the 21st century is the shift in economic thinking that began in the late 20th century with the work of Nobel Laureate in Economics Amartya Sen of Harvard and philosopher Martha Nussbaum of the University of Chicago. Sen and Nussbaum's work has been seminal in articulating the distinction between welfare and well-being or QOL. Here, *welfare* is the value assigned by the individual to income or, more generally, to the contribution to his or her well-being from those goods and services that he or she can buy with money.[1]

Sen and Nussbaum developed the *capabilities approach* to human well-being, which focuses on what human beings can do and be instead of on what they have. They defined *capabilities* as the abilities, the power of individuals to do certain things, to obtain what they desire, to achieve desired states of being, to utilize the resources they have in the way they desire, and to be who they want to be. While *goods* are the things that individuals possess, *capabilities* facilitate using goods in ways that are meaningful to individuals.[2]

Reflecting the capabilities approach to assessing how goods are used in ways that are meaningful to individuals, the Asia Barometer conducted surveys of QOL over a 5-year period in 32 countries in East Asia, Southeast Asia, South Asia, and Central Asia. These surveys took the position that the daily lives of ordinary people are central to them and that politics and economics, let alone international affairs, are peripheral. This led the Asia Barometer to focus primarily on the daily lives and concerns of ordinary people, and then shift to ask more peripheral questions about democracy and government performance.[3]

Unsurprisingly, in this most diverse region of the world, what emerged was how very different the countries and regions of Asia are in how people value aspects of their life, their material status, and their personal and family values. Clearly, this great diversity in values and priorities across Asia underscores the benefit of activating traditions that have local meaning and familiarity, and that can serve as trusted pathways to wellness in a way that strengthens the fabric of local society. Accordingly, a regional perspective on pathways to wellness for Asia must

1 D.A. Crocker. 1992. Functioning and Capability: The Foundations of Sen's and Nussbaum's Development Ethic. *Political Theory*. 20 (4). pp. 584–612.

2 A. Sen. 1999. Sen's Capability Approach. *Internet Encyclopedia of Philosophy*. pp. 70–71. https://www.iep.utm.edu/sen-cap.

3 T. Inoguchi and S Fujii. 2013. The Quality of Life in Asia: A Comparison of the Quality of Life in Asia. *The Quality of Life in Asia*. 1. Dordrecht: Springer Science + Business Media; and T. Inoguchi. 2015. Multiple Modes of Wellbeing in Asia. In W. Glatzer, L. Camfield, V. Møller, and M. Rojas, eds. *Global Handbook of Quality of Life. International Handbooks of Quality of Life*. Dordrecht: Springer Science + Business Media.

be one that is not one-size-fits-all but represents instead a set of principles and pathways that reflect local values, priorities, and heritage.

Broad Categories for Pathways to Wellness

There is now a substantial body of evidence on the benefits to physical and mental well-being of a range of health practices that might be classified as wellness practices or wellness pathways.

In view of research into conception, pregnancy, and what has come to be identified as the first 1,000 days of life, a life span approach to wellness is essential.

It turns out that certain factors that take place even before conception can have an impact on people's lives. It is known now that the health of the parents prior to and at the time of conception will influence a person's life course and some determinants of both health and lifestyle diseases. The first 2 years of life are critical in shaping future physical and mental health. Parenting styles, nutrition, and air quality are some of the factors that shape future patterns of health and mental well-being.

A series in *The Lancet* on preconception health has highlighted the study of preconception health as of foundational importance in understanding and shaping future health.[4] One article in the series, titled "Before the Beginning," notes that "observational studies show strong links between health before pregnancy and maternal and child health outcomes, with consequences that can extend across generations."[5]

At the other end of the life span, replacing half an hour to an hour of sedentariness with light exercise, including housework, each day is enough to significantly reduce the risk of mortality.[6] A growing number of studies on wellness modalities, e.g., meditation, yoga, and dance, are finding positive changes in the brains of regular practitioners, which translate into improved mental well-being and cognitive performance. Dance has been shown to enhance memory, communication, and cognition among people with dementia.[7]

Looking at nutrition and recognizing the great diversity of culinary traditions of Asia and the high use of pharmacologically potent herbs and spices, a healthy, largely organic diet is being shown to be foundational in enhancing both physical and mental wellness. This is beneficial from many different angles, including reducing inflammation, boosting immunity, and preventing metabolic disorders, and has been found to be modulated by an influential pathway between the gut and the brain, known as the gut-brain axis.

Sleep and meditation are different forms of experiencing the rest that is essential for the body to renew itself on a daily basis. Evidence shows that enhanced health, cardiovascular functioning, mental well-being, and cognitive performance are associated with meditation.

It turns out that the arts, including music, the visual arts, and writing, as well as dance, all have documented benefits for mental health and well-being. Laughter or just the experience of laughing, not at or about anything, but laughing with others, creates health and happiness that are measurable in physiological terms.

4 *The Lancet*. 2018. Preconception Health series. http://www.thelancet.com/series/preconception-health?dgcid=etoc-edschoice-email_tlwpreconhealth18.

5 J. Stephenson et al. 2018. Before the Beginning: Nutrition and Lifestyle in the Preconception Period and Its Importance for Future Health. *The Lancet*. DOI: https://doi.org/10.1016/S0140-6736(18)30311-8.

6 I. Dohrn et al. 2018. Replacing Sedentary Time with Physical Activity: A 15-Year Follow-up of Mortality in a National Cohort. *Clinical Epidemiology*. 10: 179. doi: 10.2147/CLEP.S151613.

7 K. Charrasa et al. 2020. Dance Intervention for People with Dementia: Lessons Learned from a Small-Sample Crossover Explorative Study. *The Arts in Psychotherapy*. 70: 101676.

Clearly, there are many pathways to wellness that are beneficial across a long life span. The major broad categories under which clusters of wellness pathways exist are nutrition, movement, physical health and well-being, mental wellness, and environment.

Nutrition

As the world's rapidly growing burden of obesity and diabetes threatens health systems and national economies, the Westernization of diets worldwide is in the spotlight as a major causal factor. Using data from the Food and Agriculture Organization (FAO), Vandevijvere et al. report that an increase in national food energy production is a powerful predictor of the obesity levels of a nation. While proposed policies include managing increased food energy and promoting physical activity, others assert that qualitative changes in food choices play an equally important role in the increase in chronic illness: "Strong evidence and broad consensus exists for such food-based dietary patterns and should inform dietary recommendations instead of relying on the outdated emphases on SFA, total fat, and calorie counting."[8]

With support from the United Nations Human Rights Council and the Special Rapporteur on the Right to Food, Consumers International's 2014 Recommendations Towards a Global Convention to Protect and Promote Healthy Diets promotes the participation of local communities in the development and implementation of socially and culturally appropriate strategies and programs, drawing on local agricultural and culinary traditions.[9]

Asia

With 4.44 billion people, about 60% of the world's population, Asia is the world's largest and most populous continent. Great variation exists across Asia's ethnicities and their traditions of farming, food processing, and diet. Yet rapid economic growth has been accompanied by a "nutrition transition." The traditional dominance of rice, vegetables, and other staples is shifting toward a dominance of wheat, high protein, fats, and energy dense foods. This is associated with a rise in diabetes and obesity, with some Asian countries having obesity rates of more than 40%.[10]

Central to the problem of dietary risk factors for NCDs is the fact that, as income levels increase in developing countries, exposure to the global "urban" eating pattern increases, resulting in the consumption of many Western-style foods.[11] Asian countries in economic and demographic transition are already showing dramatic changes in food consumption patterns.

Association of Southeast Asian Nations Food Imports

Agriculture in the Association of Southeast Asian Nations (ASEAN) is largely concentrated on rice production. Rice's gross value share of total agriculture production varies widely, including 25% in the Philippines and 60%

8 S. Vandevijvere et al. 2015. Increased Food Energy Supply as a Major Driver of the Obesity Epidemic: A Global Analysis. *Bulletin of the World Health Organization*. 93. pp. 446–456.

9 World Obesity Federation & Consumers International. 2014. Recommendations towards a Global Convention to Protect and Promote Healthy Diets. http://www.consumersinternational.org/media/1475072/recommendations-for-a-convention-on-healthy-diets-low-res-for-web.pdf.

10 P. Pingali. 2007. Westernization of Asian Diets and the Transformation of Food Systems: Implications for Research and Policy. *Food Policy*. 32 (3). pp. 281–298.

11 P. Pingali. 2007. Westernization of Asian Diets and the Transformation of Food Systems: Implications for Research and Policy. *Food Policy*. 32 (3). pp. 281–298; and J. Kearney. 2010. Food Consumption Trends and Drivers. *Philosophical Transactions of the Royal Society of London. Series B, Biological Science*. 365 (1554). pp. 2793–2807.

in Cambodia. Malaysia remains a key exception, with the majority of its agricultural production concentrated on palm oil.[12] It is also the largest food importer in ASEAN; 25% of food is imported. According to Malaysia's former minister of health, Malaysia is also the fattest nation in Asia.[13] Additionally, Malaysia has ASEAN's highest rate of diabetes.[14]

Unhealthy dietary patterns include high energy intake from total fats, excessive use of cooking oil with high saturated fat (including indigenous oils such as palm oil and coconut oil), high consumption of sugars and sweetened beverages, high intake of dietary salt, and low consumption of fruit and vegetables.

Increasingly, the Mediterranean diet is touted as the dietary pattern to counter chronic lifestyle diseases. However, as noted elsewhere, the Mediterranean diet "can be seen as a Western diet, studied by Westerners on Westerners—now being recommended for the world, 75% of which is non-Western."[15]

Clearly, cultures other than those in the Mediterranean region have evolved healthy eating patterns using foods available to them and often unique preparation methods. A growing body of research on Asian food traditions merits wider global attention if we are to understand the potential of dietary patterns and traditions in controlling obesity, diabetes, and other NCDs.

Asia's Dietary Traditions

Asian diets are diverse in vegetables and fruits and include many plant foods rich in pharmacologically active compounds that are beneficial to health. Among these are *reishi* mushrooms and *goji* in East Asia, and turmeric and bitter gourd in South Asia and Southeast Asia. Many food preparation methods utilize microorganisms, now understood as critical to healthy digestion and physical function.

A growing body of evidence indicates that, in parallel with losing touch with ancestral food traditions, comes an increase in chronic disease.

At the same time, there has been an awakening of interest and concern about the lack of documentation of traditional and indigenous food cultures, which are important not only for their own sake but for the legacy of food knowledge, which they can confer on future generations, provided they are not lost. "By and large, there is a remarkable resilience and ingenuity of people and their food systems."[16]

What could be added to this view is that Asian diets incorporate medicinal ingredients into the food. This is well established in Japanese, Chinese, and Indian cuisine, e.g., *reishi* mushrooms in Japanese cuisine, *goji* berries in Chinese food, and turmeric and other potent medicinal species in India menus. Malaysia has its *ulam,* a unique and pharmacologically potent medicinal herbal salad. Indonesia has its *jamu,* herbal beverages based around nature's most powerful anti-inflammatory agent, turmeric, and a powerful digestive agent, ginger.

12 M. Whitehead. 2018. ASEAN's Agri Imports and Exports in Five Charts. *Bluenotes.* https://bluenotes.anz.com/posts/2018/03/ASEANs-agri-imports-and-exports-in-five-charts.

13 *Straits Times.* 2014. Malaysia Battles the Bulge as Southeast Asia's Fattest Country Wakes Up to Health Bomb. 27 November. http://www.straitstimes.com/asia/se-asia/malaysia-battles-the-bulge-as-southeast-asias-fattest-country-wakes-up-to-health-bomb.

14 *The Star.* 2013. Number of Diabetics in Malaysia Alarming. 14 June. http://www.thestar.com.my/news/nation/2013/06/14/number-of-diabetics-in-malaysia-alarming.

15 G. Bodeker and F. Kronenberg. 2015. Tackling Obesity: Challenges Ahead. *The Lancet.* 386. pp. 740–741.

16 M.L. Wahlqvist and M.S. Lee. 2007. Regional Food Culture and Development. *Asia Pacific Journal and Clinical Nutrition.* 16 (Suppl 1). pp. 2–7.

Research has shown that the lower amount of calories in plant-rich foods and the high intake of plant-based nutrients and antioxidants in traditional diets all contribute to preventing the development of such NCDs as obesity, diabetes, heart disease, cancer, and rheumatism.

East Asia

People's Republic of China. The 7th century Common Era (CE) physician and medical scholar Sun Simiao favored food as the first line of intervention in preventing and treating disease. Predating WHO's NCD guidelines by about a millennium and a half, Sun Simiao prioritized food hygiene, advised against rich or greasy food, promoted thorough cooking and avoiding excessive drinking, and recommended taking a walk after a meal.

As Chinese communities lose touch with ancestral traditions, changes in disease patterns occur. A study of weight loss found that those eating a traditional Chinese diet, compared to a standard Western diet, lost more weight despite eating an equal number of calories.[17] They also lost less lean muscle mass and did not feel as hungry. Eating according to traditional food theories is being shown to enhance health and well-being, with potential to slow the escalating obesity rates in the People's Republic of China (PRC).

Japan. Japanese people, particularly in Okinawa, are more likely than any others to reach age 100, a fact attributed to their diet. A traditional Okinawan diet is characterized by root vegetables, other vegetables, and soy-based foods, with moderate consumption of seafood, including seaweeds, lean meat, fruits, spices, healthy fats, and tea. It is relatively low in calories and high in phytonutrients. As a result, Okinawans have a low risk of arteriosclerosis and stomach cancer and a very low risk of hormone-dependent cancers such as breast and prostate cancer. In Asia, the Japanese diet is well studied and there are commonalities with the Mediterranean diet. These include high intake of unrefined carbohydrates, moderate intake of protein, healthy fat profile, low glycemic load, less inflammation and oxidative stress, and potential modulation of aging-related pathways. A point of difference is that Asian diets typically include pharmacologically potent ingredients, such as turmeric in South Asia and Southeast Asia; *umeboshi* plums and *reishi* mushrooms in Japan; *goji* berries, ginkgo, and licorice root in the PRC; ginseng in the Republic of Korea (ROK); and the medicinal herb *Centella asiatica* in Thailand and Malaysia.

Republic of Korea. In the ROK, socioeconomic and lifestyle changes since the 1970s were accompanied by changes in food choices. Animal products replaced plant foods that had been plentiful in the traditional diet, causing not just changes in energy consumption but also qualitative changes. A traditional Korean diet, compared with a contemporary (Westernized) diet, has been found to improve blood pressure, glycemic control, and cardiovascular risk factors despite slightly larger average caloric intake and a high carbohydrate content, including steamed rice and plant foods. Explanations include health-promoting compounds in the food, and effects from the fermentation central to Korean cuisine.

South Asia and Southeast Asia

India. South Asian traditions have not drawn the same attention as East Asian dietary practices. India's dietary tradition, which has an influence on those throughout Southeast Asia, has its roots in Ayurvedic theory and practice. These offer comprehensive and personalized dietary guidelines for promoting health and managing illness.

[17] F. Leonettia et al. 2016. Effects of Basic Traditional Chinese Diet on Body Mass Index, Lean Body Mass, and Eating and Hunger Behaviours in Overweight or Obese Individuals. *Journal of Traditional Chinese Medicine*. 36 (4). pp. 456–463.

Ayurveda's theory of personalized nutritional, lifestyle, and medicinal guidelines is consistent with an emerging 21st-century prioritization of personalized medicine, and it is strengthened by a growing body of research on the related genomics.

There has been considerable research on food ingredients and spices used in South Asia and Southeast Asian cuisine, including turmeric (*Curcuma longa*), one of the best known natural anti-inflammatory agents. Widely used throughout South Asia and Southeast Asia, turmeric contributes to a dietary approach of preventing and managing type 2 diabetes as well as having well-documented anti-cancer, cardioprotective, and anti-Alzheimer's properties.

Pharmacoactive ingredients are abundant in herbs and spices used in South Asian and Southeast Asian cuisine, including black pepper, chilis, coriander, allspice, and nutmeg. Studies of fruits of the region have identified antioxidant, anti-inflammatory, anti-bacterial, anti-fungal, hypoglycemic, and other beneficial properties.

Clearly, the traditional foods of Asian cultures have valuable health benefits. At the same time, tea, a staple across Asia and so beneficial in East Asia, has become a health risk in South Asia and Southeast Asia because of heavy sweetening.

Malaysia. Malaysia's *ulam* is a unique and pharmacologically potent medicinal herbal salad.

Indonesia. *Jamu,* Indonesia's widely valued herbal beverage tradition, has long been the mainstay for local disease prevention strategies and for the management of common illnesses. Originating in Java and made with turmeric and ginger, which are both potent medicinals, as base ingredients, *jamu* beverages have been found to be powerful anti-inflammatory and antioxidant agents. A well-known wonder herb, turmeric is one of nature's most powerful anti-inflammatory agents. In more than 2,000 studies, turmeric has been shown to reduce and prevent conditions associated with inflammation, such as heart disease, rheumatoid conditions, and even potentially Alzheimer's disease.

From the classic cane basket of glass bottles with rolled leaf stoppers, carried on the backs of women *jamu* sellers throughout Java, *jamu* drinks are now emerging as a commercialized, packaged drink in Southeast Asia.

Rice: Asia's Food Staple

Although bread (i.e., wheat) is a staple in West Asia and parts of South Asia, Asia as a whole represents the world's largest consumer of rice. According to FAO data, in developing countries, rice accounts for 715 kilocalories per day, 27% of the dietary energy supply, 20% of dietary protein, and 3% of dietary fat.

FAO's calculations of food energy, and hence of obesity risk, as presented by Vandevijvere et al., include high rice consumption across Asia.[18] Yet the rice included in these calculations bears little resemblance to the rice that sustained peoples over the centuries.

Ancient (around 10,000-year-old) traditions of rice production, preparation, and consumption exist across Asia. From its beginnings, rice has served as a source of food energy for population growth and health.

Ayurvedic texts describe different rice varieties according to their respective health promotional effects. In India, ethnographic research has documented more than 30 nutritionally valuable varieties of traditional rice and eight

[18] S. Vandevijvere et al. 2015. Increased Food Energy Supply as a Major Driver of the Obesity Epidemic: A Global Analysis. *Bulletin of the World Health Organization*. 93. pp. 446–456.

medicinally valuable varieties. While classical methods of rice preparation included de-husking, farmers did not typically polish the grain by removing the endosperm, as is done in modern industrial processing to produce white rice. It is estimated that polishing rice results in loss of 29% of the protein, 79% of the fat, and 67% of the iron. More importantly, the endosperm contains amino acids, B vitamins, and other nutrients. Without the endosperm, nutrients in rice are depleted while the starch (a polysaccharide) remains intact. White rice, then, becomes a source of high polysaccharide intake, heightening the risk of diabetes and obesity.

A meta-analysis of studies found that white rice consumption is associated with a significantly increased risk of type 2 diabetes. The association was higher in East Asians (Chinese and Japanese) than in populations in West Asia.[19] In South Asia, research has shown that almost half of daily calories come from refined grains. Among these, white rice, which is consumed on a daily basis during the three main meals, is predominant.

In Bangladesh, it has been found that the effect of rice on blood sugar levels differs widely among varieties and "the higher the glycaemic value of a specific variety, the higher its probability to cause diabetes." While high-yielding varieties have greatly increased rice production in Bangladesh, "production is dominated by varieties that lead to sharp rises in blood-sugar levels," i.e., that produce diabetes.[20]

The results from three prospective cohort studies have shown that higher consumption of total whole grains and several commonly eaten whole grain foods, including whole grain breakfast cereal, oatmeal, dark bread, brown rice, added bran, and wheat germ, was significantly associated with a lower risk of type 2 diabetes.[21]

Traditional Rice and the Green Revolution

Naturally, concerns will be raised about this emphasis on traditional crop varieties being a potential backward step, given the perceived transformative effects of the green revolution on food supply, agricultural productivity, and nutrition.

In citing the case of India, which was at the forefront of countries that embraced the green revolution, critics of the green revolution note that the heavy reliance on use of chemical fertilizers and pesticides has resulted in (i) environmental degradation, including loss of soil fertility, erosion of soil, soil toxicity, diminishing water resources, pollution of underground water, and salinity of underground water; and (ii) health consequences, such as a high incidence of cancer, hyperthyroidism, and birth defects in a sizable segment of the population, notably in the agricultural state of Punjab. The key question being asked by policy analysts and critics is whether this food security that resulted from the green revolution has been worth the toll it has taken in terms of human health and a degraded environment.

Of particular concern to critics has been that, while the production of wheat and rice doubled post–green revolution, the production of other food crops, such as indigenous rice varieties and millets, declined. This has led to the loss of distinct indigenous crops from cultivation and has also caused extinction. Researchers have pointed out that many indigenous varieties of rice and millets are resistant to drought, salinity, and floods.[22]

---

19 E.A. Hu et al. 2012. White Rice Consumption and Risk of Type 2 Diabetes: Meta-analysis and Systematic Review. *BMJ*. 344: e1454.

20 Food Planning and Monitoring Unit, Ministry of Food and Disaster Management of the Government of Bangladesh. *Healthy Rice for Healthy Lives*. http://fpmu.gov.bd/agridrupal/sites/default/files/Healthy%20rice_Final.pdf.

21 Y. Hu. 2020. Intake of Whole Grain Foods and Risk of Type 2 Diabetes: Results from Three Prospective Cohort Studies. *BMJ*. 370: m2206. doi: 10.1136/bmj.m2206.

22 R.H. Richharia and S. Govindasamy. 1990. *Rices of India*. Karjat: Academy of Development Science.

Traditional rice cultivars have also been found to have higher nutritional values than hybrid rice varieties,[23] being a rich source of minerals and vitamins such as niacin, thiamine, iron, riboflavin, vitamin D, and calcium, and possessing higher fiber. These cultivars also possess several health benefits, such as reducing the risk of developing type 2 diabetes, obesity, and cardiovascular diseases by lowering the glycemic and insulin responses.[24]

The largest potential improvement of nutritional well-being in Asia could be a shift toward regular consumption of traditional rice varieties. Typically, these are high in essential nutrients and many have lower glycemic indices than commercial varieties. Additionally, their production could be beneficial for biodiversity conservation, agricultural practice, and landscape preservation, as well as for widespread prevention of NCDs and the promotion of nutritional well-being.

The Importance of Documenting Food and Dietary Traditions

Documenting food and dietary traditions is a high-profile demonstration of a commitment to locally sourced food, cultural preservation and promotion, organic sourcing, and contribution to improve local livelihoods, and will create benefit to both the rural and urban levels of society. In addition to recording ingredients and recipes to preserve cultural traditions and create unique new wellness menu offerings, this approach can identify culturally established foods that

(i) combat specific health problems and improve health;
(ii) preserve local traditions that may become lost to imported and fast-food influences; and
(iii) attach science to food traditions so that the new, scientific generation can see tradition in terms of modern insights and understand the science behind the wisdom of their elders.

Through this kind of understanding, food traditions will be more highly valued and passed on to future generations, offering the promise of new eating patterns, new agricultural directions, and new wellness products as part of the $4.5 trillion global wellness economy.[25]

Tapping into the food and beverage market rather than the far tougher medicine market has been profitable for herbal companies and fits well with the booming wellness trends globally. Of course, regulatory hurdles are never far behind new market trends and the climate seems to be getting a little tougher, with good science being the basis for success. In the words of the well-respected trend monitoring group, Euromonitor: "The world is getting older and fatter. As such, health and wellness remain as viable as ever, irrespective of broader economic concerns. Consumers around the world still demand viable health and wellness solutions of ever greater specificity, including gut health and immune system support, weight management, inner beauty, and heart health. However, at least in the near term, tightening regulations represent a significant stumbling block, and further highlight the importance of solid science."[26]

[23] F.M. Bhat. 2015. Health Benefits of Traditional Rice Varieties of Temperate Regions. *Medicinal and Aromatic Plants Research Journal*. 4: 3. http://dx.doi.org/10.4172/2167-0412.1000198.

[24] M. Umadevi et al. 2012. Rice-Traditional Medicinal Plant. *Journal of Pharmacognosy and Phytochemistry*. 1 (1). pp. 6–12.

[25] Global Wellness Institute. *Wellness Industry Statistics & Facts*. https://globalwellnessinstitute.org/press-room/statistics-and-facts.

[26] Euromonitor International. 2010. *Navigating Wellbeing: Today and Tomorrow in Functional Food and Drinks*. http://www.euromonitor.com/navigating-wellbeing-today-and-tomorrow-in-functional-food-and-drinks/report.

Another growing trend in the field of culturally relevant wellness practices is the emergence of what has come to be known as Islamic wellness traditions. Here, traditional foods, beverages, and herbs are being re-evaluated in a fresh light as a means of combating the rising tide of lifestyle diseases in the Middle East and elsewhere throughout the Islamic world, whose population now comprises more than 20% of global population.[27]

What does all of this mean for countries with herbal traditions? How can herbal industries be repositioned to look into these new horizons?

First, there are new opportunities for traditional products to become commercial crops, especially using organic production and fair-trade principles. Wellness consumers favor products with these conditions on the labels of products and are often willing to pay more for these. Companies such as Himalaya Herbals and Organic India in India, and Pukka Herbs in the United Kingdom, have built their product range and consumer base around ethical values, product purity, and environmental sustainability.

Related to this is the potential for medicinal plant ecotourism, a popular and growing segment of the burgeoning global wellness tourism market, which grew to $494 billion in revenues in 2013, a 12.5% gain over 2012.[28]

This can support forestry conservation initiatives that have sustainable medicinal plant projects—both in situ and ex situ—as their focus.

In conclusion, a wellness approach to health nutrition and healthy aging across Asia would focus on

(i) identifying traditional and nutritious varieties of rice to promote as a means of combating the mounting diabetes epidemic across Asia that is linked by research to the consumption of hybrid white rice;
(ii) promoting new and traditional uses of heritage foods, herbs, spices, and seasonings, all of which have potent pharmacological properties for enhancing health and well-being;
(iii) documenting heritage traditions of nutrition and food production, and positioning these toward both an informed domestic market as well as global gourmet and wellness markets that are looking for exactly such products;
(iv) through the school system as well as via conventional and social media, educating people about the benefits of heritage foods and beverages, accompanied by relevant science;
(v) providing incentives to farmers and the agriculture sector more widely to expand production to heritage foods and traditional nutrition;
(vi) building export markets and branding around each country and region's unique heritage foods and their nutritional value; and
(vii) creating unique herbal products for each region, building on traditional knowledge and local production, targeted Asia's booming wellness economy as well as the $1 trillion global personal care, beauty, and anti-aging market, and the $700 billion healthy eating, wellness nutrition, and weight-loss market.[29]

[27] SpaFinder. 2015. Wellness Traditions from the Islamic World. 1 November. www.spafinder.com/blog/health-and-well-being/wellness-traditions-from-the-islamic-world.
[28] Global Wellness Summit. *Industry Research & Trends.* http://www.globalwellnesssummit.com/industry-resource.
[29] See Chapter 2, Figure 2.2.

Movement

There are many well-documented effects of exercise on quality of life (QOL) and longevity (Table 9.1).

Table 9.1 **Health Benefits of Exercise**

1	Help control weight.
2	Reduce the risk of heart diseases.
3	Help the body manage blood sugar and insulin levels, thus mitigating the risks and effects of type 2 diabetes.
4	Help in quitting smoking.
5	Improve mental health and mood.
6	Help keep thinking, learning, and judgment skills sharp with age.
7	Strengthen bones and muscles.
8	Reduce risk of some cancers (including colon, breast, uterine, and lung cancer).
9	Reduce risk of falls in the elderly.
10	Improve sleep.
11	Improve sexual health.
12	Increase chances of living longer.

Source: MedlinePlus. *Benefits of Exercise*. https://medlineplus.gov/benefitsofexercise.html.

Specifically, in a prospective study in rural and urban areas of 17 countries (Argentina, Bangladesh, Brazil, Canada, Chile, Colombia, India, Iran, Malaysia, Pakistan, Poland, the PRC, South Africa, Sweden, Turkey, the United Arab Emirates, and Zimbabwe),[30] Lear et al. found that higher recreational and non-recreational physical activities were associated with a lower risk of mortality and cardiovascular disease (CVD) events in individuals from low-income, middle-income, and high-income countries. Based on this, the researchers pointed out that increasing physical activity is a simple, widely applicable, low-cost global strategy that could reduce deaths and CVD in middle age.

Yet, especially in light of the growing global trend toward gym-based exercise, there are cautions that need to be noted. According to data collected by the US Consumer Product Safety Commission, almost 460,000 people were sent to hospitals in 2012 for injuries related to exercise equipment. The vast majority—nearly 428,000—were treated and released for their injuries. But about 32,000 were hospitalized or were dead on arrival. Of the serious injuries involving exercise equipment, treadmills are among the most common causes seen in emergency rooms. In 2014, hospital emergency departments across the US treated some 24,400 treadmill-related injuries.[31]

According to the Global Wellness Institute's research report *Move to Be Well*,[32] the US and the PRC are by far the world's largest national consumer markets for recreational physical activities, together accounting for 45% of global expenditures. Japan and the ROK are also included in the top 10 recreational physical activity markets globally (Table 9.2).

[30] S.A. Lear et al. 2017. The Effect of Physical Activity on Mortality and Cardiovascular Disease in 130,000 People from 17 High-Income, Middle-Income, and Low-Income Countries: The PURE Study. *The Lancet*. DOI: http://dx.doi.org/10.1016/S0140-6736(17)31634-3.

[31] *USA Today*. 2015. Treadmill Injuries Send Thousands to the ER Every Year. 4 May. https://www.usatoday.com/story/news/2015/05/04/treadmill-emergency-room-injuries-exercise-equipment/26898487.

[32] Global Wellness Institute. 2019. *Move to Be Well*.

Table 9.2 **Top 10 Recreational Physical Activity Markets**

Country	Value ($)
United States	264.6 billion
People's Republic of China	109.3 billion
Japan	43.9 billion
United Kingdom	40.9 billion
Germany	39.4 billion
France	26.3 billion
Republic of Korea	23.5 billion
Italy	19.3 billion
Canada	18.9 billion
Australia	16.7 billion

Source: Global Wellness Institute.

A new and important body of research examines the possibility that benefits from exercise can be inherited. Noting that epigenetics is the study of gene expression changes that occur in the absence of altered genotype, a 2017 review presents experimental evidence indicating that environmentally induced alterations to epigenetic modifications lead to changes in health and disease across generations.[33]

Looking ahead, if exercise can be established to confer benefits to successive generations, surely there is a need for research on the many Asian exercise modalities referenced here and elsewhere to determine if these also benefit not only the practitioner, but their descendants as well. This would be a research agenda designed to support the need for this generation to take action, not only for its own health and well-being but, through this, for the improvement of Asia's health and well-being in the future.

Yoga

The US National Institutes of Health's National Center for Complementary and Integrative Health states: "Recent studies in people with chronic low-back pain suggest that a carefully adapted set of yoga poses may help reduce pain and improve function (the ability to walk and move). Studies also suggest that practicing yoga (as well as other forms of regular exercise) might have other health benefits such as reducing heart rate and blood pressure and may also help relieve anxiety and depression."[34]

According to scientific research, yoga may reduce stress, relieve anxiety, help manage depression, decrease lower back pain, improve QOL in those with chronic conditions or acute illnesses, stimulate brain function, and help prevent heart disease.[35] An estimated $80 billion is spent on yoga worldwide,[36] illustrating how an Asian exercise program can globalize and become a substantial source of revenue.

33 J. Denham. 2017. Exercise and Epigenetic Inheritance of Disease Risk. *Acta Physiologica*. doi:10.1111/apha.12881.

34 National Center for Complementary and Integrative Health. Yoga: What You Need to Know. https://nccih.nih.gov/health/yoga/introduction.htm.

35 Harvard Mental Health Letter. 2020. Yoga for Anxiety and Depression. Updated: October 13, 2020. www.health.harvard.edu/mind-and-mood/yoga-for-anxiety-and-depression.

36 The Good Body. *Yoga Statistics*. https://www.thegoodbody.com/yoga-statistics.

Tai Chi

The National Health Service of the United Kingdom describes the traditional Chinese movement traditions as follows: "Tai chi, also called tai chi chuan, combines deep breathing and relaxation with flowing movements. Originally developed as a martial art in 13th-century [PRC], tai chi is now practised around the world as a health-promoting exercise" and a means of developing self-awareness.[37]

As balance while in motion is the core goal of tai chi, it is not surprising that tai chi has been used as a means of developing and maintaining balance among those at most risk of falling and incurring often life-damaging injuries, namely, the elderly. A meta-analysis of studies on the effects of tai chi in preventing falling in the elderly found that tai chi exercise is indeed effective for preventing falls in older adults. The preventive effect seems to increase with the frequency of tai chi practice. Interestingly, the study found a difference in effect with different styles of tai chi. Yang-style tai chi (created in the 19th century and the most widespread form of tai chi today) seemed to be more effective than Sun-style tai chi, the most recently created form of tai chi.[38]

Veterans with post-traumatic stress symptoms took part in a four-session introduction to tai chi in Boston. In addition to reporting a high degree of satisfaction with the program, participants reported feeling very engaged during the sessions, and found tai chi to be helpful for managing distressing symptoms (i.e., intrusive thoughts, concentration difficulties, and physiological arousal).[39]

In 2016, a map of 107 systematic reviews of tai chi was published. The map identified a number of areas with evidence of a potentially positive treatment effect on patient outcomes, including tai chi for hypertension, fall prevention outside of institutions, cognitive performance, osteoarthritis, depression, chronic obstructive pulmonary disease, pain, balance confidence, and muscle strength.[40] As with all systematic reviews, there was a call for further research to be done to fine-tune these findings.

While yoga and tai chi have become globalized from their origins in India and the PRC, across Asia, there is a multitude of diverse exercise traditions, most derived from local martial arts practices and each usually accompanied by medical knowledge and music and dance for practice. Yoga is perhaps an exception as it derives from meditative movement rather than a martial arts tradition.

Physical Health and Well-Being: Asian Traditional Medicine

Traditional medicine is widely used globally and, since WHO's 1978 Alma-Ata Declaration on Primary Health Care, traditional health systems have been a formal focus of policy development at national and international levels.

The Alma-Ata Declaration,[41] adopted by WHO and the United Nations Children's Fund (UNICEF), stated that:

(i) Primary health care (PHC) is essential health care based on practical, scientifically sound, and socially acceptable methods; and technology made universally accessible to individual and families in the community through their full participation and at a cost that the community and country can afford.

[37] National Health Service. 2018. *A Guide to Tai Chi*. http://www.nhs.uk/Livewell/fitness/Pages/taichi.aspx.
[38] Z.G. Huang et al. 2017. Systematic Review and Meta-analysis: Tai Chi for Preventing Falls in Older Adults. *BMJ Open*. 7 (2).
[39] B.L. Niles et al. Feasibility, Qualitative Findings and Satisfaction of a Brief Tai Chi Mind–Body Programme for Veterans with Post-traumatic Stress Symptoms. *BMJ Open*. 6 (11).
[40] M.R. Solloway et al. 2016. An Evidence Map of the Effect of Tai Chi on Health Outcomes. *Systematic Reviews*. 5: 126.
[41] Declaration of Alma-Ata. 1978. International Conference on Primary Health Care, Alma-Ata, USSR. 6–12 September. www.who.int/docs/default-source/documents/almaata-declaration-en.pdf?sfvrsn=7b3c2167_2.

(ii) PHC forms an integral part both of the country's health system, of which it is the central function and main focus, and of the overall social and economic development of the community. It is the first level of contact of individuals, the family, and community.
(iii) PHC relies, at local and referral levels, on health workers, including physicians, nurses, midwives, auxiliaries, and community workers as applicable, as well as traditional practitioners as needed, suitably trained socially and technically to work as a health team and to respond to the expressed health needs of the community.

Most traditional medicine systems have a theoretical basis, a *materia medica*, a range of therapeutic modalities, an empirical approach to treatment, and a tradition of training. Extensive scientific research has been conducted and published on traditional medicine.

Some traditional medicine practices have been proven safe and effective through controlled clinical trials. Others have been shown to be dangerous (e.g., hepatotoxicity or herb–drug interactions) or ineffective.

In both rural and urban areas, the key point is that there is demand for traditional medicine, and people seek guidance in selecting from traditional and modern health-care options. Increasingly, in line with WHO's policies, partnerships are developing between modern and traditional health practitioners.

The WHO *Global Atlas of Traditional Complementary and Alternative Medicine*[42] provided the first global overview of utilization and policy development in the traditional medicine sector. It was found that more than half of the world's population uses these approaches on a regular basis and pays out of pocket to do so. By this standard, there is nothing "alternative" about these approaches to health care. Rather, they constitute a collective majority body of health practices.

In Asia, more than half of the population is reported to use traditional medicine on a regular basis, varying in usage across urban and rural areas (higher in rural areas) and educational levels. A bimodal curve exists, with high use at low educational and income levels and also with regular usage consistently at the highest educational and income levels.

WHO has produced a strategy on traditional and complementary medicine, which looks ahead to the year 2023.[43] WHO's Traditional Medicine Strategy 2014–2023 has two key goals:

(i) to support member states in harnessing the potential contribution of traditional and complementary medicine (T&CM) to health, wellness, and people-centered health care; and
(ii) to promote the safe and effective use of T&CM through the regulation of products, practices, and practitioners.

Much of the use of traditional medicine by those with higher levels of income and education is for the purpose of health promotion and disease prevention, more widely referred to as wellness.

Traditional Medicine: Models of Integration in Asia

In Asia, there always has been widespread acceptance of traditional medicine at the community level and formal recognition for several decades. In 1956, Viet Nam was the first country in Asia to formally incorporate its traditional medicine system into national health care. The PRC did the same in 1958 and India in 1970. Yet,

[42] G. Bodeker et al. 2005. *WHO Global Atlas of Traditional, Complementary and Alternative Medicine*. Kobe, Japan: WHO Centre for Health Development.
[43] WHO. 2013. WHO Traditional Medicine Strategy: 2014–2023. World Health Organization. https://apps.who.int/iris/handle/10665/92455.

by and large, this has been a system of two parallel tracks, with consumers making the choice between them. It has not been an integrated clinical model of care, offering the best of both systems to consumers according to their needs. This is beginning to change now. Collaborative research in the PRC into traditionally used medicines for fever (febrifuges) led to the identification of the plant *Artemisia annua* used to manage hot-cold fevers, identified as malaria, and thus to the identification of the sesquiterpene lactone *artemisinin*. This paved the way for the development of an entire new class of antimalarial drugs and the awarding of the 2015 Nobel Prize for Medicine to Professor Tu Youyou of the PRC's Yunnan Institute of Pharmacy and Shandong Institutes of Parasitology. Tu discovered a method to extract the active ingredient from *Artemisia annua*, isolated that active ingredient for structural studies, and conducted the first clinical trial of *Artemisia* extract in human patients.

India

India is home to several historical traditions of health care that far predate the introduction of Western medicine. Ayurveda is the main traditional system and is used by the majority of India's population, Hindu, Muslim, and Christian.

Theoretically linked with Ayurveda, yoga is a lifestyle system that includes meditation, physical practices, diet, breathing exercises, and lifelong learning.

The Tamil health-care tradition is called Siddha and is similar to Ayurveda in both theory and clinical practice.

Unani is the Graeco-Arabic health-care tradition that came to India with Muslim conquerors from Afghanistan and Persia from the 8th century to the 16th century.

The arrival in India of homeopathy in the early 19th century led to homeopathy being recognized as a traditional system within Indian health care in 1973, along with Ayurveda, yoga, Unani, and Siddha, which were formally made a part of Indian health care under the Indian Medicine Central Council Act of 1970.

These first letter of each of these five systems—**A**yurveda, **Y**oga, **U**nani, **S**iddha, and **H**omeopathy—have been used to form the acronym **AYUSH**, which is now the name of the Ministry of Ayurveda, Yoga & Naturopathy, Unani, Siddha Homeopathy (Ministry of AYUSH), which is responsible for the development of traditional medicine in India and its integration into formal health-care services.

On 25 September 2018, India's Prime Minister, Narendra Modi, launched the nation's new National Health Protection Scheme, known as Ayushman Bharat Yojana.

The backdrop to this has been highlighted in part by a series of recent research by the Global Burden of Disease (GBD) Study on the epidemiology of selected health conditions in India. Published by *The Lancet* as a series of articles in September 2018, the GBD group concluded that India has a disproportionately high burden of diseases in a number of areas: chronic respiratory diseases, CVD, and cancer. Strikingly, the GBD study found that 32.0% of total global disability-adjusted life years in 2016 occurred in India because of chronic respiratory diseases. CVD is rising in all states of India, with prevalence of ischemic heart disease being highest in the less-developed states. The GBD study found that 8.3% of total deaths and 5.0% of total disability-adjusted life years in India in 2016 were because of cancer. This was double the contribution of cancer in 1990.[44]

With this as the backdrop, the Ayushman Bharat program has been designed to cover more than 100 million vulnerable families, totaling about half a billion beneficiaries, and provide health care up to ₹500,000 per family per year. A beneficiary covered under the scheme will be allowed to take cashless benefits from any public and/or private hospitals registered with the program across the country. The scheme aims to target the lowest-income sectors of Indian society and will cover pre-hospitalization and post-hospitalization expenses. At the time of writing, 14 states had finalized their memoranda of understanding with the central government.

Critics of the program point out that, currently, it is focused on tertiary care, whereas the need in India's rural areas is for PHC services. However, this is also part of the planned rollout with 15 million PHC wellness centers to be in place by 2022. However, to date the AYUSH systems have not been included in planning for Ayushman Bharat. Leading scholars and practitioners of Ayurveda are petitioning the Prime Minister to cover AYUSH under the Ayushman Bharat program as more than 70% people in the country directly or indirectly depend on herbs or plants from which medicines are prepared.

Separate from this public sector debate over whether to integrate Ayurveda into all levels of the formal health system, both private sector and nongovernment organization initiatives have been moving down the road of integration of services for a decade or more. The following is a model in which prevention and home management with Ayurveda are brought together with modern medicine in a rural dermatology setting. This is the other end of the wellness user spectrum—those who are rural, have low income, and are able to benefit from lifestyle changes and interventions drawing from their tradition.

Apollo Hospitals Enterprise Limited, India

While India's Ayushman Bharat program has begun rolling out tertiary care access to the poor of India, but has not yet included the AYUSH system, India's private sector, led by the Apollo hospital group, has moved quite a way down the road of integrated hospital services, offering Ayurveda alongside modern medicine for the treatment of a range of medical conditions, especially cancer.

Founded in 1983, the Apollo hospital group is widely recognized for pioneering the private health care revolution in the country. Apollo health professionals offer therapies drawing on Ayurveda, naturopathy, acupressure, and other complementary traditions.[45]

[44] GBD. 2018. The Increasing Burden of Diabetes and Variations among the States of India: The Global Burden of Disease Study 1990–2016. *The Lancet Global Health*. doi: https://doi.org/10.1016/S2214-109X(18)30387-5; GBD. 2018. The Changing Patterns of Cardiovascular Diseases and Their Risk Factors in the States of India: The Global Burden of Disease Study 1990–2016. *The Lancet Global Health*. doi: https://doi.org/10.1016/S2214-109X(18)30407-8; GBD. 2018. The Burden of Cancers and Their Variations across the States of India: The Global Burden of Disease Study 1990–2016. *The Lancet Oncology*. doi: https://doi.org/10.1016/S1470-2045(18)30447-9; and GBD. 2018. The Burden of Chronic Respiratory Diseases and Their Heterogeneity across the States of India: The Global Burden of Disease Study 1990–2016. *The Lancet Global Health*. doi: https://doi.org/10.1016/S2214-109X(18)30409-1.

[45] Apollo Hospitals. 2019. Together, Working Towards a Healthier World: The Apollo Excellence Report 2019. https://www.apollohospitals.com/apollo_pdf/apollo-excellence-report-2019-e-version.pdf.

People's Republic of China

The PRC formally incorporated traditional Chinese medicine (TCM) into national health care in the late 1950s. Over the past 2 decades, the PRC has taken a proactive position in promoting TCM both within the PRC and internationally. WHO's Traditional Medicine Division has received funding from the PRC for many years and has developed standards for TCM diagnosis, clinical practice, and herbal formulation. A September 2018 report in *Nature* announced that TCM disease classifications were to be included as Chapter 26 in WHO's 2019 International Statistical Classification of Diseases and Related Health Problems.[46]

Guang'anmen Hospital of Traditional Chinese Medicine, Beijing

One major area where the integration of TCM and modern medicine has advanced is in cancer care. In Beijing, the Guang'anmen Hospital of Traditional Chinese Medicine is affiliated with the China Academy of Traditional Chinese Medicine. The Oncology Department of Guang'anmen Hospital was established in 1963 and from the outset has integrated Chinese and Western medicine. In February 1997, it became the National TCM Oncology Specialist Medical Center.[47]

The Oncology Department of Guang'anmen Hospital has specialized clinical treatment groups for lung cancer, gastrointestinal cancer, liver cancer, and breast cancer and has conducted in-depth research on comprehensive treatment of various cancers. TCM medicines are prepared in the hospital's pharmacies and are reported to have no obvious side effects. Doctors choose treatments according to the patient's condition and disease type.

Ongoing research has shown that this program significantly improves the clinical outcomes of cancer patients, reduces pain, and prolongs survival time. The Oncology Department of Guang'anmen Hospital also runs regular training programs for both Chinese and international physicians in methodologies for integrating TCM into cancer care.

In Guang'anmen patients with early-stage pancreatic cancer, research has found superior survival benefits using integrative medicine treatment compared to solely TCM.[48] TCM has also been found to have parallels with immunotherapy, a new and effective form of cancer therapy.[49]

Community-Level Intervention with Noncommunicable Diseases

A study carried out by researchers from universities in Nanjing assessed the impact of both community-based integrated TCM and Western medicine approaches in treating metabolic syndrome among rural residents in southern Jiangsu Province, PRC.

According to the GBD study, in terms of the number of years of life lost because of premature death in the PRC, cerebrovascular disease, ischemic heart disease, and chronic obstructive pulmonary disease were the highest-ranking causes in 2010. The leading risk factor in the PRC is dietary risks.[50]

---

[46] D. Cryanoski. 2018. Why Chinese Medicine Is Heading for Clinics around the World. *Nature*. 561. pp. 448–450. doi: 10.1038/d41586-018-06782-7.

[47] Guang'anmen Hospital. Hospital Overview. http://www.gamhospital.ac.cn/ywb/about.html.

[48] M. Li et al. 2018. Different Survival Benefits of Chinese Medicine for Pancreatic Cancer: How to Choose? *Chinese Journal of Integrative Medicine*. 24 (3). pp. 178–184.

[49] G. Bodeker. 2012. Integrative Oncology Meets Immunotherapy: New Prospects for Combination Therapy Grounded in Eastern Medical Knowledge. *Chinese Journal of Integrative Medicine*. 18 (9). pp. 652–662.

[50] GBD. 2010. *GBD Profile: China*. https://www.healthdata.org/sites/default/files/files/country_profiles/GBD/ihme_gbd_country_report_china.pdf (accessed 18 October 2018).

In the study on metabolic syndrome among rural residents in Southern Jiangsu, the research team designed a "healthy life self-help program" using TCM and appropriate technologies for the subjects.[51]

The researchers reported that, after 2 years of intervention using integrated traditional Chinese and Western medicine approaches, 57.0% (341 persons) of the subjects no longer suffered from metabolic syndrome. The recovery rate of body mass index, blood pressure, fasting blood glucose (FBG), triglycerides (TG), and high-density lipoprotein (HDL) cholesterol were 22.1%, 40.5%, 37.9%, 32.8%, and 62.4%, respectively. There were statistically significant differences in exercise, smoking, and alcohol drinking between baseline and 2 years later. This led to the conclusion that the integrated traditional Chinese and Western medicine metabolic syndrome intervention was effective in decreasing most of the parameters of metabolic syndrome, especially blood pressure, and helping people to do more exercise. They concluded that the program would be useful to implement in other similar populations.

From rural communities reducing their household expenditures on medicines to tertiary care hospitals offering a combination traditional and modern medicine as well as traditional lifestyle guidelines to prevent recurrence of illness and to promote wellness, Asia is taking a global lead in forging models of integrative care that draw on traditions that have wellness and thriving at the heart of their philosophies and treatment regimens. Supported by WHO policy, this is an area that can be rolled out further across Asia, backed by rigorous scientific evaluation and evidence, to create a wellness-based approach to health care, grounded in tradition.

Mental Wellness

As noted in Chapter 8, "Mental Wellness," there is a wide range of individual and community approaches to reducing the burden of mental illness by promoting the adoption of evidence-based pathways that are familiar within Asia culturally and can prevent stress, reduce depression and anxiety, and promote mental well-being throughout the life span. That chapter presents new directions for improving mental wellness across Asia in accord with the principles of de-institutionalization, patient-centered care, personal responsibility for mental and physical health, community support systems, and evidence as the basis for strengthening the widespread adoption of culturally familiar pathways to mental wellness.

Meditation, massage, social support, music, dance, and laughter are all important pathways to mental well-being, and the Asian cultural dimensions of these have been addressed in the chapter on mental wellness.

Environment

Clearly, a wellness agenda drawing on Asian traditions must address the growing problem of air pollution as Asia urbanizes. WHO notes: "As the world gets hotter and more crowded, our engines continue to pump out dirty emissions, and half the world has no access to clean fuels or technologies (e.g. stoves, lamps), the very air we breathe is growing dangerously polluted: nine out of ten people now breathe polluted air, which kills 7 million people every year." WHO goes on to explain, "The health effects of air pollution are serious—one third of deaths from stroke, lung cancer and heart disease are due to air pollution. This is having an equivalent effect to that of smoking tobacco, and much higher than, say, the effects of eating too much salt."[52]

[51] Y. Wang et al. 2015. Impact of Community-Based Integrated Traditional Chinese and Western Medicine Metabolic Syndrome Intervention Technology in Rural Residents in Southern Jiangsu, People's Republic of China. *Medical Science Monitor*. 21. pp. 2163–2169. doi: 10.12659/MSM.893972 PMCID: PMC4520418 PMID: 26210819.

[52] WHO. How Air Pollution Is Destroying Our Health. https://www.who.int/airpollution/news-and-events/how-air-pollution-is-destroying-our-health.

A systematic review of global data has found that people living with air pollution have higher rates of depression and suicide.[53]

Research from the PRC, which is home to 16 of the 20 most polluted cities in the world according to the United Nations' list, has found that bad air quality contributes to poor mental health and unhappiness. Researchers looked at the impact of air pollution on several key dimensions, including mental health status, depressive symptoms, moment-to-moment happiness, and evaluative happiness (i.e., overall life satisfaction). What they found was that air pollution reduces all forms of happiness and increases the rate of depressive symptoms over time.[54]

Conversely, people tend to live longer when they have access to green space, and perceived neighborhood greenness is strongly associated with better mental and physical health.[55] Those living in highly green areas are much more likely to have better physical and mental health than those living near open areas that are not highly green.[56]

Nature near home is particularly important for children, increasing their ability to cope with stressful life events, directed attention, and cognitive function.[57] Exposure and connectedness to nature have been found to be associated with body appreciation and self-esteem in women and men.[58]

New research has reported that gentle woodland sounds, such as birdsong and the breeze rustling leaves in the trees, are more relaxing than meditation recordings. Researchers exposed participants to three soundtracks: a woodland, a woman guiding a meditation session, and deep silence. When asked to listen to the woodland sounds for one minute, people felt 30% more relaxed, while stress and anxiety dropped. There was no change in the level of relaxation people felt after listening to the meditation or the silence.[59]

Reducing pollution, building green cities, and creating access to nature for Asia's burgeoning population will need to be a foundational component of wellness planning and development throughout the 21st century.

Conclusion

The majority of the world's population lives in Asia. From West Asia to East Asia, societies reflect an enormous array of cultural diversity. A capabilities approach to economic analysis highlights the power of individuals to do certain things, to obtain what they desire, to achieve desired states of being, to utilize the resources they have in the way they desire, and to be who they want to be. From this perspective, Asia has a varying landscape of wants, satisfactions, and aspirations that is different from country to country and across the vast subregions of Asia. What is common is that the desire to enhance quality of life (QOL), not just the amount of goods possessed,

---

[53] I. Braithwaite et al. 2019. Air Pollution (Particulate Matter) Exposure and Associations with Depression, Anxiety, Bipolar, Psychosis and Suicide Risk: A Systematic Review and Meta-Analysis. *Environmental Health Perspectives*. 127 (12). CID: 126002. https://doi.org/10.1289/EHP4595.

[54] X. Zhang, X. Zhang, and X. Chen. 2017. Happiness in the Air: How Does a Dirty Sky Affect Mental Health and Subjective Well-being? *Journal of Environmental Economics and Management*. (85). pp. 81–94.

[55] T. Tanako, K. Nakamura, and M. Watanabar. 2002. Urban Residential Environments and Senior Citizens Longevity in Megacity Areas: The Importance of Walkable Green Spaces. *Journal of Epidemiology and Community Health*. 56. pp. 913–918.

[56] T. Sugiyama et al. 2008. Associations of Neighbourhood Greenness with Physical and Mental Health: Do Walking, Social Coherence and Local Social Interaction Explain the Relationships? *Journal of Epidemiology and Community Health*. 62: e9. 10.1136/jech.2007.064287.

[57] N. Wells. 2000. At Home with Nature Effects of "Greenness" on Children's Cognitive Functioning. *Environment and Behavior*. 32. pp. 775–795. 10.1177/00139160021972793.

[58] V. Swami et al. 2016. Bodies in Nature: Associations between Exposure to Nature, Connectedness to Nature, and Body Image in U.S. Adults. *Body Image*. 18. pp. 153–61. doi: 10.1016/j.bodyim.2016.07.002. Epub 2016 Jul 29.

[59] National Trust. 2019. *Places That Make Us*. https://nt.global.ssl.fastly.net/documents/places-that-make-us-research-report.pdf.

is constant across Asian societies. Yet modernization, which is largely Westernization, has created trends in health, environment, and mental health that reflect declining standards of well-being. Asia's own traditions offer nutritional and medical pathways that are consistent with evidence-based optimal wellness.

With the mounting body of evidence in support of the health value of Asia's wellness traditions, it is time for governments, civil society, families, and community leaders to bring these heritage traditions to the fore. Asia's deep traditions of wellness can enhance the well-being of individuals and societies and create new commercial opportunities across the board, both domestically and internationally.

Further Reading

V. B. Preethi Sudha et al. 2012. Storing Drinking Water in Copper Pots Kills Contaminating Diarrhoeagenic Bacteria. *Journal of Health, Population and Nutrition*. 30 (1). pp. 17–21. doi: 10.3329/jhpn.v30i1.11271.

Y.Y. Zhu et al. 2000. Genetic Diversity and Disease Control in Rice. *Nature*. 406. pp. 718–722.

CHAPTER 10

Aging and Wellness in Asia

Gerard Bodeker, Madhavi Pundit, Pilipinas Quising, and Shu Tian

All of the world's societies are in the midst of a longevity revolution. Older people account for more than one-fifth of the population in 17 countries today, and projections for the end of the century anticipate that this will be the case for 155 countries in 2100, covering a majority (61%) of the world's population. This chapter takes a closer look at aging. It examines the demographic impact of aging on the global wellness industry, the connection between retirement and well-being, different wellness pathways, and policies to promote healthy aging

Introduction

As noted in *World Population Prospects 2019*, by 2050, 1 in 6 people in the world will be over the age of 65, up from 1 in 11 in 2019. *World Population Ageing 2019* explains that:[1]

> All societies in the world are in the midst of this longevity revolution—some are at its early stages and some are more advanced. But all will pass through this extraordinary transition, in which the chance of surviving to age 65 rises from less than 50%, as was the case in Sweden in the 1890s, to more than 90%, as it is at present in countries with the highest life expectancy. What is more, the proportion of adult life spent beyond age 65 increased from less than a fifth in the 1960s to a quarter or more in most developed countries today.
>
> These changes for individuals are mirrored in societal changes. Older persons are a growing demographic group in society and account for more than one-fifth of the population in 17 countries today. Projections for the end of the century indicate that this will be the case for 155 countries in 2100, covering a majority (61%) of the world's population [See Figure 10.1.]
>
> Traditionally, most researchers have used measures and indicators of population aging that are mostly or entirely based on chronological age, defining older persons as those aged 60 or 65 years or over. This provides a simple, clear, and easily replicable way of measuring and tracking various indicators of population aging.

The recent development of alternatives to measures and indicators of population aging offers a more nuanced perspective of what population aging means in different contexts. New measures and concepts of population

[1] United Nations. 2019. *2019 Revision of World Population Prospects*. https://population.un.org/wpp; United Nations, Department of Economic and Social Affairs, Population Division. 2019. *World Population Ageing 2019*: Highlights (ST/ESA/SER.A/430).

aging have significant implications for assessing the living conditions and living arrangements of older persons, their productive and other contributions to society, and their needs for social protection and health care.

Aging in Asia

"Population ageing is poised to become one of the most significant social transformations of the twenty-first century, with implications for nearly all sectors of society, including labour and financial markets, the demand for goods and services, such as housing, transportation and social protection, as well as family structures and intergenerational ties."
—United Nations

Asian economies are aging, and some quite rapidly. Between 2020 and 2030, the number of people in developing Asia aged 65 years or over is projected to grow by 46.2%, from 353 million to 516 million. By 2050, the population of older persons is projected to more than double its size, reaching nearly 839 million. In 2020, in terms of proportion to the whole population, 9% of the region's population was older than 65, up from 6% in 2010, and this is expected to double to 18% by 2050. Figure 10.1 shows the distribution of various age groups by gender in the population of developing Asia from 1990 to 2020, and the United Nations population projections until 2050. The figure illustrates a striking demographic shift from a typical pyramid shape to a structure that is more top-heavy as the population is aging. This means that, while in 2010, 1 in 16 persons living in developing Asia was over 65 years old, by 2050 it could be 1 in 6 (Figure 10.2). Looking across genders, in 2020 women accounted for about 53% of the population aged 65 years or over, and this share is expected to stay stable.

Figure 10.1 **Population Distribution, Developing Asia**

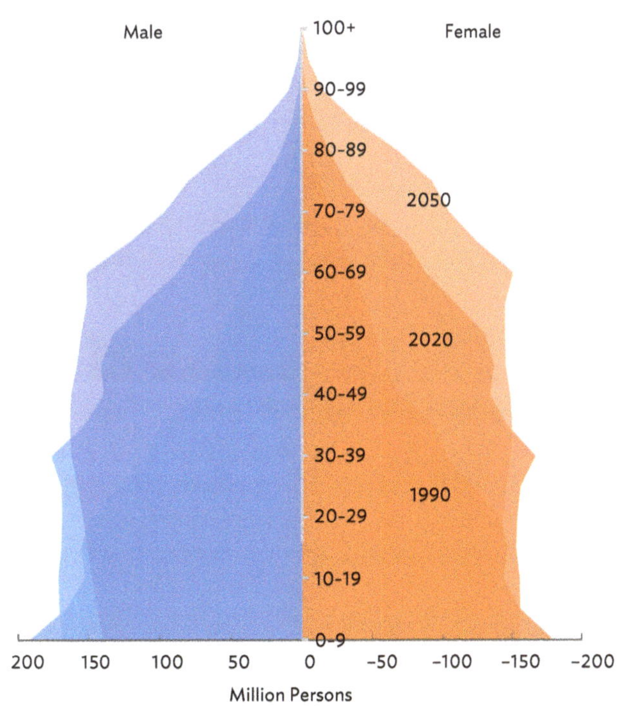

Source: United Nations Population Projections. https://population.un.org/wpp/Download/Standard/Population (accessed 15 January 2020).

Among the subregions, East Asia has the highest proportion of population aged 65 or above, with more than half the number of developing Asia's older people residing there (Figure 10.3). Projections indicate that the proportion of people aged 65 years or over will increase by 8.9 percentage points over the next 15 years, compared with the 4.6 percentage point increase that occurred between 2005 and 2020. Compared with East Asia, the proportion of older persons is expected to grow fastest in Southeast Asia (4.9 percentage points) between 2020 and 2035, followed by Central Asia (3.8), South Asia (2.8), and the Pacific (1.4).

Figure 10.2 **Proportion of Population Aged 65 and Over**

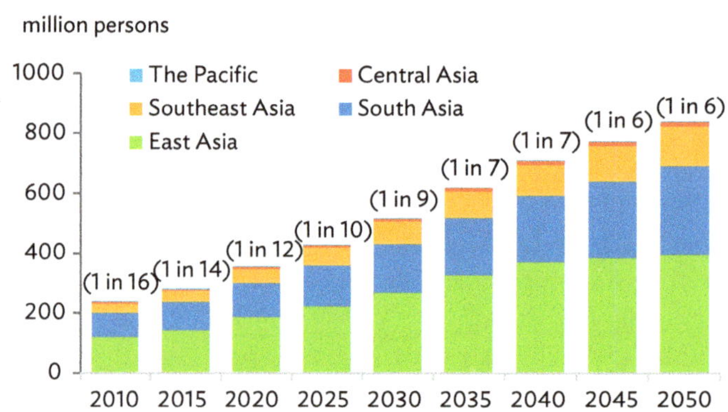

Source: United Nations Population Projections. https://population.un.org/wpp/Download/Standard/Population (accessed 15 January 2020).

Figure 10.3 **Share of Population Aged 65 and Over by Subregion**

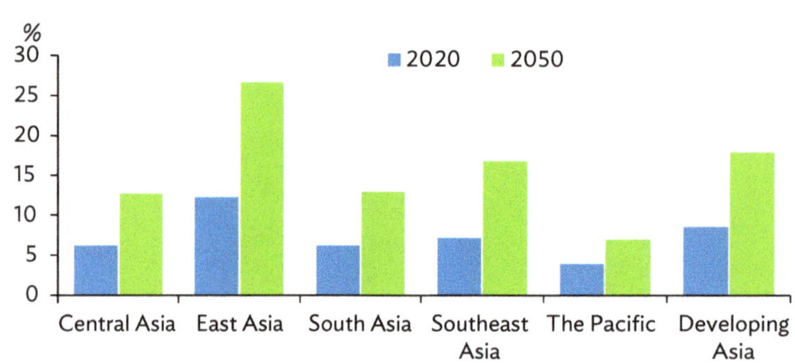

Source: United Nations Population Projections. https://population.un.org/wpp/Download/Standard/Population (accessed 15 January 2020).

While demographic shifts are evident across subregions, the development stage varies in economies even within a subregion. This is evident in the evolution of the old-age dependency ratio, i.e., the share of population aged 65 years or older compared to the working age population (15–64 years). For instance, the Republic of Korea and Hong Kong, China can be classified at an advanced stage of demographic transition, with an old-age dependency ratio of more than 22% in 2020, which is expected to go up to 64% by 2050 (Figure 10.4). In the middle stage are India and Indonesia, with about a 9% dependency ratio in 2020 that will increase to 20% by 2050. On the other hand, Tajikistan is classified at an early stage, with a stable old-age dependency ratio.

Figure 10.4 **Old-Age Dependency Ratio, Selected Asian Economies**

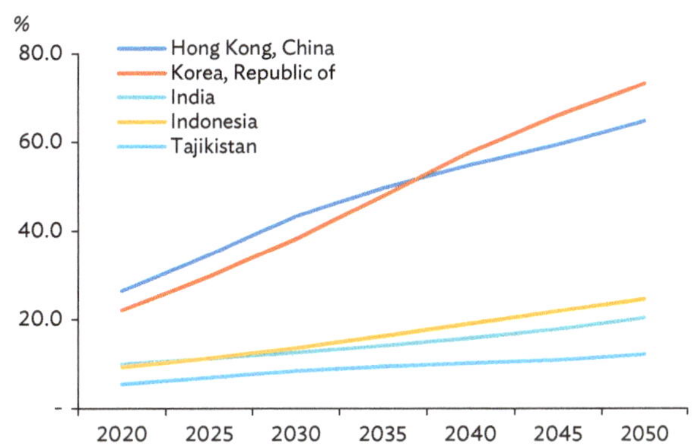

Note: The old-age dependency ratio is the share of population aged 65 and over to working-age population (15–64 years old).

Source: Population Division, Department of Economic and Social Affairs, United Nations Secretariat. *World Population Prospects: The 2019 Revision.*

In other parts of the world, the shifts in demographic structure can be attributed partly to declining rates of fertility (Figure 10.5). Changes in fertility and mortality are associated with economic progress and development, and help to predict the present and future rates of growth of the older population. In Asia, a rapid decline in fertility began in the mid-1960s, which will result in a drop in the growth rate of older persons after 2025. However, more longevity will increase the number of survivors to older ages. So, while in 1990, a 60-year-old person in developing Asia could expect to live an additional 4.8 years on average, by 2020, this number had improved to 13.5 years, and by 2050, it will be 17.9 years. For many Asian economies, particularly those in the advanced stages of demographic transition, the fertility rate is expected to decline slightly, and life expectancy rates that are already high will increase steadily (Table 10.1). This suggests that the demographic shifts for these economies can be mainly attributed to increased longevity.

Figure 10.5 **Fertility, Selected Asian Economies**
(average number of live births per woman)

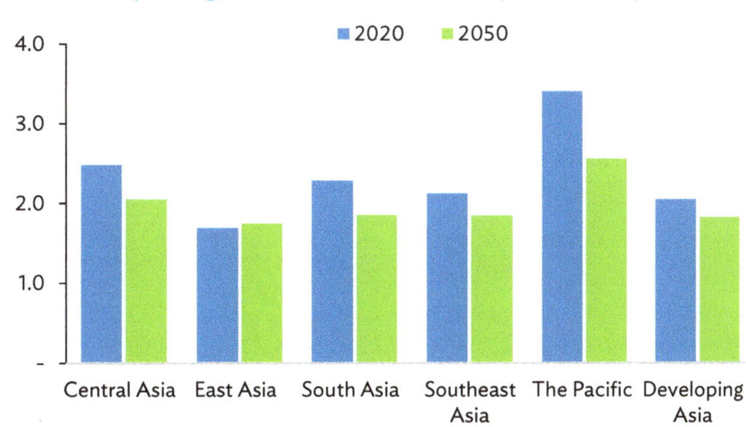

Source: Population Division, Department of Economic and Social Affairs, United Nations Secretariat. *World Population Prospects: The 2019 Revision.*

Table 10.1 **Life Expectancy at Birth**

	Total		Male		Female	
	2020	**2050**	**2020**	**2050**	**2020**	**2050**
Central Asia	72.5	76.2	69.4	73.2	75.5	79.2
East Asia	77.7	82.5	75.5	81.0	80.0	84.0
South Asia	70.4	75.2	69.1	73.4	71.8	77.1
Southeast Asia	73.1	77.6	70.2	74.9	76.2	80.3
The Pacific	66.8	71.1	65.2	69.2	68.4	73.2
Developing Asia	**73.5**	**77.9**	**71.6**	**76.0**	**75.6**	**79.8**

Note: Weighted average using population as weights.

Source: Population Division, Department of Economic and Social Affairs, United Nations Secretariat. *World Population Prospects: The 2019 Revision.*

Aging or Healthy Aging?

Of the total global burden of disease, 23% is attributable to disorders in people aged 60 years and older. Although the proportion of the burden attributable to older people (≥60 years) is highest in high-income regions, disability-adjusted life years (DALYs) per capita are 40% higher in low-income and middle-income regions, accounted for by the increased burden per capita of population arising from cardiovascular diseases, and sensory, respiratory, and infectious disorders.[2]

The leading contributors to disease burden in older people are cardiovascular diseases (30.3% of the total burden in people aged 60 years and older), malignant neoplasms (15.1%), chronic respiratory diseases (9.5%), musculoskeletal diseases (7.5%), and neurological and mental disorders (6.6%).

Governments worldwide are moving with urgency to introduce policies that address population aging. The Global Burden of Disease (GBD) study has noted that whether increased longevity is an opportunity or a threat to the stability of societies depends not only on whether populations are living longer, but on whether they are experiencing the negative health effects of aging. The negative health effects of aging are characterized by progressive loss of physical, mental, and cognitive integrity, leading to impaired functions and increased vulnerability to morbidity and mortality.[3]

In a 2019 study published in *The Lancet*, the GBD project used new metrics to calculate the risk to societies of the negative health effects of aging. They began by taking the global average of 65-year-olds as the reference population, and calculated their equivalent age in terms of age-related disease burden for all countries or territories. This enabled the authors to describe how countries with similar levels of overall age-related burden experience different onsets of aging.

The results showed:

(i) A total of 92 diseases were identified as age-related, accounting for 51.3% (95% uncertainty intervals 48.5–53.9) of all global burden among adults in 2017.

(ii) The rate of age-related burden ranged from 137.8 DALYs (128.9–148.3) per 1,000 adults in high Social Development Index countries to 265.9 DALYs (251.0–280.1) in low Social Development Index countries.

[2] P. Wu et al. 2014. The Burden of Disease in Older People and Implications for Health Policy and Practice. *The Lancet*. 385 (9967).

[3] A. Chang et al. 2019. Measuring Population Ageing: An Analysis of the Global Burden of Disease Study 2017. *The Lancet Public Health*. 4. pp. e159–167.

(iii) The equivalent age to average 65-year-olds globally spanned from 76.1 years (75.6–76.7) in Japan to 45.6 years (42.6–48.2) in Papua New Guinea.

This new metric provides a means to facilitate a shift from thinking not just about chronological age, but about the health status and disease severity of aging populations. The finding is striking: countries with similar levels of overall age-related burden experience different onsets of aging. For example, 76-year-olds in Japan and 46-year-olds in Papua New Guinea have the same level of age-related disease burden as the global average 65-year-old (footnote 3).

Related research has highlighted the importance of mental health and behavioral problems in setting in motion the development of a range of socioeconomically patterned physical illnesses. Across the three main socioeconomic position indicators and after adjustment for lifestyle factors, compared with more advantaged groups, low socioeconomic status was found to be associated with increased risk for 18 (32.1%) of 56 identified conditions. Sixteen diseases formed a cascade of interrelated health conditions with a hazard ratio greater than 5. This sequence began with psychiatric disorders, substance abuse, and self-harm, which were associated with later liver and renal diseases, ischemic heart disease, cerebral infarction, chronic obstructive bronchitis, lung cancer, and dementia.

While primary prevention in adults aged younger than 60 years old will improve health in successive cohorts of older people, much of the potential to reduce disease burden will come from more effective primary, secondary, and tertiary prevention that targets older people. Policy and health-care practices that address psychological health issues in social context and early in the life course could be effective strategies for reducing health inequalities.

In countries where public transfers from taxation and benefits are relatively low, such as many in South Asia and Southeast Asia, individuals and families face greater pressure to finance their consumption during old age. It is important to establish social protection programs that can be sustained over the long term to prevent poverty, reduce inequality, and promote social inclusion among older persons.

From an Asia-wide policy perspective, these findings underscore the importance of identifying exemplary policies and strategies that reduce DALYs and enhance quality of life so that these can serve as reference points for nationally tailored public health interventions to mitigate the negative effects of aging, and to enhance opportunities for healthy aging. If promoted across the life span, these strategies will be most effective.

Life span approaches to well-being place preeminent importance on a cluster of factors that contribute to quality of life as being central in ensuring a life journey toward fulfilled and healthy aging. These include regular exercise, good nutrition, meaningful social relationships, ability to contribute to society, connection with nature through gardening and nature walks, and a positive mindset.

Aging and Its Demographic Impact on the Global Wellness Industry

The Wellness Industry and Possible Driving Factors

Wellness relates to the concepts of well-being, happiness, and quality of life. With increasing awareness and attention paid to wellness, more demand for wellness products and services emerges in the market and contributes to people's wellness around the world. Thus, it is important to understand what factors drive the expansion of the wellness industry across markets, so that related policies can be formed to foster its further development and boost people's wellness.

The most recognized determinant of wellness, which therefore relates to the wellness industry, is income level. People with higher income are in a better position to boost their own wellness. A positive association between income level, captured by real gross domestic product (GDP) per capita, and wellness has been documented in the literature.[4] Related to income level, consumption is also positively associated with wellness.[5] In addition, good economic performance also enhances wellness by improving people's income, job security, social safety, business opportunities, and overall life quality.

Wellness is not fully determined by economic progress, individual income, and consumption. Socioeconomic and socioenvironmental factors also affect wellness. These include culture and kinship, health and nutrition, employment and working conditions, social support networks, education, social relationships, environment, marriage, work–life balance, social comparison, status anxiety, and individual lifestyle factors.[6]

This study utilizes GDP growth, GDP per capita, and consumption expenditure per capita as possible economic factors alongside the following social factors: aging (percentage of 65+-year-olds in total population), healthy living (life expectancy at birth), employment, medical and educational situation (urbanization), and stability of socioeconomic conditions, and examines their impacts on the development of the wellness industry.

Data and Methodology

The Global Wellness Institute is the primary source of data for the wellness industry. In this analysis, the number and revenue of hot springs, spa establishments, and wellness tourist arrivals for 124 economies in 2017 are used to capture wellness industry development.

Data on GDP growth rate, GDP per capita, financial consumption expenditure per capita, urban population percentage of total population, and life expectancy at birth are collected from the World Bank's World Development Indicators. The ratio of people 65 years old and up to total population is from the United Nations Population Division. The political risk rating of socioeconomic conditions is collected from the PRS Group's International Country Risk Guide. The risk rating score has three subcomponents: unemployment, consumer confidence, and poverty. Each subcomponent has a maximum score of 4, indicating very low risk, and a minimum score of 0, indicating very high risk, and the socioeconomic condition score is the sum of the three. The economic and social factors data are as of 2016. The descriptive statistics of the sample are provided in Table 10.2.

The wellness industry development in each country is regressed on a vector of economic and social factors to understand the association between economic and social factors and development of the wellness industry.

Results and Discussions

Table 10.2 shows the results for the determinants of the wellness industry for the sampled countries. It can be seen that the socioeconomic indicator that combines unemployment, consumer confidence, and poverty shows

4 For example, D. Sacks, B. Stevenson, and J. Wolfers. 2010. Subjective Well-being, Income. *Economic Development and Growth*. No. w16441. National Bureau of Economic Research; and C. Jones and P. Klenow. 2016. Beyond GDP? Welfare across Countries and Time. *American Economic Review*. 106 (9). pp. 2426–2457.

5 B. Headey, R. Muffels, and M. Wooden. 2008. Money Does Not Buy Happiness: Or Does It? A Reassessment Based on the Combined Effects of Wealth, Income and Consumption. *Social Indicators Research*. 87. pp. 65–82. doi: 10.1007/s11205-007-9146-y.

6 J. Delhey and G. Dragolov. 2014. Why Inequality Makes Europeans Less Happy: The Role of Distrust, Status Anxiety, and Perceived Conflict. *European Sociological Review*. 30 (2). pp. 151–165; K.J. Yi et al. 2015. Factors Influencing the Health and Wellness of Urban Aboriginal Youths in Canada: Insights of In-service Professionals, Care Providers, and Stakeholders. *American Journal of Public Health*. 105 (5). pp. 881–890; V. Reyes-García et al. 2015. Subjective Wellbeing and Income: Empirical Patterns in the Rural Developing World. *Journal of Happiness Studies*. 17 (2). pp. 773–791; and S. Schneider. 2016. Income Inequality and Subjective Wellbeing: Trends, Challenges, and Research Directions. *Journal of Happiness Studies*. 17 (4). pp. 1719–1739.

Table 10.2 **Summary Statistics of the Sample Data**

Variables	Observation	Mean	Median	Minimum	Maximum	Standard Deviation
Dependent variables						
Log number of hot spring establishments	89	3.33	3.37	0.00	9.95	1.99
Log number of spa establishments	124	5.57	5.54	0.69	10.18	1.79
Log number of wellness tourist arrivals	124	13.41	13.57	6.08	18.99	2.59
Log revenue of hot spring establishments	88	17.41	17.47	9.35	23.59	2.69
Log revenue of spa establishments	124	18.52	18.71	12.64	23.76	2.19
Log revenue of wellness tourist arrivals	124	19.89	20.08	13.44	26.14	2.55
Explanatory variables						
GDP growth (annual %)	124	2.91	2.94	-17.04	13.40	3.16
Log GDP per capita (constant 2010 US$)	124	8.90	8.95	5.97	11.61	1.49
Log final consumption expenditure per capita (constant 2010 US$)	124	8.62	8.74	5.72	10.99	1.37
Ratio of old 65 and up to total population	124	9.37	6.76	0.93	26.02	6.39
Life expectancy at birth, total (years)	124	73.38	75.23	53.44	84.23	7.85
Socioeconomic condition	124	5.95	5.81	0.83	10.83	2.39
Urban population % of total population	124	65.24	67.98	16.29	100.00	20.92

GDP = gross domestic product.

Source: Authors' computation.

quite a strong impact on the wellness industry, indicating the relevance of a sound socioeconomic environment to wellness industry development.

In terms of hot spring establishments, a higher ratio of 65 years old and up to total population is significantly and positively associated with an increased number and revenue of hot spring establishments. An increase of 1% more of the total population with ages of 65 years and above will raise the number of hot spring establishments by 0.20% and increase the revenue from hot spring establishments by 0.29%. Also, a more stable socioeconomic condition significantly relates to the revenue of hot spring establishments. This evidence indicates that an older population may lead to greater demand for wellness industry establishments such as hot springs to boost wellness.

Regarding spa establishments, higher life expectancy and socioeconomic conditions are both found to be significantly and positively associated with the number and revenue of spa establishments. This result indicates that both healthy lifestyles and stable socioeconomic conditions foster the demand for wellness industry establishments such as spas. Looking at wellness tourist arrivals, economies with higher life expectancy and stable socioeconomic conditions attract more wellness tourist arrivals. This shows that the wellness industry will benefit from a local market's higher quality of life and favorable socioeconomic conditions.

Overall, the analysis reveals that both economic and social factors show significant association with the size of the wellness industry in global markets. Different wellness businesses that target customers bearing various social characteristics will see ample opportunities in the future. This study sheds lights on how the global wellness industry may cater to various customer demands in different local market conditions.

Table 10.3 **The Association between Economic and Social Factors and the Development of the Wellness Industry**

Variables	Log Number of Hot Spring Establishments	Log Revenue of Hot Spring Establishments	Log Number of Spa Establishments	Log Revenue of Spa Establishments	Log Number of Wellness Tourist Arrivals	Log Revenue of Wellness Tourist Arrivals
GDP growth (annual %)	-0.07693	-0.03432	-0.06820	0.00958	-0.02925	0.01272
	(0.04774)	(0.06305)	(0.04119)	(0.06186)	(0.05752)	(0.06375)
Log GDP per capita (constant)	0.75762	0.58996	-0.16238	-0.05531	-0.84861	-0.82380
	(1.31562)	(1.62989)	(0.73611)	(0.77567)	(0.96237)	(0.88543)
Log final consumption expenditure per capita	-1.86566	-1.17719	0.13801	0.36477	0.75314	1.09454
	(1.50178)	(1.81109)	(0.88920)	(0.92281)	(1.10229)	(1.03172)
Urbanization ration % of total population	0.01105	0.01740	-0.01575	-0.01543	-0.01905	-0.02068*
	(0.01295)	(0.01557)	(0.00952)	(0.00985)	(0.01249)	(0.01168)
Ratio of age 65 and up to total population	0.19599***	0.28665***	0.03724	0.02202	0.06236	0.00493
	(0.05653)	(0.05906)	(0.03202)	(0.03209)	(0.03824)	(0.03516)
Life expectancy at birth (years)	0.05954	0.00445	0.09010**	0.11876***	0.16708***	0.17284***
	(0.05031)	(0.06374)	(0.03555)	(0.04004)	(0.04550)	(0.04504)
Socioeconomic conditions	0.24451	0.31747*	0.24560**	0.22452*	0.35797**	0.29856*
	(0.15102)	(0.18607)	(0.12149)	(0.12762)	(0.17719)	(0.16033)
Constant	4.20818	15.83431***	-1.37116	6.58783***	0.82694	4.59015*
	(3.54788)	(4.67621)	(2.10799)	(2.25177)	(2.73669)	(2.53069)
Observations	89	88	124	124	124	124
R-squared	0.26031	0.47284	0.44697	0.58919	0.57342	0.61168
Adjusted R-squared	0.196	0.427	0.414	0.564	0.548	0.588

GDP = gross domestic product, *** p<0.01, ** p<0.05, * p<0.1.

Note: Robust standard errors are in parentheses.

Source: Authors' computation.

Retirement and Well-Being

Retirement can be either an advantageous or a disadvantageous period for those who retire. For many, it is a much-awaited reward for years of hard work—a time for relaxation and reaping the benefits of one's previous work life, unburdened by the daily grind. For others, though, retirement can be a time of economic, emotional, or social loss—a period that may be marked by deteriorating health and increasing limitations. For years, researchers have been investigating the effects of retirement. Is retirement good, bad, or neutral for health? Or can a continuation of work keep people healthy?

Definition of Retirement

Moon et al. described retirement as "a life course transition involving environmental changes that reshape health behaviors, social interactions, and psychosocial stresses."[7] It is also a subjective developmental and social psychological change in identity and preferences,[8] which requires the restructuring of daily routines and social contacts.[9] From these definitions, we can see that retirement is not just an event but a process that involves change.

The Retirement–Health Nexus

There are two conflicting theories in the literature as to how retirement can affect well-being.[10] The first views work as a central part of people's being, so that they are likely to suffer psychologically if they no longer can see themselves as productive, contributing members of a society. This could result in a gradual withdrawal from social participation, which leads to isolation, illness, and a decline in happiness and life satisfaction. The second views work as a "stressor," and emphasizes the importance of doing other things. Retirement is thus seen as an opportunity to restart life with more freedom and time to build relationships and engage in health-improving activities.

There is no dearth of studies that investigate the link between retirement and health. Whereas most researchers agree as to how health affects the individual's retirement behavior, very little conclusive evidence exists on the question of how retirement affects health.[11] This is not surprising, given our definition above of retirement as a process involving change. Because people will have different pre-retirement conditions and situations, available resources, abilities to adjust to retirement, and attitudes toward retirement, the impact of retirement will vary.

Many studies have confirmed that retirement has a beneficial effect on health. In some ways, however, retirement can have a negative effect on health through several channels such as disruptions in life course, loss of key social roles, and loss of income, among others.[12] Symptoms of depression are more prominent among women retirees, especially those who retired involuntary and with spouses who cannot fully support them.[13]

---

7 J.R. Moon et al. 2012. Transition to Retirement and Risk of Cardiovascular Disease: Prospective Analysis of the US Health and Retirement Study. *Social science and medicine*. 75 (3). pp. 526–530. https://doi.org/10.1016/j.socscimed.2012.04.004.

8 D. Dannefer. 1984. Adult Development and Social Theory: A Paradigmatic Reappraisal. *American Sociological Review*. 49 (1). https://doi.org/10.2307/2095560.

9 B. Kubicek et al. 2011. Psychological Well-being in Retirement: The Effects of Personal and Gendered Contextual Resources. *Journal of Occupational Health Psychology*. 16 (2). pp. 230–246. https://doi.org/10.1037/a0022334.

10 K. Charles. 2004. Is Retirement Depressing? Labor Force Inactivity and Psychological Well-being in Later Life. *Research in Labor Economics*. 23. pp. 269–299.

11 For a survey of these studies, see I. van der Heide et al. 2013. Is Retirement Good for Your Health? A Systematic Review of Longitudinal Studies. BMC Public Health. 13: 1180. http://dx.doi.org/10.1186/1471-2458-13-1180; and E.M. Zantinge et al. 2014. Retirement and a Healthy Lifestyle: Opportunity or Pitfall? A Narrative Review of the Literature. European Journal of Public Health. 24. pp. 433–439. http://dx.doi.org/10.1093/eurpub/ckt157. For a discussion of the methodological reasons that account for these conflicting results, see E. Horner and M. Cullen. 2016. The Impact of Retirement on Health: Quasi-experimental Methods Using Administrative Data. BMC Health Services Research. 16. pp. 1–9; T. Oshio and M. Kan. 2017. The Dynamic Impact of Retirement on Health: Evidence from a Nationwide Ten-Year Panel Survey in Japan. *Preventive Medicine*. 100. pp. 287–293; and P. Hessel. 2016. Does Retirement (Really) Lead to Worse Health among European Men and Women across All Educational Levels? *Social Science & Medicine*. 151. pp. 19–26.

12 A. Gorry, D. Gorry, and S.N. Slavov. 2018. Does Retirement Improve Health and Life Satisfaction? *Health Economics*. 27. pp. 2067–2086. Almost all studies have focused on the effect of retirement on individuals' health without assessing potential spillover effects within the couple. But studies have shown that the husband's retirement affects the health of the wife negatively. See M. Bertoni and G. Brunello. 2017. Pappa ante portas: The Effect of the Husband's Retirement on the Wife's Mental Health in Japan. *Social Science & Medicine*. 175. pp. 135–142; K. Atalay and Zhu, R. 2018. The Effect of a Wife's Retirement on Her Husband's Mental Health. *Applied Economics*. 50: 43. DOI: 10.1080/00036846.2018.1458198; and P.J. Messe and F.C. Wolff. 2019. The Short-term Effects of Retirement on Health within Couples: Evidence from France. *Social Science & Medicine*. 221. pp. 27–39.

13 M. Szinovacz and A. Davey. 2004. Retirement Transitions and Spouse Disability: Effects on Depressive Symptoms. *The Journals of Gerontology: Series B*. 59 (6). https://doi.org/10.1093/geronb/59.6.S333.

Determinants of Retirement Satisfaction

While there is a tendency in economics to focus on the economic well-being of the retiree (i.e., in terms of the retiree's income and wealth), mounting research has shown that both financial and nonfinancial variables affect subjective well-being.[14] Factors such as demographic characteristics (gender, marital status); personal resources (health, education, economic situation, and interpersonal relationships); characteristics of retirement (voluntary retirement, retirement time); retirement planning; leisure activities; and social integration and engagement determine well-being in retirement. Social engagement[15] and participation in leisure activities[16] positively affect life satisfaction in retirement. In a cohort study conducted by Hajek et al.,[17] the authors report that social engagement decreased depressive symptoms in adults aged 75 and over. As education plays an important role in determining cognitive abilities in retirement,[18] planning for retirement increases retirement satisfaction.[19] Even after controlling for pension income and wealth, retirees are found to have preferences for the type of pension they have.[20] Panis finds that annuities from pensions increase retirement satisfaction and reduce the number of depression symptoms.[21]

Implications

The issue of how retirement affects the health of individuals has grave public policy implications. With continued growth in life expectancies and aging, many countries are facing large increases in the proportion of the population that are eligible to receive a publicly provided retirement pension. Investigating the consequences of retirement decisions is one of the first steps in addressing the mounting costs of supporting an aging population. Governments need to identify areas for intervention to assure higher levels of well-being for retirees. Strategies for retirement planning can include increasing opportunities for leisure activities, bridge employment for involuntary retirement, social engagement including volunteerism, beginning a new career, or even remaining in the same career on adjusted hours. As education has been found to play an important role in explaining heterogeneity in the level of cognitive abilities and its age-related decline (footnote 18), retirees should be

[14] Amorim and Franca present a systematic literature review of studies investigating variables that would improve well-being in retirement. S.M. Amorim and L.H. França. 2019. Reasons for Retirement and Retirement Satisfaction. *Psicologia: Teoria e Pesquisa*. 35. e3558. Epub. https://doi.org/10.1590/0102.3772e3558.

[15] Social engagement includes participation in community meetings, voluntary labor, religious activities, and programs to improve neighborhoods and cooperatives. B. Butrica and S. Schaner. 2005. Satisfaction and Engagement in Retirement. *Perspectives on Productive Aging*. 2. https://www.urban.org/sites/default/files/publication/50466/311202-Satisfaction-and-Engagement-in-Retirement.PDF; C. Tiernan et al. 2013. Community Engagement: An Essential Component of Well-being in Older African-American Adults. *The International Journal of Aging and Human Development*. 77. pp. 233–257. http://doi.org/10.2190/AG.77.3.d; S. Kim and D.C. Feldman. 2014. Working in Retirement: The Antecedents of Bridge Employment and Its Consequences for Quality of Life in Retirement. *Academy of Management Journal*. 43 (6). p. 1195–1210; and J.L. D'Silva and A.A. Samah. 2018. Holistic Well-being of Japanese Retirees in Malaysia. *Journal of International Studies*. 11 (3). pp. 95–103. doi: https://doi.org/10.14254/2071-8330.2018/11-3/8.

[16] S. Kim and D.C. Feldman. 2014. Working in Retirement: The Antecedents of Bridge Employment and Its Consequences for Quality of Life in Retirement. *Academy of Management Journal*. 43 (6). pp. 1195–1210; A. Sener, R.G. Terzioglu, and E. Karabulut. 2007. Life Satisfaction and Leisure Activities during Men's Retirement: A Turkish Sample. *Aging & Mental Health*. 11 (1). pp. 30–36. doi: https://doi.org/10.1080/13607860600736349; and G. Nimrod. 2007. Retirees' Leisure: Activities, Benefits, and Their Contribution to Life Satisfaction. *Leisure Studies*. 26 (1). pp. 65–80. doi: https://doi.org/10.1080/02614360500333937.

[17] A. Hajek et al. 2017. The Impact of Social Engagement on Health-Related Quality of Life and Depressive Symptoms in Old Age—Evidence from a Multicenter Prospective Cohort Study in Germany. *Health and Quality of Life Outcomes*. 15 (1). DOI:10.1186/s12955-017-0715-8.

[18] F. Mazzonna and F. Peracchi. 2012. Ageing, Cognitive Abilities And Retirement. *European Economic Review*. 56 (4). pp. 691–710. https://www.sciencedirect.com/science/article/abs/pii/S0014292112000463.

[19] J. Noone, C. Stephens, and F. Alpass. 2009. Preretirement Planning and Well-being in Later Life: A Prospective Study. *Research on Aging*. 31 (3). DOI: 10.1177/0164027508330718.

[20] K.A. Bender. 2012. An Analysis of Well-being in Retirement: The Role of Pensions, Health, and "Voluntariness" of Retirement. *Journal of Socio-Economics*. 41 (4). https://doi.org/10.1016/j.socec.2011.05.010.

[21] C. Panis. 2003. *Annuities and Retirement Satisfaction*. https://www.researchgate.net/publication/24120307_Annuities_and_Retirement_Satisfaction.

encouraged to continue seeking knowledge and engaging in activities that will challenge their mental capacities. Advanced planning for retirement is clearly an important practice that should be established as young people enter the job market.[22]

Wellness Pathways

Nutrition

Reflecting a life span perspective, the World Health Organization (WHO) has noted that many of the diseases suffered by older persons are the result of dietary factors, some of which have been operating since infancy. These factors are compounded by changes that naturally occur with the aging process.[23]

Elevated serum cholesterol, a risk factor for coronary heart disease in both men and women, is common in older people and this relationship persists into very old age.

Dietary changes seem to affect risk-factor levels throughout life, and may have an even greater impact in older people. Relatively modest reductions in saturated fat and salt intake, which would reduce blood pressure and cholesterol concentrations, could have a substantial effect on reducing the burden of cardiovascular disease. Increasing consumption of fruit and vegetables by one to two servings daily could cut cardiovascular risk by 30%.

Older adults are at increased risk of malnutrition, for a variety of physiological and psychological reasons. In turn, this has implications for health, quality of life, independence, and economic circumstances. Improvements in nutrition are known to bring tangible benefits to older people, and many age-related diseases and conditions can be prevented, modulated, or ameliorated by good nutrition.

The link between good nutrition and good mental health is also important to the mental well-being of older people. New research has been focusing on understanding the pathways that mediate relationships between diet, nutrition, and mental health. Findings point to the immune system, oxidative biology, brain plasticity, and the microbiome-gut-brain axis as key targets for nutritional interventions.

Writing for *The Lancet Psychiatry*, Jerome Sarris and colleagues at the International Society for Nutritional Psychiatry Research report:

> A traditional whole-food diet, consisting of higher intakes of foods such as vegetables, fruits, seafood, whole grains, lean meat, nuts, and legumes, with avoidance of processed foods, is more likely to provide the nutrients that afford resiliency against the pathogenesis of mental disorders. The mechanisms by which nutrition might affect mental health are, at least superficially, quite obvious: the human brain operates at a very high metabolic rate, and uses a substantial proportion of total energy and nutrient intake; in both structure and function (including intracellular and intercellular communication), it is reliant on amino acids, fats, vitamins, and minerals or trace elements. Dietary habits modulate the functioning of the immune system, which also moderates the risk for depression. The

[22] L.H.F.P. França. 2012. Envelhecimento dos trabalhadores nas organizações [Aging of company's workers]. In L.H.F.P. França and D. Stepansky, eds. *Propostas Multidisplinares para o Bem-estar na Aposentadoria*. pp. 25–52. Rio de Janeiro, RJ: Quartet; and L.H.F.P França et al. 2013. Aposentar-se ou continuar trabalhando? O que infl uencia essa decisão? [Should I retire or continue to work?]. *Psicologia: Ciência e Profi ssão*. 33 (3). pp. 548–563. doi: 10.1590/S1414-98932013000300004.

[23] WHO. 2020. *Nutrition for Older Persons*. https://www.who.int/nutrition/topics/ageing/en/index1.html.

> antioxidant defence system, which is also implicated in mental disorders, operates with the support of nutrient cofactors and phytochemicals. Additionally, neurotrophic factors make essential contributions to neuronal plasticity and repair mechanisms throughout life, and these too are affected by nutritional factors.[24]

In a study on cognitive functioning and brain aging, higher levels of B-family vitamins, as well as vitamins C, D, and E, were all associated with higher scores on cognitive tests. The same positive relationship was found for omega-3 fatty acids, which have previously been linked to better brain health. Those with higher levels of trans fats, found in a variety of junk foods, performed more poorly in thinking and memory tests. Their magnetic resonance imaging scans also revealed more brain shrinkage than in people who had lower trans fats levels. The study found that, overall, nutrition accounted for 37% of the variation in brain volume.[25]

A landmark study has found that inexpensive B vitamins stopped shrinkage in the area of the brain that defines Alzheimer's disease, called the medial temporal lobe. The study, led by David Smith from the University of Oxford, gave a combination of vitamin B_6 (20 milligrams), B_{12} (500 micrograms), and folic acid (800 micrograms) or placebo pills to people with mild cognitive impairment, the stage before a diagnosis of dementia or Alzheimer's. In those with high homocysteine levels, the specific areas of the brain associated with Alzheimer's disease shrank eight times more slowly in those taking B vitamins than in those on the placebo. This is strongly indicative that the B vitamins may be substantially slowing down, or even potentially arresting, the disease process in those with early stage cognitive decline. This is the first treatment that has been shown to do this.[26]

The Mediterranean diet is promoted globally as the dietary solution to noncommunicable diseases (NCDs). While it is clearly a beneficial dietary pathway to reduce inflammation and promote healthy nutrition, it is also a Western diet, studied by Westerners on Westerners, and it is being recommended for 75% of the world's population that is not Western.[27]

In Asia, the Japanese diet is well studied, and there are commonalities with the Mediterranean diet. They share high intake of unrefined carbohydrates, moderate intake of protein, healthy fat profile, low glycemic load, less inflammation and oxidative stress, and potential modulation of aging-related pathways. A point of difference is that Asian diets typically include pharmacologically potent ingredients, such as turmeric in South Asia and Southeast Asia; *umeboshi* plums and *reishi* mushrooms in Japan; *goji* berry, ginkgo, and licorice root in the People's Republic of China; ginseng in the Republic of Korea; and the medicinal herb *Centella asiatica* in Thailand and Malaysia.

The Prospective Urban Rural Epidemiology study, published in *The Lancet* in August 2017, collected data on more than 135,000 individuals from 18 countries for 4 to 7 years. The study assessed the association of nutrients with cardiovascular disease and mortality in low-income and middle-income populations. Findings showed that higher intakes of fats (including saturated fatty acids, monounsaturated fatty acids, and total polyunsaturated fatty acids) and animal protein were each associated with lower mortality. Carbohydrate intake was associated with increased mortality.[28]

[24] J. Sarris et al. 2015. Nutritional Medicine as Mainstream in Psychiatry. *Lancet Psychiatry*. 2 (3). pp. 271–74. http://dx.doi.org/10.1016/ 2215-0366(14)00051-0.

[25] G.L. Bowman. 2012. Nutrient Biomarker Patterns, Cognitive Function, and MRI Measures of Brain Aging. *Neurology*. 78 (4). pp. 241–249. doi: 10.1212/WNL.0b013e3182436598.

[26] D. Gwenaëlle et al. 2013. Preventing Alzheimer's Disease-Related Gray Matter Atrophy by B-Vitamin Treatment. *Proceedings of the National Academy of Sciences of the United States of America*. 110 (23). pp. 9523–9528. doi: 10.1073/pnas.1301816110.

[27] G. Bodeker and F. Kronenberg. 2015. Tackling Obesity: Challenges Ahead. *The Lancet*. 386 (9995). pp. 740–741. doi: 10.1016/S0140-6736(15)61539-2.

[28] M. Dehghan et al. 2017. Associations of Fats and Carbohydrate Intake with Cardiovascular Disease and Mortality in 18 Countries from Five Continents (PURE): A Prospective Cohort Study. *The Lancet*. http://dx.doi.org/10.1016/S0140-6736(17)32252-3.

The risk of total and non-cardiovascular mortality was in the order of 22%–23% lower for people who consume at least three servings per day of fruits, vegetables, and legumes, compared with participants who consumed less than one serving per day of these foods.[29]

Exercise

Aging populations have the potential for rapid increases in the incidence of health problems associated with aging, such as falls, dementia, osteoporosis, and osteoarthritis. An essential change of focus that is required with population aging is to support prevention-focused approaches, which means that the future aging population will age better than the current older population. Health promotion and prevention programs also have the potential to help older people with multiple comorbidities age well within the context of their existing health problems. Health promotion and prevention approaches are essential across the full spectrum of health of older populations. Exercise is one health promotion and prevention approach that has excellent potential to help aging populations to age well.[30]

Yoga

Researcher Tiffany Field, director of the Touch Research Institute at the University of Miami, has published a review and a book on clinical research on yoga.[31] The following is a summary of her findings on the impact of yoga.

Psychological effects. Field notes that at least two studies have demonstrated significant increase in mindfulness. Studies of yoga's effects on anxiety are common, with significant series and single-session effects on measures of stress, anxiety, fatigue and depression, well-being, and vigor.

Pain syndromes. Field notes findings of significant pain reduction and less analgesic and opiate use in yoga than control groups, and these findings hold regardless of gender or age differences among participants.

Cardiovascular conditions. Field describes several studies addressing coronary artery disease and hypertension. In each, yoga was found to improve cholesterol and serum low-density lipid levels significantly. Yoga groups also had fewer anginal episodes, improved exercise capacity, decreased body weight, and lowered triglyceride levels than control groups. Blood pressure and blood glucose were reduced, and self-reported well-being and quality of life were increased.

Immune conditions. Field notes that for immune (and autoimmune) conditions such as asthma, diabetes, multiple sclerosis, lymphoma, and breast cancer, yoga has been associated with several beneficial effects.

Tai Chi

The National Health Service of the United Kingdom describes the traditional Chinese movement traditions as follows: "Tai chi, also called tai chi chuan, combines deep breathing and relaxation with flowing movements. Originally developed as a martial art in 13th-century [People's Republic of] China, tai chi is now practised around the world as a health-promoting exercise" and a means of developing self-awareness.[32]

[29] V. Miller et al. 2017. Fruit, Vegetable, and Legume Intake, and Cardiovascular Disease and Deaths in 18 Countries. PURE: A Prospective Cohort Study. *The Lancet*. http://dx.doi.org/10.1016/S0140-6736(17)32253-5.

[30] K.D. Hill. 2021. Health Benefits of Exercise for Older People: The Research Evidence and Approaches to Maximize Participation. In C. Goh, G. Bodeker, and K. Kariippanon, eds. *Healthy Ageing in Asia*. Taylor & Francis.

[31] T. Field. 2011. Yoga Clinical Research Review. *Complementary Therapies in Clinical Practice*. 17 (1). pp. 1–8; and T. Field. 2012. *Yoga Research*. Bloomington, Indiana: Xlibris Corporation.

[32] National Health Services. 2018. *A Guide to Tai Chi*. http://www.nhs.uk/Livewell/fitness/Pages/taichi.aspx.

Tai chi has been shown to result in improved strength, balance, function, and balance confidence, as well as improvement in some cardiovascular measures, even in the presence of health problems such as lower limb osteoarthritis. However, some forms of tai chi are more challenging (e.g., from a balance or fitness perspective), and therefore are most suitable for more healthy older people (e.g., Yang style), while other forms of tai chi such as the Sun style, including tai chi for arthritis, are more suitable and safe for people with comorbidities, such as lower limb arthritis or reduced balance.[33]

Dance

Research across the age span has highlighted the differing benefits of dance for different age groups. Research on the benefits of dance, as summarized in a Global Wellness Institute white paper on mental wellness,[34] has found benefits across the life span.

Older-aged dance participants with Parkinson's disease have shown improvements in mobility, reduced tremor, and improved social outreach. Dance for Parkinson's Disease is an international program that began in New York and has spread to many countries. It offers dance as a means of enhancing quality of life and improving symptoms in people with Parkinson's disease.

A study in the *New England Journal of Medicine* examined physical and cognitive activities associated with reduced risk of developing Alzheimer's disease. Researchers found that cognitive activities such as reading, playing board games, and playing musical instruments were associated with a lower risk of dementia. However, of 11 physical activities, "dancing was the only physical activity associated with a lower risk of dementia."[35]

A new and comprehensive review of the neurobiology of dance found that dancing triggers the release of reward-related neurotransmitters, including endorphins and opioids. Dance, like all physical exercise, enhances immuno-reactivity and improves caloric equilibrium, coordination, muscle tone, and cardiovascular health. In addition, dance practice provides strong psychobiological learning opportunities. In this regard, dance provides socio-emotional coping skills to increase self-confidence and boost self-esteem.

The Arts

Music

New research has found that music therapy can improve anxiety and depression, and enhance cognition in Alzheimer's patients.[36] Music played while patients are in intensive care units has been found to abate the stress response, decrease anxiety during mechanical ventilation, and induce an overall relaxation response without the use of medication. Music may also improve sleep quality and reduce patients' pain with a subsequent decrease in sedative exposure leading to an accelerated ventilator weaning process and a speedier recovery.[37]

[33] Z.G. Huang et al. 2017. Systematic Review and Meta-analysis: Tai Chi for Preventing Falls in Older Adults. *BMJ Open*. 7 (2): e013661; and R. Song et al. 2007. Effects of a Sun-Style Tai Chi Exercise on Arthritic Symptoms, Motivation and the Performance of Health Behaviors in Women with Osteoarthritis. *Taehan Kanho Hakhoe chi*. 37 (2). pp. 249–256.

[34] G. Bodeker. 2018. Dance. In G. Bodeker, ed. *Mental Wellness: Pathways, Evidence, Horizons*. Miami: Global Wellness Institute.

[35] J. Verghese et al. 2003. Leisure Activities and the Risk of Dementia in the Elderly. *New England Journal of Medicine*. 348 (25), pp. 2508–2516.

[36] J.E. de la Rubia Orti et al. 2018. Does Music Therapy Improve Anxiety and Depression in Alzheimer's Patients? *Journal of Alternative and Complementary Medicine*. 24 (1). pp. 33–36. doi: 10.1089/acm.2016.0346; G.M. Gomez and G.J. Gomez. 2016. Music Therapy and Alzheimer's Disease: Cognitive, Psychological, and Behavioural Effects. *Neurologia*. 16. pp. 4–9; and R. Fang et al. 2017. Music Therapy Is a Potential Intervention for Cognition of Alzheimer's Disease: A Mini-review. *Translational Neurodegeneration*. 6: 2. https://doi.org/10.1186/s40035-017-0073-9.

[37] A. Mofredj et al. 2016. Music Therapy, a Review of the Potential Therapeutic Benefits for the Critically Ill. *Journal of Critical Care*. 35. pp. 195–199.

Findings from multiple studies that have been recently reviewed show that patients with severe mental illness, including difficulties in expression and communication, obtained benefits when they participated in music therapy programs.[38]

Art and Art Therapy

In a systematic review of art therapy and mental health, Uttley et al. reported the following:[39]

Depression. Among nine studies examining depression, art therapy resulted in significant reduction in depression in six studies. In four of these six studies, art therapy was significantly more effective than the control.

Anxiety. Among seven studies examining anxiety, art therapy resulted in significant reduction of anxiety in six studies. In these six studies, art therapy was significantly more effective than the control.

Mood. Among four studies examining mood or affect, art therapy resulted in significant positive improvements to mood in three studies. In these three studies, art therapy was significantly more effective than the control.

Trauma. Among three studies examining trauma, art therapy resulted in significant reduction of symptoms of trauma in all studies. While trauma improved from baseline, there was no significant difference between the art therapy and control groups in any of the three studies.

Distress. Among three studies examining distress, art therapy resulted in significant reduction of distress in all studies. In two studies, art therapy was significantly more effective than the control group.

Quality of life. In four studies examining quality of life, art therapy resulted in significant improvements to some but not all components of the quality of life measures in all studies. In all studies, art therapy was significantly more effective than the control.

Coping. Among three studies examining coping, art therapy resulted in significant improvements to coping resources in all studies. In one study, art therapy was significantly more effective than the control. In another study, there was no difference between groups. In the third study, significant differences between the art therapy and control groups were not reported.

Cognition. In one study examining cognition, the control group (simple calculations) exhibited significant improvements in cognitive function relative to the art therapy group.

Self-esteem. In one study examining self-esteem, art therapy resulted in significant improvements in self-esteem relative to the control group.

Social Support

Aging is associated with an increased reliance on health-related and support services. Old age often goes hand in hand with increasingly complex and often interrelated problems, encompassing physical, psychological, and social health.

[38] M. Montánchez Torres et al. 2016. Benefits of Using Music Therapy in Mental Disorders. *Journal of Biomusical Engineering*. 4: 116. doi:10.4172/2090-2719.1000116.

[39] L. Uttley et al. 2015. Chapter 2: Clinical Effectiveness of Art Therapy: Quantitative Systematic Review. In Systematic Review and Economic Modelling of the Clinical Effectiveness and Cost-Effectiveness of Art Therapy among People with Non-psychotic Mental Health Disorders. *Health Technology Assessment*. 19.18. https://www.ncbi.nlm.nih.gov/books/NBK279641.

A study comparing the elderly in two provinces in East Asia (Tainan in Taipei,China and Fuzhou in the People's Republic of China) found that participants identified children as the most important source of objective and subjective support, followed by spouse and relatives.[40]

Tainan's elderly received more daily life assistance and emotional support, showed stronger awareness of the need to seek help, and maintained a higher frequency of social interactions compared with the elderly in Fuzhou. The mean objective support, subjective support, and support utilization scores as well as the overall social support among Tainan's elderly were significantly high compared with the scores among Fuzhou's elderly. Correlation analysis showed that social support was significantly correlated with city, age, living conditions, marital status, and self-rated health.

The *World Happiness Report 2017* has identified four factors as best representing different aspects of the social foundations of well-being. These are (i) social support, (ii) freedom to make life choices, (iii) generosity, and (iv) absence of corruption in government and business.[41]

Having someone to count on has a large impact on life evaluations even after allowing for the effects due to higher incomes and better health.

Nature and the Environment

An approach to exercise for older people that has not been the focus of much research until recently is exercising outdoors. Exercising outdoors can provide the same benefits as exercising indoors, but may have additional benefits, such as improved social interaction and mood, as well as sunlight exposure to improve vitamin D levels.

Being in nature as a means of restoring mental well-being is not new. The master of Chinese medicine, Sun Simiao, advised that fresh air, daily walks in natural landscapes, and food from a fresh and wholesome garden—cultivated in part by the owner—were the fundamentals of creating and maintaining good health. Sun Simiao was born around 581 CE and died in 682 CE after completing his 30-volume *Encyclopedia of Medicine*, the first few volumes of which were not dedicated to medicine at all, but to lifestyle, diet, and exercise. The Chinese poet and scholar Tao Yuanming, later known as Tao Qian (365–427), resigned his post as a civil administrator and chose a life of poetry, farming, family, friendships, wine, and, above all, a connection with the deep pulse of life, which is known in Chinese tradition as the Tao. Both Sun Simiao and Tao Qian have become Chinese icons of an ideal life in nature.

The ancient Indian tradition of going to the Himalayas for cold water bathing and doing morning exercises with the rising sun also have their roots in the healing power of nature and in humans balancing their lives by connecting with nature.

In Japan, there is the tradition of *shinrin-yoku*, a term that means "taking in the forest atmosphere" or "forest bathing." The group Shinrin-Yoku.org lists confirmed results of *shinrin-yoku*: (i) boosted immune system functioning, with an increase in the count of the body's natural killer cells; (ii) reduced blood pressure; (iii) reduced stress; (iv) improved mood; (v) increased ability to focus, even in children with attention deficit hyperactivity disorder (ADHD); (vi) accelerated recovery from surgery or illness; (vii) increased energy levels; and (viii) improved sleep.[42]

[40] Y. Dai et al. 2016. Social Support and the Self-Rated Health of Older People. 95 (24): e3881. doi: 10.1097/MD.0000000000003881.
[41] J. Helliwell, R. Layard, and J. Sachs. 2017. *World Happiness Report 2017*. New York: Sustainable Development Solutions Network .
[42] B.J. Park et al. 2010. The Physiological Effects of Shinrin-yoku (Taking in the Forest Atmosphere or Forest Bathing): Evidence from Field Experiments in 24 Forests across Japan. *Environmental Health and Preventive Medicine*. 15 (1). pp. 18–26. doi: 10.1007/s12199-009-0086-9.

People tend to live longer when they have access to green space, and perceived neighborhood greenness is strongly associated with better mental and physical health. Those living in highly green areas are much more likely to have better physical and mental health than those living near open areas that are not highly green.

Hope in Bloom is a nonprofit group that plants gardens for breast cancer sufferers. They note: "Healing gardens have been proven to be therapeutic sanctuaries offering both comfort and hope to meet the emotional and psychological needs of patients and their families. Many of our recipients are now in remission and attribute their good fortune in part to their gardens. Others report their gardens help reduce stress and anxiety, which strengthens their resolve to face an often-grueling treatment regimen."[43]

Japan's *Ikigai*

In Japan, *ikigai* is written by combining the kanji characters that mean "life" with "to be worthwhile." *Ikigai* is a Japanese concept that means "reason for being." It is the heart of things, the motivation at the center of our existence: the source of value in a person's life or the things that makes them put one foot in front of the other each day.

Two Western researchers, Héctor García and Francesc Miralles, identified the characteristics and principles of Japanese who live longer with happiness. Their book *Ikigai: The Japanese Secret to a Long and Happy Life* defines the rules of *ikigai.* The authors conducted a total of 100 interviews in Ogimi, Okinawa, to try to understand the longevity secrets of centenarians and supercentenarians. They write, "What do Japanese artisans, engineers, Zen philosophy, and cuisine have in common? Simplicity and attention to detail."

A deep connection with, and appreciation for, *ikigai* is one probable reason for the remarkable longevity of the Japanese, particularly those residing in Okinawa. Here, there are 24.55 people over the age of 100 for every 100,000 inhabitants, far more than the worldwide average. The authors speculate that there are many factors that might collude to explain Okinawa's disproportionate populace of centenarians: their uncommon sense of community; a non-exclusionary sense of oneness wherein even strangers are treated like brothers; access to lush hills and crystalline waters; Moringa tea; a light, nutritious diet; and moderate exercise, even after retirement.[44]

Aging in Place

Jean Woo of the Department of Medicine & Therapeutics, Chinese University of Hong Kong, an authority on aging in Asia, has highlighted the fact that many health-care systems do not include systematic screening for aging-related needs, in particular early identification of common geriatric syndromes such as frailty, sarcopenia, anorexia, mild cognitive impairment, and depression.[45] These conditions may predispose people to functional decline, hence the call for rapid geriatric assessments in the community. A recent survey among 2,400 older persons aged 60 years and over who attend community centers in Hong Kong, China, showed high prevalence of unmet needs, with memory problems (74%), chewing difficulties (63%), and pre-frailty and frailty (38%) being the most common problems, while about 20% reported low subjective well-being and had problems with instrumental activities of daily living, as well as insufficient income.

Woo argues that aging in place is only desirable if conditions are met to optimize function to enable coping with common chronic disabling diseases, such as arthritis and stroke, as well as age-related syndromes such as sensory

[43] Hope in Bloom, Inc. https://www.hopeinbloom.org.

[44] *Water for Health.* 2019. Ten Rules of Ikigai: A Blueprint for a Fuller, Healthier Life? 12 March. https://www.water-for-health.co.uk/our-blog/2019/03/ten-rules-of-ikigai-a-blueprint-for-a-fuller-healthier-life.

[45] J. Woo. 2021. Ageing in Place. In C. Goh, G. Bodeker, and K. Kariippanon, eds. *Healthy Ageing in Asia.* Taylor & Francis.

impairment; chewing difficulties; cognitive impairments (such as deficits in the domains of memory, processing speed, and executive function); impairments in instrumental activities of daily living; physical function; and psychosocial needs.

Aging in place requires understanding needs from the older person's perspective and must be personalized.

Age-Friendly Environments Outside of the Home

Age-friendly environments outside of the home should also be considered. The overall principles of age-friendly environments are summarized by WHO's concept of age-friendly cities, covering age-friendly transport, housing, respect and social inclusion, civic participation and employment, health and community services, information and communication, social participation, and outdoor spaces and building. Since many older people live in cities, attention to these principles may make a difference to promoting healthy aging instead of being obstacles.

Currently, social experiments are being carried out to redesign age-friendly communities in Kashiwa and Fukui in Japan, which incorporates all the age-friendly city domains.[46]

Conclusion

Healthy aging needs to begin in childhood. Policies to support this make most sense when embedded within the rationale of an overarching life span framework such as Japan's 100-Year Life program. Early nutritional, environmental, social, and exercise experiences have lasting effects on the health of adults throughout their life span. These effects can be intergenerational. The concept of retirement is being rethought globally, with 70 or 75 now being considered as a realistic retirement age for people who may live for 20–30 years beyond this retirement date. The question of how these years can be lived in health is facing every economy in Asia. New research shows that aging takes place at different rates across societies in Asia, with a "global 65 years" being experienced at age 45 in Papua New Guinea and at age 75 in Japan. This disparity in aging rates means that different countries will have different levels of health care burdens according to the rate at which their populations age.

Nutrition is of fundamental importance in reducing the risks associated with noncommunicable diseases (NCDs) and their growing burden on society and national health-care budgets. It turns out that traditional Asian diets have much to offer that aligns with recognized best nutritional guidelines for the prevention of NCDs. Agricultural, market, and health promotion policies need to be aligned to this reality to support the expansion of healthy aging across Asia.

Exercise is also of primary importance in reducing the risk of people developing NCDs. Exercising outdoors in a non-polluted space can be of double benefit because being in nature has well-documented benefits on cardiovascular health, immunity, and mental well-being. Dance has been shown to be an especially beneficial form of exercise for older people in that it promotes social exchange and is a form of movement that is focused on communication, thus activating communication areas of the brain. Dance has shown benefits in reducing the symptoms of both Parkinson's disease and Alzheimer's.

Social support, especially friendship and meaningful social interaction, are vital for ensuring mental well-being in later life. The Japanese philosophy of *ikigai* highlights the impact that a purposeful life, good nutrition, regular movement, good social networks, a positive outlook, and a smile all have on optimal aging into later years.

[46] Research Institute of Science and Technology for Society. Redesigning Communities for Aged Society. https://www.jst.go.jp/ristex//en/e_examin/korei.html.

Across Asia, there are a wealth of traditional well-being practices that can be drawn upon to enhance nutrition, movement, social interaction, and inner well-being. Healthy aging is of vital importance for the economies of the region as citizens live longer and also as many spend their later years afflicted by NCDs. A wellness path to personal and national health needs to be at the heart of trans-sectoral planning in Asian economies, harnessing the productive capacity of seniors, reducing needless disability from the effects of poor dietary and other lifestyle choices, and creating the knowledge and foundations for lifelong well-being in younger generations.

Further Reading

Asian Developmnet Bank. 2018. *Strategy 2030: Achieving a Prosperous, Inclusive, Resilient, and Sustainable Asia and the Pacific*. Manila.

C. Benoit et al. 2015. Dietary Emulsifiers Impact the Mouse Gut Microbiota Promoting Colitis and Metabolic Syndrome. *Nature* 519. pp. 92–96. doi: 10.1038/nature14232.

P. Bingley and A. Martinello. 2013. Mental Retirement and Schooling. *European Economic Review*. 63 (C). pp. 292–298. https://EconPapers.repec.org/RePEc:eee:eecrev:v:63:y:2013:i:c:p:292-298.

M.E. Clegg and E.A. Williams. 2018. Optimizing Nutrition in Older People. *Maturitas*. 112. pp. 34–38. doi: 10.1016/j.maturitas.2018.04.001. Electronic Publication.

S. Edwards. 2016. *Dancing and the Brain, On the Brain: The Harvard Mahoney Neuroscience Institute Newsletter*. http://neuro.hms.harvard.edu/harvard-mahoney-neuroscience-institute/brain-newsletter/and-brainseries/dancing-and-brain (accessed 21 September 2017).

K. Krinski et al. 2017. Let's Walk Outdoors! Self-Paced Walking Outdoors Improves Future Intention to Exercise in Women With Obesity. *Journal of Sport and Exercise Psychology*. 39 (2). pp. 145–157.

P. Levinger et al. 2018. Outdoor Physical Activity for Older People—the Senior Exercise Park: Current Research, Challenges and Future Directions. *The Health Promotion Journal of Australia*. 29 (3). pp. 353–359.

D. Omigie and S. Samson. 2014. A Protective Effect of Musical Expertise on Cognitive Outcome Following Brain Damage? *Neuropsychology Review*. 24 (4). pp. 445–460.

M. Rogerson et al. 2016. Influences of Green Outdoors versus Indoors Environmental Settings on Psychological and Social Outcomes of Controlled Exercise. *International Journal of Environmental Research and Public Health*. 13 (4). p. 363.

M. Sales et al. 2017. A Novel Exercise Initiative for Seniors to Improve Balance and Physical Function. *Journal of Aging and Health*. 29 (8). pp. 1424–1443.

M. Sales et al. 2018. Older Adults' Perceptions of a Novel Outdoor Exercise Initiative: A Qualitative Analysis. *The Journal of Aging and Social Change*. 8 (1). pp. 61–78.

J. Sarris, D. Mischoulon, and I. Schweitzer. 2012. Omega-3 for Bipolar Disorder: Meta-analyses of Use in Mania and Bipolar Depression. *The Journal of Clinical Psychiatry*. 73. pp. 81–86.

C. Sherrington et al. 2019. Exercise for Preventing Falls in Older People Living in the Community. *Cochrane Database of Systematic Reviews*. 1 (CD012424). doi: 10.1002/14651858.CD012424.pub2.

M.R. Solloway, et al. 2016. An Evidence Map of the Effect of Tai Chi on Health Outcomes. *Systematic Review.* 5 (1). doi:10.1186/s13643-016-0300-y.

L. Uttley et al. 2015. The Clinical and Cost Effectiveness of Group Art Therapy for People with Non-psychotic Mental Health Disorders: A Systematic Review and Cost-effectiveness Analysis. *BMC Psychiatry*. 15 (151). https://doi.org/10.1186/s12888-015-0528-4.

A. Voukelatos et al. 2015. The Impact of a Home-Based Walking Programme on Falls in Older People: The Easy Steps Randomised Controlled Trial. *Age and Ageing*. 44 (3). pp. 377–383.

J. Woo et al. 2017. Urban Characteristics Influencing Health of Older People: What Matters. *International Journal of Innovative Research in Medical Science.* 2 (12). pp. 1561–1568.

R. Yu et al. 2017. Associations between Perceived Neighborhood Walkability and Walking Time, Wellbeing, and Loneliness in Community-Dwelling Older Chinese People in Hong Kong. *International Journal of Environmental Research and Public Health.* 14 (10).

CHAPTER 11

Analysis of the Global and Asian Wellness Tourism Sector

Scott Wayne with Emma Russell

The travel and tourism industry has been one of the most resilient and fastest-growing economic sectors globally and within the Asia and Pacific region. The wellness tourism sector, which has a self-reinforcing and thus self-perpetuating dimension, has been a key driver of this growth. Wellness activities, including wellness tourism, help create a healthier population, which in turn becomes an economically more productive population, one with more spending power, disposable income, and desire to travel. However, the outbreak of coronavirus disease (COVID-19) severely tested the wellness and thus sustainability of tourism globally, but especially in the People's Republic of China (PRC) and the rest of Asia. This chapter analyzes the wellness tourism sector with a specific focus on the Asia and Pacific market. This is followed by case studies covering Thailand, India, and Sri Lanka, and recommendations for Asian governments on how to further develop this sector in the aftermath of the COVID-19 pandemic.

Introduction

The travel and tourism industry has been one of the most resilient and fastest-growing economic sectors globally and within the Asia and Pacific region. This paper summarizes the key overall trends driving this growth, especially the wellness tourism sector, which has a self-reinforcing and thus self-perpetuating dimension. Wellness activities, including wellness tourism, help create a healthier population, which in turn becomes an economically more productive population, one with more spending power, disposable income, and desire to travel.

Increasing numbers of people travel to realize greater wellness in their lives. They endeavor to maintain a healthy lifestyle, reduce stress, prevent disease, and enhance their overall physical and mental well-being. Some people travel mainly in pursuit of wellness, while others seek to add a wellness activity or service to their trips. These pursuits span a wide range of wellness activities and services, which can include spiritual and emotional well-being, personal care, beauty and anti-aging, healthy eating, nutrition and weight loss, fitness, and mind–body activities, preventive and personalized medicine and public health, traditional and complementary medicine, wellness lifestyle real estate, and workplace wellness. These are often the main motives for traveling to destinations that offer these activities and services.

In addition, the wellness industry offers of many destinations often depend on protected natural assets and cultural traditions, such as hot springs and traditional yoga and acupuncture practices. Many wellness-motivated travelers are attracted by these assets and traditions, as well as the broader cultural and natural heritage attractions of destinations. By visiting these destinations and buying locally made wellness products and wellness services and activities, these travelers are also contributing to generating local employment, preserving and protecting heritage, and strengthening the overall sustainability of the destination.

Overview of the Global Tourism Industry

Global Tourism Trends

The travel and tourism industry was one of the world's largest and fastest-growing industries with a global economic contribution (direct, indirect, and induced) of more than $8.9 trillion by the end of 2019 (Figure 11.1). The direct economic impact of the industry, including but not limited to accommodation, transportation, entertainment, and attractions, was about $2.77 trillion.[1] Much of this economic impact was generated by international tourists, who totaled about 1.46 billion in 2019,[2] a number that had grown 135% since 1996 and was forecast in 2019 to continue growing to an estimated 2.2 billion arrivals by 2029.[3]

Figure 11.1 Tourism Gross Domestic Product Growth

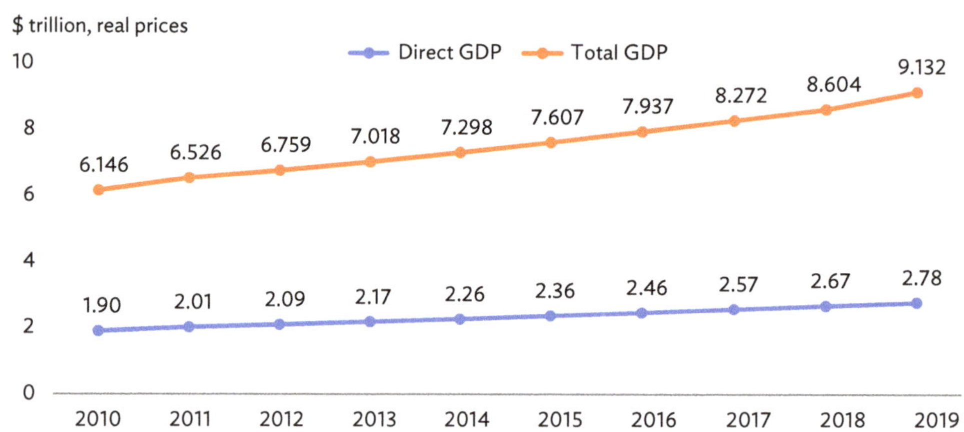

GDP = gross domestic product.

Source: World Travel and Tourism Council Online Data Tool. https://tool.wttc.org (accessed 6 November 2020).

Main Drivers of Tourism

According to the United Nations World Tourism Organization (UNWTO), in 2018 more than half of the world's travel and tourism was driven by travelers seeking leisure, recreation, and holidays (56%); followed by 27% traveling for visits with friends and relatives, religion, and health (Figure 11.2).

In their 2019 report *Understanding the Socioeconomic Drivers of Megatrends*, Euromonitor International cited 20 of the "most influential megatrends set to influence the world."[4] They also stated that these trends were influencing the travel and tourism industry. Among those that particularly impacted the industry were:

(i) healthy living, which includes increased focus on wellness and the sharing economy (i.e., Airbnb and Uber);

---

1 World Travel and Tourism Council Data Tool. tool.wttc.org (accessed 6 November 2020).

2 UN World Tourism Organization (UNWTO). 2020. *UNWTO World Tourism Barometer*. Madrid, Spain. https://www.e-unwto.org/toc/wtobarometereng/18/1.

3 World Travel and Tourism Council. 2019. *Travel & Tourism Economic Impact 2019 World*. London, United Kingdom. This estimate was done before the outbreak of COVID-19.

4 Euromonitor International. 2019. *Understanding the Socioeconomic Drivers of Megatrends*. London.

Figure 11.2 **Purpose of Visit, 2019**

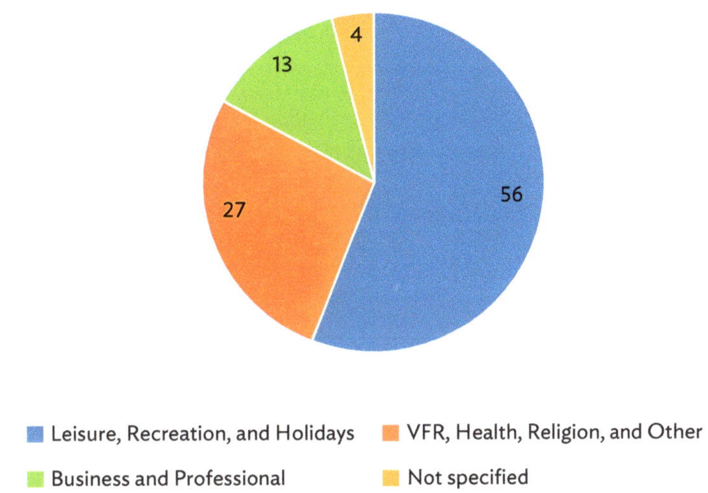

VFR = visiting friends and relatives.

Source: United Nations World Tourism Organization. 2019. *UNWTO Tourism Highlights, 2019*. Madrid, Spain.

(ii) ethical living, including striving for and preservation of authenticity;
(iii) connected consumers, which is both the result and cause of increased multiculturalism and personalization; and
(iv) shopping reinvented with online shopping fast growing globally.

All of these megatrends also reflected increased interest in and demand for sustainable products and services that respect and strengthen environmental and sociocultural conservation and protection. For travel and tourism, these megatrends were reflected in the following key drivers:

(i) **Adventure travel.** The Adventure Travel Trade Association values adventure experiences at $683 billion yearly with a 21% compound annual growth rate since 2012.
(ii) **Cultural tourism.** According to the UNWTO, cultural tourism is one of the largest and fastest-developing markets, with an estimated 4 out of 10 tourists choosing their destination based on cultural offerings.
(iii) **Gastronomy or culinary travel.** The World Food Travel Association's 2020 *State of the Food Travel Industry Report* predicts substantial growth in food and wine festivals and active combination experiences such as culinary bike tours. Their research shows that most travelers spend at least 25% of their travel budgets on food and beverages.
(iv) **Wellness tourism.** The wellness tourism market is also an increasingly prominent driver of travel and tourism, accounting for an estimated total (direct, indirect, and induced) spending of $683 billion in 2018, according to the report of the Global Wellness Institute (GWI), which is described in more detail below.

Given the magnitude of these sector estimates, it is also important to remember that there is some overlap between these segments, as wellness tourism depends on a healthy environment with many activities related to natural products and nature-based activities. Also, wellness tourism was, and is expected to continue being post-COVID-19, an integral part of resort- and leisure-based offers.

Pre-COVID-19, wellness was becoming an important consideration for the lodging industry. For example, Hyatt incorporated elements of wellness into its entire business and had a senior vice-president for "global wellbeing" to lead this effort, Mia Kyricos. According to Kyricos, "We view well-being as more than spas, fitness centers, and

Table 11.1 **International Tourist Arrivals (million)**

Region	2010	2015	2016	2017	2018	2019	Market Share (% of global)	19/18 (% change)
Asia and Pacific region	208.2	284.6	306.0	324.1	347.7	360.4	24.7	3.6
Northeast Asia	111.5	142.1	154.3	159.5	169.2	170.3	11.7	0.8
Southeast Asia	70.5	104.2	110.8	120.6	128.6	138.6	9.4	6.4
Oceania	11.5	14.3	15.6	16.6	17.1	17.5	1.2	2.4
South Asia	14.7	23.5	25.9	27.5	32.8	35.2	2.4	7.4

Source: United Nations World Tourism Organization. 2012–2021 editions of *World Tourism Barometer*.

healthy food options...ultimately driven by our purpose—we care for people so they can be their best...[with] wellness as the road and well-being as the destination."

Asia and Pacific Region: Tourism Trends

The Asia and Pacific region had been one of the fastest-growing tourism regions, with 208 million international arrivals in 2010, increasing 75% to 360 million by 2019 (Table 11.1). Much of the growth has been led by Northeast Asia,[5] which grew from 111.5 million international arrivals in 2010 to 171 million by 2019. Southeast Asia also grew substantially, nearly doubling from 70.5 million to 139 million international arrivals. Other regions also grew substantially, but with fewer arrivals—Oceania from 11.5 million to 17.5 million, and South Asia from 14.7 million to 35.2 million.

Description, Definition, and Analysis of Wellness Tourism

What Is Wellness Tourism?

Wellness is becoming a high priority, globally and particularly in Asia. While there is no universal definition of wellness, GWI defines wellness as "the active pursuit of activities, choices, and lifestyles that lead to a state of holistic health."[6] They further define wellness tourism as "travel associated with the goal of maintaining or enhancing one's personal well-being and includes the pursuit of physical, mental, spiritual or environmental 'wellness' while traveling for either leisure or business."[7]

Figure 11.3 expands on this definition and shows the diversity of wellness tourism products, services, and experiences that help define and comprise the wellness tourism industry. The "pursuit" of wellness tourism proactively provides these to people of all ages with rising disposable incomes and growing interest in healthy living.

[5] UNWTO considers Northeast Asia as comprising the Democratic People's Republic of Korea; Hong Kong, China; Japan; Macau, China; Mongolia; the People's Republic of China; the Republic of Korea; and Taipei,China.

[6] GWI. 2018. *What Is Wellness Tourism?* https://globalwellnessinstitute.org/what-is-wellness/what-is-wellness-tourism.

[7] GWI. 2014. *Global Wellness Tourism Economy 2013.* Global Wellness Institute.

Figure 11.3 **Diversity of Wellness Tourism Products**

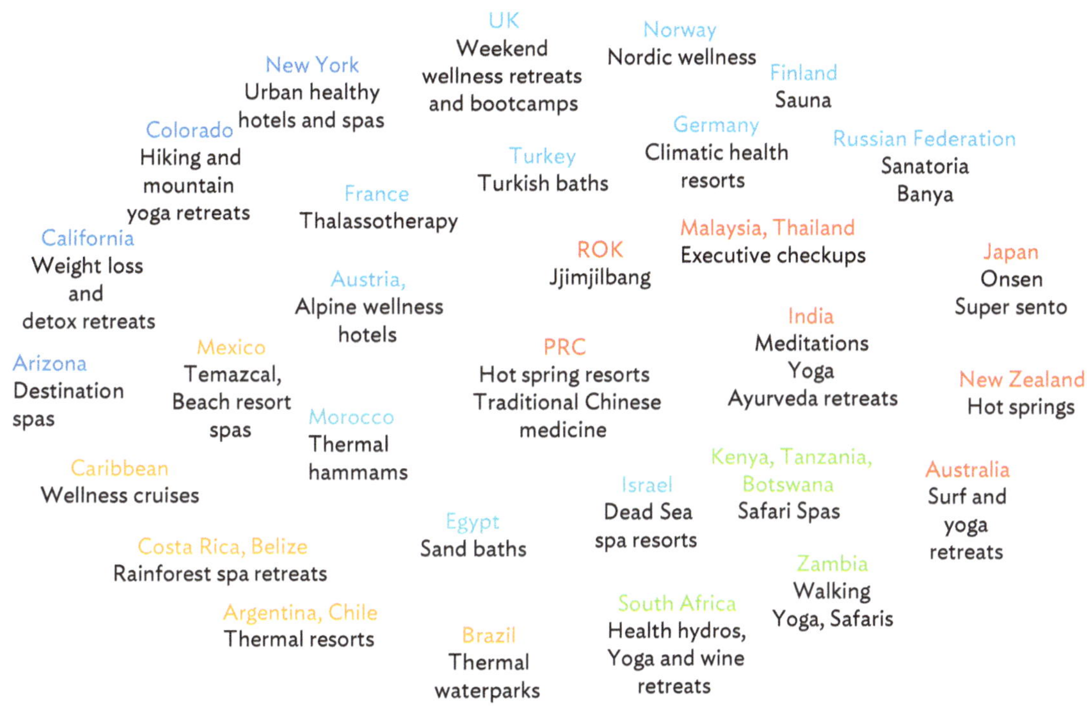

PRC = People's Republic of China, ROK = Republic of Korea, UK = United Kingdom.
Source: Global Wellness Institute. 2018. *Global Wellness Tourism Economy*.

More people travel and tour to maintain a healthy lifestyle, reduce stress, prevent disease, and enhance their well-being. Some people travel mainly in pursuit of wellness while others add a wellness activity or service to their trips. These travelers represent a broad and diverse group of people with different motivations, interests, and values. Offerings are often linked to a destination's local culture, natural assets, environmental conditions, and food. A well-preserved and protected natural environment is often part of the wellness tourism allure, thus contributing to a destination's cultural and nature-based sustainability.

Economic Impact of Wellness Tourism

The wellness tourism sector is estimated to have generated $639.4 billion in gross domestic product (GDP) and 17.9 million jobs worldwide in 2017, according to GWI. Over the past 4 years, the sector's GDP impact grew 6.5% annually and, according to the *Global Wellness Tourism Economy* report, was forecast to continue growing 7.5% annually over the next 3 years to $919 billion by 2022. This growth rate of 43% was more than double tourism's overall growth rate. The impact of COVID-19, which depressed international tourism in 2020 by more than 70% as of October 2020, will alter subsequent forecasts.

For 2019, UNWTO estimated total international travel and tourism receipts at nearly $1.5 trillion. Among these segments and probably others are activities and elements that can be considered wellness-oriented, and thus are counted as wellness tourism, which at least partially accounts for what must be some double-counting.

The economic impact of wellness tourism is magnified by the many types of product and service offers and linkages. The following chart from GWI (Figure 11.3) depicts the array of wellness-related products offered by destinations around the world, which demonstrates both the existing and the potential wellness tourism market.

The GWI estimated the total wellness economy at $4.5 trillion, which included the $639 billion generated from wellness tourism mentioned previously.

Beyond wellness tourism, the key sectors and economic impacts highlighted by GWI included:

(i) personal care, beauty, and anti-aging ($1,083 billion);
(ii) healthy eating, nutrition, and weight loss ($702 billion);
(iii) fitness and mind–body ($595 billion);
(iv) preventive and personalized medicine and public health ($575 billion);
(v) traditional and complementary medicine ($360 billion);
(vi) wellness lifestyle real estate ($134 billion);
(vii) spa economy ($119 billion);
(viii) thermal and mineral springs ($56 billion); and
(ix) workplace wellness ($48 billion).

All of these sectors intersect with wellness tourism. For example, personal-care products often are integral to spa experiences and often are included among hotel and airline amenities. Healthy eating is a core offer of wellness tourism, as well as spas, thermal springs, and fitness.

Diversity and Drivers of Wellness Tourism Offers

The wellness offers of Virtuoso, an international network of 1,000 travel agency partners and 20,000 travel advisors in 50 countries, illustrated how wellness permeates a wide range of travel and tourism segments. Here are a few "wellness tourism" examples from their network:

(i) "organic spa cuisine" where guests pick their own fresh vegetables at the Golden Door Resort in California and then can choose spa treatments, hiking and walking trails, yoga, and other experiences;
(ii) "signature experiences" at resorts such as the Indian wellness resort Ananda in the Himalayas, which emphasizes meditation programs and yoga sessions to "unleash psychic energy" and focus on breathing;
(iii) cruises with wellness options such as Regent's Seven Seas Explorer, which offers yoga on deck, and Uniworld's river cruises, which offer onshore hiking and cycling and onboard wellness instructors;
(iv) green-space visits at airports, such as at Chicago's O'Hare, Amsterdam, Dubai, and Singapore; and
(v) nature-based physical activities that include white water rafting, zip-lining, and cycling.[8]

These examples, as well as the many other wellness tourism offers of Virtuoso and other providers, depend on well-protected and preserved natural and cultural heritage. The wellness offers of many destinations depend on protected natural assets and cultural traditions, such as hot springs and traditional yoga and acupuncture practices. Many wellness-motivated travelers are attracted by these assets and traditions, as well as the broader cultural and natural heritage attractions of destinations. In visiting these destinations and buying locally made wellness products and wellness services and activities, these travelers are contributing to the preservation and protection of this heritage, as well as the overall sustainability of the destination. In so doing, these travelers and the providers are also reinforcing efforts to realize the United Nations Sustainable Development Goals (SDGs). Table 11.2 presents how wellness tourism contributes to the SDGs.[9]

[8] Miscellaneous offers from the Virtuoso online database: https://tinyurl.com/yfneqjjw.
[9] The first two columns of this table are extracted from UNWTO. 2018. *Tourism for Development—Volume II Success Stories*. Madrid. pp. 6–7.

Table 11.2 **United Nations Sustainable Development Goals, Tourism, and Wellness Tourism**

United Nations Sustainable Development Goals (SDGs)	Tourism and SDGs	Wellness Tourism and SDGs
SDG 1: End poverty in all its forms everywhere.	Tourism provides income through job creation at local and community levels. It can be linked with national poverty reduction strategies and entrepreneurship. Low skills requirements and local recruitment can empower less-favored groups, particularly youth and women.	Wellness tourism can be generated by wellness, especially in destinations where local cultural traditions offer wellness, such as meditation, healthy cuisine, which in turn can generate a variety of local employment and entrepreneurial opportunities.
SDG 2: End hunger, achieve food security and nutrition, and promote sustainable agriculture.	Tourism can spur sustainable agriculture by promoting the production of supplies for hotels, and sales of local products to tourists. Agri-tourism can generate additional income while enhancing the value of the tourism experience.	Healthy, often organic food is integral to wellness tourism experiences. Movements such as "farm to table" and "slow food" are very much part of wellness tourism.
SDG 3: Ensure healthy lives and promote well-being for all at all ages.	Tax income generated from tourism can be reinvested in health care and services, improving maternal health, reducing child mortality, and preventing diseases. Visitor fees collected in protected areas can contribute to health services as well.	Wellness tourism not only contributes to and strengthens the wellness of visitors, but it can serve as an example of wellness and a source of income for residents.
SDG 4: Ensure inclusive and equitable quality education and promote lifelong learning for all.	Tourism has the potential to promote inclusiveness. A skilled workforce is crucial for tourism to prosper. The tourism sector provides opportunities for direct and indirect jobs for the youth, women, and those with special needs, who should benefit through educational means.	Wellness tourism experiences often include learning opportunities, which again could be opportunities for visitors to learn about local culture and customs and for local people to learn and become more involved in this fast-growing segment.
SDG 5: Achieve gender equality and empower all women and girls.	Tourism can empower women, particularly through the provision of direct jobs and income-generation from memorable, meaningful experiences in tourism and hospitality-related enterprises. Tourism can be a tool for women to become fully engaged and lead in every aspect of society.	Same as SDG4.
SDG 6: Ensure availability and sustainable management of water and sanitation for all.	Tourism investment requirements for providing utilities can play a critical role in achieving water access and security, as well as hygiene and sanitation for all. The efficient use of water in tourism, pollution control, and technology efficiency can be key to safeguarding our most precious resource.	Wellness tourism depends on safe and clean water, and thus can stimulate investments in ensuring quality management of water and sanitation.
SDG 7: Ensure access to affordable, reliable, sustainable, and modern energy for all.	As an energy-intensive sector, tourism can accelerate the shift toward increased renewable energy shares in the global energy mix. By promoting investments in clean energy sources, tourism can help to reduce greenhouse gases, mitigate climate change, and contribute to access of energy for all.	By nature, wellness tourism is clean and green, so its consumers tend to favor clean and renewable energy sources, which reinforce the sustainability of the destination.
SDG 8: Promote sustained, inclusive, and sustainable economic growth, employment, and decent work for all.	As a service trade, tourism is one of the top four export earners globally, currently providing 1 in 10 jobs worldwide. Decent work opportunities in tourism, particularly for youth and women, and policies that favor better diversification through tourism value chains, can enhance tourism's positive socioeconomic impacts.	The wellness tourism value chain offers diverse and direct employment opportunities for youth, women, and disabled people in the workforce.

continued on next page

Table 11.2 *(continued)*

United Nations Sustainable Development Goals (SDGs)	Tourism and SDGs	Wellness Tourism and SDGs
SDG 9: Build resilient infrastructure, promote inclusive and sustainable industrialization, and foster innovation.	Tourism development relies on good public and private infrastructure. The sector can influence public policy for infrastructure upgrades and retrofits, making them more sustainable, innovative, and resource-efficient; it can also encourage movement toward low-carbon growth, thus attracting tourists and other sources of foreign investment.	Wellness tourism both requires and stimulates investment in quality infrastructure, especially in energy efficiency and sustainable management of waste and water.
SDG 10: Reduce inequality within and among countries.	Tourism can be a powerful tool for reducing inequalities if it engages local populations and all key stakeholders in its development. Tourism can contribute to urban renewal and rural development by giving people the opportunity to prosper in their place of origin. Tourism is an effective means for economic integration and diversification.	Wellness tourism can occur in both urban and rural environments—from city neighborhoods to remote game parks. In some destinations such as India, visitor spending can generate income and employment for local communities and also help preserve local wellness traditions, such as Ayurvedic medicine.
SDG 11: Make cities and human settlements inclusive, safe, resilient, and sustainable.	Tourism can advance urban infrastructure and accessibility, promote regeneration, and preserve cultural and natural heritage, assets on which tourism depends. Investment in green infrastructure (more efficient transport, reduced air pollution) should result in smarter and greener cities not only for residents but also for tourists.	Similar to the above SDGs.
SDG 12: Ensure sustainable consumption and production patterns.	The tourism sector needs to adopt sustainable consumption and production modes, accelerating the shift toward sustainability. Tools to monitor sustainable development impacts for tourism, including for energy, water, waste, biodiversity, and job creation, will result in enhanced economic, social, and environmental outcomes.	By nature, wellness tourism is a lead sector that ensures sustainable consumption. Through maximizing sustainability measures, wellness tourism becomes an even more attractive offer.
SDG 13: Take urgent action to combat climate change and its impacts.	Tourism contributes to and is affected by climate change. Tourism stakeholders should play a leading role in the global response to climate change. By reducing its carbon footprint in the transport and accommodation sector, tourism can benefit from low-carbon growth and help tackle one of the most pressing challenges of our time.	Wellness tourism can be a lead sector in increasing sustainability measures for transport and accommodations.
SDG 14: Conserve and sustainably use the oceans, seas, and marine resources for sustainable development.	Coastal and maritime tourism rely on healthy marine ecosystems. Tourism development must be a part of integrated coastal zone management to help conserve and preserve fragile marine ecosystems and serve as a vehicle to promote a blue economy that contributes to the sustainable use of marine resources.	Many wellness tourism opportunities are at coastal destinations, so healthy marine ecosystems are critical to these and can reinforce efforts to protect marine ecosystems.
SDG 15: Protect, restore, and promote sustainable use of terrestrial ecosystems and halt biodiversity loss.	Rich biodiversity and natural heritage are often the main reasons tourists visit a destination. Tourism can play a major role if sustainably managed in fragile zones, not only in conserving and preserving biodiversity, but also in generating revenue as an alternative livelihood to local communities.	As with marine ecosystems, many wellness tourism offers are inland in or near protected areas where conservation of local biodiversity is critical.

Table 11.2 *(continued)*

United Nations Sustainable Development Goals (SDGs)	Tourism and SDGs	Wellness Tourism and SDGs
SDG 16: Promote peaceful and inclusive societies, provide access to justice for all, and build inclusive institutions.	As tourism revolves around billions of encounters between people of diverse cultural backgrounds, the sector can foster multicultural and interfaith tolerance and understanding, laying the foundation for more peaceful societies. Tourism, which benefits and engages local communities, can also consolidate peace in post-conflict societies.	Wellness tourism is all about maximizing well-being and healthy environments, both for the visitor and the visited.
SDG 17: Strengthen the means of implementation and revitalize the global partnership for sustainable development.	Because of its cross-sectoral nature, tourism can strengthen private–public partnerships and engage multiple stakeholders (international, national, regional, and local) to work together to achieve the SDGs and other common goals. Public policy and innovative financing are at the core for achieving the 2030 Agenda for Sustainable Development and the SDGs.	Wellness tourism flourishes where public policy can help ensure quality standards, and the private sector invests and operates quality offers.

SDG = Sustainable Development Goal.

Sources: United Nations. https://sustainabledevelopment.un.org/?menu=1300; and Global Wellness Institute 2018. *Global Wellness Tourism Economy*. Global Wellness Institute. The first two columns of this table are extracted from United Nations World Tourism Organization. 2018. *Tourism for Development—Volume II Success Stories*. Madrid. pp. 6–7.

Virtuoso cites the 2015 *Spafinder Wellness 365 Survey* and *State of Wellness Travel Report*[10] to demonstrate the broadness and growing popularity of the segment.

Travel agents surveyed for the Spafinder report, many of whom were probably Virtuoso agents, cited the following factors that are driving increased demand:

(i) increased overall consumer concern with health and wellness;
(ii) people's rising stress levels;
(iii) increased knowledge of, and media attention about, wellness travel as a category;
(iv) more wellness-focused vacation properties, with more diverse offerings and price ranges;
(v) people are working harder, and vacations are more precious; and
(vi) an aging population.

Of the agents surveyed, 83% said that their clients were willing to pay a premium for wellness travel and/or access to health products and services while traveling. So, as the GWI report emphasized, it is not surprising that wellness travelers generally spend more than other types of travelers—an average of $1,528 per international trip in 2017, about 58% more than other international travelers.

Among wellness travelers, spa destinations and activities were one of the fastest-growing segments of wellness tourism. GWI estimated that, in 2017, there were more than 149,000 spas globally, earning $93.6 billion in revenues and employing nearly 2.5 million workers. This segment grew 9.9% annually from 2015 to 2017 and is projected to reach $128 billion by 2022.

[10] Available at https://www.spabusiness.com/wellness-news/Survey-shows-record-number-of-travel-agents-expect-growth-in-wellness-travel/318101.

Table 11. 3 **Top United States and International Wellness Tourism Destinations, 2018**

United States Wellness Destinations	Global Wellness Destinations
1. Sedona, Arizona	1. Bali, Indonesia
2. Hawley, Pennsylvania	2. Rishikesh, India
3. Ojai, California	3. Sedona, Arizona, United States
4. Amelia Island, Florida	4. Hepburn Springs, Australia
5. Calistoga, California	5. Ko Samui, Thailand
6. Lenox, Massachusetts	6. Costa Rica
7. Palm Springs, California	7. Goa, India
8. Park City, California	8. Zermatt, Switzerland
9. Stowe, Vermont	9. Maldives
10. Wailea, Hawaii	10. Ibiza, Spain

Source: L. Hill. 2018. TripAdvisor Names Top Destinations for Wellness Tourism as Segment Continues to Experience Exponential Growth. *Welltodo Global Wellness News*. June. https://www.welltodoglobal.com/tripadvisor-names-top-destinations-for-wellness-tourism-as-segment-continues-to-experience-exponential-growth.

Skift, an international travel research firm, estimated that about 78% of affluent travelers in the United States would like to incorporate wellness into their trips.[11] The Wellness Tourism Association's Wellness Travel Survey[12] further revealed that 63% of respondents had taken a "wellness vacation" and the remaining 37% also indicated interest in taking a wellness trip. To further reinforce the trend, a Facebook poll by TripAdvisor found that more than 25% of its online followers were interested in taking a wellness trip over the next 12 months.[13]

The top 10 wellness destinations in the United States and globally, based on TripAdvisor research, are presented in Table 11.3.

It is notable that TripAdvisor indicated that 6 of the 10 most popular wellness destinations globally were in Asia. Beyond TripAdvisor, GWI research showed that wellness tourism was also heavily concentrated in Germany, the PRC, France, and Japan, which ranked among the top five wellness tourism destinations and represented 59% of the global market (Table 11.4). However, the PRC and India's wellness tourism rankings are rising rapidly. The PRC went from 11th in 2014 to third in 2018 and India from 16th to seventh.[14] The report estimated that emerging markets will drive more than half of overall wellness tourism growth expenditures and three-quarters of wellness trip growth in the next 5 years in the following regions: Asia and Pacific, Latin America–Caribbean, Middle East–North Africa, and sub-Saharan Africa (footnote 14).

[11] M. Carty. 2019. *US Affluent Traveler Trends 2019*. New York: New Skift Research.
[12] Wellness Tourism Association. https://www.wellnesstourismassociation.org.
[13] *TripAdvisor*. 2018. TripAdvisor Names Most Blissful Destinations for Wellness Travel. 12 June. http://ir.tripadvisor.com/news-releases/news-release-details/tripadvisor-names-most-blissful-destinations-wellness-travel; and reported on *CBS Morning*, 21 July 2018.
[14] GWI. 2018. *Global Wellness Tourism Economy*. Global Wellness Institute.

Table 11.4 **Leading Growth Markets for Wellness Tourism, 2015–2017**

	Number of Wellness Arrivals/Trips Added (million)	Average Annual Growth Rate
People's Republic of China	21.9	20.6%
India	17.3	20.3%
United States	15.4	4.7%
Germany	7.5	6.2%
Spain	5.2	17.5%
Mexico	3.3	10.3%
Malaysia	3.3	28.6%
Viet Nam	3.2	22.8%
Chile	3.2	29.3%
Thailand	2.7	13.1%
Japan	2.7	3.5%
Italy	2.7	12.2%
Indonesia	2.7	21.5%
United Kingdom	2.6	6.1%
Russian Federation	2.3	8.4%
Czech Republic	2.2	18.1%
Austria	2.2	7.3%
Canada	2.2	4.2%
Poland	2.0	14.7%
Brazil	1.9	10.4%
France	1.8	2.8%
Republic of Korea	1.6	4.5%
Australia	1.5	8.3%
Slovakia	1.4	36.9%
Philippines	1.1	31.1%

Note: These figures combine both international/inbound and domestic wellness tourism spending and include both primary and secondary wellness trips. These are estimates by the Global Wellness Institute based on tourism industry data from Euromonitor International.

Source: Global Wellness Institute. 2018. *New Study Reveals Wellness Tourism Now a $639 Billion Market*. https://globalwellnessinstitute.org/press-room/press-releases/new-study-reveals-wellness-tourism-now-a-639-billion-market.

Transformative Travel

Underlying demand for wellness tourism is related to the growing trend of transformative travel, which is rooted in the idea that travel experiences have the power to transform one's life; to be life-changing; and to empower people to make meaningful, lasting changes in their lives. As the cofounder of the Transformational Travel Council, Michael Bennett, explained on the council's website: "Ultimately, it's a new philosophy on travel [that] connects travelers to their truest self and to others, cultivating a sense of purpose and belonging."[15] He listed seven key themes that form the foundation for transformative travel:

(i) answering the call to adventure and traveling with intention,
(ii) crossing the threshold and entering a "zone unknown,"
(iii) being open to experiences and transformation,
(iv) consciously seeking out extraordinary and challenging experiences,
(v) engaging in meaningful interactions and conversations,
(vi) taking time for reflection and "meaning-making," and
(vii) launching into purposeful action.

Not surprisingly, many of these travelers are attracted to destinations that can offer self-actualization, self-improvement and personal transformation and growth, and deeper experiences, which all lead to wellness. This trend has grown in popularity so much in recent years that travel trade publisher Skift identified "transformative travel" as one of its 2018 megatrends. GWI describes transformational travel as experiential travel to a deeper, more emotional level.

Explorer X, a Seattle-based tour operator whose owners founded the Transformational Travel Council, offers tours that, according to the owners, help define transformative travel and wellness tourism. They offer tours worldwide, including three in Asia: in Nepal, "A Sacred Journey in the Himalayas"; in Sri Lanka, "Family Adventure"; and in Bhutan, "A Pilgrimage with Phil Cousineau." Some highlights of these "journeys" provide examples of what wellness and transformative travel might look like in terms of actual trips and tours:

(i) Nepal: A 13-day "journey" that promises to "revitalize your head, heart, and mind..." and offers an opportunity to "commune with monks, and learn from a meditation wizard..."
(ii) Sri Lanka: An 11-day journey that is "family-focused" offering "wildlife safaris, 'tuk tuk' rides, enormous Buddhist temples...a global perspective for you and your family by spending time with local kids and families."
(iii) Bhutan: An 11-day tour with Phil Cousineau, author of *The Art of Pilgrimage*, who introduces visitors to religious and architectural heritage, such as dzongs and fortified monasteries; visitors also learn from a government official about Gross National Happiness.

From the perspective of a former travel writer (Lonely Planet) and longtime travel and tourism market expert with a focus on authentic experiences and sustainable tourism, none of the itineraries of these or other transformative journeys seemed novel or potentially life-changing, unless they were first-time travel experiences. However, even as first-time experiences, they seemed somewhat contrived and "off-the-shelf." Nevertheless, these journeys bring tourist spending to small communities that might not otherwise receive it. As a result, the transformation is potentially greater for the visited rather than for the visitor, since even a small amount of spending and time with visitors from the other side of the planet has potentially greater positive impacts.

Asia's Wellness Tourism Market

As of April 2021, Asian travel was still affected by the COVID-19 outbreak.[16] Wellness tourism will undoubtedly also experience declines in the region, although it is expected to recover after the crisis passes. The full impact on

[15] Transformational Travel Council. *Why Transformational Travel?* https://www.transformational.travel/about-tt-page.

[16] The UNWTO's latest data on international tourist arrivals in Asia and the Pacific used in this this report were released in October 2020 but based on the status as of August 2020.

the wellness tourism sector is not yet known, but since flights throughout the region have been severely curtailed, this sector and every other tourism sector has been negatively impacted.

Wellness tourism has been a high priority in Asia with most economies in the region experiencing major growth in the wellness industry and the PRC leading the way (Appendix 8 and Table 11.4 provide further details). From 2015 to 2017, the PRC's number of wellness trips increased by about 22 million, and India followed with an increase of about 17 million wellness trips. Travelers to and within Asia accounted for $136.7 billion (21.1%) of total wellness tourism revenue and a 10.9% compound annual growth rate. For the PRC, the wellness tourism market is mostly internal and not yet considered a main attraction for international visitors. However, for outbound Chinese travelers, traveling for wellness is important.

Significant annual growth was also observed in the Philippines, Malaysia, and Viet Nam. Ten of the world's top wellness tourism destination markets are in Asia and the Pacific (in order from largest to smallest): the PRC, India, Malaysia, Viet Nam, Thailand, Japan, Indonesia, the Republic of Korea (ROK), Australia, and the Philippines (Table 11.4). The popularity of wellness tourism in these countries is not surprising because, historically, these societies have emphasized mind–body connections, such as traditional medicine in the PRC and the ROK, tai chi in the PRC, Hindu meditation and Ayurveda in India, and the deep spiritualism and oneness with nature of Buddhism throughout the region.

According to the GWI report, wellness tourism was included in the national tourism strategies of the PRC, India, Malaysia, Viet Nam, Thailand, the ROK, and the Philippines. India and Thailand are profiled in the case studies, as well as Sri Lanka.[17] In addition, wellness tourism has been a target for national investment promotion in all these economies as well as in Bhutan; Fiji; Maldives; New Zealand; and Taipei,China. India, for example, set up a National Medical & Wellness Tourism Promotion Board to provide policy advice and measures to support wellness tourism, such as guidelines for quality and training, financial assistance, and investment promotion for wellness centers catering to tourists.

Highlights of wellness tourism in the PRC and ROK are explored in the following section.

People's Republic of China

Until COVID-19 became a crisis for the country, wellness tourism was regarded as a fast-growing segment both within the country and for outbound Chinese travelers. In 2016, the government launched the Healthy China 2030 initiative through which President Xi Jinping has prioritized health, healthy lifestyles, and wellness as central to the country's development. Demand for and interest in wellness and wellness tourism were growing prior to this initiative, which stimulated increased national demand for nature-based activities, wellness heritage and healing systems, and fitness. At the core of this interest have been age-old traditions in herbal medicine, qigong, meditation, and martial arts.

An important facet of wellness tourism in the PRC has been the country's hot springs, which GWI describes as "mainly cater[ing] to domestic visitors...[with] remnants of historic Soviet-style sanatoria, rustic day-use hot springs/traditional bathhouses, and privately-owned and operated hot springs resorts and towns focused on recreation and family holidays." The government established a national hot spring committee and regulations related to water quality, safety management, and the rating of "hot springs towns." GWI explains that "increased private investment [has been] encouraged by rising consumer interest in healthy lifestyles and wellness tourism on the one hand, and government support for preventive health on the other hand."

[17] Footnote 14, p. 69.

The publication *2019 Wellness Trends, from Global Wellness Summit* also indicates that interest in wellness activities has been growing among outbound Chinese travelers: "According to a 2017 survey from one of the PRC's leading travel powerhouses, over 70% of travelers are seeking local experiences or wellness-related activities, such as culinary exploration, outdoor recreation, gallery and museum visits, nature/ecological tours, beauty and spa treatments...and hot springs."[18]

Republic of Korea

Wellness travel is a key segment for the ROK's Ministry of Culture, Sports and Tourism and the Korea Tourism Organization. Through their website,[19] they market and promote 25 must-visit wellness attractions in the ROK, which they herald as "the best destination to improve your physical and mental health and wellbeing." These attractions are categorized into beauty and spa, traditional Korean medicine, nature and forest, and healing and meditation destinations. One attraction, for example, the Herb Lab Bom Dong in Seoul, Republic of Korea, serves visitors "medical teas that match their individual physical states." Another attraction, the Suncheonman Bay National Garden & Wetland Reserve in Suncheon, is "the perfect place to de-stress and enjoy some peace and quiet, and you can also enjoy a herbarium, a traditional Korean medicine experience center."

Three Wellness Tourism Case Studies

Wellness tourism case studies from India, Thailand, and Sri Lanka show the wide variety of opportunities offered by different countries' wellness tourism sectors.

India

According to GWI's 2018 *Global Wellness Tourism Economy* report, the wellness tourism sector is strong in India, due in part to the country's offerings of meditation, yoga, and Ayurveda retreats.

In the global wellness tourism segment, India ranked seventh as a wellness tourism destination in 2017 with a wellness tourism expenditure of $16.3 billion, which directly supported 3.8 million jobs, or 14% of all tourism employment. India had 56 million wellness tourist arrivals in 2017, 51 million of which were domestic arrivals (footnote 14). India's wellness tourism market is estimated to be growing by 22% annually, which makes it the fastest-growing in the world. A growing number of hotel and resort spas in India, including traditional Ayurvedic resorts, are becoming destination spas and wellness retreats that provide a holistic package of services, experiences, and journeys. The India-based Carnoustie Group's resorts are a prime example.

The Carnoustie Group is known for its Ayurveda and wellness resorts in India, which are particularly popular in the state of Kerala. Kerala has developed what is considered an authentic and place-based wellness tourism product and brand. Kerala branded itself as the "Land of Ayurveda" 2 decades ago, and now 40% of their tourism revenue is generated by Ayurveda-related offers.[20]

Similarly, the state of Uttarakhand has become renowned for its yoga study center of Rishikesh, which is replete with ashrams and is described by the Uttarakhand Tourism Development Board as "a most tranquil place." The center attracted the Beatles in the 1960s for a stay with their guru, the Maharishi Mahesh Yogi (footnote 14).

[18] GWI. 2019. *2019 Wellness Trends, from the Global Wellness Summit*. Miami. p. 75.

[19] See https://gokorea.co.uk/portfolio-view/wellness-tourism/#.

[20] A. Nishad. *Development of Medical Tourism in Kerala with Special Reference to Ayurvedic Tourism*. 2015. https://www.linkedin.com/pulse/development-medical-tourism-kerala-special-reference-ayurvedic-a; and GWI. 2018. *Global Wellness Tourism Economy*.

As the wellness segment grows, it is also faced with key challenges: a shortage of skilled staff for spas and other wellness services, and a lack of staff training to meet international standards. Several wellness-related associations are working to better support this growing segment, including the International Indian Wellness and Medical Tourism Association, the Indian Medical Travel Association, the Spa Association of India, Spas India, and the Spa and Wellness Association of India. The Government of India has also implemented strategies to promote wellness and medical tourism, including the establishment of a National Medical & Wellness Tourism Promotion Board, which provides policy advice to this sector, including guidelines for quality and training, financial assistance, and investment promotion for wellness centers.

India's strategies also included revamping its branding and marketing initiatives, "Incredible India!" and "Athiti Devo Bhava," and the 2018 release of the Incredible India mobile app for trip planning. Wellness is an integral offer via the app, which promotes "major experiences such as spirituality, heritage, adventure, culture, yoga, wellness, and more."[21] Earlier in 2015, the Government of India established the Ministry of Ayurveda, Yoga & Naturopathy, Unani, Siddha and Homoeopathy and the national government issued Revised Guidelines for the Promotion of Wellness and Medical as Niche Tourism Products, which offer a marketing development assistance (MDA) scheme and financial assistance to accredited providers.

Based on the revised guidelines, the types of support include:

- 50% financing for publicity and promotional materials;
- financial assistance for organizing workshops, events, meetings, and seminars promoting wellness and medical tourism for 100+ participants, at least half of whom are non-Indian;
- financial assistance for shows with exhibits, suppliers, and buyers for the promotion of wellness and medical tourism for 75+ participants, 40% of whom are non-Indian buyers; and
- financial support for training courses on skills development and certification courses in the wellness and medical tourism sectors per Ministry of Tourism guidelines.

Many lessons can be drawn from this case study of wellness tourism in India:

- The Government of India and some states, such as Kerala and Uttarakhand, support the growth of the wellness tourism sector through a national-level MDA and financial assistance to accredited providers.
- It is not possible to precisely gauge the success of MDA for wellness tourism providers, but the fast growth in the sector suggests that it has contributed to growth. For example, according to statistics from the Uttarakhand Tourism Development Board, in 2009 the state received more than 23 million total visitors, with 1.1 million foreign visitors and the rest domestic. By 2018, the state recorded more than 37 million visitors, with 1.5 million foreign visitors.
- Private sector associations dedicated to the wellness sector also are facilitating development and growth through marketing and training and are eligible for MDA.

Sri Lanka

Sri Lanka, like India, has many hotel and resort spas and traditional Ayurvedic resorts that are becoming (or have become) destination spas and wellness retreats and provide holistic "wellness" packages. In marketing and promotion, Sri Lanka combines wellness tourism, some with an Ayurvedic emphasis, with the country's diverse nature-based historical and cultural offerings. These include yoga, meditation, spirituality, pilgrimages, indigenous medicine, faith healing, and well-being.

[21] The app can be downloaded from https://tourism.gov.in/important-links-latest-program-application-download/android.

Supporting this sector, the Government of Sri Lanka has implemented strategies to promote wellness and medical tourism, including economic incentives and simplified project approval procedures for companies investing in wellness-related developments. The country's National Export Strategy (2018–2022) also supports the wellness tourism sector.[22] The strategy's three goals include (i) coordinated development of traditional and modern health and medical tourism, (ii) establishing a quality assurance system for wellness and traditional health systems, and (iii) providing an information system for the Sri Lankan health tourism sector and its target markets. A Wellness Tourism Strategy is part of the National Export Strategy.

The Wellness Tourism Strategy was produced for the period 2018–2022 and seeks to establish Sri Lanka as a major wellness tourism hub for the region. The strategy indicates that the goal is to "develop the sector strategically by addressing constraints in a comprehensive manner and by defining concrete opportunities that can be realized through the specific steps detailed in the Strategy's 'Strategic Framework' and Plan of Action (PoA)." The strategic framework and plan of action are intended to be a road map for helping to achieve the following strategic objectives:

- develop coordination in traditional and Western health tourism;
- set up a quality assurance system for wellness and traditional health systems; and
- build information about the Sri Lankan health tourism sector and about its target markets.

In line with these objectives and the overall strategy, the country's Export Development Board (EDB) has identified health and wellness tourism services as a key growth sector. Both the overall strategy and the EDB are driven by a vision of "Sri Lanka: The Preferred Destination for Well-being." To help realize this vision, the EDB is (i) working with the health and wellness tourism sector and government institutions on targeted marketing and promotion campaigns; and (ii) also studying how to link with European Union wellness travel and insurance companies (footnote 22).

The government is also exploring the establishment of a national certification system for wellness and traditional medicine service providers. This would be complemented by international certification options to support the Western medicine segment, as well as a new regulatory and licensing system for spas, including amended regulations particularly for the Ayurveda segment. It is also a potentially promising development that the EDB and the government have been working on strict guidelines for international hotel and spa investors interested in wellness tourism (footnote 22). The government wants to ensure that the highest possible quality standards are maintained.

Finally, to facilitate and maximize private sector involvement and investment, in early 2020, the EDB helped establish the Sri Lanka Wellness Tourism Association, which was formed with more than 50 stakeholders, including Western medicine companies, indigenous Ayurveda practitioners, and many others engaged in wellness tourism–related activities.

Many lessons can be drawn from this case study of wellness tourism in Sri Lanka:

- The Government of Sri Lanka recognizes that wellness tourism is a leading high-growth and high-value sector for the country, and thus requires a stronger and more strategic approach through investment in development and implementation of a strategy that is specifically for wellness tourism.
- Importantly, the strategy includes an emphasis on introducing and implementing national regulations and standards, while also increasing wellness tourism marketing for both national and international markets.

[22] *International Medical Travel Journal*. 2020. Plans to Regulate Wellness Tourism in Sri Lanka. 6 February. https://www.imtj.com/news/plans-regulate-wellness-tourism-sri-lanka.

- The government-led EDB worked with private sector stakeholders to create the Sri Lanka Wellness Tourism Association. Prior to January 2020, no such association existed, so it is expected that this will help boost investment and coordinated training and marketing programs.
- To further attract and incentivize investment in the wellness tourism sector, the government facilitates fast-track approval and investment procedures.

Thailand

GWI estimates that Thailand earned about $12 billion from wellness tourism from 12.5 million wellness-related arrivals, thus ranking the country 13th as a wellness tourism destination market, in 2017. International arrivals for wellness tourism grew more than 13% from 2015 to 2017, which was about 50% more than the rate of overall international arrivals.[23] Notably, with 6.8 million wellness-related domestic arrivals, this amounts to nearly 46% of the total wellness tourism market (footnote 14). This market also directly supports more than 500,000 jobs in the country, thus 20% of direct jobs in travel and tourism.

Thailand's main wellness tourism offers are based on spa resorts, with the Tourism Authority of Thailand (TAT) promoting 41 spa and wellness resorts in the country. These resorts are especially known for offering traditional Thai massage, which is influenced by traditional medicine and is promoted by TAT for relieving physical and mental tension, as well as reducing migraines, sprains, bruises, and anxiety, and improving flexibility.

In 2014, TAT launched a health and wellness marketing strategy in cooperation with Thai Airways International; Asia Web Direct; and more than 30 providers of health, beauty, and spa treatments. The strategy focused on a digital marketing initiative for health and wellness that was aimed at women in the Asia and Pacific region. Under the slogan of "Find Your Fabulous," the campaign helped promote more than 150 packages of wellness and beauty treatments, spa packages, and hotel stays throughout the country. The government also began to develop the country's thermal springs, with a lead pilot "spa city" development in Khlong Thom District in Krabi Province. The campaign is believed to have succeeded based on the strong growth of the market. The campaign also prompted the creation of the annual Thailand Health and Wellness Trade Meeting that brings international buyers to meet Thai sellers of medical and wellness services.[24]

The high demand for spa facilities and experiences also led to the creation of the nonprofit Thai Spa Association, which promotes the industry and works to ensure high standards in staff training, spa management, and equipment. High standards in the sector have positively impacted the development of the industry and its reputation for excellent customer service. The Thai Spa Association also offers its members:

- educational opportunities;
- access to the latest trends and information on wellness and the spa sector;
- discounted professional training courses, seminars, and workshops;
- networking opportunities with spa professionals from all over Thailand and beyond;
- member-only spa tours, excursions, and events;
- plans for spa accreditation; and
- a "Seal of Approval" that offers recognition to spas that demonstrate the industry's best practice standards.

[23] UNWTO. 2020. *UNWTO World Tourism Barometer*. Madrid, Spain. January. https://www.e-unwto.org/toc/wtobarometereng/18/1.

[24] *Bangkok Post*. 2015. World of Wellness. 3 August.

There are several other related associations that offer similar services, including the Thai Massage Association, the Federation of Thai Spa & Wellness Association,[25] and the Thai Medical and Wellness Tourism Association.[26] These associations work to ensure high quality standards and offers.

Many lessons can be drawn from this case study of wellness tourism in Thailand:

- The Government of Thailand supports the growth of the wellness tourism sector through increased marketing, which has been widely successful.
- The government has also taken proactive steps to increase wellness tourism, including by developing hot-spring areas and creating the annual Thailand Health and Wellness Tourism Trade Meeting to connect international buyers with local sellers.
- The high degree of private sector organization in associations has helped wellness tourism, especially via coordinated training and marketing.

Strategic Recommendations for COVID-19 Response and Recovery

As described above, the tourism industry overall, especially its wellness tourism segment in East Asia and Southeast Asia, was thriving and growing at one of the fastest rates in the world until the COVID-19 outbreak. Wellness tourism has proved to be an important driver of economic growth and employment for tourism and national economies overall. After the outbreak subsides, wellness tourism might offer a faster path to recovery than other segments. Wellness tourism emphasizes healthy living, well-being, and the preservation of nature and culture-based heritage, with some of the highest-spending tourists, and it also reinforces efforts to achieve the United Nations SDGs.

As of April 2021, the COVID-19 outbreak was still impacting the travel and tourism industry globally and was expected to continue limiting travel into 2022. This impact has been felt substantially in Asia, with every segment of the economy affected. Before the outbreak, preparing for medical crises was not a top priority issue for tourism, but this has become central to strategies and planning going forward.

The following strategic recommendations for the wellness tourism industry as it responds to and recovers from the effects of COVID-19 are organized according to immediate, medium-term (6–12 months), and longer-term actions.

Immediate Actions

Public information campaigns. Wellness tourism is a valuable sector for destination countries. As discussed above, wellness travelers spend on average about 58% more than other types of travelers. While in 2020 due to the COVID-19 pandemic it was increasingly difficult, if not impossible, to ensure that conditions were safe and healthy or at least stable, continual and comprehensive public information campaigns at the local and national levels by government agencies, as well as by accommodations and tour providers, will be essential going forward. These campaigns should provide the facts about the number of COVID-19 cases and recommendations for hygiene, prevention, and protection. Campaigns such as what the TAT does at a national level and for the wellness destination of Krabi are proactive and positive.

The "Krabi We Care" project strengthens the town's wellness tourism opportunities by demonstrating community-wide cooperation to prevent COVID-19. The project is part of the local tourist office and industry efforts to promote responsible tourism.

[25] The Federation of Thai Spa & Wellness Association. https://www.federationspaandwellness.com.

[26] Thai Medical and Wellness Tourism Association. https://www.facebook.com/ThaiMedicalAndWellnessTourismAssociation.

Proactive marketing and promotion of wellness tourism destinations to strengthen health, hygiene, and well-being. Wellness tourism emphasizes sustainable activities that strengthen health, hygiene, and well-being, which could serve as examples for non-wellness destinations. Quality certification schemes, such as those that exist in Thailand, Sri Lanka, and other countries, should be reviewed, and perhaps instituted with other tourism segments.

In addition, international and national wellness, spa, and wellness tourism associations should be actively communicating the strengths of wellness tourism. For example, while the Wellness Tourism Association is promoting virtual experiences among some of their members, there did not appear to be any guidelines about how the segment can be proactive in the battle against COVID-19.

Other stakeholder organizations and businesses could be involved in communicating the strengths of wellness tourism, i.e., Virtuoso, Hyatt Hotels, and "green space" airports such as Singapore.

Financial relief. The governments of the PRC, the ROK, Singapore, and other countries are providing economic stimulus aid to help industries survive the outbreak. Similar support should be considered for wellness tourism destinations that are impacted by COVID-19 so that they can survive, as well as possibly serve as models of quality health, hygiene, and well-being standards for the industry overall. Singapore, for example, estimated that arrivals fell by 84.4% in 2020. Their support for tourism provides some ideas for consideration:

- License fees for hotels, travel agents, and tour guides are being waived.
- The Singapore Tourism Board is defraying the cleaning and disinfecting cost of hotels that provide accommodation to confirmed and suspected COVID-19 cases.
- Property tax rebates are provided for licensed hotels and serviced apartments, meeting, incentive, conference, and exhibition venues, ferry terminals, and integrated resorts.
- A Temporary Bridging Loan Program will be introduced to provide more cash flow for enterprises in the tourism sector.
- Eligible employers will be able to apply for the Leave of Absence Support Program, which provides the employer $100 daily per affected worker for the duration of the leave of absence.

Rapid risk assessments of COVID-19's impacts on the wellness tourism segment in member states. Given the high value and potential for serving as a positive model for the entire industry, member states and their wellness tourism providers would benefit from rapid assessments of the impacts of COVID-19 on the segment. The assessments could be used to prioritize risks and plan for immediate and medium-term actions to fast-track recovery efforts and/or ensure the sustainability of the segment.

Medium-Term Actions

Inclusion of wellness tourism in country-level tourism strategies based on rapid assessments. As of 2018, the following Asian countries included wellness tourism in their national tourism strategies: Bhutan, the PRC, India, Malaysia, Maldives, the ROK, Sri Lanka (as of 2019), the Philippines, Thailand, and Viet Nam. In 2018, these countries received almost 32 million Chinese arrivals. According to GWI, the wellness tourism segment in 2017 generated substantial receipts for the following countries with wellness in their strategies: the PRC ($31 billion), India ($16.3 billion), Thailand ($12 billion), the ROK ($7.2 billion), Malaysia ($5 billion), and Viet Nam ($4 billion). Other countries could follow their lead and include wellness tourism in their tourism strategies.

COVID-19 wellness tourism survey. A survey of Asian wellness tourism destinations about the impacts and preventive actions being taken to reduce COVID-19 exposure would be helpful.

Longer-Term Actions

Wellness tourism strategies or wellness tourism as an integral part of tourism strategies. Where there were wellness tourism strategies or wellness tourism was part of overall tourism strategies (as of August 2018), the segment proved to succeed in generating growing numbers of visitors, often both domestic and international. (The list from GWI as of August 2018 is provided in Appendix 7.) Sri Lanka recognized the importance of the segment with the launch of their Wellness Tourism Strategy for 2018–2022, which seeks to establish Sri Lanka as a major wellness tourism hub for the region.

Ensure high quality and model international standards through national certification. As India and Sri Lanka demonstrated, government-led certification programs help ensure high quality, which in turn reinforces national and international marketing efforts. Coordinated agreement and implementation of international standards would be helpful for knowledge sharing and international promotion of the segment as the highest-quality segment of tourism.

Broaden the application of the hazard analysis and critical control point (HACCP) system to wellness tourism destinations and facilities. The seven-step HACCP process could be adapted to wellness tourism destination certification, and thus further strengthen the segment as a model source of hygiene, health, and well-being. Steps would include:

(i) Conduct a hazard analysis to identify potential hazards.
(ii) Identify the critical control points (CCPs), those points in the process where the potential hazards could occur and can be prevented and/or controlled.
(iii) Establish critical limits for preventive measures associated with each CCP. A critical limit is a criterion that must be met for each CCP.
(iv) Establish CCP monitoring requirements to ensure that each CCP stays within its limit. Monitoring may require materials or devices to measure or otherwise evaluate the process at CCPs.
(v) Establish corrective actions if monitoring determines a CCP is not within the established limits.
(vi) Establish effective record-keeping procedures that document the HACCP system is working properly.
(vii) Establish procedures for verifying that the HACCP system is working properly. Verification procedures may include reviewing the HACCP plan, CCP records, and critical limits.

Prior to COVID-19. increasing numbers of people were traveling to realize greater wellness in their lives. They sought healthier lifestyles, reduced stress, ways to prevent disease, and enhance physical and mental well-being. As Asia and the Pacific emerge from COVID-19, people will want to travel again, but with more caution and attention to health and safety issues. As described above, wellness focuses on health and well-being, so this sector is well-positioned to help people and places recover and restore livelihoods in ways that benefit the entire society. The strategic recommendations provide departure points for advancing this process.

Further Reading

Airbnb Newsroom. 2017. *The U.S. Midwest, Ryokans and Brazilian Beaches: Airbnb's 2018 Travel Trends*. https://news.airbnb.com/the-u-s-midwest-ryokans-and-brazilian-beaches-airbnbs-2018-travel-trends.

M. Carty. 2019. *U.S. Affluent Travelers Plan More Wellness Trips This Year: Skift Research*. https://skift.com/2019/05/07/u-s-affluent-travelers-plan-more-wellness-trips-this-year-skift-research.

Centers for Disease Control. 2020. *Update: Public Health Response to the Coronavirus Disease 2019 Outbreak—United States*, 24 February. https://www.cdc.gov/mmwr/volumes/69/wr/mm6908e1.htm#suggestedcitation.

China Outbound Tourism Research Institute. China Outbound Latest. https://china-outbound.com/info.

J. Haywood et al. 2017. *Airbnb & Hotel Performance. STR Research Inc., 2017*. Hendersonville, Tennessee.

Hilton Worldwide Holdings, Inc. Form 10-K for Fiscal Year Ended December 31st, 2018. EDGAR. Securities and Exchange Commission, 2019, https://otp.tools.investis.com/clients/us/hilton_worldwide2/SEC/sec-show.aspx?Type=html&FilingId=13217616&CIK=0001585689&Index=10000#Q42018HWH10-K_HTM_S5C817A068FDB557A9AEEF58562499E8E.

International Association of Amusement Parks and Attractions. 2019. Global Theme and Amusement Park Outlook. Florida.

Marriott International, Inc. Form 10-K for Fiscal Year Ended December 31st, 2019. EDGAR. Securities and Exchange Commission, 2019, https://www.sec.gov/Archives/edgar/data/1048286/000162828020002376/mar-q42019x10k.htm#sD3179DC31AC555469AFF84342F6A41DA.

J. Rubin, ed. *TEA/AECOM 2018 Theme Index and Museum Index: The Global Attractions Attendance Report*. Burbank, California: Themed Entertainment Association (TEA), 2019 and Los Angeles: AECOM, 2019.

Sri Lanka Tourism Development Authority. 2019 and 2020. Monthly Tourist Arrivals Reports. Colombo.

Statista. 2019. Number of international tourist arrivals worldwide from 1996 to 2017 (in millions). https://www.statista.com/statistics/209334/total-number-of-international-tourist-arrivals.

UN World Tourism Organization (UNWTO). 2006. *WTO World Tourism Barometer*. Madrid, Spain. January.

______. 2018. *Tourism for Development—Volume II Success Stories*. Madrid.

______. 2019. *UNWTO World Tourism Barometer*. Madrid, Spain. November.

______. 2020. 100% of Global Destinations Now Have COVID-19 Travel Restrictions, UNWTO Reports. 28 April. https://www.unwto.org/news/covid-19-travel-restrictions.

UNWTO and Global Tourism Economy Research Centre. 2019. *UNWTO/GTERC Asia Tourism Trends 2019 Edition*. Madrid, Spain.

World Tourism Organization. 2003. *WTO World Tourism Barometer*. Madrid, Spain. January.

______. 2005. *WTO World Tourism Barometer*. Madrid, Spain. January.

PART 5

Wellness for Happiness and Inclusion

CHAPTER 12

Wellness for Happiness in Developing Asia

Shun Wang

The wellness sector of Asian economies can potentially contribute to national happiness, either through its contribution to economic performance or through noneconomic channels. This chapter exploits recent data on six wellness sectors from the Global Wellness Institute and self-reported happiness from the Gallup World Poll to assess the wellness–happiness nexus empirically. Simple ordinary least squares (OLS) regressions show that workplace wellness spending by employers is statistically and economically significant for national happiness, both globally and within developing Asia. Wellness real estate development and spending on recreational physical activities are also correlated with a population's happiness, but only in the global sample.

Introduction

Interest in happiness has been growing since Richard Easterlin showed that income growth may not always lead to a higher level of self-reported happiness.[1] Over the past few decades, the economics of happiness has been one of the fastest-growing fields in economics, particularly in the last 10 years.[2] In addition to the exploding increase in academic research on happiness, there is a growing interest in happiness among policy makers worldwide. Gradually, happiness is being viewed as a new and important measure of people's well-being and a policy target[3] that is complementary to traditional income measures.

In July 2011, the United Nations General Assembly passed a historic resolution, "Happiness: Towards a Holistic Approach to Development, A/RES/65/309." Member countries are invited to measure their citizens' happiness and to use this to guide their policies. In April 2012, the first United Nations high-level meeting on happiness and well-being was held, chaired by the Prime Minister of Bhutan. The first *World Happiness Report,* edited by John F. Helliwell, Richard Layard, and Jeffrey Sachs, was released during the meeting, followed by a series of annual

Note: The author is grateful to the Global Wellness Institute for sharing its wellness data with him, and thanks Donghyun Park for his invaluable comments.

1 R. Easterlin. 1974. Does Economic Growth Improve the Human Lot? Some Empirical Evidence. In P.A. David and M.W. Reder, eds. *Nations and Households in Economic Growth*. New York: Academic Press. pp. 89–125.

2 A.E. Clark. 2018. Four Decades of the Economics of Happiness: Where Next? *The Review of Income and Wealth*. 64 (2). pp. 245–269; A.E. Clark et al. 2018. *The Origins of Happiness: The Science of Well-being over the Life Course*. Princeton University Press; and B.S. Frey. 2020. What Are the Opportunities for Future Happiness Research? *International Review of Economics*. 67. pp. 5–12.

3 Global Happiness Council. 2018. *Global Happiness Policy Report 2018*.

reports. In 2013, the Organisation for Economic Co-operation and Development (OECD) published its guidelines on the measurement of well-being to encourage and facilitate government actions.[4]

At the national level, the Office of National Statistics (ONS) in the United Kingdom (UK) has sampled citizens of the UK randomly on happiness since 2012 and used the data to guide policy making. The Government of New Zealand has been engaged in a Quality of Life Project to monitor well-being and study how to use it more systematically for policy analysis. In February 2016, the United Arab Emirates created the Ministry of State for Happiness and Wellbeing and appointed Her Excellency Ohood bint Khalfan Al Roumi as the first minister. The role of the ministry was to harmonize government plans, programs, and policies to achieve a happier society. Happiness is also becoming a higher priority in developing Asia.[5] Bhutan is probably the best known example where the government has adopted the Gross National Happiness Index as its national objective. The 14th Congress of the People's Republic of China (PRC) has laid out the people's happiness (*xingfu gan*) as one of its strategic national goals. The current Seoul metropolitan government turned to sustainable development and happiness as its main goals.

Among the many factors fostering a population's happiness, the booming wellness sector may contribute to happiness, either through its contribution to employment and economic growth, or through noneconomic channels. This chapter aims to introduce the measurement of happiness and the development of the wellness industry in developing Asia, and explore the relationship between the wellness industry and happiness.

Recently, the Global Wellness Institute (GWI) defined wellness as "the active pursuit of activities, choices, and lifestyles that lead to a state of holistic health."[6] It is similar to what the National Wellness Institute provides: "wellness is an active process through which people become aware of, and make choices toward, a more successful existence." The wellness industry is defined as "industries that enable consumers to incorporate wellness activities and lifestyles into their daily lives" (footnote 6). Compared with the traditional health care industry, which mainly focuses on disease treatment and control, the wellness industry is proactive and preventive.

As discussed above, wellness is the process of seeking health and well-being. Thus, it is distinguished from the concept of health or well-being, which is an outcome or a static state of being. The World Health Organization defines health as a state of complete physical, mental, and social well-being, and not merely the absence of disease or infirmity. Well-being generally includes objective well-being (as measured by gross domestic product [GDP], gross national income, and the Human Development Index) and subjective well-being (which is often called "happiness," as measured by life evaluations, eudaimonia, and emotions).

The growing interest in wellness reflects Asia's transformation into an overwhelmingly middle-income or above region with many high-income countries. There were only two countries (Afghanistan and Nepal) that were categorized as low-income countries in 2016, according to World Development Indicators. The urbanization rate is also relatively high compared with other developing regions, as almost half of Asian countries are above the

[4] OECD. 2013. *OECD Guidelines on Measuring Subjective Well-being*. OECD Publishing.

[5] Developing Asia consists of the following 46 economies as of April 2019, which are further categorized into five groups by the Asian Development Bank: (i) Central Asia comprises Armenia, Azerbaijan, Georgia, Kazakhstan, the Kyrgyz Republic, Tajikistan, Turkmenistan, and Uzbekistan; (ii) East Asia comprises Hong Kong, China; Mongolia; the People's Republic of China (PRC); the Republic of Korea (ROK); and Taipei,China; (iii) South Asia comprises Afghanistan, Bangladesh, Bhutan, India, Maldives, Nepal, Pakistan, and Sri Lanka; (iv) Southeast Asia comprises Brunei Darussalam, Cambodia, Indonesia, the Lao People's Democratic Republic, Malaysia, Myanmar, Niue, the Philippines, Singapore, Thailand, Timor-Leste, and Viet Nam; and (v) the Pacific comprises the Cook Islands, the Federated States of Micronesia, Fiji, Kiribati, the Marshall Islands, Nauru, Palau, Papua New Guinea, Samoa, Solomon Islands, Tonga, Tuvalu, and Vanuatu.

[6] O. Yeung and K. Johnston. 2018. *The Global Wellness Industry and Its Implications for Asia's Development*. White paper for Asian Development Bank.

world urbanization level. The large middle-income and upper classes who are mainly living in urban areas aspire to a higher quality of life (QOL). However, there are many unhealthy elements in their lives, such as automobile dependency, consumption of processed food, and exposure to pollution. Their demand for wellness naturally arose from their desire for better life and their purchasing power.

The rest of the chapter is organized as follows. The second section, "Measurement of Happiness," briefly introduces the concept and measurement of happiness. "Happiness in Developing Asia" then introduces the current status of happiness in developing Asia and compares it with other regions. "The Wellness Industry in Asia" presents the distribution of wellness sectors across the region. "Wellness for Happiness: Conceptual Framework and Literature" discusses the theoretical nexus between wellness and happiness and reviews the literature. "Wellness for Happiness: An Empirical Analysis" conducts an empirical analysis using cross-sectional data at the country/territory level, globally, and in developing Asia. The final section draws conclusions.

Measurement of Happiness

Happiness is often used as an equivalent to "subjective well-being," which refers to a range of individual self-reports of life assessments and moods. Among various measures of happiness, a primary distinction is made between cognitive life evaluations and affective well-being.[7] Eudaimonic measures, linked to the idea of having a sense of meaning or purpose in life, are sometimes also collected in some surveys.

Cognitive life evaluations refer to people's overall evaluations of their lives as a whole. This sort of question may ask how satisfied people are with their lives as a whole, or how happy they are in general, or how they position their lives on a life ladder. For example, the survey question for life satisfaction in the Gallup World Poll is: "All things considered, how satisfied are you with your life as a whole these days? Use a 0 to 10 scale, where 0 is dissatisfied and 10 is satisfied." The answer might be on a 1–5 point scale or on a 1–4 point scale in other surveys. The life ladder question in the Gallup World Poll is: "Please imagine a ladder, with steps numbered from 0 at the bottom to 10 at the top. The top of the ladder represents the best possible life for you and the bottom of the ladder represents the worst possible life for you. On which step of the ladder would you say you personally feel you stand at this time?" This sort of question was first designed by Hadley Cantril,[8] thus the life ladder score is also called Cantril ladder, or Cantril's Self-Anchoring Striving Scale. A similar overall happiness question is used in the European Social Survey: "Taking all things together, how happy would you say you are?" The answer is on a 0–10 scale, where 0 refers to "extremely unhappy," and 10 to "extremely happy."

Measures of affective well-being are often rated on multi-item scales of people's emotions in a recent time period such as last hour, previous day, or previous week. Generally, this covers the experience of both positive and negative emotions. For example, the following questions on positive and negative affect have been used in the Gallup World Poll: "Did you experience the following feelings during a lot of the day yesterday? How about enjoyment?"; "Did you smile or laugh a lot yesterday?"; "How about happiness?"; "How about worry?"; "How about stress?"; "How about anger?"; and "How about sadness?" The answer to each item is binary, where 1 is for "yes" and 0 is for "no."

[7] See, for example, J.F. Helliwell and S. Wang. 2012. The State of Happiness. In J.F. Helliwell, R. Layard, and J. Sachs, eds. *World Happiness Report 2012*. New York: The Earth Institute of Columbia University. pp. 10–57; and D. Kahneman, E. Diener, and N. Schwarz. 1999. *Well-being: The Foundations of Hedonic Psychology*. New York: Russell Sage.

[8] H. Cantril. 1965. *The Pattern of Human Concerns*. New Brunswick, New Jersey: Rutgers University Press.

In practice, the UK's ONS started to collect data on happiness in 2012, including the following four questions to cover all three broad dimensions of happiness:

(i) Overall, how satisfied are you with your life nowadays? [evaluative well-being]
(ii) Overall, how happy did you feel yesterday? [positive affect]
(iii) Overall, how anxious did you feel yesterday? [negative affect]
(iv) Overall, to what extent do you feel the things you do in your life are worthwhile? [eudaimonic well-being]

Published in 2013, the *OECD Guidelines on Measuring Subjective Well-being* also suggest that all three broad dimensions should be covered, though they recommend survey questions on worry and depression for negative emotion, rather than anxiety, as in the ONS surveys in the UK (footnote 4).

There have been debates over which of these dimensions of well-being should be paid more attention to. Recent studies tend to give the highest priority weighting to evaluative well-being, as they are more interested in the deeper features of a good life.

Happiness in Developing Asia

The largest comparable happiness data in developing Asia are available from the Gallup World Poll. The measure of happiness is based on the Cantril ladder, an evaluative measure that is often used for international happiness rankings in the United Nations World Happiness Report series. Happiness data used in this chapter is based on the national average of happiness from Chapter 2 of the *World Happiness Report 2019*,[9] which is mainly based on the Gallup surveys from 2016 to 2018.

Among the 45 economies in developing Asia, happiness data are available for 29. No happiness data are available for the Pacific. Figure 12.1 shows the ranking of happiness scores in these developing Asian economies. There are two important findings from these happiness rankings.

First, there are large variations in happiness scores among these developing Asian economies.

Second, the happiness levels in developing Asia are relatively low compared to the rest of the world, according to Chapter 2 of the *World Happiness Report 2019*. On a scale of 0–10, the average score in developing Asia is 5.17, which is lower than the global average of 5.46.[10] It is higher than the scores in Africa and the Middle East, but lower than in all other regions in the world. Taipei,China, being the happiest in developing Asia, is still lower than Finland as the happiest worldwide, by the magnitude of 1.323. The lowest in developing Asia is Afghanistan (3.203), which also ranks as the third lowest in the world and only slightly higher than South Sudan (2.853) and Central African Republic (3.083).

[9] J.F. Helliwell, H. Huang, and S. Wang. 2019. Changing World Happiness. In J.F. Helliwell, R. Layard, and J. Sachs, eds. *World Happiness Report 2019*. New York: United Nations Sustainable Development Solutions Network. pp. 8–49.

[10] These are unweighted averages. The adult population weighted averages for developing Asia is 4.82 and for the world is 5.23.

Figure 12.1 **Ranking of Happiness**

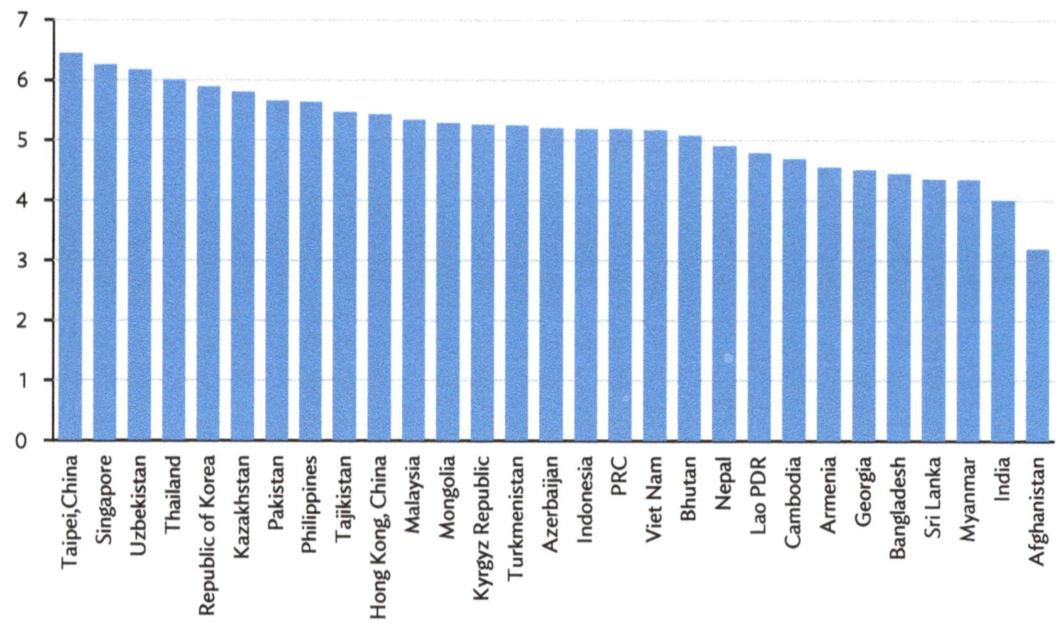

Lao PDR = Lao People's Democratic Republic, PRC = People's Republic of China.

Source: J.F. Helliwell, H. Huang, and S. Wang. 2019. Changing World Happiness. In J.F. Helliwell, R. Layard, and J. Sachs, eds. *World Happiness Report 2019*. New York: United Nations Sustainable Development Solutions Network. pp. 8–49.

The Wellness Industry in Asia

Wellness industry data at the country/territory level are available for 2017 for six sectors from the GWI: hot spring revenue, spa revenue, wellness tourism expenditures, workplace wellness spending by employers, wellness real estate construction value, and expenditures on recreational physical activities and enabling sectors. To compare the relative size of each wellness sector across economies, per capita values have been calculated for each sector. Among the 45 economies in developing Asia, there are no wellness industry data in the Cook Islands, Nauru, and Tuvalu, so they are excluded from the analysis.

Figures 12.2–12.7 illustrate the ranking of per capita values for these six sectors in 42 developing Asian economies. Figure 12.2 shows the ranking of per capita hot spring revenue. The values in this sector are quite small in magnitude for all economies, as the availability of hot springs depends highly on geographic conditions. The highest is Taipei,China, with the per capita value of $18.45. The PRC takes the second position with a value of only $12.59 and the Republic of Korea (ROK) has the third position with a value of $6.53. In addition, 15 record zero in this sector (mostly island economies), and 14 have values less than $1. Thus, we may conclude that this sector's contribution to whole economy in developing Asia is fairly small, if not negligible.

Figure 12.3 shows the ranking of per capita spa revenue. Here, Maldives and Palau are the top two, with much higher values than the rest of the economies. Moreover, the magnitude is quite large. For example, Maldives' per capita revenue is $484.66. Clearly, this is because these two countries are famous destinations for vacation.

Figure 12.2 **Per Capita Hot Spring Revenue**
($)

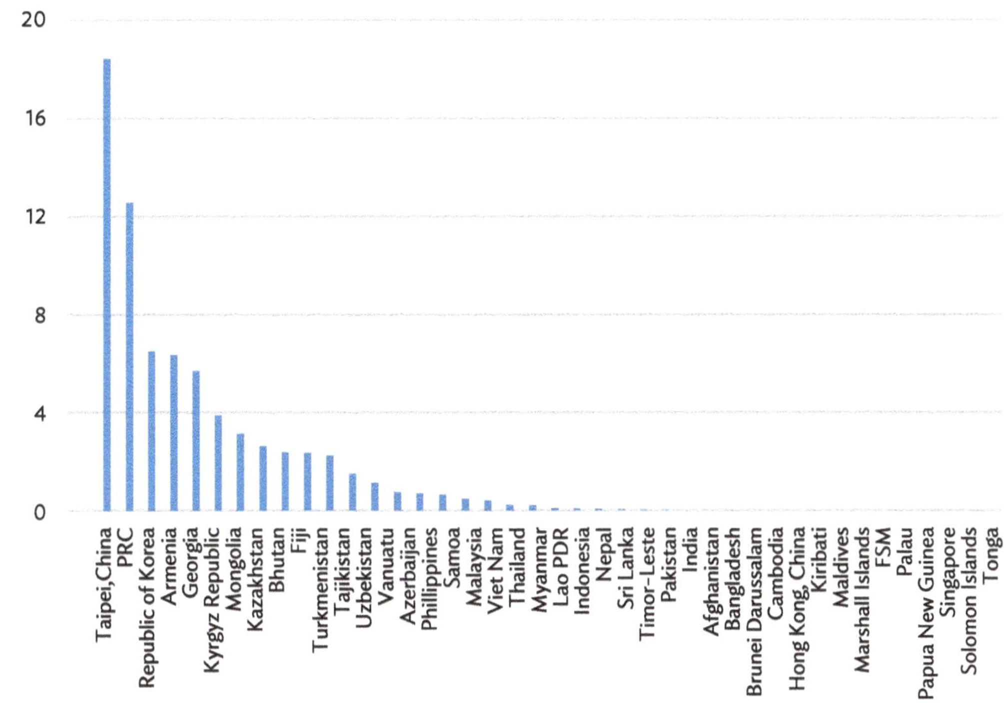

FSM = Federated States of Micronesia, Lao PDR = Lao People's Democratic Republic,
PRC = People's Republic of China.

Source: Author's calculations using 2017 wellness data at the country/territory level from the Global Wellness Institute.

Similar to the spa sector, per capita wellness tourism expenditure (Figure 12.4) is also quite high in Palau, at $5,150.85, and Maldives, at $1,890.35. Vanuatu with a value of $1,009.04, Fiji with $807.47, Samoa with $533.16, and Tonga with $504.30 follow. These values show that tourism is a very significant part of the whole economy in those countries. Countries in Central Asia are generally very low in these two sectors.

Per capita workplace wellness spending by employers (Figure 12.5) exhibits a different pattern than spa and wellness tourism. Singapore; Hong Kong, China; the ROK; Taipei,China; and Brunei Darussalam are the top five, with much higher total spending than the rest of the economies. Per capita wellness real estate construction (Figure 12.6) shows a similar pattern, with four of the top five economies overlapping the top five for workplace wellness spending. In addition, wellness real estate does not exist at all in 31 economies, showing the huge disparity in this sector. The top five in terms of per capita expenditures on recreational physical activities and enabling sectors (Figure 12.7) are exactly the same as the top five for workplace wellness spending, with a different order among them. The amount of per capita spending on recreational physical activities is quite large among the top economies. For example, the value for Hong Kong, China is $556.04; for the ROK $455.91; and for Taipei,China $327.95. Positive spending is found in all economies, even the lowest in ranking (Afghanistan, with a value of $3.45). Moreover, per capita values in this sector and the wellness tourism sector are often the highest two of the six sectors in many economies, which shows the general significance of these two sectors in developing Asia.

Figure 12.3 **Per Capita Spa Revenue**
($)

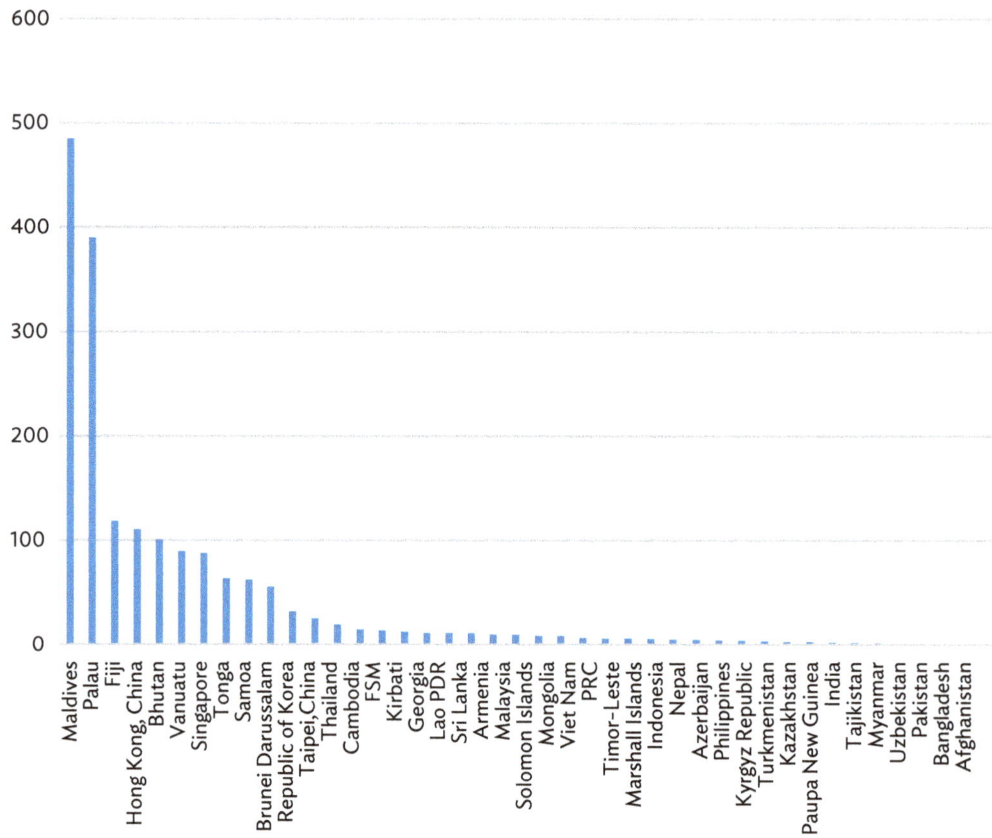

FSM = Federated States of Micronesia, Lao PDR = Lao People's Democratic Republic, PRC = People's Republic of China.

Source: Author's calculations using 2017 wellness data at the country/territory level from the Global Wellness Institute.

The pattern observed across these three sectors (workplace wellness spending, wellness real estate, and physical activities) is closely related to a higher stage of economic development. Employers in a richer economy are likely to spend more on their employees as part of employee benefits; the supply and demand of wellness real estate is likely to be higher in richer economies; and people in richer economies are more prone to spend on recreational physical activities.

In summary, the levels and distributions of the six wellness sectors in developing Asia are quite uneven, both across sectors and across economies, and are closely related to economic and geographic conditions. Specifically, there are three observations. First, the spa and wellness tourism sectors are particularly important components of island economies and are also non-negligible in many other economies. Second, the amount of spending on workplace wellness, wellness real estate, and physical activities is closely related to the level of economic development. Finally, as a fairly small sector, hot spring revenue is related to geographic and economic conditions.

Wellness for Happiness: Conceptual Framework and Literature

The development of wellness sectors is expected to play an important role in the pursuit of higher QOL, because it will likely contribute to important determinants of happiness or affect happiness directly. These important

Figure 12.4 **Per Capita Wellness Tourism Expenditures** ($)

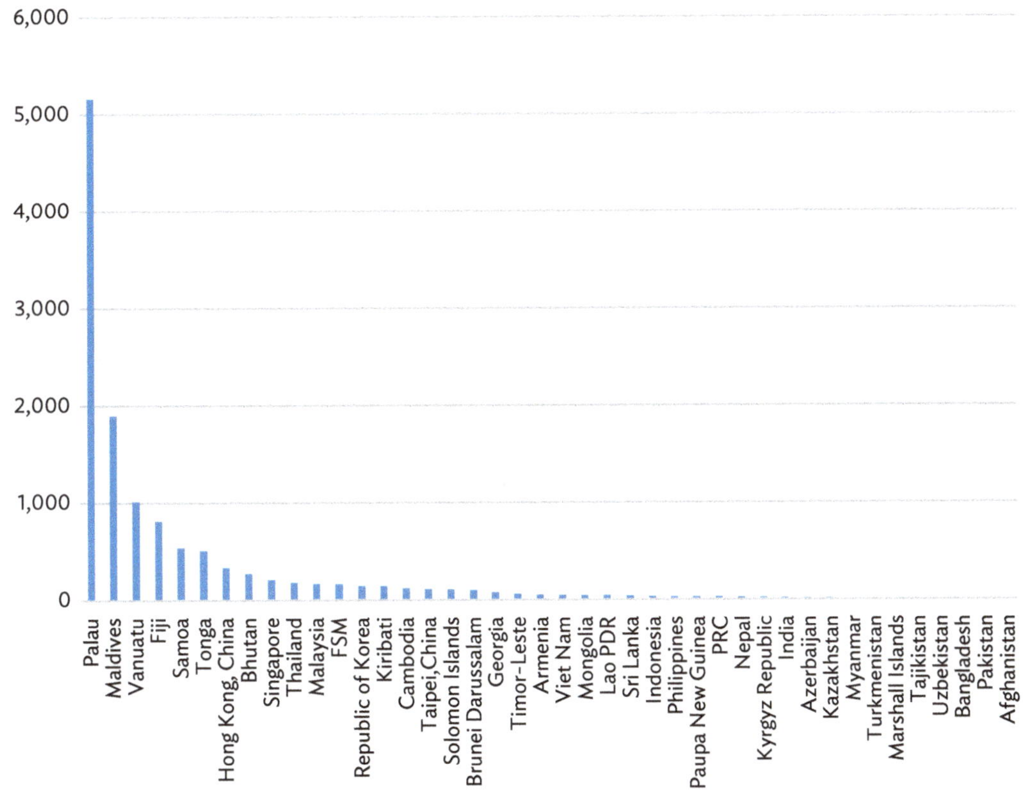

FSM = Federated States of Micronesia, Lao PDR = Lao People's Democratic Republic
PRC = People's Republic of China.

Source: Author's calculations using 2017 wellness data at the country/territory level from the Global Wellness Institute.

determinants of a population's happiness can include economic growth, employment, inflation, personal health, and leisure, among others.[11]

The development of the wellness industry may contribute to economic output, which may then further improve happiness. As shown in the previous section, wellness tourism and the spa industry are very important components of the national economy in some island countries, such as Maldives and Palau. For example, the tourism sector accounted for about 20% of Maldives' total GDP in 2016 and 2017 and was even higher in the past (as high as 27.1% back to 2006).[12] The development of these wellness sectors that mainly serve foreign tourists is highly correlated with employment and economic growth in those countries.

[11] R. Di Tella, R. MacCulloch, and A.J. Oswald. 2001. Preferences over Inflation and Unemployment: Evidence from Surveys of Happiness. *American Economic Review*. 91 (1). pp. 335–341; R. Di Tella, R. MacCulloch, and A.J. Oswald. 2003. The Macroeconomics of Happiness. *The Review of Economics and Statistics*. 85 (4). pp. 809–827; J.F. Helliwell and S. Wang. 2012. The State of Happiness. In J.F. Helliwell, R. Layard, and J. Sachs, eds. *World Happiness Report 2012*. New York: The Earth Institute of Columbia University. pp. 10–57; and J.F. Helliwell, H. Huang, and S. Wang. 2019. Changing World Happiness. In J.F. Helliwell, R. Layard, and J. Sachs, eds. *World Happiness Report 2019*. New York: United Nations Sustainable Development Solutions Network. pp. 8–49.

[12] National Bureau of Statistics, Maldives. 2018. *Statistical Pocketbook of Maldives 2018*. National Bureau of Statistics, Republic of Maldives.

Figure 12.5 **Per Capita Workplace Wellness Spending by Employers ($)**

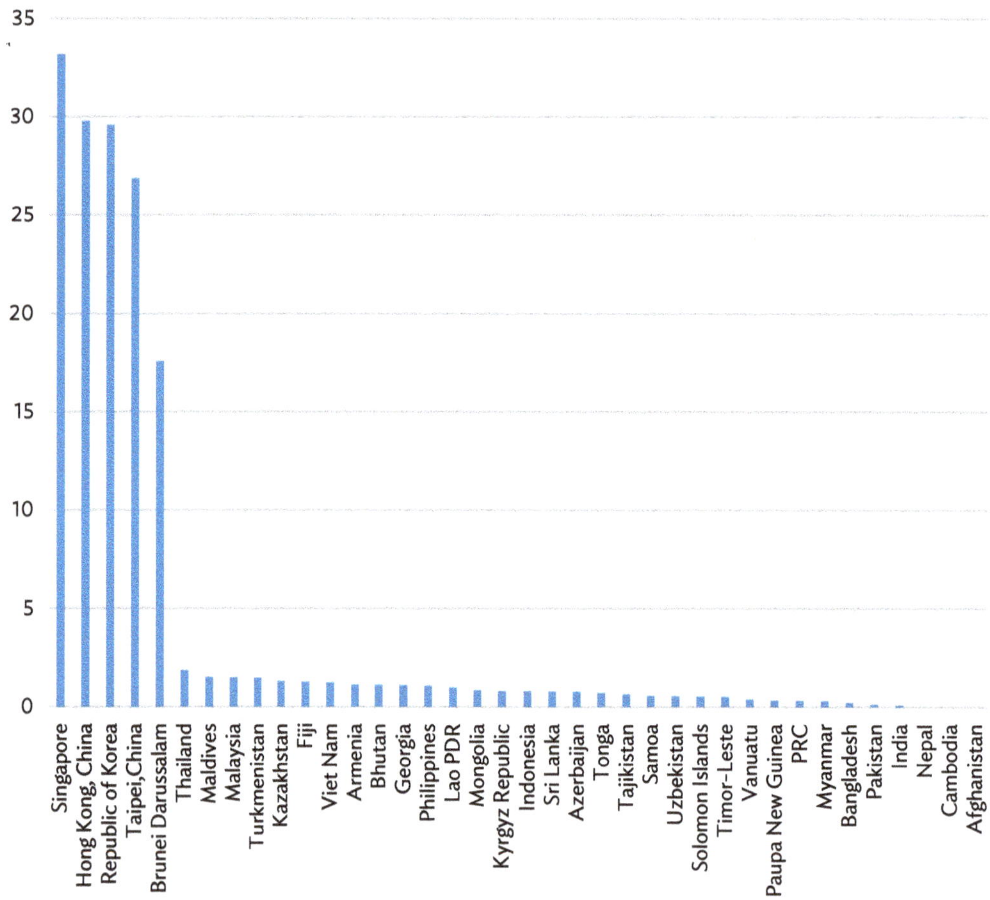

Lao PDR = Lao People's Democratic Republic, PRC = People's Republic of China.

Source: Author's calculations using 2017 wellness data at the country/territory level from the Global Wellness Institute.

Many wellness sectors, such as recreational physical activities, workplace wellness programs, and spa therapy, are linked with better health outcomes, which are an important determinant of happiness. Cohen et al.[13] show that retreat experiences lead to significant improvements in several dimensions of health and well-being that are maintained for 6 weeks. Similar results are found in Gilbert et al.[14] Klick and Stratmann[15] find that spa therapy leads to a significant reduction in both absenteeism and hospitalization, using German longitudinal data. Desveaux et al.[16] find that yoga practice can lead to significant improvements in exercise capacity and health-related QOL in a meta-analysis.

[13] M. Cohen et al. 2017. Do Wellness Tourists Get Well? An Observational Study of Multiple Dimensions of Health and Well-being after a Week-Long Retreat. *Journal of Alternative and Complementary Medicine*. 23 (2). pp. 140–148.

[14] A. Gilbert et al. 2014. A Randomized Trial Comparing a Brief Meditation Retreat to a Vacation: Effects on Daily Well-being. *Journal of Alternative and Complementary Medicine*. 20 (5): A92.

[15] J. Klick and T. Stratmann. 2008. Do Spa Visits Improve Health: Evidence from German Micro Data. *Eastern Economic Journal*. 34 (3). pp. 364–374.

[16] L. Desveaux et al. 2015. Yoga in the Management of Chronic Disease: A Systematic Review and Meta-analysis. *Medical Care*. 53 (7). pp. 653–661.

Figure 12.6 **Per Capita Wellness Real Estate Construction Value ($)**

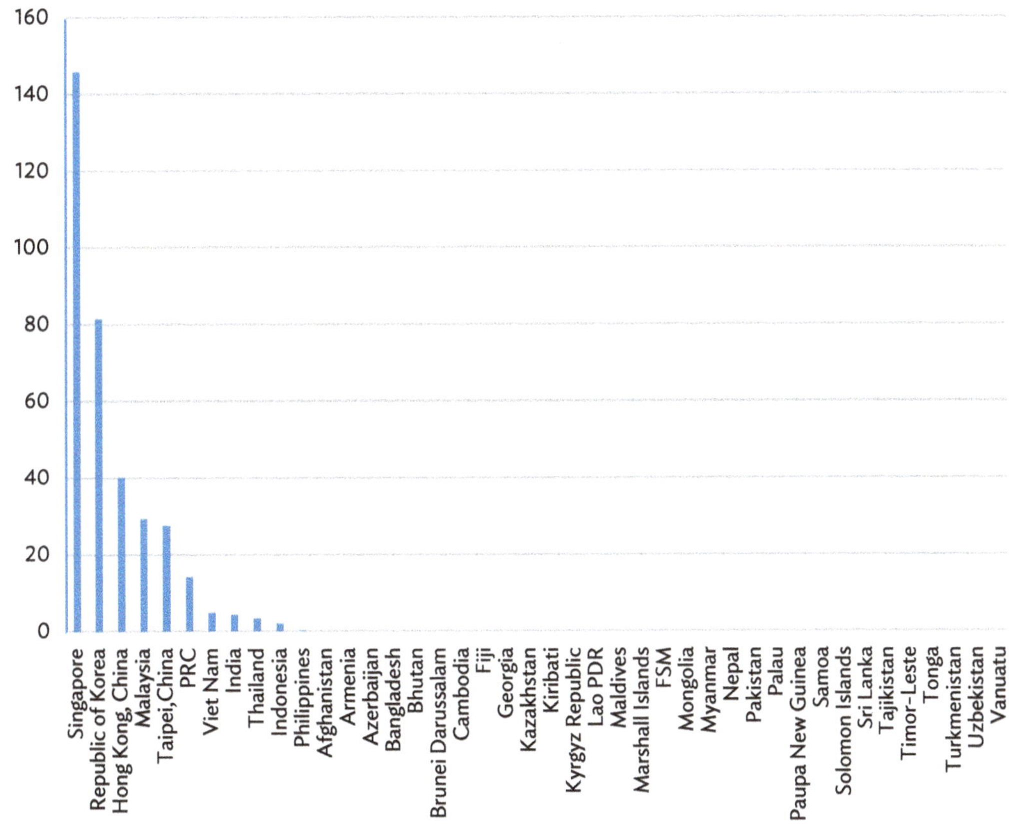

FSM = Federated States of Micronesia, Lao PDR = Lao People's Democratic Republic, PRC = People's Republic of China.

Source: Author's calculations using 2017 wellness data at the country/territory level from the Global Wellness Institute.

Workplace wellness programs are workplace-based efforts that enhance awareness, change behavior, and create environments that support "good" health practices.[17] Workplace wellness spending may affect employees' happiness though better health behaviors, improved health, or by creating a better workplace environment. Song and Baicker[18] find that a workplace wellness program led to significantly higher rates of positive health behaviors, such as engaging in regular exercise and actively managing weight, in a large United States warehouse retail company. Mills et al.[19] find that a health promotion program focused on employee health risks produced sizeable changes in health risks and productivity. Musich et al.[20] find that a well-managed comprehensive health promotion program can continue to yield significant health outcomes.

[17] S.G. Aldana. 2001. Financial Impact of Health Promotion Programs: A Comprehensive Review of the Literature. *American Journal of Health Promotion*. 15 (5). pp. 296–320.

[18] Z. Song and K. Baicker. 2019. Effect of a Workplace Wellness Program on Employee Health and Economic Outcomes: A Randomized Clinical Trial. *Journal of the American Medical Association*. 321 (15). pp. 1491–1501.

[19] P.R. Mills et al. 2007. Impact of a Health Promotion Program on Employee Health Risks and Work Productivity. *American Journal of Health Promotion*. 22 (1). pp. 45–53.

[20] S. Musich et al. 2015. An Evaluation of the Well at Dell Health Management Program: Health Risk Change and Financial Return on Investment. *American Journal of Health Promotion*. 29 (3). pp. 147–157.

Figure 12.7 **Per Capita Expenditures on Recreational Physical Activities and Enabling Sectors**
($)

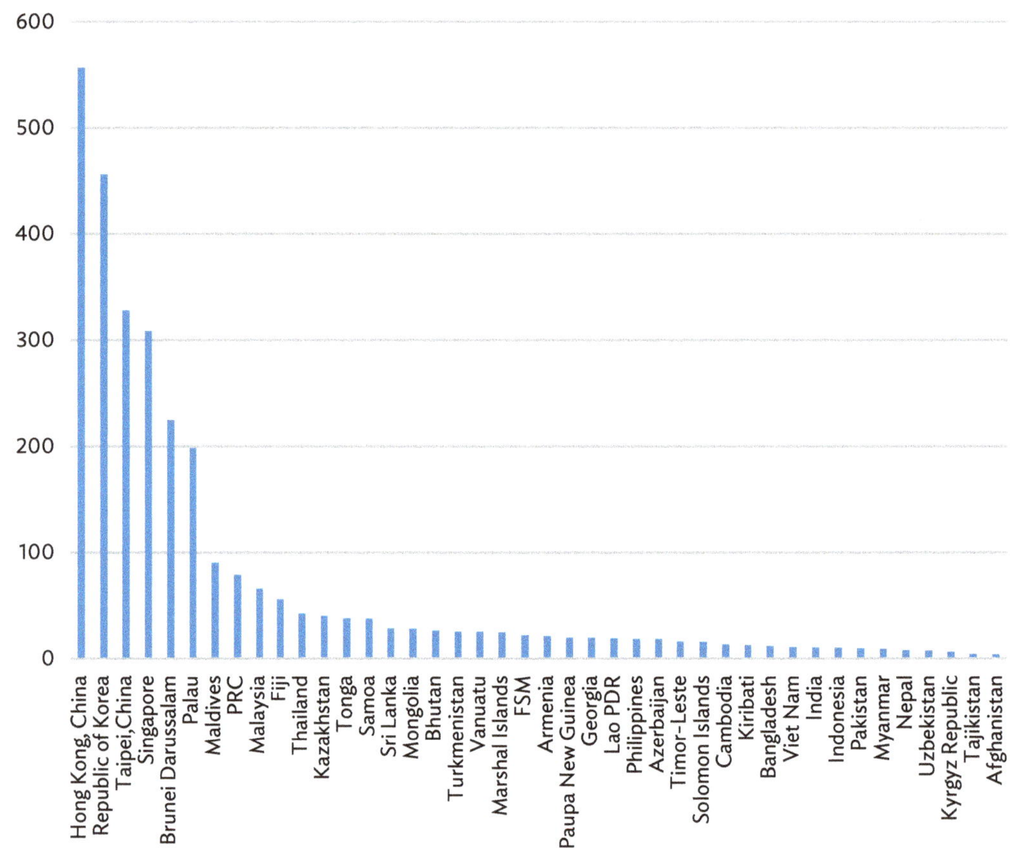

FSM = Federated States of Micronesia, Lao PDR = Lao People's Democratic Republic, PRC = People's Republic of China.

Source: Author's calculations using 2017 wellness data at the country/territory level from the Global Wellness Institute.

A recent meta-analysis shows that workplace wellness programs lead to a reduction in medical costs and absenteeism costs.[21] In addition to the majority of studies on workplace wellness that rely on observational comparisons between participants and nonparticipants,[22] there are also many randomized control trials that have focused on certain wellness activities[23] or comprehensive workplace wellness programs.[24]

[21] K. Baicker, D. Cutler, and Z. Song. 2010. Workplace Wellness Programs Can Generate Savings. *Health Affairs*. 29 (2). pp. 304–311.

[22] For reviews, see K.R. Pelletier. 2011. A Review and Analysis of the Clinical and Cost-effectiveness Studies of Comprehensive Health Promotion and Disease Management Programs at the Worksite: Update VIII 2008 to 2010. *Journal of Occupational and Environmental Medicine*. 53 (11). pp. 1310–1331; L.S. Chapman. 2005. Meta-evaluation of Worksite Health Promotion Economic Return Studies: 2005 Update. *American Journal of Health Promotion*. 19 (6). pp. 1–11; and L.S. Chapman. 2012. Meta-evaluation of Worksite Health Promotion Economic Return Studies: 2012 Update. *American Journal of Health Promotion*. 26 (4). pp. 1–12.

[23] G. Charness and U. Gneezy. 2009. Incentives to Exercise. *Econometrica*. 77 (3). pp. 909–931; H. Royer, M. Stehr, and J. Sydnor. 2015. Incentives, Commitments, and Habit Formation in Exercise: Evidence from a Field Experiment with Workers at a Fortune-500 Company. *American Economic Journal: Applied Economics*. 7 (3). pp. 51–84; and K.G. Volpp et al. 2011. Redesigning Employee Health Incentives—Lessons from Behavioral Economics. *New England Journal of Medicine*. 365 (5). pp. 388–390.

[24] D. Jones, D. Molitor, and J. Reif, 2019. What Do Workplace Wellness Programs Do? Evidence from the Illinois Workplace Wellness Study. *The Quarterly Journal of Economics*. 134 (4). pp. 1747–1791; and Z. Song and K. Baicker. 2019. Effect of a Workplace Wellness Program on Employee Health and Economic Outcomes: A Randomized Clinical Trial. *Journal of the American Medical Association*. 321 (15). pp. 1491–1501.

The studies discussed provide relative fruitful evidence that wellness is linked with the determinants of happiness, such as health; however, there are fewer studies examining the direct correlation between wellness and happiness. Health activities are one of the wellness activities that have been relatively more explored.[25] Lathia et al.[26] show that physical activity contributes to happiness for both adolescents and adults, by using a smartphone app to record information on individual physical activities and happiness. Richards et al.[27] find positive correlation between physical activity and happiness in 15 European countries, with a sample that includes both adolescents and adults. Wang et al.[28] find a similar impact in Canada. There are also some studies focusing only on adolescents that find a significant impact.[29] Physical activity also has positive effects for disabled adolescents. For example, Maher et al.[30] show that physical activity is a key predictor of QOL and happiness in children and adolescents with cerebral palsy.

There are also studies on the well-being effect of some specific physical activities. Wang et al.[31] find that tai chi, a form of mind–body exercise that originated in the PRC, has beneficial effects on psychological well-being measures. Watanabe et al.[32] show that 12 weeks of water-based aerobic exercises significantly reduces the depression of seniors.

There are a few studies showing the correlation between other wellness activities or wellness sectors and individuals' happiness. For example, Strauss-Blasche et al.[33] find that spa therapy improves emotional and health satisfaction among middle-aged adults with health impairments.

Wellness for Happiness: An Empirical Analysis

Despite the scattered evidence, which mainly consists of individual-level studies, there is no systematic evaluation of the impact of wellness activities on individuals' well-being, particularly at the macro level. Given that data is only available for six wellness sectors, it is not feasible to empirically examine the correlation between overall wellness development and national happiness. The data available for the six wellness sectors is thus used here to perform a preliminary empirical analysis on the relationship between wellness sectors and national happiness.

[25] For example, see the review in Z. Zhang and W. Chen. 2019. A Systematic Review of Measures for Psychological Well-being in Physical Activity Studies and Identification of Critical Issues. *Journal of Affective Disorders*. 256. pp. 473–485.

[26] N. Lathia et al. 2017. Happier People Live More Active Lives: Using Smartphones to Link Happiness and Physical Activity. *PLOS ONE*. 12 (1): e0160589.

[27] J. Richards et al. 2015. Don't Worry, Be Happy: Cross-sectional Associations between Physical Activity and Happiness in 15 European Countries. *BMC Public Health*. 15 (1). pp. 1–8.

[28] F. Wang et al. 2012. Long-term Association between Leisure-Time Physical Activity and Changes in Happiness: Analysis of the Prospective National Population Health Survey. *American Journal of Epidemiology*. 176 (12). pp. 1095–1100.

[29] J.H. Min et al. 2017. Physical Activity, Weight Status and Psychological Well-being among a Large National Sample of South Korean Adolescents. *Mental Health and Physical Activity*. 12. pp. 44–49; R. Norris, D. Carroll, and R. Cochrane. 1992. The Effects of Physical-Activity and Exercise Training on Psychological Stress and Well-being in an Adolescent Population. *Journal of Psychosomatic Research*. 36 (1). pp. 55–65; and V.S. Straatmann et al. 2016. Changes in Physical Activity and Screen Time Related to Psychological Well-being in Early Adolescence: Findings from Longitudinal Study ELANA. *BMC Public Health*. 16 (1). p. 977.

[30] C.A. Maher, M. Toohey, and M. Ferguson. 2016. Physical Activity Predicts Quality of Life and Happiness in Children and Adolescents with Cerebral Palsy. *Disability and Rehabilitation*. 38 (9). pp. 865–869.

[31] F. Wang et al. 2014. The Effects of Tai Chi on Depression, Anxiety, and Psychological Well-being: A Systematic Review and Meta-analysis. *International Journal of Behavioral Medicine*. 21 (4). pp. 605–617.

[32] E. Watanabe et al. 2001. Effects of Increasing Expenditure of Energy during Exercise on Psychological Well-being in Older Adults. *Perceptual and Motor Skills*. 92 (1). pp. 288–298.

[33] G. Strauss-Blasche et al. 2000. The Change of Well-being Associated with Spa Therapy. *Research in Complementary and Natural Classical Medicine*. 7 (6). pp. 269–274.

First, the simple correlation between each of the six wellness sectors and the happiness of the population in the country/territory is presented. In the sample, there are 146 economies with data on both happiness and the six wellness sectors in the global sample. However, there are only 29 with this data in developing Asia. The results of the global sample are shown in Table 12.1, and then developing Asian economies with a limited number of observations are reported in Table 12.2.

Table 12.1 shows a sizable and positive correlation in the global sample between each wellness sector and the population's level of happiness. The coefficient of correlation ranges between 0.46 for log per capita hot spring revenue and 0.81 for log per capita workplace wellness spending by employer. The correlation between log per capita expenditure on physical activities and happiness is 0.8, which is the second highest among the six wellness sectors.

Table 12.2 shows a similar pattern for each wellness sector's correlation with happiness in developing Asia. The values range between 0.3 for log per capita hot spring revenue and 0.65 for log per capita workplace wellness spending by employer. The correlation between workplace wellness and happiness is the highest for both the global and the developing Asia samples. However, the coefficients of correlation generally are smaller than the corresponding values in Table 12.1, by a magnitude of 0.16–0.39. This result may suggest that wellness sectors are even more important for a population's happiness in the rest of the world.

Next, a preliminary empirical analysis of the correlation between wellness industry and happiness is conducted, using the following ordinary least squares (OLS) model:

$$Happiness = \beta_0 + \beta_1 x + \beta_2 \, lngdp + \varepsilon,$$

where *Happiness* denotes the country/territory-level happiness score average over the period of 2016 to 2018, and x denotes the log value of each of the six wellness sectors. *lngdp* is the natural log of GDP per capita in 2017, purchasing power parity adjusted in 2011 international dollars. GDP per capita is controlled for, as it is an important determinant of happiness, and it is likely also to be highly correlated with the wellness industry. ε is the error term. β_1 denotes the coefficient of correlation between the wellness sector and happiness. The summary statistics of variables for the global sample and for developing Asia are reported in Table 12.3.

Table 12.4 shows the OLS coefficients and robust standard errors (in brackets) for the global data. There are 12 columns in total, grouped into six batches, mapping to the six wellness sectors, respectively. The odd-number columns do not control for log GDP per capita, in order to show the raw correlation between each wellness sector and happiness. Nine region dummies are controlled for in all columns, but their coefficients are not reported to save space.

Columns (1) and (2) of Table 12.4 show the coefficients of log per capita hot spring revenue, for the model without and with log GDP per capita, respectively. In both cases, the coefficients are positive, but not statistically significant at a conventional significance level. This is not surprising because, as discussed in the previous section, hot springs are quite a small sector. It would be very unlikely that this small sector would make a significant contribution to a population's happiness.

Columns (3) and (4) are for log per capita spa revenue. The coefficient is 0.19 and significant at 0.001 in the model without controlling for GDP per capita, showing that spa revenue is positively correlated with happiness. However, once we control for GDP per capita, as shown in column (4), the coefficient is reduced to 0.04 and becomes insignificant. The next two columns, for log per capita wellness tourism expenditures, show the same pattern. This may reveal that the impact of spas and wellness tourism on happiness is mainly tied to their contribution to economic growth. This is consistent with the fact that spa and wellness tourism revenue is quite high in the few island countries with tourism sectors that mainly target foreigners, while it is generally low in other countries. Foreigners may enjoy a direct happiness benefit, while local residents enjoy it through the contribution to economic performance.

Table 12.1 **Correlation Matrix in Global Sample**

	Happiness	Hot Spring Revenue	Spa Revenue	Wellness Tourism Expenditures	Workplace Wellness Spending by Employers	Wellness Real Estate Construction Value	Expenditures on Physical Activities
Happiness	1.00						
Hot spring revenue	0.46	1.00					
Spa revenue	0.71	0.59	1.00				
Wellness tourism expenditures	0.72	0.57	0.98	1.00			
Workplace wellness spending by employers	0.81	0.58	0.84	0.82	1.00		
Wellness real estate construction value	0.64	0.31	0.56	0.60	0.65	1.00	
Expenditures on physical activities	0.80	0.57	0.85	0.85	0.91	0.75	1.00

Note: The value of each wellness variable is the log per capita one.

Source: Author's calculations using data from J.F. Helliwell, H. Huang, and S. Wang. 2019. Changing World Happiness. In J.F. Helliwell, R. Layard, and J. Sachs, eds. *World Happiness Report 2019*. New York: United Nations Sustainable Development Solutions Network. pp. 8–49; and the Global Wellness Institute.

Table 12.2 **Correlation Matrix in Developing Asia**

	Happiness	Hot Spring Revenue	Spa Revenue	Wellness Tourism Expenditures	Workplace Wellness Spending by Employers	Wellness Real Estate Construction Value	Expenditures on Physical Activities
Happiness	1.00						
Hot spring revenue	0.30	1.00					
Spa revenue	0.41	0.25	1.00				
Wellness tourism expenditures	0.33	0.20	0.96	1.00			
Workplace wellness spending by employers	0.65	0.37	0.70	0.62	1.00		
Wellness real estate construction value	0.40	0.15	0.53	0.54	0.68	1.00	
Expenditures on physical activities	0.45	0.35	0.72	0.68	0.83	0.82	1.00

Note: The value of each wellness variable is the log per capita one.

Source: Author's calculations using data from J.F. Helliwell, H. Huang, and S. Wang. 2019. Changing World Happiness. In J.F. Helliwell, R. Layard, and J. Sachs, eds. *World Happiness Report 2019*. New York: United Nations Sustainable Development Solutions Network. pp. 8–49; and the Global Wellness Institute.

Table 12.3 **Summary Statistics**

Variable	Obs	Mean	Std. Dev.	Min	Max
World					
Happiness	146	5.45	1.14	2.66	7.79
Per capita hot spring revenue ($)	146	19.23	106.79	0.00	1,260.92
Per capita spa revenue ($)	146	27.55	41.70	0.01	233.52
Per capita wellness tourism expenditures ($)	146	151.99	296.50	0.03	2,030.41
Per capita workplace wellness spending by employers ($)	146	10.83	17.22	0.01	73.99
Per capita wellness real estate construction value ($)	146	19.16	52.15	0.00	384.93
Per capita expenditures on recreational physical activities and enabling sectors ($)	146	137.36	209.78	1.92	1,084.30
GDP per capita (purchasing power parity adjusted in constant 2011 international $)	146	19,382.06	18,858.64	753.82	93,101.78
Developing Asia					
Happiness	29	5.13	0.83	2.66	6.42
Per capita hot spring revenue ($)	29	2.40	4.21	0.00	18.45
Per capita spa revenue ($)	29	16.93	29.52	0.04	109.99
Per capita wellness tourism expenditures ($)	29	66.43	86.76	0.08	330.04
Per capita workplace wellness spending by employers ($)	29	4.81	10.26	0.01	33.24
Per capita wellness real estate construction value ($)	29	12.24	31.13	0.00	145.93
Per capita expenditures on recreational physical activities and enabling sectors ($)	29	74.98	143.40	3.45	556.04
GDP per capita (purchasing power parity adjusted in constant 2011 international $)	29	16,163	19,307.51	1,758.47	87,760.37

GDP = gross domestic product, Obs = observation, Std. Dev. = standard deviation.

Sources: J.F. Helliwell, H. Huang, and S. Wang. 2019. Changing World Happiness. In J.F. Helliwell, R. Layard, and J. Sachs, eds. *World Happiness Report 2019*. New York: United Nations Sustainable Development Solutions Network. pp. 8–49; World Bank. World Development Indicators online database. https://databank.worldbank.org/source/world-development-indicators (accessed 1 October 2019); and author's calculations using data from the Global Wellness Institute.

Columns (7) and (8) present the coefficients for log per capita workplace wellness spending by employers. Consistent with existing micro evidence that workplace wellness programs promote health behaviors and health,[34] there is a significant impact of workplace wellness spending on a population's happiness. The coefficient is 0.27 and significant at the 0.001 significance level in the simple model. The coefficient reduces by about half to 0.15 after controlling for GDP per capita, but remains significant at the 0.05 significance level. This implies that,

[34] For example, P.R. Mills et al. 2007. Impact of a Health Promotion Program on Employee Health Risks and Work Productivity. *American Journal of Health Promotion*. 22 (1). pp. 45–53; S. Musich et al. 2015. An Evaluation of the Well at Dell Health Management Program: Health Risk Change and Financial Return on Investment. *American Journal of Health Promotion*. 29 (3). pp. 147–157; and Z. Song and K. Baicker. 2019. Effect of a Workplace Wellness Program on Employee Health and Economic Outcomes: A Randomized Clinical Trial. *Journal of the American Medical Association*. 321 (15). pp. 1491–1501.

Table 12.4 **Wellness and Happiness in the World**

	(1)	(2)	(3)	(4)	(5)	(6)	(7)	(8)	(9)	(10)	(11)	(12)	(13)
Log per capita hot spring revenue	0.07	0.01											
	(0.06)	(0.05)											
Log per capita spa revenue			0.19***	0.04									
			(0.05)	(0.05)									
Log per capita wellness tourism expenditures					0.16***	0.03							
					(0.05)	(0.05)							
Log per capita workplace wellness spending by employers							0.27***	0.15*					
							(0.04)	(0.06)					
Log per capita wellness real estate construction value									0.40***	0.22**			
									(0.06)	(0.07)			
Log per capita expenditures on recreational physical activities											0.43***	0.30+	
											(0.08)	(0.15)	
Log GDP per capita		0.56***		0.52***		0.51***		0.31*		0.44***		0.20	0.56***
		(0.10)		(0.10)		(0.11)		(0.14)		(0.11)		(0.19)	(0.10)
Region dummies	Yes	Yes	Yes	Yes	Yes	Yes	Yes	Yes	Yes	Yes	Yes	Yes	Yes
N	146	146	146	146	146	146	146	146	146	146	146	146	146
Adjusted R-squared	0.579	0.695	0.627	0.696	0.637	0.697	0.697	0.710	0.658	0.715	0.706	0.707	0.697

+ p<0.10, * p<0.05, ** p<0.01, *** p<0.001.

GDP = gross domestic product.

Note: Robust standard errors are in parentheses.

Source: Author's estimates.

even if we control for the impact due to its contribution to GDP per capita, workplace wellness spending still has an impact on happiness. The coefficient means that, for a 1% increase in per capita workplace wellness spending, a population's happiness will increase by 0.0015 units. In other words, if per capita workplace wellness spending doubles (e.g., from the world average of $10.83 to $21.66), happiness will increase by 0.15 units, which is about 0.13 standard deviation.

A similar pattern is observed for the wellness real estate construction in columns (9) and (10): the significant coefficient of log per capita wellness real estate construction value reduces from 0.40 to 0.22 after controlling for GDP per capita, which may imply that the wellness real estate sector affects happiness beyond its contribution to GDP per capita.

Column (11) shows that expenditures on recreational physical activities are significantly correlated with happiness, with the coefficient 0.43. However, after controlling for GDP per capita in column (12), the coefficient is reduced to 0.30, but is still significant at 0.1 significance level (p=0.054). Note that there is a very high correlation between per capita expenditures on recreational physical activities and GDP per capita (r=0.94); the standard errors in this model could be potentially inflated. The coefficient 0.30 implies that a 1% increase in expenditures on recreational physical activities would be associated with a 0.003 unit increase in the happiness level, which is bigger than the impact of wellness real estate and workplace wellness spending. It also means that, if the per capita expenditures on recreational physical activities double (e.g., from the world average of $137.36 to $274.72), happiness would increase by 0.30 units, which is about 0.26 standard deviation. This finding is in line with Lathia et al. and Richards et al.,[35] who show in micro-data analysis that physical activities contribute to happiness.

Table 12.5 shows the results of the same analysis as in Table 12.4, but with the sample restricted to developing Asian economies. The sample size is reduced to 29. This small sample size means that we should interpret the results with caution. Columns (1)–(6) show that hot spring revenue, spa revenue, and wellness tourism are not correlated with happiness, no matter whether or not GDP per capita is controlled for. The results for hot springs are the same as for the global sample, confirming the marginal influence of this sector. The raw impact of spas and wellness tourism disappears, which may imply their limited contribution to the economy in developing Asia, as very few island economies record high values for these sectors. In contrast, workplace wellness spending, wellness real estate construction, and expenditures on recreational physical activities remain significant in the model without controlling for GDP per capita, as reported in columns (7), (9), and (11). However, after controlling for GDP per capita, only workplace wellness spending remains significant, as shown in column (8). Even with such a small sample size, we still observe a strong correlation between workplace wellness spending and happiness.

Conclusions

The wellness economy has become an important component of the overall economy in many developing Asian economies. However, the lack of detailed information on the size and distribution of wellness sectors constrains our understanding of its contribution to people's well-being.

This chapter uses recent data on six key sectors of the wellness economy (specifically, hot springs, spas, wellness tourism, workplace wellness, wellness real estate, and recreational physical activities and enabling sectors) to explore the distribution of wellness economy within developing Asian economies. Data from the Global Wellness

[35] N. Lathia et al. 2017. Happier People Live More Active Lives: Using Smartphones to Link Happiness and Physical Activity. *PLOS ONE*. 12 (1): e0160589; and J. Richards et al. 2015. Don't Worry, Be Happy: Cross-sectional Associations between Physical Activity and Happiness in 15 European Countries. *BMC Public Health*. 15 (1). pp. 1–8.

Table 12.5 **Wellness and Happiness in Developing Asia**

	(1)	(2)	(3)	(4)	(5)	(6)	(7)	(8)	(9)	(10)	(11)	(12)
Log per capita hot spring revenue	0.28	0.14										
	(0.17)	(0.14)										
Log per capita spa revenue			0.19	0.04								
			(0.11)	(0.12)								
Log per capita wellness tourism expenditures					0.14	-0.01						
					(0.12)	(0.12)						
Log per capita workplace wellness spending by employers							0.29***	0.33*				
							(0.07)	(0.12)				
Log per capita wellness real estate construction value									0.21**	-0.01		
									(0.07)	(0.11)		
Log per capita expenditures on recreational physical activities											0.28*	-0.18
											(0.12)	(0.18)
Log GDP per capita		0.43*		0.47***		0.42**		-0.08		0.48		0.70*
		(0.16)		(0.11)		(0.13)		(0.21)		(0.26)		(0.28)
N	29	29	29	29	29	29	29	29	29	29	29	29
Adjusted R-squared	0.055	0.257	0.078	0.235	0.139	0.239	0.402	0.382	0.128	0.235	0.174	0.249

+ p<0.10, * p<0.05, ** p<0.01, *** p<0.001.

GDP = gross domestic product.

Note: Robust standard errors are in parentheses.

Source: Author's estimates.

Institute (GWI) on the six wellness sectors show that the distribution across sectors and economies is quite uneven in Asia. Specifically, the spa and wellness tourism sectors particularly are important components of a few island economies, and are also non-negligible in many other economies. The size of workplace wellness, wellness real estate, and physical activities are closely correlated with levels of economic development. Hot springs are a fairly small sector in most Asian economies.

The use of happiness as an indicator of well-being is then examined in happiness literature, in order to explore the well-being impact of the wellness economy. Gallup World Poll's survey on the Cantril ladder (on a scale of 0–10) is used to measure happiness, as in the World Happiness Report series. The happiness scores for most Asian economies are relatively low, compared with Scandinavian countries. The variations of happiness among Asian economies are also large. The happiness score of the top performer, Taipei,China, is about double that of the lowest one, Afghanistan.

A simple OLS analysis, based on cross-section data at the country level, shows that five of the six sectors (excluding hot springs) are significantly correlated with a population's happiness in the global sample, when not considering GDP per capita. After controlling for GDP per capita, three sectors (workplace wellness, wellness real estate, and recreational physical activities and enabling sectors) are still significantly correlated with a population's happiness, statistically and economically. When the analysis is restricted to the 29 observations in developing Asia, workplace wellness spending by employers is still very significant. Based on data at the country/territory level, the preliminary analysis in this chapter shows that at least some sectors of the wellness economy are closely related to a population's happiness. However, more rigorous analysis is needed in the future when more detailed wellness data are available.

CHAPTER 13

Policy Options to Promote Wellness in Asia

Katherine Johnston, Ophelia Yeung, and Gerard Bodeker

This chapter discusses the wellness policies that governments can undertake to encourage people to make healthy choices proactively, live healthy lifestyles, and create living environments that support and encourage healthy behaviors and lifestyles. The chapter presents policy approaches in two separate sections. The first section focuses on the role of government and public policy in four wellness domains that are most critical and central to encouraging healthy behaviors and lifestyles: healthy built environments, physical activity, healthy eating, and workplace wellness. For each of these domains, the chapter discusses the ways and areas in which government and policies can have the greatest impacts. The second section presents a life span approach to wellness, highlighting the areas where governments and policy interventions can create a health-enhancing environment from the first 1,000 days of life (prenatal to early years) and school years to healthy aging.

Introduction

There has been little research on "wellness policy" or evidence that governments have adopted wellness as an overall policy goal, strategy, or priority at the national, regional, and local levels. This could be because wellness is not well understood by governments and has emerged as a primarily consumer-driven, private sector-oriented phenomenon over the last several decades. Wellness, as defined by the Global Wellness Institute (GWI), is the "active pursuit of activities, choices and lifestyles that lead to a state of holistic health." Wellness is tied to individuals' behaviors, lifestyles, choices, and agency. While wellness is holistic and has many dimensions (e.g., mental, emotional, spiritual, and physical), physical health is paramount to the concept of wellness.

"Wellness policy" is distinct from what is currently within the realms of public health and health policy. Both public health and health policy emerged from the scientific and medical advances of the 19th and 20th centuries, which enabled societies to treat and control diseases and injuries. Across the world, public health policy has accomplished a lot in the prevention and control of infectious disease (e.g., via immunization and sanitation), and in addressing other major health threats, such as workplace safety, food safety, sanitation and water safety, and motor vehicle safety.[1]

[1] Centers for Disease Control and Prevention. 2011. Ten Great Public Health Achievements—United States, 2001–2010. *Morbidity and Mortality Weekly Report*. 60 (19). pp. 619–623. https://www.cdc.gov/mmwr/preview/mmwrhtml/mm6019a5.htm; and Public Health Association Australia. 2018. *Top 10 Public Health Successes over the Last 20 Years*. PHAA Monograph Series No. 2. Canberra: Public Health Association of Australia. https://www.phaa.net.au/documents/item/3241.

In recent decades, noncommunicable diseases (NCDs) have replaced communicable and infectious diseases as the leading causes of death globally. NCDs (including heart disease, stroke, cancer, diabetes, and chronic lung disease) are collectively responsible for 71% of deaths worldwide,[2] and they account for more than one-half of the global burden of disease.[3] NCDs are sometimes labeled "lifestyle diseases" because they are largely preventable: at least 80% of heart disease, stroke, and type 2 diabetes, as well as 40% of cancers, could be prevented by addressing key risk factors related to our modern, unhealthy lifestyles (e.g., sedentary behavior, poor eating habits, stress, lack of sleep, loneliness, addiction, and environmental toxins).[4] The last 5–10 years have also brought growing awareness of a mounting global mental health crisis, including stress, anxiety, loneliness, depression, and suicide. While public health efforts have made great strides in addressing certain types of lifestyle risks and environmental diseases—such as smoking cessation and reducing childhood lead poisoning—the public health community is no match for the big business interests that promote and sell tobacco, alcohol, and unhealthy or processed foods, especially in developing countries (including in Asia).[5] Lifestyle disease and mental health issues stem from a confluence of factors, and they are closely linked with the socioeconomic and physical environments in which people live. These factors do not fit neatly within government policy "siloes," and they are typically outside the control and purview of both public health and health policy.

Although lifestyle-related disease and mental illness represent some of the greatest future challenges to global health,[6] the public health system and the medical care system are not designed or equipped to address the underlying issues that lead to these challenges, or to change the environments that shape people's health-related behaviors. For example, our ability to engage in physical activity depends on urban planning, infrastructure, transportation, parks and recreation, and youth and education policies and programs, while our eating habits are heavily shaped by agriculture, economic, trade, and food-related government agencies and policies. All of these are far outside the realm of the public health and health-care systems, and they also span multiple levels of government (from the local to the national). Simply put, the policies that shape our wellness cut across numerous government domains, and they have not been effectively put under a unifying framework for policy making or prioritization.

Wellness policy is distinct from the emerging field of well-being and happiness policy. Wellness is often conflated with well-being and happiness because all three concepts reflect human experience in a complex, subjective, and multidimensional way, including physical, mental, emotional, social, financial, environmental, spiritual, and other aspects. In recent years, subjective well-being and happiness have become growing fields of economic and academic study that have garnered interest from governments and policy communities. The measurement of happiness at the country level was initiated in Bhutan, which introduced its Gross National Happiness Index as an alternative to gross national product for assessing the country's level of progress. Country-level happiness is now measured in a global index sponsored by the United Nations (published annually in the *World Happiness and Wellbeing Policy Report*). This index has spurred interest in the role of government and policy in increasing people's happiness. In 2017, the Global Happiness Council (later renamed Global Council for Happiness and Wellbeing)

[2] World Health Organization (WHO). 2018. *Fact Sheet: Noncommunicable Diseases.* http://www.who.int/en/news-room/fact-sheets/detail/noncommunicable-diseases.

[3] C.P. Benziger, G.A. Roth, and A.E. Moran. 2016. The Global Burden of Disease Study and the Preventable Burden of NCD. *Global Heart.* 11 (4). pp. 393–397. https://doi.org/10.1016/j.gheart.2016.10.024.

[4] WHO. 2005. *Preventing Chronic Diseases: A Vital Investment—Misunderstanding #4.* https://www.who.int/chp/chronic_disease_report/part1/en/index11.html.

[5] V. Tangcharoensathien et al. 2019. Addressing NCDs: Challenges from Industry Market Promotion and Interferences. *International Journal of Health Policy and Management.* 8 (5). pp. 256–260. http://www.ijhpm.com/article_3589.html; and P. Delobelle. 2019. Big Tobacco, Alcohol, and Food and NCDs in LMICs: An Inconvenient Truth and Call to Action. *International Journal of Health Policy and Management.* 8 (12). pp. 727–731. http://www.ijhpm.com/article_3663.html.

[6] WHO. 2005. *Preventing Chronic Diseases: A Vital Investment.* http://www.who.int/chp/chronic_disease_report/contents/en; A. Adler-Waxman. 2017. This Is the Biggest Challenge to Our Health. *World Economic Forum: Shaping the Future of Health and Healthcare Initiative.* https://www.weforum.org/agenda/2017/12/healthcare-future-multiple-chronic-disease-ncd; United Nations. 2018. *New UN High-Profile Panel Set to Take on Noncommunicable Diseases, Cause of Seven in 10 Deaths Globally.* https://news.un.org/en/story/2018/02/1002921; and Council on Foreign Relations. 2014. *The Emerging Crisis: Noncommunicable Diseases in Low- and Middle-Income Countries.* https://www.cfr.org/report/emerging-global-health-crisis.

was founded by the ruler of the Emirate of Dubai. The council sponsors research on the policy approaches and best practices that could enhance happiness and individual well-being, grouping its efforts under six themes: education, workplace, personal happiness, public health, city design, and metrics.[7]

As far as we know, the only global metrics on wellness that currently exist are for the wellness economy, produced and published by the authors under the auspices of GWI. Therefore, insofar as governments are paying attention to wellness at all, they tend to view it through the lens of industry clusters that can bring economic development impacts (e.g., foreign investments, tourism receipts, employment, and tax revenues). For this reason, the wellness sector that seems to have garnered the most government attention is wellness tourism. This is an unfortunate and extremely narrow view of the potential impact of wellness on society and the economy, or the potential space for policy interventions.

Wellness brings an important perspective to policy making that is complementary to public health and health policy, and to the emerging field of happiness. The wellness paradigm and the ever-increasing consumer engagement with wellness activities suggest its strong appeal, as well as the potential for behavioral changes that can lead to healthier lifestyles and better health outcomes. The rapidly growing wellness economy, both globally and in Asia, represents a consumer response to the inadequacy and failure of many interrelated factors and systems (e.g., capitalism, economic development policies, health systems, urban planning, environmental regulations, food policies, and social protection) in enabling and supporting good health and holistic health. In turn, the consumer-centric and business-led wellness movement has spurred new interest in healthy lifestyles and wellness modalities across the world and in Asia, as well as increased public awareness that many aspects of our lives and our environments are detrimental to our health.

Compared with the happiness and well-being movement, the wellness movement places more emphasis on the physical aspects of health (such as physical movement and healthy eating). Therefore, it can draw attention to key areas that have received scant attention from the happiness movement or happiness-driven policy making. Complementary to public health, the vibrant private sector in the growing wellness economy has developed new thinking, frameworks, innovations, systems, technologies, services, and products that enable consumers to adopt healthier lifestyles, while also spurring interest in wellness traditions, particularly those that have Asian roots (e.g., traditional Chinese medicine, Ayurveda, yoga, tai chi, meditation, plant-based diets, and indigenous herbs). And yet, as with any new industry or service, the early adopters are usually the privileged class, i.e., higher-income, more educated, and urban consumers. Governments and policies have many important roles to play in wellness, such as encouraging new innovations; enabling the adoption of healthy lifestyles; scaling effective services and activities; increasing access through public investments; funding new research; collaborating with the private and nonprofit sectors; and using tax and regulatory tools, where appropriate.

Crosscutting Wellness Policy Domains

Our health outcomes are not predetermined. While we may carry genetic tendencies for many types of disease, external factors (including physical environment, socioeconomic environment, health-care environment, and our lifestyles) can account for 70%–90% of our disease risks and health outcomes. Governments exert enormous influence on all of these environmental factors. The authors define wellness policies as those that: i) nudge people toward healthier choices and habits; and ii) create living environments that encourage and enable healthy behavior and lifestyles. We segment these policies into four domains: built environment, physical activity, healthy eating, and workplaces.

[7] Global Council for Happiness and Wellbeing. 2019. *Global Happiness and Wellbeing Policy Report 2019*. New York: Sustainable Development Solutions Network. http://www.happinesscouncil.org; and Global Happiness Council. 2018. *Global Happiness Policy Report 2018*. New York: Sustainable Development Solutions Network. http://www.happinesscouncil.org/report/2018.

Create a Healthy Built Environment

Our modern built environment—both urban and suburban—is often described as obesogenic, with many factors interacting and conspiring against a physically active lifestyle and encouraging sedentary behavior. The built environment also influences our social interactions, mental wellness, and even levels of civic engagement. Several policy areas offer opportunities to counter and reverse the unwellness trends.

Prioritize Walkability and Physical Movement in Urban and Regional Planning

Across Asia, urban planning that prioritized vehicular traffic flow has led to widening of roads, stripping of sidewalks, increases in speed, and other auto-centric features that make it more difficult and less attractive for people to walk or ride bicycles, thus depriving people of the physical activity that comes with such active transportation. The People's Republic of China (PRC) offers the most extreme example of replacing millions of bicycles with cars over the span of just 1.5 generations. Better urban and regional planning by governments can help reverse this trend, and encourage and enable people to choose walking and biking instead, while reducing the environmental pollution associated with motor vehicle use. For example, in Shanghai, the PRC, the old Bund used to be the site of an 11-lane elevated highway cutting through the city center. Between 2008 and 2010, the Bund was redeveloped into a pedestrian-friendly signature waterfront area, by eliminating seven lanes and 70% of vehicular traffic, replacing elevated sections with pedestrian crosswalks, and creating a 7-kilometer nonmotorized transport zone along the river.[8] In Seoul, the Republic of Korea (ROK), the Skygarden project has redeveloped a 1970s elevated motorway into a walkway and garden, with bridges that connect to adjoining buildings and structures, creating new cafes, performance spaces, and markets for pedestrians.[9]

Create Green Spaces and Natural Sanctuaries for Urban Residents

Overcrowding, traffic, polluted air, noise, stress, and lack of green space are becoming the way of life for people who live in the largest and expanding metropolises across Asia. Yet a growing body of research shows that nature and urban green space can enhance our well-being. Positive impacts include buffering of noise and air pollution, increased physical activity, reduction of childhood obesity, and even reduced mortality, as well as improvements in cognitive abilities and moods, promotion of healing, and reduction of aggression and negative feelings.[10] Policy measures to expand green space can include planting street trees, rehabilitating vacant lots into pocket parks or community gardens, and rails-to-trails projects, as well as larger-scale initiatives to expand urban park systems, greenways, and multiuse trails.[11] Also, the building of greenways and multiuse trails helps encourage active transport and support sustainable infrastructure in urban settings. The redevelopment of the Pearl River banks in the PRC has created an ecological corridor that connects multiple biking and walking paths, resulting in 3,500 kilometers of greenway that provides a natural respite and active recreational spaces for residents.

Protect People from Harmful Indoor Built Environments and Materials

Modern construction techniques, materials, and products often expose inhabitants to numerous potentially harmful substances inside buildings, such as polyvinyl chloride and phthalates, flame retardants, volatile organic compounds, antimicrobials, bisphenol A, nanomaterials, mold, and fungus, among many others. Indoor air quality and "sick building syndrome" were identified as major concerns by the World Health Organization (WHO) more than

[8] EMBARQ Network. 2015. China's Pedestrianization: Reviving a Tradition of Walking for Healthier Cities. *Smart Cities Dive.* https://www.smartcitiesdive.com/ex/sustainablecitiescollective/china-s-pedestrianization-reviving-tradition-walking-healthier-cities/1089003.

[9] R. Moore. 2017. A Garden Bridge That Works: How Seoul Succeeded Where London Failed. *The Guardian.* https://www.theguardian.com/cities/2017/may/19/seoul-skygarden-south-korea-london-garden-bridge.

[10] For a recent review of scientific evidence, see M.C. Kondo et al. 2018. Urban Green Space and Its Impact on Human Health. *International Journal of Environmental Research and Public Health.* 13 (3). 445. https://doi.org/10.3390/ijerph15030445.

[11] For an in-depth review of urban greening policies, approaches, and case studies in Europe and North America, see I. Anguelovski et al. 2018. *Green Trajectories: Municipal Policy Trends and Strategies for Greening in Europe, Canada and United States (1990–2016).* Barcelona: Barcelona Lab for Urban and Environmental Justice and Sustainability. http://www.bcnuej.org/wp-content/uploads/2018/06/Green-Trajectories.pdf.

30 years ago, and studies have shown that indoor air pollution can be 2–5 times worse than outdoors.[12] In lower-income regions, the greatest source of indoor air pollution is the reliance on coal, kerosene, or biomass fuels for cooking and heating, causing nearly 4 million premature deaths every year.[13] The scope of things in the built environment that can impact health is vast, including construction materials and finishes; design, operation, and maintenance of ventilation and temperature control systems; cleaning products and practices; furnishings and appliances; and lighting. The environmental and sustainability movements have advanced some design and construction techniques that can enhance the wellness of both the planet and individuals, such as access to fresh air (windows that open or access to outdoor spaces); access to daylight and other natural elements indoors (windows with views or greenery and plants inside); thermal control and good air quality; and the use of environment-friendly, natural, healthy, and "toxin-free" materials. At a minimum, buildings and built environments should not make their inhabitants unhealthy or sick. Governments need to expand research to understand these impacts, as well as keep up with the latest research and clinical studies in order to update building standards and regulations.

Support Wellness Real Estate and Make Healthy Homes Affordable and Accessible

Over the past decade, a burgeoning global wellness real estate movement has drawn attention to the importance of prioritizing human health in the design and construction of homes, offices, and other buildings. The wellness real estate sector is substantial, valued by GWI in 2017 at $46.8 billion in Asia.[14] Most wellness-focused real estate projects prioritize walkability and physical activity, in addition to providing amenities such as fitness clubs, swimming pools, meditation or yoga spaces, exercise classes, social events, and green space. With poor and vulnerable populations typically at higher risk for disease, governments should find it in their interest to make healthy homes and wellness real estate accessible across the income spectrum, including in the public and subsidized housing categories. Importantly, many wellness real estate features are affordable and cost-effective with good planning and design, especially those that encourage healthy behaviors and active lifestyles, such as attractive sidewalks, walking and jogging paths, pocket parks, playgrounds, outdoor gyms, community gardens, recreational centers, and well-designed spaces that make residents feel motivated and safe to be physically active on a daily basis.

Enable and Support Physical Activity

Physical activity is essential to good health. When Asians are asked why they do not participate in recreational physical activity, the most often-cited reasons are lack of time, lack of energy, their physical and health conditions, lack of interest, and lack of access to facilities.[15] Governments can enable, encourage, and widen participation in recreational physical activity through multiple avenues.

Publicly Funded Infrastructure, Facilities, and Programs for Recreational Physical Activities

Widespread participation in recreational physical activity relies on publicly funded infrastructure, such as parks; athletic fields; running and biking paths; outdoor gyms; and community sports, recreation, and exercise facilities and programs. In Asia, recreational physical activity participation rates tend to be highest in places where governments have adopted "sports for all" approaches and aggressively invest in such public infrastructure (e.g., the ROK, Singapore, Japan). According to the authors' research, 6.5 million people in Asia utilize public, nonprofit, and public–private gyms and fitness facilities, across 7,600 locations, typically with low or subsidized membership fees. These include government-subsidized (but often privately run) gyms and leisure centers in Australia and New Zealand;

[12] US Environmental Protection Agency. n.d. *Volatile Organic Compounds' Impact on Indoor Air Quality*. https://www.epa.gov/indoor-air-quality-iaq/volatile-organic-compounds-impact-indoor-air-quality (accessed 5 February 2020).

[13] WHO. 2018. *Household Air Pollution and Health Fact Sheet*. http://www.who.int/mediacentre/factsheets/fs292/en.

[14] GWI. 2018. *Build Well to Live Well: Wellness Lifestyle Real Estate and Communities*. https://globalwellnessinstitute.org/industry-research/wellness-real-estate-communities-research.

[15] GWI. 2019. *Move to Be Well: The Global Economy of Physical Activity*. https://globalwellnessinstitute.org/industry-research/global-economy-physical-activity.

public and city-operated gyms and community centers in Japan, Singapore, the ROK, and Hong Kong, China; and nonprofit facilities such as YMCAs (Australia, New Zealand, and Japan). In addition, about 3.7 million people in Asia (mostly students and young adults) use gyms and fitness facilities on nearly 4,500 (mostly public) university campuses. In addition to dedicated fitness and recreational facilities, safe open spaces are also important. For example, in the PRC, older men and women gather daily in public parks to do tai chi, while millions of people, mostly women, engage in "plaza dancing," often spontaneously and without formal organization.

Prioritize Government Investments in Communities That Are at Higher Risk for Physical Inactivity

Physical activity participation is not evenly distributed across all groups. For example, physical activity tends to drop from youth to adulthood, and often falls further among senior populations. In some regions, there is a huge disparity in the rates of physical activity between male and female populations (e.g., in South Asia). Overall, the availability of recreational physical activity infrastructure and facilities, both private and public, tends to be concentrated in urban areas and first-tier cities in Asia, leaving other less-developed regions with limited options and fewer opportunities to exercise. Governments should target these populations in infrastructure investments and programming. For example, about 7,500 free outdoor gyms have been installed across Asia, and many of these are designed as "senior playgrounds." Facilitating group exercise among seniors in public places also helps to mitigate loneliness and social isolation. In some countries, women and girls have been discouraged from exercising outdoors for fear of harassment and even violence. In these cases, governments can create dedicated, safe places for women to exercise outdoors, or simply to get some fresh air. For example, in 2012, the city of Lahore, Pakistan, opened its first "women only" park in a 4-acre space secured behind 7-foot-high walls, with its own jogging track, gymnasium, and badminton court.[16] Other strategies may include setting aside certain hours in parks and gyms for use exclusively by women.

Prescribe Exercise as Part of Patient Care

The majority of people who exercise are fit and capable of physical activities, while those with medical or physical conditions are often marginalized by the mainstream fitness industry. Public health authorities and publicly funded health care systems can be leaders in prescribing exercise for those whose health conditions are partly caused or exacerbated by a lack of physical activity. Exercise Is Medicine (EIM) is a global initiative that advocates for physical activity to be included as a standard part of medical treatment and the patient care process.
A number of Asian economies have joined the EIM global network, including the PRC; Hong Kong, China; Taipei,China; the ROK; Japan; Indonesia; Malaysia; the Philippines; Thailand; Singapore; and Sri Lanka.[17] As part of the EIM initiative, Singapore has launched Active Health Labs, which conduct free assessments and provide personalized exercise advice, as well as take referrals from physicians to prescribe and implement appropriate physical activity for patients in order to treat, manage, and prevent common chronic health conditions.

Support Youth to Build Healthy Habits and Interest in Physical Activity

Physical education classes in schools can help children build awareness, skills, and lifelong habits of physical activity. While 90% of Asian economies have legal or de facto requirements for physical education in schools, these requirements vary greatly, and on average fall short of the 1 hour of activity per day recommended for children by WHO.[18] In some countries, the physical education requirement may drop sharply from primary to secondary school. In Asia, the culture of academic achievement and testing often relegates physical education to a lower status than

[16] S. Ali. 2012. Are Women-Only Parks the Answer to Street Harassment in Pakistan. *Independent*. https://www.independent.co.uk/voices/comment/are-women-only-parks-the-answer-to-street-harassment-in-pakistan-8223147.html; and R. Khan. 2012. Six Women's-Only Parks Being Developed. *Tribune*. https://tribune.com.pk/story/434063/harassment-protection-six-womens-only-parks-being-developed.

[17] Exercise Is Medicine Global Presence: Global Directory. https://exerciseismedicine.org/eim_map.

[18] Asian economies included in the UNESCO study include Afghanistan; Bangladesh; Bhutan; Cambodia; Hong Kong, China; India; Indonesia; Japan; Kazakhstan; the Kyrgyz Republic; the Lao People's Democratic Republic; Malaysia; Mongolia; Myanmar; Nepal; Pakistan; the ROK; the PRC; Singapore; Sri Lanka; Turkmenistan; Uzbekistan; and Viet Nam. UNESCO. 2014. *World-wide Survey of School Physical Education*. Paris. https://en.unesco.org/inclusivepolicylab/e-teams/quality-physical-education-qpe-policy-project/documents/world-wide-survey-school-physical.

academic subjects, thereby giving physical education a lower priority in terms of teacher training, funding, facilities, and consistency of holding classes. The quality of physical education facilities is reportedly inadequate in 40% of the Asian countries surveyed by the United Nations Educational, Scientific and Cultural Organization (UNESCO).[19] In some communities, girls are discouraged and may even be forbidden by parents from participating in sports or exercising outdoors. In these instances, policies and public-awareness campaigns can help promote a broader understanding of the beneficial impacts of physical education and physical activities for females.

Outside of physical education classes, sports provide the most important access point for children to learn physical skills and build a lifelong habit and love of being active. However, the global trend of youth sports becoming formalized and increasingly competitive discourages youth from participating unless they are playing at a competitive level. When they are simply considered "play" or recreation, sports are often not valued by Asian parents, especially when compared with the importance of academic studies or other "achievements." Elsewhere in the world, the most lauded and healthy approach to youth sports can be found in the Nordic countries, which treat youth sports as a major public health and welfare concern. In Norway, organized sports clubs and teams are guided by policies that prohibit high-level competition and the publishing of scores and rankings for younger children, emphasize fun and friendship, keep costs low, and encourage children to plan and execute their own activities and training. These policies have resulted in more children playing more sports for fun, more free play, overall higher levels of physical activity among youth, and a higher persistence of sports involvement into adulthood. These policies can be considered and emulated in Asian countries.[20]

Encourage Healthy Eating

Today's health and wellness challenges related to food and nutrition encompass a host of concerns, from poor nutrition, processed foods, and obesity to "food deserts," food insecurity, food equity, and food safety. While individuals are responsible for the foods they purchase and consume, unhealthy food environments, unhealthy ingredients or additives, ease of access, cost of food, and a lack of awareness facilitate poor eating choices, and government policies have a major influence on all of these factors.[21]

Improve Consumer Information and Awareness of Nutrition and Diet

Consumers need knowledge about good nutrition and healthy diets, as well as transparency in information, in order to make healthy choices. At least 90 countries (including 17 in Asia) have established national food-based dietary guidelines, which are used by governments to educate the public about healthy eating. There are challenges related to dietary guidelines as they currently exist in most countries, including whether they actually reflect the latest scientific knowledge on nutrition (e.g., few countries' guidelines recommend limits on processed foods, sugar, or caffeine); whether guidelines are unduly influenced by food industry interests; and whether guidelines are culturally relevant and adaptable for different socioeconomic and indigenous groups.[22]

[19] UNESCO. 2014. World-wide Survey of School Physical Education. Paris. https://en.unesco.org/inclusivepolicylab/e-teams/quality-physical-education-qpe-policy-project/documents/world-wide-survey-school-physical.

[20] The US-based Aspen Institute's Project Play initiative (launched in 2013) has also developed a comprehensive set of strategies that can help parents, coaches, and communities make sports a more accessible and enjoyable experience for all children. https://www.aspenprojectplay.org.

[21] D. Mozaffarian et al. 2018. Role of Government Policy in Nutrition—Barriers to and Opportunities for Healthier Eating. *BMJ*. 361. https://doi.org/10.1136/bmj.k2426; Actions for Healthy Eating. 2009. In L. Parker, et al., eds. *Local Government Actions to Prevent Childhood Obesity*. Washington, DC: National Academies Press. pp. 49–69. http://nap.edu/12674; and M.T. Gorski and C.A. Roberto. 2015. Public Health Policies to Encourage Healthy Eating Habits: Recent Perspectives. *Journal of Healthcare Leadership*. 7. pp. 81–90. https://doi.org/10.2147/JHL.S69188.

[22] A. Herforth et al. 2019. A Global Review of Food-Based Dietary Guidelines. *Advances in Nutrition*. 10 (4). pp. 590–605. https://doi.org/10.1093/advances/nmy130; and A. Jacobs. 2019. A Shadowy Industry Group Shapes Food Policy around the World. *New York Times*. 16 September. https://www.nytimes.com/2019/09/16/health/ilsi-food-policy-india-brazil-china.html.

Governments play a critical role in ensuring that food labels and warnings are clear and understandable to consumers. Many countries are now adding front-of-package labels or symbols to highlight certain nutritional qualities or "healthy choices," adding standardized warning labels for unhealthy foods or ingredients, adding color-coded or "traffic light" labels for certain ingredients, and adding labels for other qualities (such as allergens, gluten, or genetically engineered foods). In 2011, Thailand was the first Asian country to introduce mandatory front-of-package labels for snack foods. A number of Asian nations now use "healthy choice" symbols on food packaging (e.g., Singapore, Thailand, Malaysia, the PRC, and Viet Nam).[23] Labeling can also extend to restaurant menus. Singapore's voluntary Healthier Dining Programme encourages restaurants, food courts, and hawker centers to post "healthier choice" labels on healthy menu options and provides grants to partners to develop healthy dishes for their menus. According to the Health Promotion Board, after the program's launch the sales of healthier meals increased from 7.5 million in 2014 to 26 million in 2017.[24]

While dietary guidelines and labeling are important informational tools, there is limited evidence of their effectiveness in actually spurring changes in eating behaviors, especially among marginalized and high-risk groups. The greater impact of labeling policies may be that they can spur industry to voluntarily reformulate products in order to avoid negative labels (e.g., by removing harmful ingredients, or by reducing calories or portion sizes).[25] In Singapore, reformulations for packaged beverages occurred in response to increasingly strict government regulations on sugar labeling and warning symbols.[26]

Create Economic Incentives for Healthy Eating Choices

Price can have a strong influence on consumers' food purchasing decisions. Over the last decade, many national and municipal-level governments have instituted sugar, soda, and/or junk food taxes to disincentivize the purchase and consumption of unhealthy foods that contribute to obesity and chronic disease. The underlying idea behind these kinds of taxes is that they raise the price of junk foods to be closer to their true "societal cost" (i.e., accounting for negative externalities, such as their direct and indirect costs on health). Price sensitivity to junk food taxes is stronger among lower-income groups, which can help to address the nutritional disparities among these higher-risk populations. Studies indicate that junk food taxes are more effective than consumer education and package labeling at changing consumer behavior.[27] Asian countries that have imposed sugar taxes include India (2017), Sri Lanka (2017), Thailand (2017), the Philippines (2018), Malaysia (2019), and many Pacific island countries.[28] In 2016, the state government of Kerala, India, passed a 14.5% tax on fast food, and Bangladesh proposed a 10% supplementary duty on fast food in 2017 (although it is not clear if the measure was implemented).[29]

---

[23] European Food Information Council. 2018. *Global Update on Nutrition Labelling (2018 edition): Executive Summary*. https://www.eufic.org/images/uploads/healthy-living/Executive-Summary-GUNL-2018-V2.pdf.

[24] Singapore Health Promotion Board. n.d. *Healthier Dining Programme*. https://www.hpb.gov.sg/healthy-living/food-beverage/healthier-dining-programme/about-the-healthier-dining-programme; and Singapore Health Promotion Board. n.d. *Healthier Dining Programme Extended to Include Food in Hawker Centres and Coffee Shops*. https://www.hpb.gov.sg/article/healthier-dining-programme-extended-to-include-food-in-hawker-centres-and-coffee-shops.

[25] D. Mozaffarian et al. 2018. Role of Government Policy in Nutrition—Barriers to and Opportunities for Healthier Eating. *BMJ*. 361. https://doi.org/10.1136/bmj.k2426.

[26] A.H. Min. 2019. New Mandatory Nutrition Labels, Advertising Ban for Pre-packaged Drinks High in Sugar. *Channel News Asia*. https://www.channelnewsasia.com/news/singapore/high-sugar-drinks-new-nutrition-labels-advertising-ban-11987416; and A.H. Min. 2019. Manufacturers Supportive of New Regulations for Pre-packaged Sweetened Drinks. *Channel News Asia*. https://www.channelnewsasia.com/news/singapore/high-sugar-drinks-pre-packaged-manufacturers-support-measures-11988542.

[27] WHO. 2017. *Taxes on Sugary Drinks: Why Do It?* https://apps.who.int/iris/bitstream/handle/10665/260253/WHO-NMH-PND-16.5Rev.1-eng.pdf;sequence=1; and L.M. Powell et al. 2013. Assessing the Potential Effectiveness of Food and Beverage Taxes and Subsidies for Improving Public Health: A Systematic Review of Prices, Demand and Body Weight Outcomes. *Obesity Review*. 14 (2). pp. 110–128. https://doi.org/10.1111/obr.12002.

[28] Obesity Evidence Hub. 2020. *Countries That Have Implemented Taxes on Sugar-Sweetened Beverages (SSBs)*. https://www.obesityevidencehub.org.au/collections/prevention/countries-that-have-implemented-taxes-on-sugar-sweetened-beverages-ssbs.

[29] S. Menon. 2016. Why Has an Indian State Imposed a "Fat Tax"? *BBC News*. https://www.bbc.com/news/world-asia-india-36771843; and *Dhaka Tribune*. 2017. 10% Supplementary Duty on Fast Food Proposed. https://www.dhakatribune.com/business/economy/2017/06/01/duty-fast-food-proposed.

Another tool used by many governments is to embed financial incentives for healthier foods (e.g., subsidies, vouchers, or lower prices for fresh fruits and vegetables) into food assistance programs for lower-income families, children, and pregnant women, thereby improving the purchasing power of higher-risk populations to access healthy food choices. Studies indicate that cost reductions and subsidies for healthier foods (alongside junk food taxes) can have a significant impact on purchasing and consumption of these products.[30]

Create Healthier Food Environments and Expand Access for High-Risk Groups

There are many "nudge strategies" available to policy makers that can support healthy eating by making changes in the default food environment, essentially making healthier food choices the easiest and most obvious choice.[31] As populations become more urbanized, a growing number of people (especially the urban poor) live in "food deserts" where grocery stores and outlets selling fresh healthy foods are scarce or nonexistent, and fast food and packaged or convenience foods may be overabundant. Governments can address "food deserts" by supporting the construction of grocery stores and corner stores in underserved areas, as well as supporting existing stores to stock more fresh produce and healthy food options. Some cities and regions are also working to reduce access to unhealthy foods—for example, by changing zoning laws to restrict the construction of fast food outlets or convenience stores close to schools or within neighborhoods designated as "food deserts." Installing drinking fountains and water refilling stations in public spaces can also discourage consumption of unhealthy beverages by making fresh water more readily available.

Policies can also reshape the default options available within existing restaurants, stores, and food service outlets. Some strategies include removing soft drinks or French fries from children's menus in restaurants, reducing portion sizes or cup or plate sizes in restaurants, restricting free refills on soft drinks, and changing the placement of fresh and healthy foods in grocery stores. Governments (who are major employers and food purchasers) can take the lead in this regard by changing food procurement practices and menus within publicly funded facilities (including schools, military installations, parks/recreation/tourism facilities, hospitals, prisons, and government agencies). In Japan, for example, the mandatory and highly subsidized public school lunch program requires all students to eat the same school lunch each day, and meals are specially planned by nutritionists to be healthy and emphasize fresh ingredients. School lunch is viewed as an opportunity for food and nutrition education (*shokiuku*), where children can learn about healthy eating habits.[32]

Strengthen Industry Standards and Regulations for Ingredients and Marketing

In some countries and cities, governments are exploring more stringent regulations on the food and restaurant industry to support healthier population-wide eating habits, although these measures can be challenging because they are typically met with significant industry opposition. Regulations typically take three forms: restrictions on the use of certain ingredients or additives in processed or restaurant foods (e.g., trans fats or salt), restrictions on the sales of certain foods deemed unhealthy, and restrictions on marketing of certain foods. In 2019, Thailand became the first member country in the Association of Southeast Asian Nations (ASEAN) to ban imports, production, and sales of partially hydrogenated oils, the main source of artificial trans fats. In India, the government has set a goal to limit trans fats in fats and oils to no more than 2% by weight by 2022.

Many governments also target food marketing as a "softer" approach to regulating the industry, most often via restrictions on the types of foods, imagery, and advertisements that can be marketed at children. In 2010, the

[30] Tufts University. 2017. Food Subsidies, Taxes Significantly Improve Dietary Choices. *Science Daily*. https://www.sciencedaily.com/releases/2017/03/170301142157.htm; and R. An. 2013. Effectiveness of Subsidies in Promoting Healthy Food Purchases and Consumption: A Review of Field Experiments. *Public Health and Nutrition*. 16 (7). pp. 1215–1228. https://doi.org/10.1017/S1368980012004715.

[31] P.G. Hansen et al. 2016. Making Healthy Choices Easier: Regulation versus Nudging. *Annual Review of Public Health*. 37. pp. 237–251. https://doi.org/10.1146/annurev-publhealth-032315-021537.

[32] Hunter College New York City Food Policy Center. 2019. *Japan's School Lunch Program Serves Nutritious Meals with Food Education*. https://www.nycfoodpolicy.org/food-policy-snapshot-japans-school-lunch-program.

ROK instituted restrictions on TV advertisements of energy-dense and nutrient-poor foods targeting children, resulting in a measurable decrease in advertising placements and budgets for such products. In 2016, Taipei,China implemented similar limits on TV advertisements for unhealthy foods on dedicated TV channels for children, as well as banning free toys paired with unhealthy foods in restaurant and fast food meals.[33]

Implement "Food as Medicine" in Patient Care

The health-care arena is an important setting for delivering education, counseling, and incentives for healthy eating, especially for people with chronic disease or elevated risk factors. Health policy, especially in countries with nationalized or single-payer health systems, can encourage the integration of nutritional education courses, nutritionist or dietician referrals, menu planning support, and other measures to make food, eating, and nutrition a formal part of treatment and patient care protocols. Nutrition counseling can be especially effective for pregnant women and new mothers, and often includes support for breastfeeding. Asian countries with government-supported "food as medicine" initiatives include Malaysia, Singapore, Thailand, and Fiji.[34] In the United States, some cities and medical providers are experimenting with "produce prescriptions" and "food farmacy" programs, whereby doctors write "prescriptions" for reduced-price or free fresh fruits and vegetables that can be redeemed at participating stores and farmers' markets. These schemes typically target lower-income regions or at-risk patients, and are mostly funded via nonprofit partnerships, government grants, or existing government food assistance programs.[35]

Enhance Wellness in the Workplace

Workers in Asia are plagued by unwellness: rising chronic disease; workplace illness, injuries, and death; financial insecurity; rampant stress and burnout; and widespread employee disengagement. Some of these issues are closely intertwined with globalization, technological change, new business models, and the shifting relationships between workers and employers, as well as with the economy in general (e.g., the rise of the "gig economy" and short-term contract work). Within this evolving landscape, governments can help to protect and enhance workers' well-being through policies and regulations, as well as by being a leader and promoting best practices through their role as an employer of a large government workforce.

Ensure a Safe and Healthy Physical Work Environment

Every job or workplace brings with it different types of physical health hazards and risks—for example, nurses risking back injuries from lifting heavy patients; office workers with carpal tunnel syndrome; truck drivers facing road accidents; and factory workers dealing with hazardous chemicals, heavy equipment, or loud noises. Regardless of the type of work or the place of work, every worker has a basic human right to a safe and healthy working environment.[36] Governments have a responsibility to monitor and enforce existing standards, while stepping up regulations where protections are lacking. For example, Singapore's strong enforcement of workplace safety and health policies has reduced work-related fatal injuries from 4.9 per 100,000 workers in 2004 to 1.2

[33] S. Kim et al. 2013. Restriction of Television Food Advertising in South Korea: Impact on Advertising of Food Companies. *Health Promotion International*. 28 (1). pp. 17–25. https://doi.org/10.1093/heapro/das023; and World Cancer Research Fund International. 2019. *Nourishing Framework: Restrict Food Advertising and Other Forms of Commercial Promotion*. https://www.wcrf.org/sites/default/files/4_Restrict_advertising.pdf.

[34] World Cancer Research Fund International. 2019. *Nourishing Framework: Nutrition Advice and Counselling*. https://www.wcrf.org/sites/default/files/9_Nutrition_advice_and_counselling.pdf.

[35] S. Radcliffe. 2019. Why "Food Prescriptions" Are the Best Medicine for Chronic Diseases. *Healthline*. https://www.healthline.com/health-news/heres-how-healthy-food-prescriptions-could-save-lives-and-money; and C. Szabo. 2019. Food "Farmacies," Produce Prescriptions Gain Lawmaker Support. *ABC News*. https://abcnews.go.com/Politics/food-farmacies-produce-prescriptions-gain-lawmaker-support/story?id=63552564.

[36] International Labour Organization (ILO). 2009. *Health and Life at Work: A Basic Human Right—World Day for Safety and Health at Work 2009*. Geneva, Switzerland. https://www.ilo.org/safework/WCMS_108590/lang--en/index.htm.

in 2017 and 2018. Recent measures aim to reduce this rate to 1.0 per 100,000 by 2028, in part by encouraging employers to take more ownership of safety, increasing transparency about injury and fatality rates, and empowering workers to speak up about risky situations.[37]

Protect Workers from Hostile Work Environments, Overwork, and Other Triggers of Emotional and Mental Distress

The culture and social environment in a workplace can have a profound impact on workers' mental wellness. While it is impossible to mandate kind and friendly behavior, governments and policy can set a baseline by defining the behaviors that are unacceptable because they can harm others and create a hostile work environment. Behaviors that can be regulated by policy may include, but are not limited to, sexual harassment and discrimination based on race, sex, religion, sexual orientation, and disability. Sexual harassment is an important and sensitive issue in Asia, as more women are entering the workplace, and often working in informal arrangements and low-paid jobs supervised by men. While anti-harassment laws exist on the books in some Asian countries, implementation and enforcement remain weak. For example, Singapore implemented the Protection from Harassment Act in 2014, but it is not accompanied by legal enforcement mechanism. India implemented the Prevention of Sexual Harassment of Women at Workplace Act in 2013, but the guidelines and provisions are not widely known, followed, or enforced.[38]

Governments can also help to mitigate overwork and workplace stress by limiting work hours and mandating breaks. In Japan, a country known for its entrenched culture of overwork, the government enacted a "work-style reform" bill in 2018 that, among other things, caps overtime work hours at 45 hours per month and 360 hours per year, with penalties stipulated for employers that violate these regulations.[39] An additional measure in Japan is the National Stress Check Program, the first mandatory workplace policy in Japan related to mental health, requiring employers with more than 50 employees to offer the option of taking an annual stress survey. Workers with high stress levels can request a meeting with an occupational health physician to receive advice and address workplace challenges, while employers can analyze team-level data to identify and improve work environment issues.[40]

Provide Living Wages, Unemployment Benefits, and Paid Family and Sick Leave

Income insecurity can be an important source of stress and distress for workers, leading to a host of other health and well-being issues. In recent years, workers in many Asian countries have experienced stagnating wages or slower wage growth, while losing job security due to the rise of the contract work and the "gig economy." According to the International Labour Organization (ILO), wage growth in high-income Asian economies was close to zero in 2017, and a meager 2.4% in Southeast Asia and the Pacific.[41] While market wages are set through

[37] G.W. Hoe and C.K. Sing. 2019. Why Singapore's New Approach to Workplace Safety and Health Matters (to You). *Today*. https://www.todayonline.com/commentary/why-singapores-new-approach-workplace-safety-and-health-matters-you. Singapore's Ministry of Manpower and the Workplace Safety and Health Council also provide extensive resources and case studies on best practices in Asia. See https://www.mom.gov.sg/workplace-safety-and-health/wsh-best-practices and https://www.wshc.sg.

[38] National University of Singapore, Lee Kuan Yew School of Public Policy. 2018. Tackling Workplace Sexual Harassment in Asia: A Necessary Paradigm Shift. *Global-Is-Asian*. https://lkyspp.nus.edu.sg/gia/article/tackling-workplace-sexual-harassment-in-asia-a-necessary-paradigm-shift; and K. Vaswani. 2017. The Costs of Sexual Harassment in the Asian Workplace. *BBC News*. https://www.bbc.com/news/business-42218053.

[39] Japan Institute for Labour Policy and Training. Trends: Work Style Form Bill Enacted. 2018. *Japan Labor Issues*. 2 (10). https://www.jil.go.jp/english/jli/documents/2018/010-01.pdf; and D. Demetriou. 2019. New Labour Law Puts Limits on Japan's Overworking Culture. *The Telegraph*. https://www.telegraph.co.uk/news/2019/04/02/new-labour-law-puts-limits-japans-overworking-culture.

[40] Healthy Work Campaign. 2019. *Stress Check: A National Policy in Japan for Prevention of Workplace Stress*. https://healthywork.org/wp-content/uploads/2019/09/016-HWC-Website-Page-Content-Resources-Healthy-Work-Strategies-Stress-Check-Japan-v1-092019-300res-CYMK.pdf; N. Sugawara et al. 2016. What Is the Purpose of the Stress Check Program? *Journal of Occupational Health*. 58 (6). pp. 653–655. https://doi.org/10.1539/joh.16-0170-OP; and K. Imamura et al. 2018. Effect of the National Stress Check Program on Mental Health among Workers in Japan: A 1-year Retrospective Cohort Study. *Journal of Occupational Health*. 60 (4). pp. 298–306. https://doi.org/10.1539/joh.2017-0314-OA.

[41] ILO. 2018. Asia-Pacific Wage Growth Stalls but Stays Ahead of the Rest of the World. *Global Wage Report 2018/19*. https://www.ilo.org/asia/media-centre/news/WCMS_651039/lang--ja/index.htm.

the dynamics of supply and demand, a mandated minimum wage can help define the baseline for workers at the lowest rungs of the economic ladder. In recent years, several Southeast Asian countries have raised minimum wages (e.g., Cambodia, Myanmar, and the Lao People's Democratic Republic).[42] In addition to reducing stress and financial insecurity, research shows that higher minimum wages can improve workers' physical and mental health.[43] Other ways governments can improve workers' financial security are through mandated unemployment benefits and state-sponsored unemployment schemes, paid parental leave and family leave, and sick leave. Generally, however, these benefits protect workers only in formal, contract-based employment. With the rapid rise in the "gig" economy across Asia, governments are only beginning to explore what kinds of regulations or protections are needed or even feasible for these workers.[44]

Make Government a Workplace Wellness Leader and Best Practice Employer

A holistic approach to workplace wellness must go far beyond simply protecting workers from unsafe and unhealthy work conditions and workplace harassment, or ensuring fair wages and fair labor practices. True workplace wellness extends to creating a work environment that encourages healthy behaviors and habits, cultivates a collegial and supportive work culture, recognizes stress and burnout, and motivates and engages workers. What governments *can* do is to model best practices within government worksites and workplaces. Since the government is the largest employer in many places, the implementation of workplace wellness strategies within the government can affect a significant share of the workforce, while raising the standard of workplace wellness practices across the board and also providing a model for private sector employers.

Establish Legal Structures That Enable and Support "Benefit Corporations" and Environmental, Social, and Governance Reporting

An important aspect of workplace wellness is allowing employees to align work with their intrinsic motivations—their interests, values, and sense of purpose. In recent years, some businesses have begun to frame their missions and visions in terms of broader societal and environmental impacts, moving toward a purpose-driven mission rather than a profit-driven one. In recent years, a new type of corporate entity—the "benefit corporation"—has emerged, explicitly recognizing social and environmental benefits as a core corporate mission.[45] The benefit corporation movement is gaining momentum around the world, including in Asia, where benefit corporations can now be legally certified in a number of countries (e.g., Japan, the ROK, India, Australia, and New Zealand). However, in most countries, policies and regulations have yet catch up in order to clarify the duties of directors and their legal obligations and protections under this new company structure.[46]

In addition, the spread of environmental, social, and governance (ESG) reporting, the development of ESG guidelines, and the growth of socially responsible investing and impact investing are helping encourage

---

[42] J. Yap. 2018. Laos Government Approves Minimum Wage Increase. *The Laotian Times.* https://laotiantimes.com/2018/04/24/laos-government-approves-minimum-wage-increase; N.L. Aung and P.T. Phyo. 2018. Government Sets New Daily Minimum Wages at K4800. *Myanmar Times.* https://www.mmtimes.com/news/government-sets-new-daily-minimum-wage-k4800.html; P.C. Thul. 2018. Cambodia Hikes Textile Workers' Minimum Wage, Falls Short of Union Demands. *Reuters.* https://www.reuters.com/article/us-cambodia-garment/cambodia-hikes-textile-workers-minimum-wage-falls-short-of-union-demands-idUSKCN1MF18B; and Y. Nakamura et al. 2018. Minimum Wages Surge across Southeast Asia. *Nikkei Asian Review.* https://asia.nikkei.com/Economy/Minimum-wages-surge-across-Southeast-Asia.

[43] L.P. Leigh and J. Du. 2018. Effects of Minimum Wages on Population Health. *Health Affairs Health Policy Brief.* https://doi.org/10.1377/hpb20180622.107025; and American Public Health Association. 2016. *Improving Health by Increasing the Minimum Wage.* APHA Policy Statement No. 20167. https://www.apha.org/policies-and-advocacy/public-health-policy-statements/policy-database/2017/01/18/improving-health-by-increasing-minimum-wage.

[44] R. Phua. 2020. The Singapore Gig Economy: Right Balance on Regulations Needed to Unlock Its Full Potential, Say Experts. *Channel News Asia.* https://www.channelnewsasia.com/news/singapore/the-singapore-gig-economy-right-balance-on-regulations-needed-to-12235556.

[45] Fourth Sector Network. No date. *For-Benefit Corporations.* http://www.fourthsector.net/learn/for-benefit-corporations (accessed 15 January 2020); and Benefit Corporation. No date. *What Is a Benefit Corporation?* https://benefitcorp.net/what-is-a-benefit-corporation (accessed 15 January 2020).

[46] Lift Economy. 2019. *Key Developments in the B Corp Movement (Since the First Edition).* https://www.lifteconomy.com/blog/2019/4/24/key-developments-in-the-b-corp-movement-since-the-first-edition; and Benefit Corporation. No date. *Policymakers Overview.* https://benefitcorp.net/policymakers (accessed 15 January 2020).

companies to consider their business mission, practices, and impacts.[47] While ESG reporting frameworks have traditionally focused heavily on environmental metrics, there is now a growing movement to expand employee health and well-being metrics within ESG guidelines.[48] This shift is important, providing transparency on corporate practices that affect employee wellness and creating internal data to inform and improve corporate decision making on these matters. Government policies and regulations play an important role in supporting these developments by providing mandates and clear standards for ESG reporting to ensure a fair marketplace, as well as clarifying regulatory guidelines on fiduciary duties so that investors do not feel that they are prohibited from considering ESG factors in their decisions.[49] As some of the largest institutional investors in the world, governments can also support this movement by integrating ESG considerations into their own investment decisions.[50] For example, in 2015 the Government of Japan paved the way for the growth of ESG in Japan's private markets when the Government Pension Investment Fund, the world's largest public pension fund, became a signatory to the United Nations Principles for Responsible Investment and began emphasizing ESG criteria in investment decisions.[51]

In many ways, the development of benefit corporations and ESG reporting in the private sector is analogous to the nascent rise of "well-being budgeting" in the public sector. Both represent an important "top-down" shift in priorities, moving away from purely financial and economic considerations and toward an emphasis on the health and well-being of people (and the planet) as a key factor for decision making and a key metric for "success."

Life Span-Based Wellness Policy Domains

Understanding Brain Plasticity

Given all of the foundational influences on human development and mental health during infancy and childhood, is there any hope for change in adulthood? A growing number of studies on wellness modalities (e.g., meditation, yoga, and dance) are finding positive changes in the brains of regular practitioners. At the heart of this emerging body of research findings is the concept that the brain can continue to grow and develop new neural pathways and connections well into adulthood. This evidence stands in contrast to earlier views that brain development ceases in adolescence.

[47] For more information on ESG in Asia and globally, see CFA Institute and Principles for Responsible Investment. 2019. *ESG Integration in Asia Pacific: Markets, Practices, and Data.* https://www.cfainstitute.org/-/media/documents/survey/esg-integration-apac.ashx; A. Holt. 2019. Asian Companies Get Serious about ESG. *IR Magazine.* https://www.irmagazine.com/reporting/asian-companies-get-serious-about-esg; R.G. Eccles and S. Klimenko. 2019. The Investor Revolution. *Harvard Business Review.* https://hbr.org/2019/05/the-investor-revolution; and G. Kell. 2018. The Remarkable Rise of ESG. *Forbes.* https://www.forbes.com/sites/georgkell/2018/07/11/the-remarkable-rise-of-esg/#37ea24571695.

[48] M. Tulay. 2019. Executive Perspective: Corporate Sustainability Strategy Starts with Employee Health. *Thomson Reuters.* https://blogs.thomsonreuters.com/sustainability/2019/02/26/executive-perspective-corporate-sustainability-strategy-starts-with-employee-health; A. Walsh. 2019. Where Is the "Social" Wellbeing in ESG Reporting? *Reward & Employee Benefits Association (RIBA).* https://reba.global/content/the-worth-of-the-workforce-where-is-the-social-in-esg-reporting; Pensions and Lifetime Savings Association and High Pay Centre. 2019. *Hidden Talent 2: Has Workforce Reporting by the FTSE Improved?* http://highpaycentre.org/files/Hidden-Talent-2-Has-workforce-reporting-by-the-FTSE-100-improved.pdf; and Delos. 2017. The Rise of Health Metrics in ESG Investing. *GRESB.* https://gresb.com/the-rise-of-health-metrics-in-esg-investing.

[49] Organisation for Economic Co-operation and Development. 2017. *Investment Governance and the Integration of Environmental, Social and Governance Factors.* https://www.oecd.org/finance/Investment-Governance-Integration-ESG-Factors.pdf; and D. Stanley. 2018. ESG Investing and Government Regulation. *Seven Pillars Institute for Global Finance and Ethics.* https://sevenpillarsinstitute.org/esg-investing-and-government-regulation.

[50] E. Chasen. 2018. Governments Push ESG Investing Forward. *Bloomberg Briefs.* https://www.bloomberg.com/professional/blog/governments-push-esg-investment-forward.

[51] E. Woodland. 2019. Abe's Green Arrow: The Rise of ESG Investing in Japan. *AMPCapital.* https://www.ampcapital.com/au/en/insights-hub/articles/2019/october/abes-green-arrow-the-rise-of-esg-investing-in-japan; and B. Eccles. 2019. How to Further Accelerate Sustainable Investing in Japan: Taking It to Mainstream Asset Managers. *Forbes.* https://www.forbes.com/sites/bobeccles/2019/09/07/how-to-further-accelerate-sustainable-investing-in-japan-taking-it-to-mainstream-asset-managers/#20faf2e7e467.

As reported in the GWI's *Pathways, Evidence, Horizons: A White Paper on Mental Wellness,*[52] there is now substantial scientific evidence that explains how wellness habits help our brain change and rewire itself through a lifelong process termed "neuroplasticity." With the awareness, knowledge, and practice of self-directed neuroplasticity, we can achieve mental and overall wellness.[53]

Wellness in the First 1,000 Days

The arc of life, we are learning, begins before conception. The health of the parents prior to and at the time of conception is known now to influence our life course and some determinants of both health and lifestyle diseases. The first two years of life are especially critical in shaping people's future physical and mental health. Parenting styles, nutrition, and air quality are just some of the factors that shape future patterns of health and mental well-being. A 2018 *Lancet* series on preconception health highlights the study of preconception health as of foundational importance in understanding and shaping future health.[54] One article in the series, entitled "Before the Beginning," notes that "observational studies show strong links between health before pregnancy and maternal and child health outcomes, with consequences that can extend across generations."[55]

Policy Implications: Preventive Interventions in the First 1,000 Days

Today, there is agreement that the first 1,000 days of life, from conception to the second year of life, are the most important determinants of the health of individuals, and probably account for 70% of good health and wellness in the life span.[56] To date, efforts to prevent NCDs have primarily focused on adult individuals' risk factors (e.g., poor diet, physical inactivity, and smoking and alcohol consumption), while mostly ignoring the early stages of individuals' development. Effective preventive interventions for populations can be created to significantly lower the burden of health-care costs and increase the quality of life. The target of interventions needs to be an individual (the fetus and infant) who is not responsible for his or her own lifestyle, and this involves addressing that individual's environment. Policy recommendations in this field are based on six pillars of perinatal health to prevent NCDs in later life:

(i) movement;
(ii) nutrition;
(iii) mental health;
(iv) environment;
(v) fun; and
(vi) support.

The aim here is that future mothers and fathers of various socioeconomic backgrounds will be armed with knowledge about the critical lifelong impacts of parental and baby health, and will be actively engaged in positive lifestyle habits during preconception, pregnancy, and the first 2 years of life.

---

52 G. Bodeker, ed. 2018. *Pathways, Evidence, Horizons: A White Paper on Mental Wellness.* Miami, Florida: GWI. https://globalwellnessinstitute.org/wp-content/uploads/2018/10/GWI-MWI-WhitePaper2018.pdf.

53 L. Choy. 2018. Neuroplasticity and Mental Wellness: Our Path Forward. In G. Bodeker, ed. *Pathways, Evidence, Horizons: A White Paper on Mental Wellness.* pp. 18–29. Miami, Florida: GWI. https://globalwellnessinstitute.org/wp-content/uploads/2018/10/GWI-MWI-WhitePaper2018.pdf.

54 Preconception Health Series. 2018. *The Lancet.* 391 (10132). https://www.thelancet.com/series/preconception-health.

55 J. Stephenson et al. 2018. Before the Beginning: Nutrition and Lifestyle in the Preconception Period and Its Importance for Future Health. *The Lancet.* 391 (10131). pp. 1830–1841. https://doi.org/10.1016/S0140-6736(18)30311-8.

56 S. Pecorelli. 2018. The First 1,000 Days of Life. In G. Bodeker, ed. *Pathways, Evidence, Horizons: A White Paper on Mental Wellness.* pp. 13–17. Miami, Florida: GWI. https://globalwellnessinstitute.org/wp-content/uploads/2018/10/GWI-MWI-WhitePaper2018.pdf.

Wellness During School Years

In New South Wales, Australia, the state government has introduced a program to mainstream well-being throughout the school system.[57] Their policy framework puts well-being at the heart of education and includes the following:

(i) The school has a comprehensive and integrated strategy in place to support the cognitive, emotional, social, physical, and spiritual well-being of students in a context of quality teaching and learning.
(ii) The resources and expertise of the system at every level are targeted to meet the well-being needs of all students.
(iii) Teaching and learning occur in environments that celebrate differences and diversity and recognize, respect, and respond to identity and cultural backgrounds.

Wellness for Seniors

According to *World Population Prospects 2019*, by 2050, 1 in 6 people in the world will be over the age of 65, up from 1 in 11 in 2019.[58] *World Population Ageing 2019* explains that: "All societies in the world are in the midst of this longevity revolution; some are at its early stages and some are more advanced. But all will pass through this extraordinary transition, in which the chance of surviving to age 65 rises from less than 50%—as was the case in Sweden in the 1890s—to more than 90% at present in countries with the highest life expectancies. What is more, the proportion of adult life spent beyond age 65 has increased from less than one-fifth in the 1960s to one-quarter or more in most developed countries today." The negative health effects of aging are characterized by progressive loss of physical, mental, and cognitive integrity, leading to impaired functions and increased vulnerability to morbidity and mortality.[59]

Policy Implications: Lifelong Learning and Reskilling

The authors of *The 100-Year Life*, Lynda Gratton and Andrew Scott , professors of economics and business at London Business School, argue that people will have to work and reskill until age 75–85 in order to live a 100-year life.[60] They take the view that the importance of reskilling lies in its broader perspective toward life. During retirement, life after the age of 65 up to 100 is a very long time, and Gratton argues that we should consider, instead, a much more phased approach to retirement where people can work until their 70s.[61]

Developing "intangible assets." In a long life, money as a tangible asset is important, of course. But what actually helps in our 60s and 70s is not having more money, but rather having intangible assets, which are something like personal qualities. The three types of intangible assets listed in *The 100-Year Life* are:

(i) one's own capacity to be productive;
(ii) vitality, which means being physically and mentally healthy; and
(iii) transformation, which is our capacity to change.

[57] For more information, see New South Wales Department of Education and Communities. 2015. *The Wellbeing Framework for Schools*. https://education.nsw.gov.au/content/dam/main-education/student-wellbeing/whole-school-approach/media/documents/Wellbeing-Framework-for-schools-Accessible.pdf.
[58] United Nations. 2019. *2019 Revision of World Population Prospects*. https://population.un.org/wpp.
[59] United Nations, Department of Economic and Social Affairs, Population Division. 2019. *World Population Ageing 2019: Highlights* (ST/ESA/SER.A/430); A.Y. Chang et al. 2019. Measuring Population Ageing: An Analysis of the Global Burden of Disease Study 2017. *The Lancet Public Health*. 4 (3). pp. 159–167. https://doi.org/10.1016/S2468-2667(19)30019-2.
[60] L. Gratton and A. Scott. 2017. *The 100-Year Life: Living and Working in an Age of Longevity*. London: Bloomsbury Business.
[61] Future of Work: A Conversation with Lynda Gratton. 2017. *Fujitsu Insights*. https://www.fujitsu.com/global/vision/insights/201712event2.

Japan's 100-Year Life Program. In Japan, there is a gap of about 10 years between the "healthy life span" and the "average life span." The healthy life span is estimated at 72.14 years for Japanese men in 2016 (up 0.95 years from 2013), and 74.79 years for women (up 0.58 years from 2013), as reported by the Ministry of Health in March 2018. In 2016, the average life span for Japanese men stood at 80.98 years, and for Japanese women at 87.14 years. The expected lifetime after healthy years was shortened by 0.18 years for men and 0.05 years for women. Japanese people incur most of their medical expenses in the 10-year period between the healthy life span and the average life span, placing a considerable and growing pressure on the health system and the national budget as life span increases for the Japanese population.[62]

To address this challenge, Japan has introduced a 100-Year Life Program to promote wellness and a healthy life across the life span, which is being addressed cross-sectorally in Japan. During the 100-year life, there is a need to continually reskill because having a single skill or ordinary skills will not help us traverse a long life. The new approach is to acquire new skills and knowledge as people progress through life.

Japan has established a Council for Designing 100-Year Life Society to formulate policies to be implemented by the Government of Japan. Key ideas from the council include significant improvements in long-term care worker pay, a "drastic expansion of recurrent education" to expand mid-career employment, and laying the groundwork for raising employment levels of the elderly.

Policy Implications: Safe and Enabling Homes for Seniors

From a policy perspective, aging in place (typically at home) is only desirable if conditions are met to optimize function to enable coping with common chronic disabling diseases such as arthritis and stroke, as well as age-related syndromes such as sensory impairments; chewing difficulties; cognitive impairments (such as deficits in the domains of memory, processing speed, and executive function); and impairments in instrumental activities of daily living, physical function, and psychosocial needs.[63]

As one example of the implications for housing policy, Daiwa House, one of Japan's largest house builders, is transitioning into the "home reform" business. The company foresees the mass aging of Japan's construction workforce and the need for two innovations: labor-saving construction techniques and house designs that can be easily upgraded by elderly renovators.

The overall principles of age-friendly environments are summarized by WHO's concept of age-friendly cities, which encompass age-friendly transport, housing, respect and social inclusion, civic participation and employment, health and community services, information and communication, social participation, outdoor spaces, and buildings. Since many older people live in cities, attention to these principles may make a difference to promoting healthy aging instead of being obstacles.[64]

Policy Implications: Nutrition for Seniors

Reflecting a life span perspective, WHO has noted that many of the diseases suffered by older persons are the result of dietary factors, some of which have been operating since infancy. These factors are then compounded by changes that naturally occur with the aging process.[65]

---

[62] T. Maruyama. 2021. Enriching the Lives of Seniors in Japan: Ikigai Healthy Ageing Policy. In C. Goh, G. Bodeker, and K. Kariippanon, eds. *Healthy Ageing in Asia: Culture and Tradition in Prevention and Wellness.* Miami, Florida: Taylor & Francis (in preparation).

[63] J. Woo. 2021. Ageing in Place. In C. Goh, G. Bodeker, and K. Kariippanon, eds. Miami, Florida: Taylor & Francis Miami (in preparation).

[64] WHO. n.d. *Ageing and Life-Course: Global Age-Friendly Cities Project.* https://www.who.int/ageing/projects/age_friendly_cities/en.

[65] WHO. n.d. *Nutrition for Older Persons.* https://www.who.int/nutrition/topics/ageing/en/index1.html.

Of these dietary risks, the biggest contributors to the global burden of disease in 2017 were diets that are low in whole grains; high in sodium; or low in fruits, nuts, seeds, or vegetables. Additionally, higher body mass index has an effect on disease outcomes. Another factor is the price of foods rich in micronutrients, which further discourages their consumption.

Relatively modest reductions in saturated fat and salt intake, which would reduce blood pressure and cholesterol concentrations, could have a substantial effect on reducing the burden of cardiovascular disease. Increasing consumption of fruit and vegetables by one or two servings daily could cut cardiovascular risk by 30%.

WHO Nutrition Director Francesco Branca has argued that food systems and the infrastructure on which they depend must be restructured. Reforms to the supply side of food systems are needed to improve the availability of healthy, sustainable diets.[66]

Measures that affect demand for certain foods—what we buy, how we prepare it, and what we eat or throw away—are urgently needed. These should include actions to create healthy food environments, supported by nutrition education, especially in schools, to ensure that even the most vulnerable people can access healthy diets. Along with regulatory measures for food composition, marketing, labeling, and nutrition standards for food in schools and other public institutions, taxes and subsidies are among the tools available.

[66] F. Branca et al. 2019. Transforming the Food System to Fight Non-communicable Diseases. *BMJ*. 364: l296. https://doi.org/10.1136/bmj.l296.

CHAPTER 14

Conclusion—Toward Wellness for All Asians

Donghyun Park

The coronavirus disease (COVID-19) was an unprecedented global public health and economic crisis, and its effects will be felt for years to come. The disease spread across the entire world in a matter of months after it first emerged in early 2020. Its highly contagious nature also blanketed the world with fear and anxiety. Throughout 2020, to contain COVID-19, many countries partially or fully closed their borders and restricted the movement of people. In extreme cases, people were ordered to stay at home and allowed to go outside only for special purposes. While such restrictions helped to limit the spread of the pandemic, they took a heavy toll on the physical and mental health of the global population. Furthermore, they severely restricted economic activity, which caused a great deal of economic hardship, which further harmed the well-being of people around the world. Developing Asia was hit hard by the pandemic. The region's economy shrank for the first time in 6 decades, and millions of Asians suffered untold distress and suffering.

Given the pronounced impact of the pandemic on the physical and mental health of Asians, now is a most opportune time to examine the issue of wellness in Asia. Wellness is conceptually related to but distinct from happiness and well-being. While happiness and well-being refer to the subjective condition of feeling happy or well, wellness denotes the active and conscious pursuit of activities, choices, and lifestyles that leads to a state of holistic health. Put differently, wellness leads to happiness and well-being. Some concrete examples of wellness include exercising regularly, eating healthy food, and meditating. COVID-19 highlighted the importance of wellness, which can contribute to a sound mind and fit body. Medical evidence indicates that individuals with preexisting health conditions are much more vulnerable to the disease. Further, pandemic-related mobility restrictions, which cut off people from their family, friends, and acquaintances, created significant stress and anxiety among Asians.

COVID-19 is likely to further strengthen the momentum of demand for wellness among Asians. This demand was already robust well before the advent of the pandemic, as evident in the proliferation of fitness centers and the rapid growth of wellness tourism in the region. According to the analysis presented in this book, the wellness economy accounted for 11% of the region's gross domestic product in 2017 and has been growing by around 10% annually in recent years. Therefore, wellness industries such as personal care, fitness, and healthy eating can serve as a major engine of growth as Asia's economies recover from the pandemic. Furthermore, wellness can promote inclusive growth because it creates additional jobs, especially for female workers, and it opens up opportunities for micro and small enterprises in wellness industries such as wellness tourism. It is possible to participate in many wellness activities, for instance doing tai chi in public parks or playing basketball in neighborhood courts, at low or no cost. However, free activities such as these require public investment in wellness infrastructure. This implies that a key role of the government in Asia's wellness sector is to support all Asians by building wellness infrastructure so that poorer Asians too can participate in wellness activities, which contribute to physical and mental well-being.

The good news for Asia is the existence of a rich heritage of wellness traditions that it can draw upon. Some of the world's most well-known wellness traditions originated in the region. Asian wellness practices such as yoga have become popular in Western countries even as they were somewhat neglected in their birthplaces, and it is now high time for Asian countries to rediscover their wellness roots. In particular, Asia's two major systems of traditional health knowledge—Chinese traditional medicine and Ayurvedic medicine—have shaped the wellness traditions of East, South, and Southeast Asia. A healthy lifestyle that prevents poor health is the defining characteristic of both systems. Significantly, a growing body of scientific evidence confirms the substantial benefits of Asian wellness traditions for physical and mental health. Asian governments have paid attention to traditional medicine to varying degrees. For example, in 2015 the Indian government created a new Ministry of AYUSH (Ayurveda, Yoga & Naturopathy, Unani, Siddha and Homoeopathy) to develop traditional medicine and integrate it into India's formal health services. But there is plenty of scope for Asian governments to further promote traditional medicine, especially by better integrating traditional and conventional medicines.

At a broader level, Asian governments can and should do more to encourage wellness among Asians. There is a wide range of policy options available to them. One set of policy options has to do with four crosscutting policy domains. These are (ii) creating a healthy built environment that encourages physical activity; (ii) funding public infrastructure, facilities, and programs for physical activity; (iii) encouraging Asians to eat healthier food; and (iv) ensuring a safe and healthy work environment. A life span approach to wellness looks after mental and physical health from birth to old age. An overarching life span framework, such as Japan's 100-Year Life Program, recognizes that healthy aging begins in childhood and progresses through life. Taken together, crosscutting policies and life span policies can foster physical and mental wellness. In the final analysis, wellness is a conscious lifestyle that individuals must choose for themselves. The government cannot exercise regularly, eat healthier food, or get enough sleep for a person. As Asians become more aware of the benefits of wellness, or the costs of unwellness, we can expect more of them to choose healthier lifestyles.

Appendix 1: Core Asian Countries

1. Armenia
2. Azerbaijan
3. Bangladesh
4. Cambodia
5. Fiji
6. Georgia
7. India
8. Indonesia
9. Japan
10. Kazakhstan
11. Kyrgyz Republic
12. Malaysia
13. Nepal
14. Pakistan
15. Papua New Guinea
16. People's Republic of China
17. Philippines
18. Republic of Korea
19. Singapore
20. Sri Lanka
21. Tajikistan
22. Thailand
23. Turkmenistan
24. Uzbekistan
25. Viet Nam

Note: Availability of wellness data varies across indicators and locations, so in constructing the wellness index an initial step was to establish this list of "core countries of interest." The list includes 25 ADB members with a wide variation in size, economic growth, and geography that are known to have good data coverage from previous studies, such as ADB's Inclusive Green Growth Index (IGGI). These core countries were used to help guide the data collection and identification strategy.

Appendix 2: Full Wellness Index

The table presents the Wellness Index for 153 economies for which scores in all four pillars of wellness could be calculated. The table also includes additional economies with limited data availability. It reports scores for pillars for which data were available, leaving the remaining cells blank.

Economy	Physical	Intellectual	Environmental	Social	Wellness Index	Rank
Afghanistan	40.89	16.74	25.38	11.22	23.56	151
Albania	90.92	73.70	73.54	50.67	72.21	46
Algeria	85.70	51.45	54.76	41.66	58.39	82
Angola	48.73	29.95	35.18	9.91	30.94	145
Antigua and Barbuda	*88.48*	*71.94*				
Argentina	89.01	74.99	64.91	42.38	67.82	58
Armenia	87.16	81.13	61.73	62.05	73.02	43
Australia	97.47	94.55	87.85	80.89	90.19	13
Austria	96.70	94.38	82.31	83.68	89.27	14
Azerbaijan	80.35	81.03	59.85	29.78	62.76	71
Bahamas, The	*83.42*					
Bahrain	90.83	74.27	14.75	19.92	49.94	110
Bangladesh	73.88	41.05	37.47	19.82	43.06	125
Barbados	90.54	81.77	77.48	62.40	78.05	33
Belarus	88.06	91.59	70.95	53.52	76.03	38
Belgium	96.37	91.17	79.15	85.58	88.07	16
Belize	*84.76*					
Benin	49.23	19.93	53.27	47.20	42.41	127
Bhutan	76.57	32.72	91.22	67.61	67.03	59
Bolivia	74.75	68.16	69.27	32.97	61.29	75
Bosnia and Herzegovina	90.95	75.67	69.82	43.60	70.01	51
Botswana	66.03	61.13	75.40	50.99	63.39	67
Brazil	86.97	61.44	70.40	32.88	62.92	69
Brunei Darussalam	*88.15*	*71.27*				
Bulgaria	87.86	88.39	77.63	54.25	77.03	34
Burkina Faso	46.32	15.34	44.10	48.84	38.65	134
Burundi	43.75	36.77	67.28	23.84	42.91	126
Cambodia	71.36	53.83	71.98	7.51	51.17	107

continued on next page

continued

Economy	Physical	Intellectual	Environmental	Social	Wellness Index	Rank
Cameroon	46.73	44.74	18.81	27.18	34.36	140
Canada	96.34	98.08	81.59	80.62	89.16	15
Cape Verde	81.39	54.83	66.95	70.37	68.38	56
Central African Republic	0.00	11.18	31.67	13.84	14.17	152
Chad	14.00	0.00	19.51	0.00	8.38	153
Chile	93.68	78.62	61.61	57.53	72.86	44
China, People's Republic of	89.31	69.95	30.89	20.56	52.68	101
Colombia	90.15	66.03	66.21	28.23	62.65	72
Comoros	60.40	32.80	74.32	40.07	51.90	103
Congo, Republic of	*46.40*	*45.95*		*9.28*		
Costa Rica	93.24	69.46	75.11	68.19	76.50	37
Cote d'Ivoire	40.02	25.18	40.19	36.06	35.36	139
Croatia	93.07	88.11	83.61	52.34	79.28	28
Cuba	93.06	82.26	72.59	58.72	76.66	36
Cyprus	95.70	89.83	71.05	68.16	81.18	26
Czech Republic	94.39	94.28	82.26	76.89	86.96	19
Denmark	95.80	95.17	85.95	100.00	94.23	5
Djibouti	*61.41*					
Dominican Republic	79.87	54.22	74.19	22.75	57.76	85
Ecuador	87.37	66.77	74.27	30.34	64.69	65
Egypt, Arab Republic	78.36	41.56	11.56	27.44	39.73	131
El Salvador	84.03	50.47	75.88	19.57	57.49	88
Equatorial Guinea	48.72	55.01	38.31	16.42	39.61	132
Eritrea	49.86	33.34	53.84	14.55	37.90	136
Estonia	92.91	97.83	94.36	79.28	91.09	10
Ethiopia (excluding Eritrea)	58.54	18.79	57.31	27.60	40.56	130
Fiji	72.96	82.10	86.49	46.43	72.00	47
Finland	96.79	96.81	96.18	95.20	96.24	1
France	97.67	88.24	79.61	77.64	85.79	20
Gabon	64.38	64.87	47.41	41.13	54.45	95
Gambia, The	51.14	22.60	44.65	53.90	43.08	124
Georgia	83.72	84.41	60.87	58.75	71.94	48
Germany	95.60	99.30	88.15	91.94	93.75	6
Ghana	61.49	38.96	39.14	57.52	49.28	113
Greece	95.88	80.75	59.75	61.86	74.56	41
Grenada	*82.97*	*82.30*				
Guatemala	78.31	48.90	70.23	0.40	49.46	112
Guinea	38.08	16.96	47.06	31.12	33.30	141

continued on next page

continued

Economy	Physical	Intellectual	Environmental	Social	Wellness Index	Rank
Guinea-Bissau	32.58	15.76	56.48	28.31	33.29	142
Guyana	72.94	52.09	71.15	44.71	60.22	80
Haiti	41.66	30.26	61.75	8.41	35.52	138
Honduras	82.77	53.65	71.80	20.93	57.29	89
Hong Kong, China		*97.45*				
Hungary	90.37	91.07	78.00	54.20	78.41	31
Iceland	98.02	90.37	90.22	83.60	90.56	11
India	69.37	40.78	10.97	34.74	38.96	133
Indonesia	75.65	62.64	60.18	32.33	57.70	87
Iran, Islamic Republic of	87.65	67.73	27.73	21.60	51.18	106
Iraq	74.88	51.00	14.06	10.39	37.58	137
Ireland	97.04	95.79	88.28	80.22	90.34	12
Israel	*97.97*	*92.68*				
Italy	98.25	85.67	71.99	67.42	80.83	27
Jamaica	83.56	62.60	78.08	52.39	69.16	53
Japan	100.00	100.00	58.32	84.76	85.77	21
Jordan	84.41	72.31	48.26	47.56	63.14	68
Kazakhstan	84.75	93.54	66.46	45.26	72.50	45
Kenya	56.97	57.99	71.76	30.52	54.31	96
Kiribati	*61.90*					
Korea, Democratic People's Republic of	*67.81*					
Korea, Republic of	98.41	98.19	34.00	73.12	75.93	39
Kuwait	92.26	58.09	2.94	43.82	49.28	114
Kyrgyz Republic	80.37	75.37	60.88	41.34	64.49	66
Lao People's Democratic Republic	63.90	50.48	70.56	20.34	51.32	105
Latvia	88.64	95.64	87.26	70.33	85.47	22
Lebanon	88.35	64.71	36.86	33.05	55.74	93
Lesotho	32.41	47.42	68.72	49.84	49.60	111
Liberia	40.04	19.20	62.75	31.64	38.41	135
Libya	*81.47*		*46.02*			
Lithuania	*89.85*	*94.13*		*68.99*		
Luxembourg	96.76	89.86	98.62	97.61	95.71	2
Macedonia, former Yugoslav Republic of	89.43	66.20	67.68	40.92	66.06	61
Madagascar	47.04	39.26	69.01	28.67	46.00	120
Malawi	54.25	30.02	86.56	38.86	52.42	102
Malaysia	89.13	77.46	65.74	44.17	69.12	54
Maldives	91.03	64.72	95.75	47.37	74.72	40

continued on next page

continued

Economy	Physical	Intellectual	Environmental	Social	Wellness Index	Rank
Mali	40.91	1.97	37.23	39.03	29.79	146
Malta	96.04	81.39	71.09	58.23	76.69	35
Marshall Islands		*73.28*				
Mauritania	52.41	22.87	34.11	19.16	32.14	143
Mauritius	83.61	73.88	89.27	65.49	78.06	32
Mexico	87.75	67.87	56.17	32.60	61.10	77
Micronesia, Federated States of	*68.53*					
Moldova	81.23	79.60	74.57	48.91	71.08	50
Mongolia	75.00	74.94	40.54	54.42	61.22	76
Morocco	82.98	39.02	57.07	44.91	55.99	91
Mozambique	41.08	26.75	64.61	33.19	41.41	129
Myanmar	65.45	46.52	57.38	23.31	48.17	116
Namibia	59.07	57.71	61.36	45.67	55.95	92
Nepal	73.46	34.46	22.66	49.14	44.93	121
Netherlands	96.41	93.83	78.16	83.44	87.96	17
New Zealand	96.11	93.62	100.00	84.94	93.67	7
Nicaragua	82.60	51.34	77.77	16.08	56.95	90
Niger	45.00	2.58	15.62	46.64	27.46	148
Nigeria	29.24	30.44	4.29	31.03	23.75	150
Norway	97.60	92.66	94.26	93.12	94.41	4
Oman	88.87	70.54	54.94	45.90	65.06	64
Pakistan	58.17	26.99	20.20	3.58	27.24	149
Palau		*83.13*				
Panama	88.69	68.23	74.51	39.93	67.84	57
Papua New Guinea	50.97	31.50	80.11	37.32	49.98	109
Paraguay	82.02	60.76	80.36	19.75	60.72	78
Peru	87.81	66.15	54.09	33.62	60.42	79
Philippines	72.80	69.38	53.26	21.69	54.28	97
Poland	*92.67*	*95.05*				
Portugal	96.40	81.97	81.36	73.85	83.39	23
Qatar	93.48	70.63	0.00	25.61	47.43	119
Russian Federation	85.02	94.28	71.66	34.64	71.40	49
Rwanda	61.17	34.23	73.26	44.70	53.34	100
Samoa	*83.26*	*80.80*				
Sao Tome and Principe	73.50	56.81	73.17	42.87	61.59	73
Saudi Arabia	88.23	68.21	2.12	31.58	47.53	118
Senegal	64.37	26.44	37.14	50.84	44.70	122
Seychelles	82.61	75.81				
Sierra Leone	20.02	10.78	42.68	41.97	28.86	147

continued on next page

continued

Economy	Physical	Intellectual	Environmental	Social	Wellness Index	Rank
Singapore	99.68	97.60	52.79	65.77	78.96	30
Slovak Republic	91.46	91.07	88.46	59.74	82.68	24
Slovenia	96.73	94.39	99.57	78.21	92.23	9
Solomon Islands	*73.05*					
Somalia	*25.79*					
South Africa	68.12	56.60	60.31	46.15	57.80	84
Spain	98.50	84.17		74.84		
Sri Lanka	89.28	69.57	82.20	36.09	69.29	52
St. Lucia	84.42					
St. Vincent and the Grenadines	*81.53*					
Sudan	58.54	28.56	26.71	12.11	31.48	144
Suriname	78.38	66.87	74.15	44.27	65.92	62
Swaziland	45.05	59.86	80.41	15.52	50.21	108
Sweden	97.68	93.77	94.12	92.40	94.49	3
Switzerland	98.53	96.66	86.32	90.33	92.96	8
Syrian Arab Republic	*82.96*					
Tajikistan	75.66	77.94	51.63	11.20	54.11	98
Tanzania	50.91	45.32	59.94	49.48	51.41	104
Thailand	89.43	65.12	59.31	23.75	59.40	81
Togo	50.40	35.84	45.82	35.24	41.82	128
Tonga	*78.15*	*70.46*				
Trinidad and Tobago	83.05	80.69	73.80	57.63	73.79	42
Tunisia	88.23	49.33	48.87	65.07	62.88	70
Turkey	90.65	69.48	40.08	22.32	55.63	94
Turkmenistan	73.41	70.21	60.11	12.00	53.93	99
Uganda	49.56	46.23	53.68	29.17	44.66	123
Ukraine	81.98	85.83	66.60	40.22	68.66	55
United Arab Emirates	87.82	76.98	25.93	40.29	57.76	86
United Kingdom	95.35	94.53	83.77	74.58	87.06	18
United States	91.39	96.53	76.77	64.56	82.31	25
Uruguay	91.57	71.74	77.61	75.36	79.07	29
Uzbekistan	77.94	77.51	53.76	23.82	58.26	83
Vanuatu	69.38	48.60	85.70	62.75	66.61	60
Venezuela	77.91	75.38	81.40	11.65	61.58	74
Viet Nam	84.23	78.23	55.38	45.48	65.83	63
Yemen, Republic of	*55.86*					
Zambia	47.00	49.38	65.86	34.04	49.07	115
Zimbabwe	39.84	59.18	77.10	14.88	47.75	117

Source: Authors' estimates.

Appendix 3: Principal Component Analysis Weights

The following table provides the weights obtained from our principal component analysis at the pillar level. Note that there are some minor differences between statistical software. The weights used in our analysis were obtained using the “pca <variable>” command in Stata 15.

Indicator (year)	Weight	Indicator (year)	Weight
Physical Wellness		**Environmental Wellness**	
Life expectancy at birth (2018)	0.4493	Mortality rate attributed to household and ambient air pollution (2017)	0.4062
Maternal mortality rate (2017)	0.4232	PM2.5 air pollution, mean annual exposure (micrograms per cubic meter) (2017)	0.6553
Child (under 5) mortality rate (2018)	0.4448	Protected areas total (2018)	0.2103
Prevalence of undernourishment (2017)	0.361	Population weighted average NO_2 levels (2019)	0.3094
DALY noncommunicable diseases (2017)	0.3068	Imperviousness of most populous city (2015)	0.5154
DALY communicable diseases (2017)	0.4436		
Intellectual Wellness		**Social Wellness**	
Literacy rate adult (2018)	0.573	Literacy rate, youth (ages 15–24), GPI (2018)	0.1346
Mean years of schooling (2018)	0.5996	Gini index (World Bank estimate) (2018)	0.2043
Harmonized test scores (2017)	0.5586	Ratio of female-to-male labor force participation rate (%) (2018)	0.1453
		Control of corruption, estimate (2018)	0.4452
		Rule of law, estimate (2018)	0.4442
		Social class equality in respect for civil liberty	0.4587
		Social group equality in respect for civil liberties	0.4047
		Power distributed by social group	0.3865

DALY = disability-adjusted life year, GPI = gender parity index, NO_2 = nitrogen dioxide.

Note: PM2.5 refers to atmospheric particulate matter that has a diameter of less than 2.5 micrometers.

Source: Authors’ estimates.

Appendix 4: Data Definitions and Sources

Appendix 4 defines all indicators used in our analysis. Definitions are reproduced from their original sources, which are also listed. The process is also described in which multiple indicators were collated to create a new indicator.

Physical Wellness

Life expectancy at birth (2018). Life expectancy at birth indicates the number of years a newborn infant would live if prevailing patterns of mortality at the time of its birth were to stay the same throughout its life.

Source: World Bank. 2019. *World Development Indicators.* Washington, DC.

Maternal mortality rate (2017). Maternal mortality ratio is the number of women who die from pregnancy-related causes while pregnant or within 42 days of pregnancy termination per 100,000 live births. The data are estimated with a regression model using information on the proportion of maternal deaths among non-AIDS deaths in women aged 15–49, fertility, birth attendants, and gross domestic product measured using purchasing power parities.

Source: World Bank. 2019. *World Development Indicators.* Washington, DC.

Child (under 5) mortality rate (2018). Under-5 mortality rate is the probability per 1,000 that a newborn baby will die before reaching age 5, if subject to age-specific mortality rates of the specified year.

Source: World Bank. 2019. *World Development Indicators.* Washington, DC.

Prevalence of undernourishment (2017). Population below the minimum level of dietary energy consumption (also referred to as the prevalence of undernourishment) shows the percentage of the population whose food intake is insufficient to meet dietary energy requirements continuously. Data showing as 5 may signify a prevalence of undernourishment below 5%.

Source: World Bank. 2019. *World Development Indicators.* Washington, DC.

DALY noncommunicable diseases (2017). Age-standardized disability-adjusted life year (DALY) rates per 100,000 individuals from noncommunicable diseases. DALYs are used to measure total burden of disease, both from years of life lost and years lived with a disability. One DALY equals one lost year of healthy life.

Source: Global Burden of Disease Collaborative Network. 2018. *Global Burden of Disease Study 2017 (GBD 2017).* Seattle, United States: Institute for Health Metrics and Evaluation (IHME).

Intellectual Wellness

Literacy rate adult (2018). Adult literacy rate is the percentage of people ages 15 and above who can both read and write with understanding a short simple statement about their everyday life.

Source: World Bank. 2019. *World Development Indicators.* Washington, DC.

Mean years of schooling (2018). Average number of years of education received by people ages 25 and older, converted from education attainment levels using official durations of each level.

Source: United Nations Development Programme, Human Development Report (2018 Statistical Update).

Harmonized test scores (2017). Harmonized test scores from major international student achievement testing programs. They are measured in Trends in International Mathematics and Science Study (TIMSS)-equivalent units, where 300 is minimal attainment and 625 is advanced attainment. Most recent estimates are used. For more information, consult H.A. Patrinos and N. Angrist. 2018. *Global Dataset on Education Quality: A Review and Update (2000–2017).* World Bank.

Source: World Bank. 2019. *World Development Indicators.* Washington, DC.

Environmental Wellness

Mortality rate attributed to household and ambient air pollution, age-standardized (2017). Mortality rate attributed to household and ambient air pollution is the number of deaths attributable to the joint effects of household and ambient air pollution in a year per 100,000 population. The rates are age standardized.

Source: World Bank. 2019. *World Development Indicators.* Washington, DC.

PM2.5 air pollution, mean annual exposure (micrograms per cubic meter) (2017). Population-weighted exposure to ambient PM2.5 pollution is defined as the average level of exposure of a nation's population to concentrations of suspended particles measuring less than 2.5 microns in aerodynamic diameter, which are capable of penetrating deep into the respiratory tract and causing severe health damage. Exposure is calculated by weighting mean annual concentrations of PM2.5 by population in both urban and rural areas.

Note: PM2.5 refers to atmospheric particulate matter that has a diameter of less than 2.5 micrometers.
Source: World Bank. 2019. *World Development Indicators.* Washington, DC.

Protected areas total (2018). Terrestrial-protected areas are totally or partially protected areas of at least 1,000 hectares that are designated by national authorities as scientific reserves with limited public access, national parks, natural monuments, nature reserves or wildlife sanctuaries, protected landscapes, and areas managed mainly for sustainable use. Marine-protected areas are areas of intertidal or subtidal terrain—and overlying water and associated flora and fauna and historical and cultural features—that have been reserved by law or other effective means to protect part or all of the enclosed environment. Sites protected under local or provincial law are excluded.

Source: World Bank. 2019. *World Development Indicators.* Washington, DC.

Population weighted average NO_2 levels (2019). The data used for processing were the 2016 LandScan grid population data (about 1 kilometer [km] spatial resolution) and the 2019 Sentinel-5P nitrogen dioxide (NO_2) concentration temporal median (about 1.1 km spatial resolution) and both were in EPSG:4326 projection. To make each pixel match, the LandScan population data were resampled to the spatial resolution of NO_2 concentration data. Once datasets were available in both resolutions, the raster files were multiplied, and resulting in a dataset where each pixel of the resulting raster image was assigned a value of equal to population*NO_2 concentration. The Database of Global Administrative Areas (GADM) country boundary was then used to get the summation of population*NO_2 concentration pixels for each country, as well as the total grid population per country. The country-level population weighted average was then computed using the formula:

country average = summation (population*NO_2 exposure)/total grid population.

Sources: Multiple sources (see description) and in-house calculations.

Imperviousness of largest city. The data used for the processing were 2016 LandScan grid population data (about 1 km spatial resolution) and 2015 World Settlement Footprint imperviousness data (30 meters resolution pixel in EPSG:3857 web-mercator projection) for the 156 cities of interest. The World Settlement Footprint imperviousness datasets were projected to EPSG:4326 projection to make them consistent with the population data. To make each pixel match, the imperviousness data were resampled to the spatial resolution of the population data. An averaging resampling method was used for this process. The population data were clipped within the boundary of each city square. After compiling both population and imperviousness data in the same scope, projection, and resolution, the raster files were multiplied, and each pixel of the resulting raster image had a value equal to population*imperviousness. The summation of population*imperviousness pixels as well as the total grid population per city were then identified. The city/country-level population weighted average was then computed using the formula:

Population-weighted average = sum (population*imperviousness)/total grid population.

Source: Multiple sources (see description) and in-house calculations.

Social Wellness

Literacy rate, youth (ages 15–24), gender parity index (2018). Gender parity index for youth literacy rate is the ratio of females to males aged 15–24 who can both read and write with understanding a short simple statement about their everyday life.

Source: World Bank. 2019. *World Development Indicators.* Washington, DC.

Gini index (World Bank estimate) (2018). The Gini index measures the extent to which the distribution of income (or, in some cases, consumption expenditure) among individuals or households within an economy deviates from a perfectly equal distribution. A Lorenz curve plots the cumulative percentages of total income received against the cumulative number of recipients, starting with the poorest individual or household. The Gini index measures the area between the Lorenz curve and a hypothetical line of absolute equality, expressed as a percentage of the maximum area under the line. Thus, a Gini index of 0 represents perfect equality, while an index of 100 implies perfect inequality.

Source: World Bank. 2019. *World Development Indicators*. Washington, DC.

Ratio of female-to-male labor force participation rate (%) (2018). Labor force participation rate is the proportion of the population aged 15 and older that is economically active: all people who supply labor for the production of goods and services during a specified period. The ratio of female-to-male labor force participation rate is calculated by dividing female labor force participation rate by male labor force participation rate and multiplying by 100.

Source: World Bank. 2019. *World Development Indicators.* Washington, DC.

Control of corruption, estimate (2018). Control of corruption captures perceptions of the extent to which public power is exercised for private gain, including both petty and grand forms of corruption, as well as "capture" of the state by elites and private interests. The estimate gives the country's score on the aggregate indicator, in units of a standard normal distribution, i.e., ranging from about −2.5 to 2.5.

Source: World Bank. 2019. *World Development Indicators.* Washington, DC.

Rule of law, estimate (2018). Rule of law captures perceptions of the extent to which agents have confidence in and abide by the rules of society, and in particular the quality of contract enforcement, property rights, the police, and the courts, as well as the likelihood of crime and violence. The estimate gives the country's score on the aggregate indicator, in units of a standard normal distribution, i.e., ranging from about −2.5 to 2.5.

Source: World Bank. 2019. *World Development Indicators.* Washington, DC.

Social class equality in respect for civil liberty (2020). Answer to the question: Do poor people enjoy the same level of civil liberties as rich people do?

Source: M. Coppedge, et al. 2020. V-Dem [Country–Year/Country–Date] Dataset v10. Varieties. https://www.v-dem.net/en.

Social group equality in respect for civil liberties (2020). Answer to the question: Do all social groups, as distinguished by language, ethnicity, religion, race, region, or caste, enjoy the same level of civil liberties, or are some groups generally in a more favorable position?

Source: M. Coppedge et al. 2020. V-Dem [Country–Year/Country–Date] Dataset v10. Varieties. https://www.v-dem.net/en.

Power distributed by social group (2020). Answer to the question: Is political power distributed according to social group?

Source: M. Coppedge et al. 2020. V-Dem [Country–Year/Country–Date] Dataset v10. Varieties. https://www.v-dem.net/en.

Notes: Indicators used for each pillar of wellness. Definitions are taken from the source listed in the source column. Source refers to the database used to collect data; indicators may be collected by different agencies.

Appendix 5: Developing Asia Coverage

The following table lists economies in developing Asia by subregion and by the level of wellness data available. Partial coverage indicates that at least one pillar score could be calculated; no coverage indicates no score could be calculated given data limitations.

Central Asia	East Asia	South Asia	Southeast Asia	The Pacific
		Full coverage		
Armenia	Mongolia	Afghanistan	Cambodia	Fiji
Azerbaijan	People's Republic of China	Bangladesh	Indonesia	Papua New Guinea
Georgia	Republic of Korea	Bhutan	Lao People's Democratic Republic	Vanuatu
Kazakhstan		India	Malaysia	
Kyrgyz Republic		Maldives	Myanmar*	
Tajikistan		Nepal	Philippines	
Turkmenistan		Pakistan	Singapore	
Uzbekistan		Sri Lanka	Thailand	
			Viet Nam	
		Partial coverage		
	Hong Kong, China		Brunei Darussalam	Samoa
				Solomon Islands
				Tonga
				Federated States of Micronesia
				Kiribati
				Marshall Islands
				Palau
		No coverage		
	Taipei,China		Timor-Leste	Cook Islands
				Nauru
				Niue
				Tuvalu

*Estimation is based on 2014–2019 data.

Source: Authors.

Appendix 6: Industries and Activities Considered Part of the Wellness Economy

ISIC Rev. 4 Code	ISIC Industry	Wellness-Related Activities
2023	Manufacture of soap and detergents, cleaning and polishing preparations	Only activities related to the manufacture of personal care items such as beauty, sunburn, manicure, and pedicure products
2100	Manufacture of pharmaceuticals, medicinal chemical, and botanical products	All activities related to the manufacture of pharmaceutical, medicinal, and botanical products
3012	Building of pleasure and sporting boats	All activities related to the manufacture of boats for recreation and wellness purposes
3230	Manufacture of sports goods	All activities related to the manufacture of sporting goods
4100	Construction of buildings	All activities related to the construction of wellness-related and indoor-sports facilities
4290	Construction of other engineering projects	All activities related to the construction of outdoor wellness and sports facilities
4721	Retail sale of food in specialized stores	All retail sale activities of fruits and vegetables
4763	Retail sale of sporting equipment in specialized stores	Retail sale of sporting and wellness-related goods
4772	Retail sale of pharmaceutical and medical goods, cosmetic, and toilet articles in specialized stores	Retail sale of pharmaceuticals and cosmetic articles
5510	Short-term accommodation activities	Includes only the provision of short-term accommodation for holiday, wellness, and recreation purposes
5520	Camping grounds, recreational vehicle parks, and trailer parks	Includes only the provision of accommodation in recreational camps and facilities
7721	Renting and leasing of recreational and sports goods	Includes activities involving the rental and leasing services of recreational and wellness-related sports goods
7911	Travel agency activities	Includes activities of agencies engaged in selling of wellness travel, tour, transport, and accommodation services
7912	Tour operator activities	Includes activities of agencies engaged in arranging and assembling wellness-related tours
7990	Other reservation services and related activities	Other provisional wellness-travel reservation activities not included in 7911 and 7912
8130	Landscape care and maintenance service activities	All services activities related to landscape care and maintaining wellness spaces

continued on next page

continued

ISIC Rev. 4 Code	ISIC Industry	Wellness-Related Activities
8541	Sports and recreational education	Education services related to the pursuit of sports, recreation, and wellness activities such as yoga and martial arts
8610	Hospital activities	All activities
8620	Medical and dental practice activities	All activities
8690	Other human health activities	All activities
8710	Residential nursing care facilities	All activities
8720	Residential care activities for mental retardation, mental health, and substance abuse	All activities
8730	Residential care activities for elderly and disabled	All activities
8890	Other social work activities without accommodation	All other social work activities without accommodation aimed at improving wellness
9000	Creative, arts, and entertainment activities	All creative, arts, and entertainment services aimed at improving wellness
9101	Library and archive activities	Activities related to the operation of libraries
9102	Museum activities and operation of historical sites and buildings	Activities related to the operation of wellness-related sites such as spiritual spaces and museums
9103	Botanical and zoological gardens and nature reserves activities	All activities related to the operation of wellness-inducing sites such as botanical gardens
9311	Operation of sports facilities	All activities related to the operation of sports facilities
9312	Activities of sports clubs	All activities related to the operation of sports clubs that are promoting fitness
9319	Other sports activities	All other fitness-related activities excluded in 9311 and 9312
9321	Activities of amusement parks and theme parks	All activities related to the operation of amusement and theme parks
9329	Other amusement and recreational activities, n.e.c.	All other wellness-related activities excluded in 9321
9602	Hairdressing and other beauty treatment	All activities aimed at promoting beauty and wellness
9609	Other personal services activities, n.e.c.	Turkish baths, sauna and steam baths, solarium, and salons

ISIC = International Standard Industrial Classification of All Economic Activities, n.e.c. = not elsewhere classified.

Source: Authors' identification from ISIC Rev. 4. United Nations. 2008. *International Standard Industrial Classification of All Economic Activities Revision 4, Series M. No.4/Rev.4*. New York.

Appendix 7: Economies Currently Promoting Wellness Tourism

	Official Tourism Website Promotes Wellness Tourism	Tourism Strategy Addresses Wellness Tourism	Wellness Tourism Is a Target for Domestic Investment Promotion
Australia	Yes	No	No
Bhutan	Yes	Yes	Yes
Cambodia	Yes	No	No
PRC	No	Yes	Yes
Fiji	Yes	No	Yes
French Polynesia	Yes	No	No
Guam	Yes	No	No
India	Yes	Yes	Yes
Indonesia	Yes	No	No
Japan	Yes	No	No
Lao PDR	Yes	No	No
Malaysia	Yes	Yes	Yes
Maldives	Yes	Yes	Yes
Nepal	Yes	No	No
New Caledonia	Yes	No	No
New Zealand	Yes	No	Yes
Philippines	Yes	Yes	Yes
Samoa	Yes	No	No
Republic of Korea	Yes	Yes	No
Sri Lanka	Yes	No	No
Taipei,China	Yes	No	Yes
Thailand	No	Yes	No
Viet Nam	Yes	Yes	No

Lao PDR = Lao People's Democratic Republic, PRC = People's Republic of China.

Note: This list is current as of August 2018.

Source: Global Wellness Institute. 2018. *Global Wellness Tourism Economy*.

Appendix 8: Asia and Pacific Wellness Tourism Highlights, 2017

Number of wellness trips: 257.6 million (15.3% CAGR from 2015 to 2017)
Wellness tourism expenditures: $136.7 billion (10.9% CAGR from 2015 to 2017)
Projected wellness tourism expenditure CAGR (2017–2022): 13.0%
Average expenditure per trip: $1,741 for inbound/international (33% premium): $268 for domestic (120% premium)
Direct jobs: 10.1 million

Top 10 Wellness Tourism Markets in Asia and the Pacific, 2017

	Number of Arrivals/Trips ('000)			Receipts/Expenditures ($ million)
	Inbound/International	Domestic	Total	
People's Republic of China	7,724.3	62,442.2	70,166.5	31,705.9
Japan	1,585.5	38,900.0	40,485.5	22,466.1
India	4,542.4	51,426.3	55,968.6	16,299.7
Thailand	5,619.9	6,764.1	14,456.0	12,018.4
Australia	8,76.2	9,122.1	9,998.3	10,520.9
Republic of Korea	1,709.8	17,908.6	19,618.3	7,186.6
Indonesia	5,183.5	3,151.7	8,335.2	6,928.5
Malaysia	3,331.7	4,956.1	8,287.8	5,019.2
Viet Nam	3,149.5	6,465.8	9,615.3	4,001.1

CAGR = compound annual growth rate.

Note: These figures include both primary and secondary wellness trips. Expenditure data combine both international/inbound and domestic wellness tourism spending.

Source: Estimates by the Global Wellness Institute, based on tourism industry data from Euromonitor International.

Wellness Tourism Spending Premiums in the Top 10 Markets, 2017

	Average Spending per Inbound/International Trip ($)		Average Spending per Domestic Trip ($)	
	Wellness Trip	Average Trip	Wellness Trip	Average Trip
People's Republic of China	2,226	1,417	232	146
Japan	2,192	1,436	488	307
India	2,937	1,941	58	36
Thailand	1,885	1,206	191	120
Australia	2,992	2,490	866	487
Republic of Korea	2,054	1,307	205	126
Indonesia	1,184	793	251	115
Malaysia	1,109	717	267	102
Viet Nam	959	634	152	97
New Zealand	2,758	2,115	766	478

Note: These figures include both primary and secondary wellness trips.

Sources: Estimates by the Global Wellness Institute, based on tourism industry data from Euromonitor International; Global Wellness Institute. 2018. *Global Wellness Tourism Economy*.

Index

Note: Page numbers in *italics* refer to figures, page numbers in **bold** refer to tables and boxes.

www.ingramcontent.com/pod-product-compliance
Lightning Source LLC
Chambersburg PA
CBHW041752220926
51847CB00014B/182
9789292628420